CONGRESSIONAL POLICIES, PRACTICES AND PROCEDURES

BLACK LUNG PROGRAMS

MSHA, BENEFITS AND CHALLENGES

Congressional Policies, Practices and Procedures

Additional books and e-books in this series can be found on Nova's website under the Series tab.

CONGRESSIONAL POLICIES, PRACTICES AND PROCEDURES

BLACK LUNG PROGRAMS

MSHA, BENEFITS AND CHALLENGES

ROSS D. BLODGETT
EDITOR

snova
New York

Library of Congress Cataloging-in-Publication Data

ISBN: 978-1-53619-388-6

Published by Nova Science Publishers, Inc. † New York

CONTENTS

PREFACE

The federal government pays benefits to coal miners affected by coal workers' pneumoconiosis (CWP, commonly referred to as black lung disease) and other lung diseases linked to coal mining in cases where responsible mine operators are not able to pay. This book looks at the Mine Safety and Health Administration's coal dust rules and provides background information and policy options concerning the Black Lung Disability Trust Fund.

Chapter 1 - This is an edited, reformatted and augmented version of Hearing before the Subcommittee on Workforce Protections, Committee on Education and Labor, U.S. House of Representatives, One Hundred Sixteenth Congress, First Session, Serial No. 116–30, dated June 20, 2019.

Chapter 2 - In May 2018, GAO reported that the Trust Fund, which pays benefits to certain coal miners, faced financial challenges. The Trust Fund has borrowed from the U.S. Treasury's general fund almost every year since 1979 to make needed expenditures. GAO's June 2019 testimony included preliminary observations that coal operator bankruptcies were further straining Trust Fund finances because, in some cases, benefit responsibility was transferred to the Trust Fund.

This chapter examines (1) how coal mine operator bankruptcies have affected the Trust Fund, and (2) how DOL managed coal mine operator insurance to limit financial risk to the Trust Fund. GAO identified coal operators that filed for bankruptcy from 2014 through 2016 using Bloomberg data. GAO selected these years, in part, because bankruptcies were more likely to be resolved so that their effects on the Trust Fund could be assessed. GAO analyzed information on commercially- insured and self-insured coal operators, and examined workers' compensation insurance practices in four of the nation's top five coal producing states. GAO also interviewed DOL officials, coal mine operators, and insurance company representatives, among others.

Chapter 3 - With revenue of about $450 million in fiscal year 2017, the Trust Fund paid about $184 million in benefits to more than 25,000 coal miners and eligible dependents. However, the Trust Fund also borrowed about $1.3 billion from the Treasury's general fund in fiscal year 2017 to cover its debt repayment expenditures. Adding to this financial challenge, the coal tax that supports the Trust Fund is scheduled to decrease by about 55 percent beginning in 2019. GAO was asked to review the financial positon of the Trust Fund and identify options to improve it. This chapter examines (1) factors that have challenged the financial position of the Trust Fund since its inception and (2) the extent to which Trust Fund debt may change through 2050, and selected options that could improve its future financial position. GAO reviewed Trust Fund financial data from fiscal years 1979 through 2017. GAO also interviewed officials from the Departments of Labor, Treasury, Health and Human Services (HHS) and representatives of coal industry and union groups. Using assumptions, such as the about 55 percent coal tax decrease and moderately declining coal production, GAO simulated the extent to which Trust Fund debt may change through 2050. GAO also simulated how selected options, such as forgiveness of debt, could improve finances. The options simulated are not intended to be exhaustive. Further, GAO is not endorsing any particular option or combination of options. GAO provided a draft of this chapter to DOL, Treasury, and HHS. The agencies provided technical comments, which were incorporated as appropriate.

Chapter 4 - In May 2018, GAO reported that the Trust Fund, which pays disability benefits to certain coal miners, faced financial challenges. The Trust Fund has borrowed from the U.S. Treasury's general fund almost every year since 1979 to make needed expenditures. GAO's June 2019 testimony included preliminary observations that coal operator bankruptcies were further straining Trust Fund finances because, in some cases, benefit responsibility was transferred to the Trust Fund. This testimony is based on GAO's report being released today, and describes (1) how coal mine operator bankruptcies have affected the Trust Fund, and (2) how DOL managed coal mine operator insurance to limit financial risk to the Trust Fund. In producing this chapter, GAO identified coal operators that filed for bankruptcy from 2014 through 2016. GAO analyzed information on commercially-insured and self-insured coal operators, and examined workers' compensation insurance practices in four of the nation's top five coal producing states. GAO also interviewed DOL officials, coal mine operators, and insurance company representatives, among others.

Chapter 5 - The federal government pays benefits to coal miners affected by coal workers' pneumoconiosis (CWP, commonly referred to as black lung disease) and other lung diseases linked to coal mining in cases where responsible mine operators are not able to pay. In 2019, the monthly benefit for a miner with no dependents is $660.10. Benefits can be as much as $1,320.10 per month for miners with three or more dependents. Medical benefits are provided separately from disability benefits. Benefit payments and related administrative expenses in cases in which the responsible operators do not pay are paid out of the Black Lung Disability Trust Fund. The primary source of revenue for the trust fund is an excise tax on coal produced and sold domestically. If excise tax revenue is not sufficient to finance Black Lung Program benefits, the trust fund may borrow from the general fund of the Treasury. For 2018, the tax rates on coal were $1.10 per ton of underground-mined coal or $0.55 per ton of surface-mined coal, limited to 4.4% of the sales price. These rates were established in 1986. Starting in 2019, under current law, these tax rates are $0.50 per ton of underground-mined coal or $0.25 per ton of surface-mined coal, limited to 2% of the sales price. These are the rates that were set when the trust fund was established in 1977. The decline in the excise tax rates will likely put additional financial strain on a trust fund that already borrows from the general fund to meet obligations. The decline in domestic coal production, recent increases in the rate of CWP, and bankruptcies in the coal sector also contribute to the financial strain on the trust fund. The Black Lung Disability Trust Fund and associated excise tax on coal were established so that the coal industry, as opposed to taxpayers in general, would bear the burden associated with providing black lung benefits. Throughout its history, the Black Lung Disability Trust Fund has not raised revenues sufficient to meet obligations. As a result, at various points in time, Congress and the President have acted to increase the excise tax on coal, forgive or refinance trust fund debt, and modify black lung benefits eligibility. With the rate of the excise tax on coal reduced in 2019, the 116th Congress may again evaluate options for improving the fiscal condition of the Black Lung Disability Trust Fund, or other issues related to providing federal benefits to miners with black lung disease.

In: Black Lung Programs: MSHA, Benefits and Challenges ISBN: 978-1-53619-388-6
Editor: Ross D. Blodgett

Chapter 1

BREATHLESS AND BETRAYED: WHAT IS MSHA DOING TO PROTECT MINERS FROM THE RESURGENCE OF BLACK LUNG DISEASE?*

Committee on Education and Labor

Thursday, June 20, 2019
House of Representatives, Committee on Education and Labor,
Subcommittee on Workforce Protections, Washington, D.C.

The subcommittee met, pursuant to call, at 10:15 a.m., in Room 2175, Rayburn House Office Building, Hon. Alma S. Adams [Chairwoman of the subcommittee] presiding.

Present: Representatives Adams, DeSaulnier, Takano, Wild, McBath, Stevens, Byrne, Cline, and Wright.

Also Present: Representatives Scott, and Foxx.

Staff Present: Tylease Alli, Chief Clerk; Jordan Barab, Senior Labor Policy Advisor; Ilana Brunner, General Counsel -; Emma Eatman, Press Assistant; Daniel Foster, Health and Labor Council; Eli Hovland, Staff Assistant; Stephanie Lalle, Deputy Communications Director; Jaria Martin, Clerk/Assistant to the Staff Director; Kevin McDermott, Senior Labor Policy Advisor; Richard Miller, Director of Labor Policy; Max Moore, Office Aid; Veronique Pluviose, Staff Director; Banyon Vassar, Deputy Director of Information Technology; Katelyn Walker, Counsel; Cyrus Artz, Minority

* This is an edited, reformatted and augmented version of Hearing before the Subcommittee on Workforce Protections, Committee on Education and Labor, U.S. House of Representatives, One Hundred Sixteenth Congress, First Session, Serial No. 116–30, dated June 20, 2019.

Parliamentarian; Courtney Butcher, Minority Director of Coalitions and Member Services; Akash Chougule, Minority Professional Staff Member; Rob Green, Minority Director of Workforce Policy; Bridget Handy, Minority Communications Assistant; John Martin, Minority Workforce Policy Counsel; Sarah Martin, Minority Professional Staff Member; Hannah Matesic, Minority Director of Operations; Alexis Murray, Minority Professional Staff Member; Brandon Renz, Minority Staff Director; Ben Ridder, Minority Legislative Assistant; Heather Wadyka, Minority Operations Assistant, and Lauren Williams, Minority Professional Staff Member.

Chairwoman ADAMS. The Subcommittee on Workforce Protections will come to order. Welcome, everyone. Good morning. I note that a quorum is present. The committee is meeting today to receive testimony for a two panel hearing entitled "Breathless and Betrayed: What is MSHA doing to Protect Miners from the Resurgence of Black Lung Disease."

Mr. Griffin from Virginia will participate in today's hearing with the understanding that his questions will come only after all members of the Subcommittee on Workforce Protections and the full committee on both sides of the aisle who are present have an opportunity to question the witnesses.

Pursuant to committee rule 7c, opening statements are limited to the Chair and the Ranking Member. This allows us to hear from our witnesses sooner and provides all members with adequate time to ask questions.

I now recognize myself for the purpose of making an opening statement.

Today the subcommittee is going to explore three troubling developments impacting our Nation's coal miners and assess whether the Administration is making adequate efforts to protect miners' health and economic well-being.

First, we will address the resurgence of black lung disease, which has taken the lives of 78,000 coal miners since 1977 and caused suffering in thousands more. Congress codified the first enforceable limit on coal mine dust levels in the 1969 Coal Act and the rate of black lung disease began to decline in the 1970s, '80s, and '90s. More recently, the rate of black lung disease has come back with a vengeance. Nearly one in five long-tenured miners in Appalachia have been diagnosed with black lung disease. This is four times the rate anywhere else. Black lung clinics and researchers at the National Institute for Occupational Safety and Health, NIOSH, have documented a steep increase in the rate of the most severe form of the disease, called progressive massive fibrosis, or PMF.

PMF, or complicated black lung, is caused by inhalation of coal and silica dust at both underground and surface coal mines. Miners gradually lose the ability to breathe as they wheeze and gasp for air. There is no cure for black lung. It is a progressive disease and it gets worse with time.

We have a chart up that you can look at. Posted on the screen are photographs of three sets of lungs. The one on the left is a healthy lung, with a tan colored tissue. In the center, the lung with speckled black opacities, is from a coal miner with simple black lung disease whose breathing is impaired. On the right, the lung encased in solid black mass is from a miner with progressive massive fibrosis, or complicated black lung.

For some with PMF, survival requires a lung transplant, but only those healthy enough to withstand the surgery are eligible. Even then, life expectancy does not usually exceed 5 years. Most troubling, PMF is now afflicting miners at far earlier ages. Causes are being documented in miners in their 30s and 40s.

As the second slide shows, the rate of PMF declined sharply in the 1970s and kept dropping until the late 1990s. But then progress reversed and rates now exceed levels diagnosed in the 1970s. Miners' increasing silica exposure has been identified as one of the main causes of the resurgence of PMF.

Many of the thickest coals seams in central Appalachia have been mined out and the seams that remain have coal embedded in quartz-bearing rocks that contain silica.

As mining machines grind through thinner coal mine seams, they are cutting quartz and coal together. Miners who inhale this dust are inhaling larger amounts of silica, which is 20 times more toxic than coal dust alone. Let me repeat that, silica is 20 times more toxic than coal dust.

And while the Mine Safety and Health Administration, or MSHA, implemented a more stringent coal dust rule in 2014 under the Obama Administration, far more can be done. Serious problems remain to be addressed and those will be discussed during this hearing today.

This much is clear, black lung is back at epidemic levels and mine safety regulators and the industry have failed in their jobs to protect miners from this completely preventable occupational disease.

Today's hearing will also address the solvency of the Black Lung Disability Trust Fund. When miners are disabled from black lung disease they can file a claim for black lung benefits with the Department of Labor. If a mine operator shuts down or files for bankruptcy, however, benefits are paid from the Black Lung Disability Trust Fund. That Fund is financed by a small tax paid by mine operators on each ton of mined coal.

But on December 31, 2018, Congress allowed the tax rate to drop by 55 percent. If the previous tax rate is not reinstated the Government Accountability Office projects that the deficit in the Trust Fund will exceed $15 billion by 2050. While Trust Fund can borrow to pay miners' benefits and refinance its debt, allowing the tax rate to sunset effectively shifts the cost of black lung disease from the coal industry, which caused the problem, to the tax payers.

And, finally, we will examine how black lung claimants could be harmed by the Texas lawsuit that is seeking to invalidate the Affordable Care Act. That suit was brought by Republican Attorneys General and supported by the Trump Administration. A lower Court opinion already struck down the ACA on Constitutional grounds and an appeal is now pending. The Texas litigation not only threatens to eliminate the ACA's protection for people with pre-existing conditions, Federal subsidies for low income people to purchase private health insurance and Medicaid expansion, but repeal would also eliminate the so called "Byrd Amendments" to the ACA.

Those provisions, which are enacted with the support of the Black Lung Association and the United Mine Workers Union, restored important eligibility criteria that enabled miners and their families to receive compensation under the Black Lung Benefits Act.

Despite the growing surge of black lung disease, the skyrocketing red ink in the Black Lung Disability Trust Fund, and the threat to miners from the attempt to repeal the ACA, we have heard nothing from this Administration about any actions that would protect and defend the threatened health and benefits of this Nation's ailing miners.

I want to thank our witnesses for their testimony, especially those who have traveled some distance to be here.

I also want to give a special thanks to the miners who have traveled from the coal fields of West Virginia.

And now I yield to the Ranking Member, Mr. Byrne, for his opening statement.

[The information follows:]

PREPARED STATEMENT OF HON. ALMA S. ADAMS, CHAIRWOMAN, SUBCOMMITTEE ON WORKFORCE PROTECTIONS

Today, the Subcommittee is going to explore three troubling developments impacting our nation's coal miners and assess whether the Administration is making adequate efforts to protect miners' health and economic well-being.

First, we will address the resurgence of black lung disease, which has taken the lives of 78,000 coal miners since 1977 and caused suffering in thousands more.

Congress codified the first enforceable limit on coal mine dust levels in the 1969 Coal Act, and the rate of black lung disease began to decline in the 1970's, 80's and 90's. Now the rate of black lung disease is coming back with a vengeance. Nearly one in five long-tenured miners in Appalachia have been diagnosed with black lung disease. This is four times the rate elsewhere.

Black lung clinics and researchers at the National Institute for Occupational Safety and Health or NIOSH have documented a steep increase in the rate of the most severe form of the disease called Progressive Massive Fibrosis or "PMF."

PMF, or complicated black lung, is caused by inhalation of coal and silica dust at both underground and surface coal mines. Miners gradually lose the ability to breathe, as they wheeze and gasp for air. There is no cure for black lung – It is a progressive disease and gets worse with time.

Posted on the screen are photographs of three sets of lungs. On the left, is a healthy lung with tan colored tissue. In the center, the lung with speckled black opacities is from a coal miner with simple Black Lung disease, whose breathing is impaired. On the right, the lung encased in solid black mass is from a miner with progressive massive fibrosis or complicated black lung.

For some with PMF, survival requires a lung transplant. But only those healthy enough to withstand the surgery are eligible. Even then, life expectancy does not usually exceed five years. Most troubling. PMF is now afflicting miners at far earlier ages – cases are being documented in miners in their 30s and 40s.

As the second slide shows, the rate of the PMF or complicated black lung is higher now than the rate in the early 1970s. The rate of PMF declined sharply in the 1970s and kept dropping until the late 1990s, but then progress reversed, and rates now exceed levels diagnosed in the 1970s. Miners' increasing silica exposure has been identified as one of the main causes of the resurgence of PMF.

Many of the thickest coal seams in central Appalachia have been mined out, and the seams that remain have coal embedded in quartz-bearing rock that contains silica.

As mining machines grind through thinner coal mine seams, they are cutting quartz and coal together. Miners who inhale this dust are inhaling large amounts of silica, which is 20 times more toxic than coal dust alone.

Let me repeat that—silica is 20 times more toxic than coal dust.

While the Mine Safety and Health Administration or MSHA implemented a more stringent coal dust rule in 2014 under the Obama Administration in 2014, far more can be done.

Serious problems remain to be addressed and those will be discussed during this hearing. This much is clear: black lung is back at epidemic levels.

And mine safety regulators and the industry have failed in their jobs to protect miners from this completely preventable occupational disease.

Today's hearing will also address the solvency of the Black Lung Disability Trust Fund. When miners are disabled from black lung disease, they can file a claim for black lung benefits with the Department of Labor. If a mine operator shuts down or files for bankruptcy, however, benefits are paid from the Black Lung Disability Trust Fund. That Fund is financed by a small tax on each ton of mined coal.

But on December 31, 2018, Congress allowed the amount mine owners contribute to the fund to drop by 55 percent. If the previous tax rate is not reinstated, the Government Accountability Office projects that the deficit in the Trust Fund will skyrocket to $15.5 billion by 2050.

While the Trust Fund can borrow to pay miners' benefits and refinance its debt, allowing the tax rate to sunset effectively shifts the costs of black lung disease from the coal industry – which caused the problem – to the taxpayers.

Finally, we will examine how Black Lung claimants could be harmed by the Texas lawsuit, brought by Republican Attorneys General and the Trump Administration, that is seeking to invalidate the *Affordable Care Act.* A lower Court opinion already struck down the ACA on constitutional grounds, and an appeal is now pending.

The *Texas* litigation not only threatens to eliminate the ACA's protections for people with preexisting conditions, federal subsidies for low-income people to purchase private health insurance and Medicaid expansion, but repeal would also eliminate the so-called "Byrd Amendments" to the ACA that – with the support of the Black Lung Association and the United Mineworkers union – had restored important eligibility criteria that enabled miners and their families to receive compensation under the Black Lung Benefits Act.

Despite the growing insolvency of the Black Lung Disability Trust Fund and the threat to miners from the attempt to repeal the ACA, we have heard nothing from this Administration about any actions that would protect and defend the threatened benefits of this nation's ailing miners.

I want to thank our witnesses for their testimony, especially those who had to travel some distances to be here. I also want to give a special thanks to the miners who have traveled from the coal fields of West Virginia.

I yield to the Ranking Member, Mr. Byrne, for his opening statement.

Mr. BYRNE. Thank you, Madam Chairwoman, for yielding.

As the name of this subcommittee suggests, we all share the common goal of keeping hardworking Americans out of harm's way at their jobs. We want to help ensure that all workers return home to their families safe and healthy.

Workers in the mine industry have been an extremely important part of the American economy for decades. As someone who comes from a coal mining state, I have been a strong supporter of the men and women who provide for their families by working in this industry. I want us to do everything we can to ensure their safety is protected.

As such, it is essential that federal programs designed to provide benefits to these workers are effectively managed to ensure that promised protections and benefits are available now and in the future.

The Mine Safety and Health Administration, or MSHA, is responsible for protecting American mine workers by establishing and enforcing safety and health regulations governing all above ground and underground mines. It is vital that MSHA maintain high standards of safety while also allowing the industry to innovate for the benefit of mine workers and the American economy.

In 2018, MSHA reported more than 330,000 Americans were employed by the mining industries. In that same year the agency reported the second lowest number ever recorded of mining fatalities. However, one fatality is still too many. And we need to continue promoting the best possible policies to ensure a safe and healthy workplace.

When discussing the safety of mines, we cannot forget about the hazards whose effects might not be visible until years later, in the form of illnesses such as black lung disease. This illness has lasting effects that can devastate workers' bodies and make life more difficult and painful.

Today, we will hear from witnesses sharing their stories about some of their hardships. And I want to thank you for being here to provide your testimony. We all share a common goal of preventing and eliminating black lung disease.

I look forward to hearing from both panels of witnesses on how we can best accomplish this goal, and ensure those already diagnosed with the disease are receiving the proper benefits.

I am encouraged by the Trump administration's work in this area and its latest regulatory agenda, which includes a request for information on respirable crystalline silica. It is critical for the agency to determine if the current respirable dust standards are providing the best and most feasible protection for miners.

However, I think this hearing is missing a crucial voice in the examination of black lung benefits by not including the director of the Office of Workers' Compensation Programs here to testify today. As you know, this committee is responsible for oversight of the OWCP at the Department of Labor, which administers benefits for the Black Lung Disability Trust Fund and plays a key role for miners who are Trust Fund beneficiaries.

Funding for the Trust Fund, however, is provided by an excise tax on coal. While that excise tax falls under the jurisdiction of a different House committee, the Committee on Ways and Means, it would have benefitted everyone in this room to have heard directly from the OWCP so we can have a better understanding of the program.

I look forward to the testimony from all of the panelists at today's hearing. I believe we can all work together to create common sense, workable, and innovative approaches to ensuring miners have a safe and healthy workplace.

With that, Madam Chairwoman, I yield back. [The information follows:]

Prepared Statement of Hon. Bradley Byrne, Ranking Member, Subcommittee on Subcommittee on Workforce Protections

Thank you for yielding.

As the name of this subcommittee suggests, we all share the common goal of keeping hardworking Americans out of harm's way at their jobs. We want to help ensure that all workers return home to their families safe and healthy.

Workers in the mining industry have been an extremely important part of the American economy for decades. As someone who comes from a coal mining state, I have been a strong supporter of the men and women who provide for their families by working in this industry. I want us to do everything we can to ensure their safety is protected. As such, it is essential that federal programs designed to provide benefits to these workers are effectively managed to ensure that promised protections and benefits are available, now and in the future.

The Mine Safety and Health Administration (MSHA) is responsible for protecting American mine workers by establishing and enforcing safety and health regulations governing all above-ground and underground mines. It is vital that MSHA maintain high standards of safety, while also allowing the industry to innovate for the benefit of mine workers and the American economy.

In 2018, MSHA reported more than 330,000 Americans were employed by the mining industries, and that same year the agency reported the second lowest number ever recorded of mining fatalities. However, one fatality is still too many, and we need to continue promoting the best possible policies to ensure a safe and healthy workplace.

When discussing the safety of mines, we cannot forget about the hazards whose effects might not be visible until years later in the form of illnesses such as black lung disease. This illness has lasting effects that can devastate workers' bodies and make life more difficult and painful.

Today we will hear from witnesses sharing their stories about some of these hardships, and I want to thank you for being here to provide your testimony. We all share a common goal of preventing and eliminating black lung disease. I look forward to hearing from both panels of witnesses on how we can best accomplish this goal and ensure those already diagnosed with the disease are receiving the proper benefits.

I am encouraged by the Trump administration's work in this area and its latest regulatory agenda, which includes a request for information on respirable crystalline silica. It is critical for the agency to determine if the current respirable dust standards are providing the best and most feasible protection for miners.

However, I think this hearing is missing a crucial voice in the examination of black lung benefits by not including the director of the Office of Workers' Compensation Program (OWCP) here to testify today. As you know, this Committee is responsible for oversight of OWCP at the Department of Labor, which administers benefits for the Black Lung Disability Trust Fund and plays a key role for miners who are Trust Fund beneficiaries. Funding for the Trust Fund, however, is provided by an excise tax on coal. While that excise tax falls under the jurisdiction of a different House Committee, the Committee on Ways and Means, it would have benefited everyone in this room to have heard directly from OWCP so we could have a better understanding of the program.

I look forward to the testimony from all the panelists at today's hearing. I believe we can all work together to create commonsense, workable, and innovative approaches to ensuring miners have a safe and healthy workplace.

With that, I yield back.

Chairwoman ADAMS. Thank you, Mr. Byrne.

Without objection, all the members who wish to insert written statements into the record may do so by submitting them to the committee clerk electronically in Microsoft Word format by 5:00 p.m. July 5th, 2019.

I will now introduce our witnesses for panel one.

Our first witness will be Dr. Robert Cohen. Dr. Cohen is a clinical professor in the Department of Environmental and Occupational Health Sciences at the University of Illinois School of Public Health. Dr. Cohen is a leading researcher on occupational lung diseases, with a focus in workers affected by mineral dust exposure. Our next witness is Mr. Gary Hairston, who is vice president of the Fayette County Black Lung Association. Mr. Hairston is a retired coal miner who worked in the mines for 27 years before being forced to leave mining at age 48 due to black lung disease.

Since then Mr. Hairston has been active in fighting to ensure that fellow miners impacted by black lung receive the benefits they are entitled to.

Following Mr. Hairston will be Mr. Bruce Watzman. Mr. Watzman, who is testifying without affiliation, was formerly the senior vice president for regulatory affairs, National Mining Association, and their chief regulatory affairs officer before retiring last year.

Our last witness on panel one will be Mr. Cecil Roberts, president of the United Mine Workers of America. Mr. Roberts is a sixth generation coal miner and West Virginian. Since 1995 he served five terms as president of the UMWA. He started his career as a coal miner and a UMWA member in 1971.

We appreciate all of the witnesses for being here today. We look forward to your testimony.

Let me remind the witnesses that we have read your written statements and they will appear in full in the hearing record. Pursuant to committee rule 7d and the committee practice, each of you is asked to limit your oral presentation to a 5 minute summary of your written statement.

And let me remind the witnesses as well that pursuant to Title 18 of the U.S. Code Section 1001, it is illegal to knowingly and willfully falsify any statement, representation, written document, or material fact presented to Congress, or otherwise conceal or cover up a material fact.

Before you begin your testimony, please remember to press the button on the microphone in front of you so that it will turn on and members can hear you. And as you begin to speak the light in front of you will turn green. After 4 minutes the light will turn yellow to signal that you have 1 minute remaining. When the light turns red your 5 minutes have expired and we will ask you to please wrap up.

We will let the entire panel make their presentations before we move to member questions. When answering a question please remember to once again turn your microphone on.

I will first recognize Dr. Robert Cohen.

Dr. Cohen, you are recognized for 5 minutes.

TESTIMONY OF ROBERT COHEN, MD, FCCP, CLINICAL PROFESSOR, ENVIRONMENTAL AND OCCUPATIONAL HEALTH SCIENCES, UNIVERSITY OF ILLINOIS SCHOOL OF PUBLIC HEALTH

Dr. COHEN. Chairwoman Adams, Ranking Member Byrne, and distinguished members of the subcommittee, my name is Robert Cohen. I am the director of the Mining Education and Research Center at UIC, the University of Illinois at Chicago. I am also professor of medicine at the Northwestern University Feinberg School of Medicine.

I direct the Black Lung Center of Excellence and am the medical director of the National Coalition of Black Lung and Respiratory Disease Clinics, which has 60 sites across 15 states serving over 13,000 miners.

My testimony will cover three issues. First, there is a resurgence of severe black lung disease in the United States. Second, overexposure to respirable crystalline silica is an important contributing factor to this resurgence. And, third, there are short and long-term policies that MSHA, the Mine Safety Health Administration, should adopt to stem the resurgence black lung disease.

First, evidence of resurgent of black lung disease comes from reports of outbreaks of hundreds of cases of progressive massive fibrosis, or PMF, the most severe form of the disease, from former miners attending clinics in Kentucky and southwestern Virginia.

Our UIC research group, in collaboration with NIOSH, analyzed national data on former miners applying for Federal black lung benefits. And you can see on slide one that from 1970 until 1996 the numbers of PMF cases among claimants remained below 2 percent. But after 1996, this increased dramatically, reaching 8.3 percent of claims. Shockingly, there have been a total of nearly 2,500 miners determined to have PMF since 1996. Those of us who care for these young miners in our black lung clinics see them fighting for breath. They suffer from the loss of ability to do simple daily tasks, like walking to the mailbox, playing with their children and grandchildren, not to mention a loss of their careers, hobbies, and ability to support their families. They suffer from early mortality in spite of our heroic attempts to treat them, including referrals for lung transplantation.

Let me remind you, there is no cure for this disease. It confers an early death sentence.

What is the evidence that silica plays a role? Crystalline silica is present in rock strata above, below, and between coal seams. Mining activities generate freshly fractured respirable silica, which is highly toxic and causes significantly more lung scarring than coal dust. We see evidence of silica by looking at the number of miners' chest x-rays with large round scars which have been associate with silicosis. The proportion of these miners with these scars has increased in central Appalachia, paralleling the increase of severe disease in these miners.

But we go beyond chest x-ray shadows and look at the lung tissues of miners with PMF. We examine PMF lung tissue from coal miners in the NIOSH National Coal Workers Autopsy Study. On slide two you can see that we evaluated the type of PMF, whether it was a coal, mixed dust, or silicotic type, that was present to see how this disease has changed over time. Results from 376 miners showed a significant increase in the silicotic type of PMF from 24 percent of cases before 1990 to more than 40 percent after that time. This indicated that miners dying more recently were nearly twice as likely to have silicotic type of disease.

Lastly, we see evidence of the role of silica when we look at the mineral particles in the lungs of miners with PMF using the electron microscope and an x-ray probe. Data from the first eight modern miners and ten historical comparisons show that the concentration and proportion of silica particles in lung tissues was nearly double in the modern cases.

What can be done? The passage of the new 2014 MSHA dust rule was a significant step forward, but MSHA must go further and sample respirable crystalline silica more frequently than quarterly. NIOSH has developed an in-mine silica analyzer, which pared with a personal quartz monitor, provides rapid estimates of exposure to silica, such as at the end of each shift. Results of monitoring could inform inspectors and operations on the need to change ventilation or place the mine on a reduced dust standard.

MSHA should increase the frequency of monitoring for silica until a tamper proof personal quartz monitor becomes available. In addition, MSHA should adopt the current Occupational Safety and Health Administration's permissible exposure limit of 50 micrograms for silica for coal miners.

Finally, surveillance must be enhanced for miners working in the hot spots of central Appalachia. They should be offered more frequent health screening, including chest x-ray and spirometry testing every 2 to 3 years rather than every 5 years.

Thank you for the opportunity to provide this testimony and I will be pleased to answer any questions that you may have.

[The statement of Dr. Cohen follows:]

Statement of Robert Cohen, MD, FCCP, Mining Education and Research Center University of Illinois at Chicago, School of Public Health

Chairwoman Adams, Ranking Member Byrne, and distinguished members of the Subcommittee. My name is Robert Cohen and I am the Director of the Mining Education and Research Center, and Clinical Professor of Environmental and Occupational Health Sciences at the University of Illinois at Chicago, School of Public Health. I am also Professor of Medicine at the Northwestern University Feinberg School of Medicine and Direct the Occupational Lung Disease Program at Northwestern Medicine. I direct the Black Lung Center of Excellence funded by the Health Resources and Services Administration (HRSA) and serve as the medical director of the National Coalition of Black Lung and Respiratory Disease Clinics, the coalition of Black Lung Clinic Programs also funded by HRSA. There are 60 HRSA clinic sites across 15 states which serve over 13,000 coal miners [1].

My testimony will cover three issues.

First, there is extensive evidence that there is a resurgence of Black Lung in the United States, especially in its most severe forms.

Second, there is evidence indicating that over exposure to respirable crystalline silica is an important contributing factor to this resurgence.

Third, there are short and long term policies that MSHA should adopt to stem the resurgence of black lung disease.

Evidence of Resurgent Severe Pneumoconiosis in U.S. Underground Coal Miners

Surveillance of Active Miners

The NIOSH Coal Workers Health Surveillance Program (CWHSP) offers chest x-ray screening to active surface and underground coal miners to identify those miners with early signs of disease and notify them so that they might take steps to reduce exposure and prevent disease progression. Data on chest x-ray findings from the CWHSP has shown a steady decline in miners with disease dating from the passage of the Coal Mine Health and Safety Act in 1970 to the mid-1990's, falling from 30% down to a low of 5% [2]. Since then, however, there has been a significant surge in the numbers of active miners with scars on their chest radiographs. The most recent data indicates that 10% of miners have changes consistent with coal workers pneumoconiosis. Of great concern is the report that one in five coal miners with 25 or more years of mining experience from Kentucky, West Virginia, and Virginia, have evidence of disease compared to one in ten nationally [2] (See Figure 1). In 2005, an analysis of CWHSP chest x-ray data showed there were areas of the country where the disease appeared to be progressing rapidly (See Figure 2). These areas were labeled, "Hot Spots." Further reports have shown this central Appalachian region to be the epicenter of severe resurgent disease.

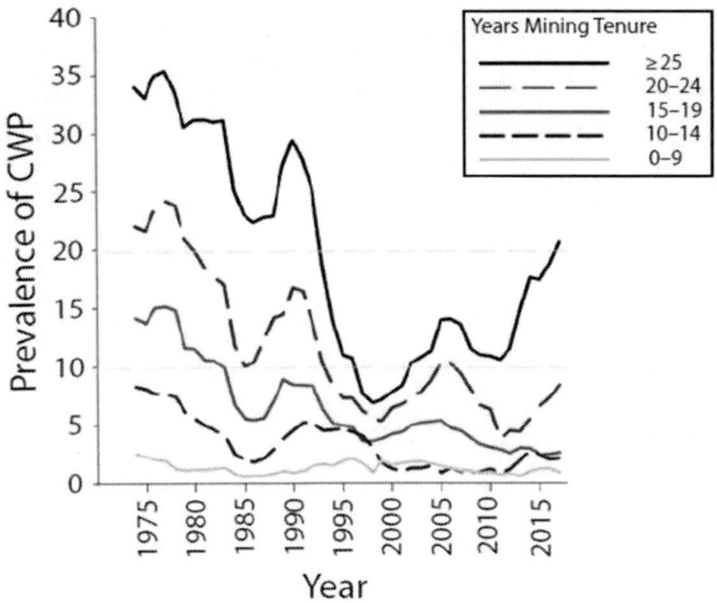

Figure 1. Prevalence of Coal Workers' Pneumoconiosis (CWP) Among Those Working Underground in Central Appalachia, Coal Workers' Health Surveillance Program, Appalachia, 1970–2017.

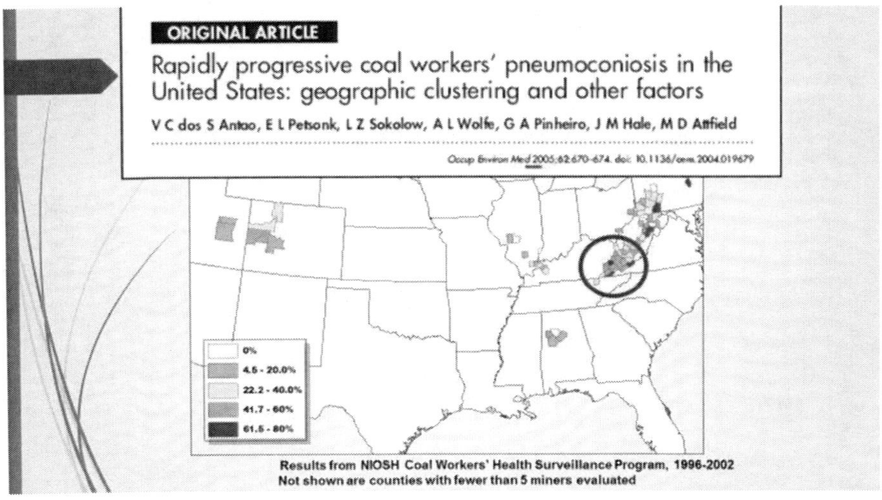

Figure 2. Geographic distribution of the proportion of miners with rapidly progressive pneumoconiosis, color coded by increasing proportion. Counties with a high proportion of cases have been labeled "HOT SPOTS." Note the clustering of Hot Spot counties in Southern WV, Eastern KY, and southwestern VA.

Disease in Former Miners

Outbreaks of hundreds of cases of the most severe form of the disease with miners exhibiting large debilitating scars, known as Progressive Massive Fibrosis (PMF) have been reported from clinics in Kentucky and southwestern Virginia [3, 4]. As a follow up study to these outbreak reports, the University of Illinois research group (UIC) in collaboration with NIOSH analyzed data from the United States Department of Labor's

Black Lung Benefits program, and for the first time ever reported national trends of PMF in thousands of former miners [5]. This study revealed that the percent of miners' with PMF remained below 2% of claims from the inception of the program in 1970 until 1996 when the proportion of severely diseased miners increased dramatically reaching 8.3% of claims by 2014 (See Figure 3). There have been a total of 2,474 miners determined to have disabling PMF since 1996. The proportion of PMF claims from 1970 through 2016 increased by 17% in the central Appalachian states of Kentucky, West Virginia, and most severely to 31% of claims in Virginia.

These numbers, while extremely disturbing, do not reflect the individual struggles that these miners with severe forms of the disease suffer through. Those of us who care for these miners in our black lung clinics on a daily basis see them fighting for breath, often with the support of supplemental oxygen as they fight to improve their condition by exercising in pulmonary rehab programs. These miners are relatively young, some as young as their 30's and 40's. They suffer from loss of their careers, hobbies, and ability to support their families. They suffer from early mortality in spite of our most heroic attempts to treat them including referrals for lung transplantation [6, 7].

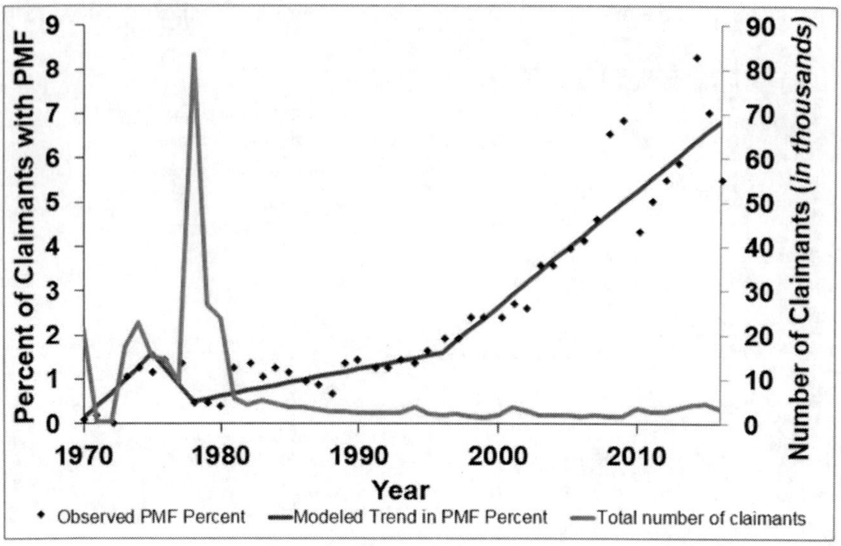

Figure 3. Number of claimants for Federal Black Lung Program benefits and the percentage of these claimants that received a determination of progressive massive fibrosis (PMF) during their claim process, 1970–2016. Data source: U.S. Department of Labor, Office of Workers' Compensation Programs, Division of Coal Mine Workers' Compensation.

Increases in Mortality

Recently the UIC research group in collaboration with NIOSH performed another important analysis. For the first time we used identifiers from miners who participated in the US DOL Black Lung Benefits Program and the CWHSP we obtained death certificates on 34,771 deceased former U.S. coal miners who had an average of 26 years of coal mine employment [8]. We analyzed causes of death and found a significant increase in proportional mortality from non-malignant respiratory diseases including COPD, emphysema, and pneumoconiosis among miners aged 65–74. Those who would have worked before 1950 had a proportional mortality for these diseases of 15%, this increased to 28-32% for those working in the mines between 1950 and 1990. The proportional mortality from pneumoconiosis in younger miners (<65 years) also increased significantly from 4-5% for those working before 1950 to 7.2% for those working between 1960 and 1990. This pattern of mortality for these preventable lung diseases should not be occurring, rather we should be seeing a decrease in proportional mortality of pneumoconiosis and for non-malignant lung disease especially since miners began working in mines operating under dust control regulations mandated by the 1969 Federal Coal Mine Health and Safety Act.

Conclusion

I believe that the evidence from surveillance of active working miners and from former miners is convincing. There is a resurgence of coal mine dust lung disease in US coal miners. We see this in chest x-ray surveillance data, black lung claims data, and in mortality data. This resurgence is most severe in the central Appalachian states of Kentucky, West Virginia, and Virginia. There is also significant evidence that the disease is not just mild, but in fact the most severe disabling forms of this preventable disease are occurring in younger miners.

What Is the Role of Silica in Resurgent Severe Coal Mine Dust Lung Disease?

Radiographic Evidence

Respirable crystalline silica (RCS) is present in rock strata, above, below, and often between coal seams. Cutting coal, securing the roof and ribs, developing tunnels and shafts, cutting overcasts, and removing overburden are all activities which generate fine respirable silica dust. Freshly fractured respirable silica is highly toxic and causes significantly more lung scarring than coal dust. Cumulative exposure to RCS was associated with increasing radiographic scarring and lung inflammation [10–13]. Larger round scars on chest x-rays have been associated with silicosis [14–16, and the proportion of these miners with these scars has increased in central Appalachia, paralleling the increase in severe disease in these miners [2, 17].

Pathologic Evidence

Chest x-rays only show a size and shape of scar/opacity that is associated with silicosis. The UIC research group decided to go beyond x-ray shadows and look at the tissues of miners with this new and more aggressive form of pneumoconiosis. In 2014 we assembled a case series of 13 miners with this disease who had undergone lung biopsies, transplant, or recent autopsy in order to look more carefully at their lung tissue. These miners from West Virginia, Kentucky, and Pennsylvania, worked in jobs with heavy exposures such as continuous miner operators and roof bolters. We published the results of this work in 2015 [18]. Under the bright light and polarizing light microscope you can clearly see the type of dust in the scar tissue. The surprising finding was that only one of these miners had a classic coal dust form of pneumoconiosis. Six miners had silicosis, or a silica predominant mixed dust disease and four additional had an evenly distributed mixed dust. These findings were clearly an alarm for our research group. The experienced occupational pulmonary pathologists who reviewed this material had not seen such severe silicosis in coal miners. This led the UIC research group to plan two follow up investigations.

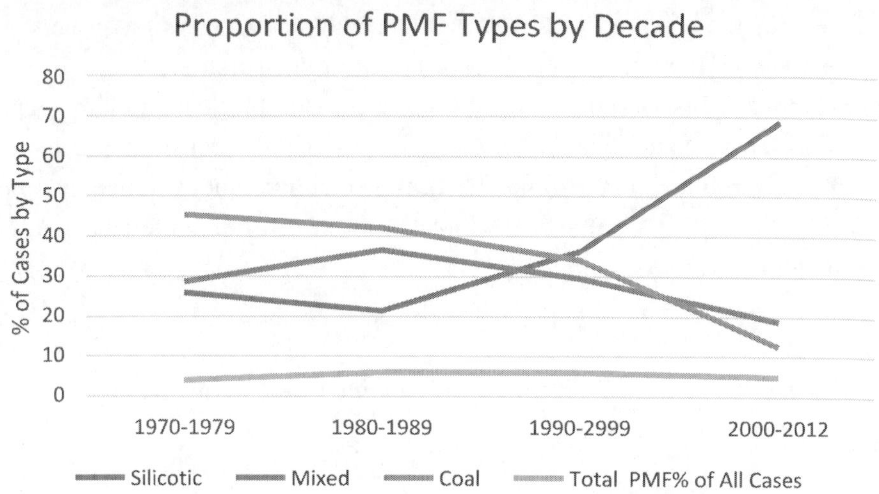

Figure 4. Proportion of PMF cases in National Coal Workers Autopsy Study by type, 1970-2012. Silicotic-type PMF - fused silicotic nodules as the predominant feature (> 75%) of the area of the lesion, mixed-type PMF - >25% but ≤ 75% silicotic nodules, coal-type PMF had ≤ 25% silicotic nodules.

We realized that NIOSH had lung pathology material from more than 7,000 coal miners whose autopsied lungs were submitted as part of the NIOSH National Coal Workers Autopsy Study. We decided to look back at these materials, search for the severe cases, and evaluate the type of PMF that was present and see if there were changes over the decades in the pattern of disease. We classified these cases as coal dust, mixed, or silicotic type of PMF [19]. This had never been done before. We examined the tissues obtained from 376 miners born between 1885 and 1961 who had an average of 33 years of mining experience. These findings were presented at the American Thoracic Society Meetings in Dallas a few weeks ago and showed that there has been a statistically significant change in the type of PMF over historical periods from only 24% of miners having a silicotic type of PMF in specimens accessioned before 1990, to more than 40% after 1990 (See Figure 4). This indicated that miners dying more recently were nearly twice as likely to have a silicotic type of disease.

Mineralogic Evidence

The next study we planned was an evaluation of the mineral particles present in the lung tissue of miners with RPP and PMF. This would allow us to determine if silica was playing an important role. We decided to go beyond light microscopy to field emission scanning electron microscopy and an x-ray probe to examine the particles in the tissue of 100 modern miners compared to 100 autopsied miners' lungs obtained prior to 1996. We have completed this work on the first eight miners recently diagnosed with rapidly progressive pneumoconiosis and PMF and ten historical comparisons. We found that the concentration and proportion of silica particles in the tissues nearly doubled and was statistically significant. These preliminary findings will be presented at the Society of Toxicologic Pathology next week in Raleigh, North Carolina.

Conclusion

I believe that the resurgent epidemic of black lung in central Appalachia is driven in significant part by excessive exposure to respirable crystalline silica. This is supported by the chest radiographic findings in surveys of active miners, the case series studies of the pathology in current miners, the change in type of PMF seen in historical cohorts of miners' lung tissues in the National Coal Workers Autopsy program, as well as our preliminary studies of the mineralogy found in the lungs of current miners compared to those from the last quarter of the twentieth century.

These findings are consistent with high exposures to silica resulting from changes in mining practices including mining thin seam mines as well as using continuous miners to develop slopes and tunnels.

Recommendations

The passage of the new 2014 dust rule, "Lowering Miners' Exposure to Respirable Coal Mine Dust, Including Continuous Personal Dust Monitors" which enacted new regulations to monitor and control dust levels in our nations mines was a significant step forward [20]. However, I believe that MSHA needs to go further and sample respirable crystalline silica more frequently than quarterly using current technologies. Current sampling technology takes days or weeks before silica exposure monitoring results are returned to the mine.

The good news is that NIOSH has developed an in-mine silica analyzer which is paired with a Personal Quartz Monitor to provide reasonable estimates of exposure to RCS, such as at the end of each shift. MSHA should require coal operators to use this technology to better understand exposures to RCS, and which will allow for a much more timely response by operators to control excessive exposures. Daily silica monitoring results could better inform MSHA inspectors on the implementation of ventilation plans or the need to place the mine on a reduced standard. This technology should be provided to miners working in mine development, and in those designated occupations associated with the most severe disease including roof bolters, continuous miner operators and helpers and long wall operators. The results of this data should be posted and made publicly available. MSHA should increase the frequency of monitoring for RCS until a tamper proof personal quartz monitor becomes available.

In addition, evidence indicates that MSHA's Permissible Exposure Limits (PEL) for coal mine dust should have a specific PEL for silica, and that this should equal the current OSHA standard of 50 micrograms/m^3. The health risks caused by exposure to silica were recently reviewed by OSHA in preparation for its new final rule [9]. The risk analysis and work done by OSHA to develop their new silica rule is directly applicable to miners exposed to this same dust.

Finally, I believe there should be enhanced surveillance for miners working in the hot spots of central Appalachia. They should be offered more frequent screening including voluntary participation in chest x-ray and spirometry testing, every 2-3 years rather than every five years. Enhanced physiologic assessment diffusion capacity, a practical lung function test that can detect early lung damage should also be strongly considered in addition to spirometry.

Thank you for the opportunity to provide this testimony. I am pleased to answer any questions you may have.

References

[1] jordana.fyne. *Black Lung Clinics Program Turns 40.* https://www.hrsa.gov/get-health-care/conditions/black-lung/40-anniversary. Published February 14, 2019. Accessed June 14, 2019.

[2] Blackley DJ, Halldin CN, Laney AS. Continued Increase in Prevalence of Coal Workers' Pneumoconiosis in the United States, 1970-2017. *Am J Public Health.* 2018;108(9):1220-1222. doi:10.2105/AJPH.2018.304517.

[3] Blackley D, Crum J, Halldin C, Storey E, Laney A. Resurgence of Progressive Massive Fibrosis in Coal Miners — Eastern Kentucky, 2016. *MMWR Morb Mortal Wkly Rep.* 2016;65:1385-1389. doi:http://dx.doi.org/10.15585/mmwr.mm6549a1.

[4] Blackley D, Reynolds L, Short C, et al. Progressive massive fibrosis in coal miners from 3 clinics in Virginia. *JAMA*. 2018;319(5):500-501. doi:10.1001/jama.2017.18444.

[5] Almberg KS, Halldin CN, Blackley DJ, et al. Progressive Massive Fibrosis Resurgence Identified in U.S. Coal Miners Filing for Black Lung Benefits, 1970-2016. *Ann Am Thorac Soc*. 2018;15(12):1420-1426. doi:10.1513/AnnalsATS.201804-261OC.

[6] Blackley DJ, Halldin CN, Cummings KJ, Laney AS. Lung transplantation is increasingly common among patients with coal workers' pneumoconiosis: Lung Transplantation for Coal Workers' Pneumoconiosis. *Am J Ind Med*. December 2015:n/a-n/a. doi:10.1002/ajim.22551.

[7] Blackley DJ, Halldin CN, Cohen RA, Cummings KJ, Storey E, Laney AS. Misclassification of occupational disease in lung transplant recipients. *J Heart Lung Transplant Off Publ Int Soc Heart Transplant*. 2017;36(5):588-590. doi:10.1016/j.healun.2017.02.021.

[8] Almberg K s., Halldin C n., Go L h. t., et al. Trends in Mortality Patterns Among U.S. Coal Miners Filing for Federal Black Lung Program Benefits, 1970 to 2016. In: *B25. Occupational Exposures Including Deployment Related, Mining, and Agriculture*. American Thoracic Society International Conference Abstracts. American Thoracic Society; 2019:A2759-A2759. doi:10.1164/ajrccm-conference.2019.199.1_MeetingAbstracts.A2759.

[9] *Occupational Exposure to Respirable Crystalline Silica*. Federal Register. https://www.federalregister.gov/documents/2016/03/25/2016-04800/occupational-exposure-to-respirable-crystalline-silica. Published March 25, 2016. Accessed February 20, 2019.

[10] Kuempel ED, Attfield MD, Vallyathan V, et al. Pulmonary inflammation and crystalline silica in respirable coal mine dust: dose-response. *J Biosci*. 2003;28(1):61-69.

[11] Centers for Disease Control and Prevention. *Current Intelligence Bulletin 64: Coal Mine Dust Exposures and Associated Health Outcomes - a Review of Information Published since 1995*. DHHS (NIOSH) Publication No. 2011–172 http://www.cdc.gov/niosh/docs/2011-172/. Accessed October 28, 2012.

[12] Fubini B, Bolis V, Cavenago A, Volante M. Physicochemical properties of crystalline silica dusts and their possible implication in various biological responses. *Scand J Work Environ Health*. 1995;21 Suppl 2:9-14.

[13] Vallyathan V, Castranova V, Pack D, et al. Freshly fractured quartz inhalation leads to enhanced lung injury and inflammation. Potential role of free radicals. *Am J Respir Crit Care Med*. 1995;152(3):1003–1009.

[14] Fernie JM, Ruckley VA. Coalworkers' pneumoconiosis: correlation between opacity profusion and number and type of dust lesions with special reference to opacity type. *Br J Ind Med*. 1987;44(4):273–277.

[15] Ruckley VA, Fernie JM, Chapman JS, et al. Comparison of radiographic appearances with associated pathology and lung dust content in a group of coalworkers. *Br J Ind Med*. 1984;41(4):459.

[16] Soutar CA, Collins HP. Classification of progressive massive fibrosis of coalminers by type of radiographic appearance. *Br J Ind Med*. 1984;41(3):334-339.

[17] Laney AS, Petsonk EL, Attfield MD. Pneumoconiosis among underground bituminous coal miners in the United States: is silicosis becoming more frequent? *Occup Environ Med*. 2010;67(10):652-656. doi:10.1136/oem.2009.047126.

[18] Cohen RA, Petsonk EL, Rose C, et al. Lung Pathology in U.S. Coal Workers with Rapidly Progressive Pneumoconiosis Implicates Silica and Silicates. *Am J Respir Crit Care Med*. October 2015. doi:10.1164/rccm.201505-1014OC.

[19] Cohen R a., Orandle M, Hubbs A f., et al. Pathologic Type of Progressive Massive Fibrosis in the National Coal Workers? Autopsy Study (NCWAS) 1971-1996. In: *B25. Occupational Exposures Including Deployment Related, Mining, and Agriculture*. American Thoracic Society International Conference Abstracts. American Thoracic Society; 2019:A2758-A2758. doi:10.1164/ajrccm-conference.2019.199.1_MeetingAbstracts.A2758.

[20] Department of Labor MS and HA. Lowering Miners' Exposure to Respirable Coal Mine Dust, Including Continuous Personal Dust Monitors; Final Rule. *Fed Regist*. 2014;79(84):24814-24994.

Chairwoman ADAMS. Thank you.

We will now recognize Mr. Hairston. You are recognized for 5 minutes, sir.

TESTIMONY OF GARY HAIRSTON, VICE PRESIDENT, FAYETTE COUNTY BLACK LUNG ASSOCIATION

Mr. HAIRSTON. Chairman Adams, Ranking Member Byrne, and the subcommittee, I would like to thank you for letting me be here today.

My name is Gary Hairston. I worked in a coal mine for 27 1/2 years. I am the vice president of Fayette County Black Lung Association. I just want to thank you for this opportunity to speak here today.

I worked for Westmoreland Coal Company. That is where I started, at Westmoreland. I was 21 years old when I went there. I was a trainee, a redhead they called us; I worked for Westmoreland 8 1/2 years. I worked for Maben Energy for 6 1/2—13 years. I worked for Maben Energy for 13 years as a—at Brushy Gap and Stoney Gap as a scoop operator and electrician. I worked 6 years with Massey Coal Company as an electrician and working on belts.

At them mines, there was plenty of dust. Maben Energy was the worst. I tell you, the dust there, you couldn't even see—when you are running equipment you couldn't even see where you are really going.

I tell you what, it was so bad at Maben Energy that we didn't even hang curtains. The only time we hung curtains is when the— we know the inspector was coming or he was around the mine. And on top of that we didn't even—we had to put our dust samplers in a good area. We couldn't put them where the dust was out so we wouldn't get a bad sample.

At Massey also there was plenty of dust where I was working at, but there the only time I really—the bad—the worst dust was when I was in the return, had to work on equipment while the mine was operating. They wouldn't shut down—they wouldn't put them out in the good air, they put them in the place where they can keep running the coal.

I was 48 years old when I had to quit work. I couldn't even play with my grandkids. Then I had to watch my wife work go out of the house and started to work to help us make the ends meet at our house. You don't know how that feels when you're balled up and people have to take care of your house. And you see your wife go out to take care of it. I never did think at this young age that I wouldn't be able to take care of my family.

But I am really here to talk about two things today for the Black Lung Association and the communities with black lungs. We are here to try to get something done about—the first thing is excise tax on coal intended to pay the cost of the run of the Black Lung program and to pay the Black Lung benefits for miners like me.

When the coal company goes bankrupt it is up to the Federal Black Lung benefit that start taking over where the coal company just quits paying. When they file bankruptcy they ain't got to pay no more black lung to us, they—we got to be turned over to the Federal Government.

After 32 years Congress allowed more than half of the excise tax to expire in January. So now the excise tax is only \$.50 instead of \$1.10, \$.25 on surface mining, where it was \$.50. According to the Government Accountability Office, this decrease will cause the Black Lung Disability Trust Fund to reach a debt of \$15.4 million in 2050. And the coal company doesn't have to worry about paying because then it will be turned over to the tax payers. You all will be paying for what the company should be paying for.

Especially at the time when more coal miners are getting black lung, the coal companies don't want to pay nothing. They are turning the excise tax over to the people.

Our second concern was the effort of the Attorneys General and the Trump Administration to end the Affordable Care Act to the court because the Act continues to—I am sorry. I am just upset.

[The statement of Mr. Hairston follows:]

Testimony of Gary Hairston, o/b/o the National Black Lung Association, U.S. House of Representation, Subcommittee on Workforce Protections, "Breathless and Betrayed: What is MSHA Doing to Protect Miners from the Resurgence of Black Lung," June 20, 2019

Chairwoman Adams, Ranking Member Byrne, and Members of the Subcommittee:

My name is Gary Hairston, and I am from Beckley, West Virginia. I serve as vice president of the Fayette County Black Lung Association and thank you for the opportunity to speak here today on behalf of the National Black Lung Association.

I was an underground coal miner in West Virginia for 27 years. I worked for Westmoreland Coal Company 8 years at their East Gulf mine, then 13 years for Maben Energy at Tommy Creek and Stoney Gap mines as an electrician and scoop operator, and the last 6 years I worked for Massey Coal Company at Brushy Eagle and Low Gap doing maintenance and repair work on the beltline.

There was plenty of dust at all those mines, but at Maben, the dust and smoke was so bad that you could hardly see. They told us not to hang ventilation curtain unless there were inspectors in the mines and to make sure the samplers were out of the dust.

At Massey, I also was exposed to a lot of dust and most of all when I had to repair the equipment that broke down in the return air filled with dust.

I was only 48 years old when I got too short of breath to do the work. When I went to the doctor, they found a mass in my lung. At first, the doctor thought it was cancer, but a biopsy showed that it was really complicated black lung.

Being disabled at such a young age nearly broke my spirit. I couldn't provide for my family. I couldn't play ball with my grandkids. And my wife had to go out and work to help support us.

With the help of a student clinic at Washington & Lee Law School, I was able to get federal black lung benefits that now helps us to make ends meet. Sometimes I can still do a few odd jobs if they don't require much exertion. I'm on the board of directors of a federally funded community health center that helps miners with black lung. I've gotten involved with other coal miners again through the Black Lung Association.

I'm here today to talk about two things that are very important to the Black Lung Association and to all coal miners with black lung:

Excise Tax on Coal

First is the Black Lung Excise Tax on coal that is intended to pay the costs of administering the black lung program and also the black lung benefits for miners like me when the responsible coal company goes bankrupt. After I became disabled, Massey Coal Company was responsible for my benefits, but Massey sold out to Alpha Coal Company. Then, Alpha went bankrupt, so now, my benefits have to come from the Trust Fund After 32 years, Congress allowed more than half of that excise tax to expire this past January. And, according to the Government Accounting Office, this decrease will cause the Black Lung Disability Trust Fund debt to reach 15.4 billion dollars in 2050 and shift the burden from the coal industry to the taxpayers.

At a time when more and more miners are getting complicated black lung and disabled like me, the Trust Fund should be fully funded, and Congress should reject the cuts in benefits being proposed by the National Mining Association. It is very important to the growing number of miners who are suffering from black lung and their families that Congress fully restore the Excise Tax Rate for at least 10 years.

Many of our members also are UMWA pensioners, so we urge you to pass legislation like the American Miners' Act of 2019 (S 27) that would restore the Excise Tax and protect our UMWA pensions.

Affordable Care Act

Our second concern is the effort by state attorney generals and the Trump administration to end the Affordable Care Act through the courts because the Act contains two amendments that are extremely important to coal miners disabled by black lung.

One provides continuing benefits to the widows and dependent children of miners who qualify for federal black lung. Without this amendment, those widows and dependent children will lose their benefits unless and until they could prove that black lung hastened the miner's death. In most cases, this would require a long legal battle at a time when widows and children are most vulnerable.

The other amendment is what we call the "15-year [rebuttable] presumption." If a coal miner has a totally disabling pulmonary impairment and 15 or more years of exposure to coal mine dust, then it is presumed that all those years of dust exposure contributed to his or her disability. This presumption is based on a lot of scientific evidence and can be rebutted if the coal company can show that the miner's disability was caused entirely by something else.

Also, the Affordable Care Act provides:

a) Medical coverage for about 225,000 West Virginians,
b) No exclusions for pre-existing conditions,
c) Coverage for children up to age 26, and
d) Funding for community health centers.

As I mentioned before, I am on the board of a community health center, and I know firsthand how important all of these provisions are to our members and to our communities.

It is a shame that our own Attorney General (Patrick Morrisey) and the current administration in Washington are trying to end the Affordable Care Act with nothing to replace these important provisions and benefits. The President made a lot of promises to West Virginia coal miners during his campaign, and we were not expecting this kind of treatment from his administration.

Thank you and I would be glad to answer your questions.

Chairwoman ADAMS. Mr. Hairston, we are going ask some questions when we finish, so thank you for your testimony, and—

Mr. HAIRSTON. Thank you all for letting me speak.

Chairwoman ADAMS.—I am just, you know, very compassionate about all that you have been through. So we thank you for just being here today and sharing your story.

Mr. HAIRSTON. Thank you.

Chairwoman ADAMS. Okay. All right.

We will now hear from Mr. Watzman. You have 5 minutes, sir.

TESTIMONY OF BRUCE WATZMAN, FORMER MEMBER, NATIONAL MINING ASSOCIATION

Mr. WATZMAN. Thank you, Madam Chair, and members of the Subcommittee. I appreciate the opportunity to be with you today to share my views based on almost four decades of experience working on issues related to miner safety and health.

In December 2018, I retired from the National Mining Association following a 37-year career. During my career, I was primarily responsible for representing the industry on issues impacting the health and safety of our nation's coal miners, including issues related to the federal Black Lung Program.

During my career, I served as a member of the National Institute for Occupational Safety and Health, Mine Safety and Health Research Advisory Committee, and participated as a member on numerous NIOSH and MSHA partnerships formed to address specific safety and health issues.

The views expressed today are solely mine. They do, however, reflect positions the industry has advanced to improve miner safety and health. I was involved in the development of those positions and I believe they would, if enacted, result in safety and health improvements beyond those we've already achieved.

At the outset, let me be clear, if we had the ability to turn back the hands of time to prevent the suffering that has been reported, I can assure you that the industry would have already done so. Unfortunately, this cannot be done. But what we can and must do is to ensure that 10, 15, or 20 years from now there will be no more suffering, nor the need for another hearing because lung disease among coal miners will have been eradicated.

The disease that is being reported on today results from exposures that occurred 10 to 20 years ago. It does not reflect the improvements of MSHA's new dust rule and the impacts of that will not be known for many years to come. What is needed today is to ensure that the actions MSHA has already taken, and those being contemplated, are based on sound science, reflect a complete understanding of the relationship of exposure and disease, provide mine operators the ability to utilize all tools available to protect the workforce, and, most importantly, are protective of miners' health. During my career, I was privileged to work with many talented individuals in industry and academia who work day-in-and-day-out to ensure that every miner returns safely to his or her loved ones and who upon their retirement would be able to enjoy the fruits of their labors. Much success has occurred, injury and fatality rates are down. But what was missed, and everyone bears some responsibility, is that we ignored certain warning signs that should have caused us to broaden our examination of the emerging increases in black lung disease.

I recall several meetings I attended, with people within NIOSH and others, where early warning signs were indicated. We talked about rapid progression CWP in a meeting with NIOSH. We sought additional information so we could further examine it when I was part of the industry. Unfortunately, the requests were denied due to HIPAA concerns.

We talked about the clustering that has occurred in southern Appalachia, the area which has become characterized as the "hot spot" region because of keen interest of the cases of PMF were being diagnosed following a latency period far shorter than traditional coal workers' pneumoconiosis. It was following this that researchers, including those at NIOSH, began to identify silica as the culprit resulting in these cases of early onset disease.

During this same time, we worked collaboratively with NIOSH and MSHA in the development of the personal continuous dust monitor. I will tell you that is a game-changer as it relates to dust sampling in the industry. But as reliable as the CPDM is in measuring coal dust concentrations, it unfortunately does not provide real time silica sampling. A renewed effort to develop a real-time silica monitor must be a priority.

But there are additional things that must be done. We must change so that mandatory surveillance, mandatory x-ray surveillance is applied across the industry. We have no baseline understanding today of the prevalence of the disease because only approximately one-third of the miners participate in the x-ray surveillance program. Without that basic information employers can't work with their employees to help them during their working career.

In tandem with this, the Part 90 program that MSHA administers must be changed. Exercising a Part 90 right under the law is at the discretion of miners. Studies have shown that only approximately 15 percent of the miners exercise this right to be moved to a less dusty workplace at no loss of pay. The law needs to be changed to accommodate that.

Thirdly, the use of administrative controls and personal protection must be recognized for mining. It is recognized in other industries and it is long overdue for mining.

Madam Chairwoman, I thank you for the time. I look forward to your questions.

[The statement of Mr. Watzman follows:]

Testimony of Bruce Watzman, Before the Subcommittee on Workforce Protections, U.S. House Representatives on "Breathless and Betrayed: What Is MSHA Doing to Protect Miners from the Resurgence of Black Lung Disease?" June 20, 2019

Thank you, Madam Chair, and members of the Subcommittee. I appreciate the opportunity to be with you today to share my views based on my years of experience working on issues related to miner safety and health. In December 2018 I retired following a 37-year career with the National Mining Association and one of its predecessor organizations, the National Coal Association. During my career, I was primarily responsible for representing the industry on issues impacting the health and safety of our nation's coal miners, including issues related to the federal black lung program. During my employment I served as a member of the National Institute for Occupational Safety and Health (NIOSH), Mine Safety and Health Research Advisory Committee and participated as a member on numerous NIOSH and Mine Safety and Health Administration (MSHA) partnerships formed to address specific safety and health problems. The views expressed today are solely mine. They do however reflect positions the industry has advanced to improve miner safety and health, as I was involved in the development of those positions and believe they would, if enacted, result in safety and health improvements beyond those already achieved.

At the outset let me be clear, if we had the ability to turn back the hands of time to prevent the suffering that has been reported I can assure you that the industry would have already done so. Unfortunately, this cannot be done but what can and must be done is to ensure that 10, 15 or 20 years from now there will be no more suffering nor the need for another hearing because lung disease among coal miners has been eradicated. The disease being reported on recently results from exposures that occurred 10 to 20-years ago. It does not reflect the improvements brought about by MSHA's new dust rule and the impacts of that will not be known for many years to come. What is needed today is to ensure that the actions MSHA has already taken, and those being contemplated, are based on sound science, reflect a complete understanding of the relationship of exposure and disease, provide mine operators the ability to utilize all the tools available to protect their workforce, and most importantly are protective of miners' health.

During my career I was privileged to work with many talented individuals in the industry and academia who worked day-in-and-day-out to ensure that every miner returned safely to his or her loved ones each day and who, upon their retirement, would be able to enjoy the fruits of his or her labors. Given the fact that the number of mine fatalities and injuries continues to decline and the goal of zero fatalities is within reach, I believe these efforts have been largely, although not entirely successful. What we missed, and everyone bears some responsibility, is that we ignored certain warning signs that should have caused us to broaden our examination of the emerging increases in cases of lung disease.

I recall being invited to a meeting at NIOSH during which NIOSH researchers presented the results of research into what they characterized as "rapid progression coal workers pneumoconiosis." In short, the researchers were identifying the onset of lung disease following latency periods far shorter than had been experienced in the past. In an effort to better understand this phenomenon, industry requested more detailed information on the identified cases. Unfortunately, the requests were denied due to HIPAA concerns.

The next event was NIOSH's designation, based on the results of the institute's limited x-ray surveillance program, of a geographic clustering of cases of progressive massive fibrosis (PMF) in the region of Southern West Virginia, Southwest Virginia and Eastern Kentucky. This area, which became characterized as the "Hot Spot" region, became of keen interest as cases of PMF were being diagnosed following a latency period far shorter than traditional coal workers pneumoconiosis. It was following this that researchers, including those within NIOSH, began to identify silica as the culprit resulting in these cases of early on-set lung disease.

During this same period the industry, in conjunction with researchers, initiated a detailed program to improve the sampling technology for coal mine dust. This multi-year effort culminated in the development and production of a commercially available Continuous Personal Dust Monitor (CPDM). The new CPDM represented a massive change in the technology from the prior system, providing real-time exposure results so miners and mine operators could take actions, if necessary, during the miner's working shift to prevent end-of-shift over-exposures. NIOSH's financial participation in funding development of this technology and their technical expertise were central to this effort. I was fortunate to have participated with these dedicated professionals. As reliable as the CPDM is in measuring coal dust concentrations it, unfortunately, does not able to provide real-time silica sampling and the industry must continue to rely on an antiquated system that requires MSHA collected samples to be sent to the MSHA lab for analysis. A renewed effort to develop a real-time silica sampler must be a priority. While I know you are not the appropriators, I implore you to encourage your colleagues on the Appropriations Committee to ensure that sufficient funding is provided to NIOSH to further ongoing efforts to develop and commercialize a real-time silica sampler.

In addition to the development of a real-time silica sampler others changes to MSHA regulations and policy are necessary to eradicate lung disease among coal miners. Under current law these changes cannot be accommodated. Congress has a constructive role to play in achieving our shared goal and I encourage you to consider targeted revisions that promote miner safety and health rather than ones designed to punish who some believe are recalcitrant operators. Politics needs to be set-aside if we are to achieve the goal of ending lung disease among coal miners.

There are steps that can be taken beyond what is already underway. First, there is no baseline understanding of the prevalence of black lung disease. The one-third participation in NIOSH's x-ray surveillance program across the entirety of the workforce does not provide a realistic appraisal of disease frequency across the workforce. To overcome this, participation in NIOSH's x-ray surveillance can no longer be voluntary. Screening must be mandatory so that intervention actions, if necessary, can be taken during the miners working career.

Second, and in tandem with a mandatory surveillance program, a process must be established for miners showing evidence of disease to share these results with their employer. Under the Mine Act miners who have evidence of black lung have the option, at their discretion, to utilize their rights under Part 90 to switch to a job in a less dusty environment at no loss in pay. Unfortunately, the current process is solely at the discretion of the miner. Throughout the history of this program few miners have exercised this right even though the Mine Act provides protection. Recent studies found that less than 15 percent of miners eligible for transfer notified their employers. Employers must be afforded the opportunity to help their employees by transferring them to alternate locations or offering additional personal protection equipment.

Third, the use of administrative controls and an approved respiratory protection program that utilizes personal protective equipment (PPE) should be recognized and encouraged. The Act recognizes neither work practices nor PPE as tools to reduce miner's exposure to dust. Respiratory equipment is a recognized control measure to mitigate health risks in many industrial work environments. The same protections should be extended to miners. Some operators voluntarily provide PPE to their workforce but to the detriment of miner health, MSHA does not recognize their use in mining.

Lastly, MSHA should recognize the utility of having personal dust monitoring devices that provide real time measurement of dust exposures by permitting mines to implement worker rotation programs. Such programs could be designed to reduce worker exposure independent of occupational or environmental dust concentrations. In many cases, representative dust sampling techniques are adequate for ensuring workers are protected from overexposure to dust. However, in some cases, worker rotation guided by the data obtained from personal dust monitoring devices could offer greater protection. Regulations should be modified to allow miners to rotate with personal dust monitors to provide accurate sampling of individual exposures across shifts.

Madam Chair, thank you for the opportunity to be here today. I look forward to your questions.

Chairwoman ADAMS. Thank you, sir.

We will now recognize Mr. Roberts. You have 5 minutes, sir.

TESTIMONY OF CECIL ROBERTS, PRESIDENT, UNITED MINE WORKERS OF AMERICA

Mr. ROBERTS. Thank you, Madam Chairwoman, for this opportunity and also Ranking Member Byrne.

My name is Cecil Roberts. I am president of United Mine Workers. I have represented coal miners now for 42 years. Prior to that I was a coal miner for 5 1/2 years.

In my career I have worked closely with the medical community, particularly Dr. Cohen, and before him, Dr. Rasmussen, who is revered in the coal fields of southern West Virginia. Unfortunately, he has passed away. I have also worked with the Black Lung Associations.

And let me just comment on my friend, Mr. Hairston. And I want to thank him for his courage to come here today, suffering from pneumoconiosis and having the courage to testify before this committee.

I have also worked with all of the clinics throughout the coal fields, and I am a board member of the Cabin Creek Clinic in southern West Virginia. So I am a native West Virginian, and I come here with a vast amount of time that I have spent on this issue. And I must say, in all due respect and honesty, the views of workers in the coal fields are not good with respect at how they have been treated by their government, whether it is at the state level or the Federal level. And I don't have to point very much further than how we got the first Act to protect coal miners in 1969. It took 159 years, by the way, before this government decided they ought to try to keep miners safe. And that was when the first law was passed in 1969. It would not have passed in 1969, Madam Chairwoman and members of this committee, if 78 miners had not lost their lives at Farmington in northern

West Virginia in the blink of an eye. And all the widows and all their friends gathered around that mine portal, shown on television in 50 states in the United States of America. That would never have happened if the country had not witnessed this.

Along with the passage of health and safety language, we got the first recognition—the first time in 1969, after 159 years, the first time that anyone in this government said there was such a thing as pneumoconiosis. For years and years there had been a denial that there was such a thing. Miners knew they were sick. Miners were dying in their 40s. They thought they had something called miners' asthma because the medical community never identified it as an occupational illness and neither did their government.

So there is a long tough history here. It wasn't long after the passage of this Act—in the '80s, there was vast fraud throughout this coal industry. Over 500 companies were cited for fraud, taking samples of miners who work for them, and over 4,000 citations issued. That wasn't the first time this happened. This has happened repeatedly throughout history.

I want to go quickly, Madam Chairwoman, because I don't want to just talk about this problem, I want to talk about some solutions here. And beginning on page 56 of my very lengthy testimony that we have submitted, we suggest that Congress needs to take necessary action, number one, to require the Federal Mine Safety and Health Administration to assume the responsibility for conducting respirable dust sampling. We can no longer allow coal companies to do this. That is like me calling up the police and say I am speeding on 79. It saves a lot of money, but I am not going to do that. And the coal industry can no longer be responsible for administering the protections these miners needs about what kind of dust they are exposed to. Remember, it is the coal companies that take these samples and there is a long history of fraud here.

Number two, Congress needs to take action to require the Federal Mine Safety and Health Administration to promulgate an emergency temporary standard that recreates a permissible exposure limit for silica. Dr. Cohen spoke to this. We can all come here today and act like we need some more time, but coal miners don't have any time. They are dying in West Virginia and they are dying in Kentucky and they are dying in Virginia, and they don't have any more time to wait here. We need an exposure limit for how much silica you can be exposed to.

Number three, Congress needs to take the necessary actions to require the Federal Mine Safety and Health Administration to promulgate an emergency temporary standard that expands the walk around rights to allow coal miners to be part of this sampling. They are not part of this, only the coal companies take these samples. So coal miners need to be part of this.

Number four, Congress needs to take the actions that are necessary to address the problem of miner representation and participation, not represented by organized labor. Organized labor, we take care of this ourselves because of our contract, but non union miners don't have these protections.

Number five, Congress must take immediate action to restore an increase to funding stream necessary to pay for benefits owed to coal miners from the Black Lung Disability Trust Fund.

And with that, Madam Chairwoman, I would just point out that I have presented to this committee a lengthy presentation. Every committee that has ever been established in this Congress to deal with this, have failed to do so, so I hope today that we take some action to protect these miners.

Thank you.

[The statement of Mr. Roberts follows:]

TESTIMONY OF CECIL E. ROBERTS, BEFORE THE UNITED STATES HOUSE OF REPRESENTATIVES, COMMITTEE ON EDUCATION AND LABOR, SUBCOMMITTEE ON WORKFORCE PROTECTIONS, JUNE 20, 2019

Good morning Chairwoman Adams; Ranking Member Byrne and the members of the Committee on Education and Labor in attendance today. My name is Cecil E. Roberts, International President of the United Mine Workers of America ("UMWA"). In that capacity I represent the largest unionized group of active and retired coal miners in North America. However, today Madam Chairman, I come before the members of this distinguished Committee as the representative of every coal miner in this nation, whether an active dues-paying member, a retiree of the UMWA or a coal miner who is working in the industry and has not yet joined the ranks of the Union. In short, I am here to be the voice of the miners who have risked their lives and health to energize and build this nation, no matter where they live and no matter their affiliation with organized labor.

The testimony I will present to this Committee today will outline, in great detail, the struggles that coal miners face every day in this country. These struggles exist for miners who are actively employed in the industry and those who have left the mines, whether they retire after years of hard work in dusty and dangerous conditions or they are forced from their jobs by occupational injury or illness. I will focus my testimony on the specific topic of this very important hearing: the effects of Coal Workers' Pneumoconiosis ("CWP" or "Black Lung disease") on the lives of America's coal miners.

The purpose of this hearing is to discuss the resurgence in reported cases of Black Lung across the coalfields of the country. According to data from the Center for Disease Control ("CDC"), the National Institute for Occupational Safety and Health ("NIOSH"), the Mine Safety and Health Administration ("MSHA" or "Agency") and a host of independent studies, the highest concentration of these historic increases in the disease are occurring in the central Appalachian Region of the United States (attachments 1-4).

This area includes all or parts of Kentucky, Ohio, Pennsylvania, Virginia and West Virginia.

I hope that this Committee will forgive me if I repeat myself in my testimony today. I ask at the outset for your indulgence if you hear me say something at this hearing that you have heard me say before. But the truth is, I cannot help but repeat myself. This is not the first time I have climbed the steps of the Capitol to speak on behalf of coal miners regarding the dangers of Black Lung disease. While the Union would agree that recent studies show there has been an alarming resurgence in the number of Black Lung cases, including the most severe form of the disease known as Progressive Massive Fibrosis ("PMF"), I have been here before to discuss that risk. The industry, and the Federal government have known for years of this resurgence. I have testified in the past about the failures of MSHA's dust control rules and policies. I have testified before about the nefarious methods that operators have used to circumvent mandatory dust monitoring. The UMWA has recommended methods and ways of improving the sampling system and that might have helped head off this resurgence. But no action has been taken.

And so, I repeat myself. I repeat myself because I come here today not explain to you a new or unprecedented danger in the nation's coalfields. We know this disease, we know what causes it, and we know how to prevent it. We do not lack information. What we lack today is the same thing we lacked all the other times I came to speak to Congress regarding the dangers of Black Lung: we lack the will to act.

Therefore, I do not apologize. I will never apologize for raising the uncomfortable truth that this government has all the data and the tools necessary to end the Black Lung epidemic in the nation's coalfields, but has consistently failed to act. If you hear me say something that I already raised in May of 2003, the first time I testified before a Congressional Committee on this issue, consider it an indictment of this government's failure to take seriously the known threat of Black Lung disease. Know that I repeat myself today because, since May 2003, over 18,000 miners have died in this country from Black Lung (attachment 5). And if Congress again fails to act, that number is expected to skyrocket in the coming decades. I will not stop repeating these truths until Congress listens. Until Congress passes legislation that requires MSHA to promulgate specific standards that protect miners, and corrects the shortcomings of the current dust standards, nothing is going to change.

The Union would argue that the seeds of the recent wave of CWP were sown by the actions of Federal agencies and coal operators whose primary job is to protect the health and safety of the nation's miners. This epidemic was further propagated by medical and legal professionals that profited from the misery of those miners unfortunate enough to contract this horrible disease. The fact is Madam Chairman, CWP is a preventable occupational disease (attachment 6) that would have been eradicated from the industry years ago, but for the greed of the industry and the failings of those who are charged to protect the nation's miners.

The History of Black Lung in the United States

It is important to understand the scope of this problem in a historical sense if we are to understand the situation we find ourselves facing today. The problem we are discussing has been plaguing the coal industry and has been a horrific reality for miners since the industry began large scale industrial mining in the mid-1800's. According to the research done by Nash Dunn (attachment 7), a Communications Specialist at North Carolina State University, more than 200,000 miners have died from Black Lung disease since the turn of the last century. A separate report *Undermining Safety: A Report on Coal Mine Safety* by Christopher W. Shaw (attachment 8), a policy analyst at the Center for Study of Responsive Law, claims, that historically "there were at least 365,000 deaths from pneumoconiosis (prior to the passage of the Coal Act of 1969), and a further 120,000 miners succumbed to the disease over the next thirty years." We should all take a moment and allow that number to sink in.

As we think about these numbers, we should not lose sight of what we are really talking about here. No matter what number you choose to accept, these miners were fathers and sons, mothers and daughters, they were grandmothers and grandfathers, aunts and uncles, they were part of a family and members of the community. These lives were cut short in the most gruesome way imaginable. These miners died struggling for their final breath, literally suffocating as a result of a preventable disease. Madam Chairman and members of the Committee, I submit to you that when it comes to protecting miners from exposure to coal mine dust, something has been very wrong for a very long time.

There are credible reports throughout history of doctors and mine operators extolling the benefits of breathing coal dust, noting the coughing experienced by miners would in fact clear their lungs. Much like evidence regarding the dangers of smoking cigarettes, industry and government downplayed the hazard of respirable coal dust. The coal industry was making profits and the victims were simply expendable. Despite evidence to the contrary and the efforts of the United Mine Workers, this type of thinking continued in this country through the 1960's.

It was not until the Farmington #9 Mine Disaster on November 20, 1968, where 78 miners were killed in a series of explosions, of which 19 miners remain entombed in the #9 mine today, that the Federal Government was finally forced to take action. To be honest Madam Chairman, had it not been for the fact that the #9 Disaster was the first mine explosion carried live on television across the nation and around the world, it is doubtful any substantive action would have resulted from even that tragic event. The American people were publicly outraged and called for Congress to take action. It is an unfortunate reality that miners in this country must die in large numbers, and the suffering of miners and their families must be shown on television, before anything is done to protect them from the hazards that this industry allows to exist.

I bring this up, Madam Chairman, because it was not until December of 1969 that President Richard Nixon reluctantly signed the Coal Mine Health and Safety Act ("Coal Act"). Included in the Coal Act was language limiting the amount of respirable coal mine dust permitted in the mine atmosphere. By that time, according to reports, hundreds of thousands of miners had died from Black Lung disease in the United States. These miners died alone, one at a time in the seclusion of their homes or hospital rooms. They were isolated from the world, only their families knew of their suffering. Industry leaders and the federal government turned a blind eye to that suffering. No television cameras chronicled their final, gasping moments.

The Coal Act was a monumental piece of legislation and I do not wish to diminish the protections it afforded miners. However, there were pieces of that legislation that were ripe for fraud and deception. The most obvious problem in that regard deals specifically with the important matter we are here to discuss today, the enforcement and policing of the Respirable Dust Sampling Program. To put it bluntly, the incidence of fraud on the part of the mine operators and lack of adequate enforcement by MSHA has been a problem from the inception of the program. I understand that this statement may seem inflammatory to many people, however, I intend to demonstrate these facts through my testimony.

The initial problem with the dust sampling program was created when the Mine Safety and Health Administration promulgated a rule allowing the mine operators to run the program (attachment 9, Section 202 of the Coal Act). Despite the Union's objections and the vocal opposition of active miners, the routine sampling of miners was placed in the hands of mine management. In the eyes of the miners and their representatives, allowing the mine operators to administer the program doomed it from the beginning. These are the very same individuals who callously placed miners in excessively dusty areas of the mine with no regard for the long-term damage they were causing to their health.

Even in the earliest days of the sampling program it was common knowledge among miners that dust sampling by the mine operators was not being done in a manner that would reduce exposure to excessive respirable dust or enhance their health. The gravimetric sampling devices were often carried by company personnel in outby,[1] meaning less dusty, areas of the mine or hung in cleaner intake air entries.[2] This not only continued to place miners lives at risk, it further eroded the credibility of the program and the miners' faith in MSHA.

---

[1] Locations in mines are described by their position relative to the cutting face of the coal. If a miner is standing in the middle of the mine, halfway between the portal (entrance) and the face, the face is "inby" and the portal is "outby." If a miner is standing directly at the face, the entire mine behind him/her is "outby." Miners sometimes refer to "outby areas" when referring to areas far from the working face, where there is less dust.

[2] Intake air entries are the passageways in the mine where fresh air is pumped towards the face. Because these entries contain fresh air and are "upstream" from the face, they are less dusty.

All White Center Tampering (AWC) Case

While the Union suspected for many years that mine operators were tampering with the sampling devices and sending fraudulent data to the Agency in order to meet the requirements of the law, the first conclusive evidence of deception was uncovered in the late 1980's (attachment 10). The Agency became aware that more than 500 coal companies had tampered with dust samples at more than 850 operations. MSHA issued 4,710 citations and $6.5 million in fines to coal operators.

In this case, the dust sampling cassettes used by the company to monitor miners' exposure were sent to MSHA as required by regulation for weighing and evaluation. During that testing MSHA technicians discovered the filters inside many of the cassettes all displayed a strange characteristic. The center of the filters were absent of dust, creating a "doughnut hole," almost like this area of the filter was new, despite being underground and operating in the mine atmosphere. It was determined at the time that the only possible way for this to occur would be if someone blew air through the cassette to dislodge and purge the dust from the filter. This phenomenon became known as the "Abnormal White Center" ("AWC") case and the tampering ended any shred of faith miners had in the program.

The Coal Mine Respirable Dust Task Group

In May 1991, in the aftermath of the AWC case, the Honorable Lynn Martin, Secretary of Labor, directed MSHA to conduct a review of the Respirable Dust Sampling Program. In response to the Secretary's directive, the Agency created the *Coal Mine Respirable Dust Task Group* (Task Group) to review all aspects of the sampling program (attachment 11, pertinent excerpts from the Task Group). Notably, the Task Group did not include representatives from Labor, Industry, NIOSH or other interested parties connected to the mining industry. In essence, the Secretary was permitting the Agency that had failed to adequately protect miners from the deceptive actions by coal mine operators to investigate itself.

Despite the fact that they were given no formal role in the Task Group, miners and many mine health and safety experts expressed their concern that mine operators could not be trusted to administer the coal dust sampling program. They contended that, "there is simply too great an incentive to manipulate the program, and a lack of adequate MSHA oversight makes it far too easy for some operators to do so." These critics also, "urged that MSHA assume responsibility for the collection of all samples of the mine environment used for compliance determinations."

While the Task Group offered recommendations, most would prove to be superficial and therefore ineffective. As to the question of MSHA taking responsibility for all compliance sampling, the Task Group failed to even make a recommendation. They instead kicked the can down the road arguing that MSHA took strong action after operator abuse and that it would require the Agency to redirect significant resources towards that goal. Perhaps the most disingenuous reason for the Task Groups refusal to make such a recommendation was that, "the future adoption of a program based on continuous fixed-site monitoring would significantly reduce the need for either the operator or MSHA to conduct periodic sampling."

The Task Group then doubled down on its decision not to wrest control of the sampling program by stating, "The Task Group believes that the existing operator sampling program can provide adequate assurance that miners will not be exposed to unhealthful levels of respirable coal mine dust until continuous monitoring is feasible, if appropriate improvements are made in the program." This was particularly absurd given the fact that the AWC case, among other incidents, proved that "adequate assurances" were not present. Further, the Task Group did not address the fact that the technology for continuous monitoring was still decades away. That meant that in light of the coal industry's demonstrated circumvention of the respirable dust standards, the Task Group's solution was a few more decades of operator-administered dust tests. In short, no change.

The Task Group failed in its primary mission to make practical and necessary recommendations that would protect coal miners from continued exposure to excessive respirable coal mine dust. Instead they made inconsequential recommendations that did not alter the worsening trajectory of the dust control program. Worse, they devalued the life of every miner in the country by not taking bold and decisive action. They determined the financial cost of providing protection for the miner was too high. This was an abdication of responsibility by a group made up of individuals working for the Agency charged by law to protect the health and safety of the nation's miners.

Advisory Committee on the Elimination of Pneumoconiosis among the Nation's Coal Workers

Five years later, the Advisory Committee on the Elimination of Pneumoconiosis among Coal Mine Workers ("Advisory Committee") was established by the Honorable Robert B. Reich, Secretary of Labor, on January 31, 1995. The Committee was chartered to "make recommendations for improving the program to control respirable coal mine dust in underground and surface mines in the United States." The Committee was to "examine how to eradicate pneumoconiosis through the control of coal mine respirable dust and the reduction of miners' exposure to achieve the purpose of the Federal Coal Mine Health and Safety Act of 1969 and the 1977 Mine Act amendments" and to "review information and experience in the United States and abroad concerning the prevention of pneumoconiosis among coal miners; the availability of current state-of-the-art engineering controls to prevent overexposure to respirable coal mine dust; and the existing strategies for monitoring of coal mine dust exposures." The Committee was charged to "make recommendations to the Secretary for improved standards, or other appropriate actions, on permissible exposure limits to eliminate black lung disease and silicosis; the means to control respirable coal mine dust levels; improved monitoring of respirable coal mine dust levels and the role of the miner in that monitoring; and the adequacy of the operator's current sampling program to determine the actual levels of dust concentrations to which miners are exposed."

Unlike the Task Group, the Advisory Committee appointees did not include employees of any government agency. Instead, the Committee consisted of five members from academia and the medical profession, two representing the interests of labor and two representing the interests of industry. The Advisory Committee did consult individuals from MSHA, NIOSH, the Pittsburgh Research Center (PRC) and other government agencies as necessary. However, none of those consulted were voting members of the Committee.

In 1996, the Advisory Committee completed its work and submitted a report to the Secretary of Labor (attachment 12, pertinent exerts from the Advisory Committee report). The Union was generally pleased with the work of the Advisory Committee. Its members were able to identify many of the more difficult challenges inherent in the Respirable Dust Sampling Program without the encumbrance of self-examination that hampered the previous internal review. The Advisory Committee researched some of the more controversial issues surrounding the Respirable Dust Sampling Program and offered concrete recommendations to correct them.

It will be helpful to look at some of the Advisory Committee's recommendations, and review how MSHA has acted, or failed to act on them. In the Committee's first area of concern, members made recommendations regarding actual amount of dust present in mine atmosphere. Specifically, they advocated reducing the overall level of respirable dust permitted in the mine atmosphere, creating and enforcing separate Permissible Exposure Limit (PEL) for silica and coal mine dust, and directing MSHA to seek input from NIOSH for advice on lowering the current silica exposure of miners. The Committee also recommended adjusting the PEL to take into consideration extended work weeks (recommendation 16a).

When the Advisory Committee issued its report in 1996, NIOSH recommended a standard of 1.0 mg/m (milligrams per cubic meter of air) of respirable dust. NIOSH also recommended a 50 μg/m (micrograms per cubic meter of air), PEL for silica. At the time, MSHA was enforcing a 2.0mg/m respirable dust standard. The 2.0mg/m was reduced if silica (quartz) was present in the mine atmosphere. There was (and is) no separate silica standard in the mining industry. It was not until 2014, 18 years later, that the Agency promulgated a new regulation that reduced the dust standard from 2.0mg/m to 1.5mg/m and accounted for extended work days and work weeks (attachment 13, Summary of

2014 Dust Rule). This was still higher by 0.5mg/m than NIOSH recommended in 1996. The Agency has still not taken up the Committee recommendation to create a separate PEL for silica, nor has it lowered the exposure limit. MSHA continues to maintain the PEL for silica at 100μg/m, twice the NIOSH recommended exposure limit. In 2018 OSHA established a reduced silica standard of 50μg/m.

As noted above, the Advisory Committee recommended adjusting the PEL to consider extended work weeks. The Advisory Committee was concerned that, even at lower levels of exposure, more hours worked would result in dangerous levels of cumulative exposure. Today, there remains some question as to the actual exposure to respirable dust that miners receive at the 1.5mg/m over a 12 or 14-hour shift. The Union has expressed its concern that such respirable dust exposure during longer shifts may exceed the standard set by Congress in the Mine Act.

In other recommendations, the Advisory Committee attempted to tackle the overriding issues of fraud and tampering inherent in the Respirable Dust Sampling Program. They also recommended ending operator control of the sampling process.

The Committee determined in recommendation 16c, by a unanimous vote, that they considered it, "a high priority that MSHA take full responsibility for all compliance sampling at a level which assures representative samples of respirable dust exposures under usual conditions of work. In this regard, MSHA should explore all possible means to secure adequate resources to achieve this end without adverse impact on the remainder of the Agency's resources and responsibilities." Note that both industry representatives voted in favor of this recommendation (attachment 14, Committee votes).

In 16b, the Committee noted that there were methods available to MSHA to obtain necessary resources that would permit the Agency to conduct all compliance sampling and eliminate operator participation in that aspect of the Sampling Program. The Committee stated that it believed, "…that any MSHA resource constraints should be overcome by mine operator support for MSHA compliance sampling. The Committee recommends that to the degree that MSHA's resources cannot alone serve the objective identified, resource constraints should be overcome by mine operator funding for such incremental MSHA compliance sampling. One means for obtaining this support could be a reasonable and fair operator fee, based on hours worked, or other equivalent means designed to cover the costs of compliance sampling." The recommendation passed the Committee 8-0-1, the lone abstention was cast by a representative of industry. Significantly, one of the industry representatives voted in favor of this recommendation.

The Advisory Committee noted several times the importance of having representatives of the miners actively participate in all aspects of the Respirable Dust Sampling Program. In order to facilitate their input, the committee repeatedly recommended that miners be afforded the rights provided in Section 103(f) of the Mine Act (attachment 15). This would allow miners to receive compensation, at their regular rate of pay, while taking an active role in the Respirable Dust Sampling Program.

Unfortunately, these particular Advisory Committee recommendations, recommendations that the Union believes are key to affording miners the protections Congress intended, have never been acted on by MSHA. The Agency continues to argue that the recommendations are too expensive, too burdensome and will not result in substantial improvement in the Respirable Dust Sampling Program. MSHA argues, without support, that the recommendations offer no significant health benefits to miners. The Union vehemently disagrees with the Agency's decision regarding these recommendations and further argues that the Agency's logic for making such a decision is incorrect and detrimental to the health and safety of the nation's miners.

The Union believes that if the Agency imposed a mandatory fee for service on each operator to conduct all compliance sampling, while at the same time relieving the operator of the expense associated with performing this sampling under the current statute, both parties would benefit from the arrangement. MSHA could then be certain that all the respirable dust sampling was done in accordance with the law and that all the samples were accurate. Mine operators would save valuable assets both in terms of manpower and money. Significantly, operators would no longer be tempted to submit fraudulent samples or tamper with sampling devices in order to comply with the law. One beneficiary of this system would be conscientious operators, who would know that their competitors could not gain a competitive advantage by gaming the system. However, the individuals who will benefit the most by eliminating the mine operator from the sampling equation is the miner. This action would further the initial objective of the Mine Act by better protecting the industry's most precious resource – the miner.

The Union would also encourage MSHA to accept the Advisory Committee's recommendation to afford the Representative of the Miners the right to participate fully in the Respirable Dust Sampling Program. The Agency should modify its interpretation of the Mine Act to allow miners to utilize Section 103(f) "Walk Around Rights" at all times, regardless of the reason a Representative of the Secretary is on mine property. That would include granting walkaround rights for the purpose of compliance sampling. The participation of miners at mining operation is critical to the overall success of Mine Act in general and the health and safety of the workers at the facility in particular.

Finally, Congress and MSHA need to carefully examine a problem the Union has recognized for decades and the Advisory Committee addressed in recommendation 19f. The Committee stated that it recognized, "the problem of miner representation and participation in the dust control programs at mines not represented by a recognized labor organization and recommends that MSHA target such mines for compliance sampling. MSHA targeting should be active in nature and should consider many factors including miner input, compliance history, and medical surveillance data. Given the seriousness of this problem, MSHA should immediately start auditing and appropriately targeting these types of operations." This has been a historic problem in the industry that cuts at the very heart of the Mine Act's ability to be applied equally at all mining operations. The nature of the industry and MSHA's inability to adequately police non-compliant operators creates a bifurcated enforcement system that does not afford equal protection for all miners. The safest mines are Union-represented operations, where workers have a legitimate voice on the job.

Stanford Review

You do not have to simply take my word, or the word of the Advisory Committee, for the proposition that union represented mines are safer and more healthful than nonunion mines. The numbers bear that out, as shown in an article published by Stanford Law Professor Alison D. Morantz, entitled *Coal Mine Safety: Do Unions Make a Difference?* Vol. 66 Industrial and Labor Relations Review, No. 1 (2013) (attachment 16). Professor Morantz conducted a statistical analysis of injury reporting at underground, bituminous coal mines between 1993 and 2010. She researched both union and non-union mines to determine whether unionization reduced mine injuries or fatalities. The results of her inquiry were stark, but not surprising to those of us who work to improve miner health and safety every day.

Specifically, Professor Morantz found that unionization results in a "sizeable (more than 20%) and highly significant decline in traumatic injuries. . ." Similarly, she found "unionization is associated with an even larger (more than 50%) fall in fatal injuries . . ." That is, miners in union mines were far less likely to suffer traumatic or fatal injury. In analyzing this data, Professor Morantz concluded that traumatic and fatal injuries were the least prone to "reporting bias" therefore demonstrating "real" union safety effect in U.S. underground coal mines. While Professor Morantz was studying injuries (rather than occupational disease), I would argue that her findings are highly significant for the topic we are discussing today. First and foremost, the statistics show that union mines are safer than nonunion mines. Miners are less likely to die or suffer traumatic injury when they work in a union represented mine.

And the reason why this is the case is illustrated by the statistics regarding non-traumatic injuries. Specifically, while showing that union represented mines were far less likely to have fatal and traumatic injuries, the statistics also showed that union mines were "associated with a very sizeable (more than 25), robust, and statistically significant *increase* in non-traumatic injuries . . ." (emphasis in original). However, in explaining this counterintuitive result, Professor Morantz concluded that her findings lend "credence to claims that injury reporting practice differ significantly across union and nonunion mines." Put simply – nonunion miners were not less likely to suffer non-traumatic injuries; they were just less likely to report them. They reported higher levels of fatal and traumatic injuries, because those sorts of injuries are harder to hide.

These findings demonstrate what any union miner already knows: union represented mines are safer because union miners feel empowered to actively participate in their own safety. Union miners report lower numbers of fatal and traumatic injury because union miners know they can refuse to perform unsafe acts and can demand that their employer follow the rules. Further, union miners are more likely to report non-traumatic injury because they know that if the company retaliates against them for reporting the injury, that their union brothers and sisters will have their back. Nonunion miners reasonably fear retaliation from operators. They cannot afford to insist that their employers follow the rules and they cannot risk reporting minor injuries.

There is no reason to believe that this dynamic is any different as it relates to respirable dust. Union miners will insist that their employers follow the laws and ventilation plans to control respirable dust. When union miners see a problem, they will speak up. Non-union miners do not have the support systems necessary to take that risk. Instead, they will silently suffer while they breathe in the coal and silica dust that will slowly kill them.

Louisville Courier Journal

Following the issuance of the Task Group and Advisory Committee reports, The problems associated with the Respirable Dust Sampling Program continued. While this is not surprising, considering the fact that no action was taken to improve conditions in the mines, it is nonetheless disheartening. And the nation learned about it from a newspaper. Beginning on April 19, 1998, the *Louisville Courier Journal* ("*Courier Journal*") published the results of a year-long investigative report into the problem. The newspaper printed a 5-part series, *Dust, Deception and Death; Why Black Lung Hasn't Been Wiped Out* (attachment 17, relevant articles). I am sure many of you, especially those from the coalfield areas of northern Appalachia, are familiar with the reporting. But I believe it is important to revisit some of what the newspaper uncovered, to understand the depth of the problem miners have been dealing with for years. It is also critical that we realize the efforts to subvert the Respirable Dust Sampling Program by many operators and the inability of MSHA to adequately address these problems was not isolated to any particular area of the country, that it was not ended by the notoriety and MSHA fines that occurred as a result of the AWC case, and that it still occurs today.

The subheading for the first edition of the Journal story was, "*Cheating on coal-dust test widespread in nation's mines.*" While that blaring indictment naturally makes us think about the abhorrent actions of the coal companies, I would like to ask each member of this Committee to think about the people actually harmed. Think about the miners whose health was permanently ruined by this cheating.

Let me highlight one of those miners, whose experience was chronicled in the *Courier Journal*. After serving in the U.S. Army for 3 years, Leslie Blevins started his mining career in a low seam coal mine (36 inches) in 1972 at the age of 23. Blevins spent a lot of his 21 years in the mine operating a continuous mining machine, one of the dustiest jobs in any mine. It involved operating a massive piece of machinery designed to tear coal from the solid mine walls. For two years he was assigned to cut through solid rock in the mine, a common occurrence in many operations. The rock is much harder than coal and generates huge amounts of silica dust, which in much more toxic and damaging to the lungs. "Sometimes, I would have to shut the miner down and go in the fresh air and puke," stated Blevins. "My boss would tell me to get back in." But Blevins' story gets worse. Blevins was operating a miner, an occupation MSHA requires to be sampled for respirable mine dust. When he was asked about the sampling practices at the mine Blevins stated, "There would be times when I took company samples and the foreman would turn off" the sampling machine. "Or I'd come out of the mine, and they'd say, 'you took a sample today' and I'd say. 'I did? Where was it?' and they'd say, 'in the intake (clean air).'" The situation Mr. Blevins was subjected to is disgraceful. What is truly disgusting is that these same incidents still occur today.

Let me take a moment and explain exactly what, according to the *Courier Journal*, Mr. Blevins' employer and other coal operators were doing to avoid their obligations to provide healthy work environments for their employees. MSHA's dust program requires miners to be sampled on a routine basis while performing their normal duties at the mine. The sampling device was to be worn for 8 hours while the miner was in the mine. However, in an effort to have the company appear to be in compliance with the mine's dust plan, many mine operators devised countless ways to game the system.

Miners were told that the dust samples, that were supposed to be used to give an honest assessment of the amount of dust in the mine's atmosphere, must come out of the mine "clean," or within permissible limits. So instead of wearing the devices and risk disciplinary action by the mine operator, the sampling devices were routinely hung in fresh air intakes, placed in other less dusty areas or placed in the miners' lunch bucket. In one report in the *Courier Journal*, a miner remembers the only time he ever wore a dust sampling device. "I got a bad sample, and they told me in front of everybody that I would be carrying that thing for the rest of my life if I didn't get a good sample. So, I took it in the next day and set it at the breaker box in clean air and got a good sample." There should be no doubt in anyone's mind that the message from mine management to this individual was not a single incident. These types of actions by coal operators are as old as the Dust Rule and are in fact still occurring today. There is no doubt in my mind, that if that miner had continued to bring out accurate samples that were not in compliance, he would have been fired.

In one particularly incredible scenario, miners at A.T. Massey Coal Company's Crystal Fuels mine took 45 dust samples at the mine face, the area where the solid coal is mined. Thirty-four of those samples, or 76 percent, contained just 0.1 mg of dust per cubic meter of air sampled. This is an outcome that by all accounts, including the opinions of experts with years of experience, is impossible to achieve. I would submit to this Committee that a miner working all day in intake air would not be able to attain such sampling results. And yet, the Union was unable to find any investigation or inquiry by MSHA questioning the validity of these sampling results. Let me put it bluntly: A.T. Massey obviously and transparently cheated on their dust sampling, but MSHA ignored these obvious "red flags."

Despite this evidence of rampant tampering, not to mention the 23-year-old recommendations of the Advisory Committee, coal operators are still charged with administering the Respirable Dust Sampling Program. As a result, MSHA must bear a major share of the blame for the current state of that Program. As I stated earlier, the seeds for the program's failure were apparent from the start, and those seeds have clearly taken root. Little has changed since the *Courier Journal* wrote its scathing report. The words of former Assistant Secretary for Mine Safety and Health Davitt McAteer at the time still ring very true. McAteer stated that, "Expecting operators to police themselves defies human nature…the system is broken." Recognizing that fact, McAteer was seeking to increase testing by federal inspectors and relying less on mine operator sampling. That idea, like so many other proposals, never came to fruition. Despite being able to concretely identify the shortcomings in the system, MSHA has done little to remedy the most blatant problems.

I realize that up to this point much of my testimony has focused on, what many would consider, the distant past. However, as I will point out, those sins of the past have never stopped plaguing the nation's coal miners.

Previous Congressional Hearings

On July 13, 2010 and again on March 27, 2012, I came before the House Committee on Education and Labor and the House Committee on Education and the Workforce, respectively, to discuss the disaster at Massey Energy's Upper Big Branch Mine South ("Upper Big Branch" or "UBB") in Montcoal, Raleigh County, West Virginia (attachments 18-19). While the overriding context of that testimony dealt with the events leading up to the mine explosion and its aftermath, the information I submitted and the testimony I gave predicted, that if action was not taken by Congress and the Agency, we would witness the Black Lung crisis we are discussing today. The Union has been raising the concerns routinely for years. I have enclosed the past several years of the *UMW Journal* (attachments 20-29), the official publication of the Union, that chronicles the Union's continual attempts to bring these problems to the forefront of public debate.

However, like so many other efforts to protect workers, the legitimate warnings about Black Lung the Union has raised have been ignored by industry, MSHA and Congress.

The conditions in the Upper Big Branch mine, specifically the amount of coal dust that exploded and killed 29 miners, presents a microcosm of the dust problem that has haunted the industry for almost two centuries. While the UBB disaster could still provide fodder for hundreds of Congressional hearings, what is important to the topic we are here to discuss today is that the thick layers of coal dust that filled the entries of the UBB were not restricted only to the mine surfaces. This respirable and deadly dust also lined the lungs of the workers at that operation, slowly but surely killing the miners. In my 2012 testimony, I specifically referred to the fact that autopsies performed on the miners at UBB showed the majority of those killed had some level of Black Lung Disease. This is true of some of the youngest miners who lost their lives in the disaster.

Further, the report issued by the Union after the disaster, *Industrial Homicide,* (attachment 30, relevant pages) stated, "The fact that miners worked in such a dusty atmosphere offers great insight into the prevalence of black lung disease in many of the miners killed in the disaster. Of the 24 miners, between the ages of 24 and 61 whose lungs could be examined during autopsy, 17 or 71 percent, showed some stage of black lung." With respect to the mining practices at UBB, the report noted that the practice of running the longwall shearer without the required water sprays amounted to, "…reckless disregard for the law…And over the long term, exposure to uncontrolled coal mine dust greatly increases miners' chances of contracting black lung disease."

Madam Chairman, the UBB disaster occurred on April 5, 2010. It is not ancient history. More importantly based on the information that is available, it is clear that this type of illegal activity on the part of many coal operators are accepted practices in the industry. There is a clear and uninterrupted pattern of behavior on the part of the coal industry that runs back to the earliest days of the Respirable Dust Sampling Program. Tragically, even the spotlight shone on the issue by martyrs of UBB could not put an end to the industry's reckless behavior.

National Public Radio and Center for Public Integrity

In 2012, an investigation by National Public Radio (NPR) and the Center for Public Integrity (CPI) found that the Black Lung disease has spiked in the last decade, especially in portions of Kentucky, West Virginia and Virginia (attachment 31). NPR and CPI documented weak enforcement by federal regulators and cheating by mining companies involving the system that is supposed to limit exposure to coal mine dust. If you have heard this all before, you are not alone.

NPR followed up on the story in December of 2016 when it printed data obtained from Black Lung Clinics in Central Appalachia (attachment 32). The story demonstrates the correlation between the industry's and the government's failure to curb excessive exposure to coal dust and the effects on miners' health.

NPR reported that recent studies showed that the occurrence Black Lung disease among coal miners across the nation had skyrocketed beyond anything ever seen before in the industry. Younger, less experienced miners were contracting the disease at an earlier age, subjecting them to a shortened and debilitating existence until they ultimately succumb to the ravages of the illness.

NPR reported that data from Black Lung Clinics across Appalachia, studies from NIOSH, and information that they uncovered all came to the same conclusion: the occurrence of Black Lung and PMF was being diagnosed in unprecedented numbers across the region. Perhaps even more alarming, many of the individuals contracting the disease were younger miners with less than 20 years of mining experience.

The information obtained from eleven Black Lung Clinics in Pennsylvania, West Virginia, Virginia and Ohio discovered 962 cases of the disease from 2010 to 2015. This is nearly ten times the number of cases reported by NIOSH during those five years. NPR also stressed that the frequency rate could be even higher because some clinics had incomplete records and other clinics refused to provide information.

At long last, on April 23, 2014, MSHA, perhaps responding to public outcry generated by the earlier NPR reports and pressure from the UMWA, published a final rule titled "Lowering Miners' Exposure to Respirable Coal Mine Dust, Including Continuous Personal Dust Monitors." After decades of turning a blind eye, MSHA was finally taking some action on respirable dust. The rule became effective on August 1, 2014, and was phased in over a two-year period. It included a reduction in the concentration of respirable coal mine dust permitted in the mine atmosphere from 2mg/m to 1.5 mg/m, use of the personal dust monitor (PDM), required full shift sampling of specific designated occupations (DOs) and designated areas (DAs) and permitted MSHA to cite a mine operators for violating the law based on a single shift sample. The Rule did not include, nor did it contemplate, including the requirement for a separate, legally enforceable, PEL for silica.

At the time, the UMWA offered "qualified" support for the rule noting, "There are aspects of the rule the Union believes will help lower miners' exposure to mine dust and reduce the chances they will contract black lung. However, there are other issues we believe MSHA should have included in the final rule to better protect miners." The Union went on to state that, "The PDM is cutting edge technology, but MSHA did not require it be used to sample all miners." and that "MSHA enforcement of the new rule will be critical to its ultimate success, which would be more likely had the Agency taken over the sampling procedures." While the Union continues to stand by that assessment, we must face the unfortunate reality that operator fraud and tampering along with inadequate enforcement has once again doomed the respirable dust sampling program.

According to a report published in the September, 2018 edition of the *American Journal of Public Health,* one in every ten coal miners who have worked for at least 25 years in the industry has been identified as suffering from Black Lung disease (attachment 33). The situation in West Virginia, Kentucky and Virginia is much worse. NIOSH data has determined that one in five miners with two and a half decades mining experience in central Appalachia have contracted some level of the disease. NIOSH also noted that the number of miners diagnosed with progressive massive fibrosis (PMF), the most severe form of the disease, will likely increase at the same rate in the coming years. To put this health crisis in perspective, the number of cases of Black Lung diagnosed through 2016 in West Virginia and Kentucky have increased over 16 percent compared to 1970. In Virginia, the same year comparison shows an increase of over 31 percent. Doctors from the National Institute for Occupational Safety and Health have described the incidence rates as nothing short of an epidemic.

Armstrong Coal Company

Madam Chairman, in the event that any person on this Committee is inclined to think that coal industry changed after the tragedies I have discussed today, I would offer a review of a recent indictment of both the coal industry and MSHA. The case I am referring to came to a head just last year and is currently being prosecuted by the United States Attorney for the western District of Kentucky. A federal grand jury indicted nine officials from the Armstrong Coal Company on charges of conspiring to commit dust fraud. Those nine officials were Glendal "Buddy" Harison, the Manager of all of Armstrong's western Kentucky Mines; Charles Barber, superintendent of the Parkway Mine; Brian Keith Casebier, Parkway Mine safety director; Steven Demoss, Parkway Mine assistant safety director; Billie Harold, Parkway Mine section chief; Ron Ivy, Kronos Mine safety director; John Ellis Scott, worked in the safety department at Parkway Mine; Dwight Fulkerson, Parkway Mine section chief and Jeremy Hackney, Parkway Mine section chief. The grand jury charged that each individual, "…knowingly and willingly altered the company's required dust-sampling procedures, by circumventing the dust-sampling regulations, submitting false samples and making false statements on dust certification cards." The fraud and deception occurred between January 1, 2013 and August 8, 2015, through the time frame when MSHA's new dust rule was being implemented. The indictments were made public in July 2018. New charges related to the alleged fraud were added in February of this year (attachments 34-35).

While the Union is pleased the alleged perpetrators of these crimes were indicted, it is important to note that MSHA enforcement activity did not play a role in initiating this case. Rather, the miners at the operation who contracted Black Lung or were experiencing shortness of breath brought the damning information to the attention of the Huffington Post, resulting in an investigation by the Agency. Miners at the operation reported that the company officials at Armstrong used many of the same tactics that other coal operators have used since the inception of the Respirable Dust Sampling Program. Dust pumps were hung in intake entries, company officials falsified tests on days the mine was not even operating, workers wearing dust sampling devices were removed from dusty areas or occupations and replaced by miners not wearing the devices. The devices were also wrapped in cloth to restrict dusty airflow into the pumps.

So, Madam Chairman and members of the Committee as we sit in this beautiful hearing room, breathing in clean fresh air, I am disappointed to report that nothing much has changed in the coal industry. There is a new respirable dust rule, there is a new Assistant Secretary at MSHA, there is new continuous dust monitoring devices in the nation's mines and the industry is still willfully, knowingly and with impunity causing the slow and horrific death of thousands of miners every year. The dollar they put into their pocket at the expense of these miners' lives is apparently worth the harm they are causing.

Allow me to repeat myself; after nearly two centuries of mining coal in the United States very little has changed.

Madam Chairman, it has been brought to my attention that at the conclusion of this panel, the Committee intends to hear from a representative of the mining industry and the Assistant Secretary for Mine Safety and Health Administration, Mr. Zatezalo. I cannot be certain about the exact details of the testimony they will be offering the Committee. However, based on my knowledge of this issue and from what I have read and seen in other sources, I can confidently speculate that their views will not align very closely with what I have stated today.

I am certain that industry will attempt to explain the continued occurrence of Black Lung disease among today's miners as a remnant of the past. The leftover casualties of a time before operators became enlightened, followed the letter of the law, and looked out for the health of the miner. There will be attempts to show this Committee that the industry has changed and only a few rogue operators are still placing the lives of miners at risk. I could not disagree more.

The failure of the Respirable Dust Sampling Program is apparent. There is no question that in order to gain a competitive advantage over a competitor or increase their profit margin, today's mine operators will resort to the same tactics the have used for years to game the system. If left to their own devices and permitted to retain control of the sampling program, coal operators will continue to expose miners to excessive and deadly coal dust with no regard for the lives they are destroying.

The Mine Safety and Health Administration will attempt to demonstrate the success of the Respirable Dust Sampling Program by reciting the number of dust samples that have been taken and the percentage that are in compliance since the inception of the new dust rule. If I am not mistaken, those figures will reflect that between MSHA and mine operators 138,768 samples have been taken and that over 99 percent are below the Permissible Exposure Limit. The data will also show the average concentration of these samples are at a historic low of 0.61mg/m . The Agency will attempt to paint the new sampling system as successful, based on this data. Unfortunately, this data has been removed from MSHA's web site.

From the prospective of the UMWA, based of years of experience and the history of the industry, we simply do not accept or trust the data being presented by the Agency. Unfortunately, the overwhelming evidence of tampering and fraud by coal operators and the lack of adequate oversight by MSHA leaves the Union no other choice but to dismiss this information as subjective and not scientifically sound. Given the history of what I have recounted today, what would give this Committee, or any reasonable observer, any confidence that the numbers cited by MSHA are accurate?

In the end, I believe both industry and MSHA will seek to delay any attempts to strengthen the protections afforded to miners though Congress or by rulemaking. They will request more time to establish whether the new rule is working sufficiently. Madam Chairman they may have more time for studies and information gathering, but the nation's miners do not. Additional time for miners under the present conditions is, simply put, additional time to contract Black Lung. Time is something miners do not have when it comes to protecting their health and safety.

It is not my intention to impugn the sincerity of the testimony any individual will present to this Committee, although I would not hesitate to question the factual basis for their remarks. I believe that MSHA honestly wants its Respirable Dust Sampling Program to work. But, the Union's views are clear on this matter. The Program does not work. We know why. We know ways to fix it. It is time to take action.

After the Diagnosis

Madam Chairman, this is not the end of the problems created by the broken Respirable Dust Sampling Program that miners are forced to work under. To the contrary, for most miners who have contracted the disease, the difficult and deadly process is only just beginning. The realty of the situation for miners is that rather than accept the responsibility for their actions and seek to compensate disabled miners and mitigate the effect of the disease, coal operators and others do everything in their power to shirk that responsibility. It is not confined to dust sampling and Black Lung. If the Committee had time, I could fill the congressional record with stories of operators disclaiming responsibility for anything and everything that happens to miners they are charged to protect. But when it comes to Black Lung, it seems that the excuses and evasions never end. Operators will stop at nothing to avoid paying for Black Lung benefits. It's a sad situation that just keeps playing out over and over again.

There are countless stories of miners who have contracted the most severe form of Black Lung disease, PMF, but were unable to receive the benefits they were owed. These miners are examined by medical experts from the U.S. Department of Labor and their own doctor to confirm their worst fears only to see their employer contest their eligibility in administrative proceedings, sometimes for decades. The truth is that, almost without exception and despite overwhelming evidence supporting the miner, coal operators still refuse to recognize the miners' disability. The premise behind the operator's decision to deny benefits is simple: The delaying effort allows them to rely on time and money, two things most miners with the disease don't have. The morality of their actions is also simple: it is reprehensible.

The expense of pursuing the claim can cost the miner tens of thousands of dollars they simply do not have and most lawyers familiar with the Black Lung legal system know the return on their investment in time and research is meager at best. So, after an initial filing and a series of hearings before the administrative law judge, most miners cannot afford to continue the fight. The case is dropped, the company wins and the miner suffers in obscurity until the disease causes their lungs to fill with liquid and they drown.

Perhaps one reason the company wins so many Black Lung claims is a rule employed by the Department of Labor's Administrative Law Judges ("ALJs"), and the Benefits Review Board that oversees those ALJs, that denies benefits when the evidence supporting and the evidence refuting a claimant's Black Lung diagnosis is equal. Under the adversarial system created to administer of the Black Lung Benefits Act, claimants and their former employers will each submit a certain number of x-ray readings, a certain number of spirometry and blood gas results, and a certain number of medical reports to prove their case. The miners will present evidence showing they have Black Lung and are disabled. Operators will present evidence showing they are not sick or are not disabled. As I will discuss later, the evidence presented by operators is sometimes inaccurate or downright fraudulent. Nonetheless, it is easy for an ALJ to look at the evidence, determine that all the doctors involved have equally impressive credentials, and decide the evidence is equal. And, finding the evidence is "in equipoise" those ALJs then deny the claim. In short, if an ALJ cannot or will not make up his or her mind about the existence of disabling Black Lung, the miner pays the price.

Madam Chairman, in the 115th Congress, H.R. 1912, was introduced by Representative Matt Cartwright and was entitled the "Black Lung Benefits Improvement Act." That bill would have, among other things, changed the Black Lung Benefits Act to state, "[i]n determining the validity of a claim under this title, an adjudicator who finds that the evidence is evenly balanced on an issue shall resolve any resulting doubt in the claimant's favor and find that the claimant has met the burden of persuasion on such issue." That change, and other changes contained in H.R. 1912 would have been significant improvements. I would like to thank Representative Cartwright, and the co-sponsors for their work on that bill. I would also like to thank Senator Robert Casey, Jr. and his co-sponsors, who introduced a similar bill in the Senate. Unfortunately, the bills were not passed and miners continue to suffer under the current system.

Under the current circumstances, should a miner have enough resources and find an attorney willing to accept and stick with their case to continue the fight for benefits, the employer's legal team relies on the passage of time to settle the case. Miners with PMF have a limited time left on this earth. Through court hearings, delays, appeals and any number of stalling tactics, the miners' time is slowly drained away as the case languishes in the system. Ultimately, the miner will suffocate and die. But, for the mine operator and his legal team, the case is over and no benefits are paid. It's a win no matter what the cost in human tragedy!

Unfortunately, the truth about these despicable tactics by mine operators and the law firms they hire with the profits from the miners' labor is that, they work.

A Special Place in Hell

The intervention and deceitful dealings of the operators' lawyers, and in many instances the less than truthful medical personnel they hire to do the companies bidding, must also be taken into account. While miners, their lawyers and the UMWA have always suspected that an unethical and unholy alliance came together that would resort to whatever means necessary to defeat the miners' claims for benefits, the fact is, there is evidence to confirm our suspicions. It all came to light in a report issued by CPI (attachments 36-38).

The most notorious case concerns one of the largest legal firms representing coal companies, Jackson Kelly, PLLC and one of the most prestigious medical institutions in the nation, Johns Hopkins University Medical Center. The two institutions know each other well. They have worked together on Black Lung cases for decades. Their collaboration and interaction with coal operators around the country have been extremely damaging to miners seeking compensation for the illness that is ravaging their bodies and destroying their lives.

Jackson Kelly has spent nearly two centuries catering to the coal industry. This has made them the go-to law firm for the giants in the business. The firm's aggressive and ruthless approach to defending their coal industry clients is apparent, but a report by CPI raised serious ethical questions about the firm's tactics. In a very limited review of cases handled by Jackson Kelly, CPI found at least eleven cases that the firm was "…found to have withheld potentially relevant evidence [of Black Lung] and, in six cases, the firm offered to pay the claim rather than turn over documents as ordered by a judge." In one case in particular, a miner underwent a biopsy to determine if he was suffering from lung cancer. The tissue was examined by a pathologist and was ruled negative for the disease. However, without the knowledge of the miner, Jackson Kelly obtained the medical slides of the biopsy and sent it to two pathologist the firm had previously contracted to consult on Black Lung cases. Both reported that the tissue from the biopsy was likely complicated Black Lung disease. The report that definitively proved the miner had Black Lung, which only Jackson Kelly had, was suppressed, hidden away and never shared with the miner, his doctor or his attorney at trial. The miner's benefits were denied.

The report also discovered that, according to Jackson Kelly's own documents, the firm has a history of withholding evidence unfavorable to its clients and "shaped the opinions of its reviewing doctors by providing only what they wanted them to see." The firm claims that they are not required to disclose such information because it is "attorney work product." Meanwhile, as miners continued to suffer and die from the incurable effects of the disease, Jackson Kelly continued to defend the practice. In court filings, Counsel for the firm noted, "there is nothing wrong with its approach and that its proper role is to submit evidence most favorable to its clients." In the end, truth be damned, miners are collateral damage in the industry and Jackson Kelly must win no matter what the cost.

Of course, Jackson Kelly, and other company lawyers, could not subvert the process on their own. They are lawyers, not doctors. Unfortunately, coal companies found willing allies in white lab coats. A small unit of radiologists in one of the nation's most prestigious medical schools was willing to do the bidding of coal companies in their attempts to deny miners Black Lung claims for decades. For 40 years, medical professionals at Johns Hopkins Medical Center reviewed x-rays of miners suffering from Black Lung disease. Almost without exception these individuals, whose x-ray interpretations cost up to 10 times the rate typically paid for such services, have never diagnosed the most severe form of the disease, Massive Pulmonary Fibrosis.

To get the full picture of the impact that Johns Hopkin's Black Lung program has had on miners across the country, you need only look at the work of one man who ran the operation for the hospital, Dr. Paul Wheeler. Wheeler, who retired after the story by CPI was printed, was considered by many to be a leading authority on lung disease. With a medical degree from Harvard University, and the prestige associated with Hopkin's Medical Center, judges took his evaluations of patients as gospel. Some sided with the coal company's medical professional because he [Wheeler] is, "…the best qualified radiologist" and stating their decisions were because of Wheeler's testimony noting, "I defer to Dr. Wheeler's interpretation because of his superior credentials."

But, a deeper look into Wheeler's expertise revealed some alarming problems. The Center's reporting found that, "In more than 1,500 cases decided since 2000 in which Wheeler read at least one x-ray, he never found the severe form of the disease, Complicated Coal Workers' Pneumoconiosis." However, in more than 100 of the cases

Wheeler determined to be negative, biopsies and autopsies provided indisputable evidence of Black Lung.

The doctor may have many reasons for his findings, beyond the fact that coal companies are the clients. His own words seem to indicate as much. For whatever reason, he believed miners do not have Black Lung and are being wrongfully compensated. He stated, "They're getting payment for a disease that they're claiming is some other disease." Wheeler generally blamed miners' lung problems on tuberculosis or histoplasmosis (an illness caused by a fungus in bat and bird droppings). His arrogance, however, did not end there. He made it clear that despite what the law says, miners should be required to prove the existence of Black Lung. When confronted with his misinterpretation of the law, Wheeler's contempt reached a new level when he stated, "I don't care about the law." Johns Hopkins was so embarrassed by the report of Dr. Wheeler's actions that it terminated its Black Lung program.

The story by CPI was an enlightening look into the less than honorable and sometimes unethical levels coal operators and their surrogates will go to in order to win. Miners stand little chance of proving their case when the odds are so heavily stacked in favor of big business and bigger money. The tragedy lives on until the miner finally dies, but the "professionals" who oppose them go home to comfort and with another notch in their belt.

Madam Chairman and members of the Committee, there can be no doubt that miners continue to suffer from the inadequacies of a system that, at almost every turn, is stacked against them. They have known for years that the coal operators who employ them have cheated and scammed the system. They have witnessed the blatant fraud and outright lying by the operators whose objective has always been more production at any cost. I would defy anyone from the industry to bring facts to the table that shows otherwise. Industry officials of today may be more sophisticated and speak in nobler terms about the evolution of the industry and the concern that they have for the miners, but they have not moved far from the coal barons who preceded them. Their actions prove that profits continue to trump health and safety at every turn.

Likewise, we must all understand that MSHA's incessant need to demonstrate success, in spite of facts to the contrary, leaves them with little recourse to correct their situation. This persistent need to prove that it is meeting the requirements of the Mine Act or that the rules it has promulgated are effective, even in the face of the fact and the testimony I have presented that proves otherwise, shows the disconnect between the Agency and its true mission. They must know the system, even as it exists today, is horribly broken, yet for whatever institutional reasons that may exist, they cannot and will not admit it. This inability to conduct a thorough and honest evaluation of its own failings and to take the necessary corrective action continues to cost miners their lives.

We must also find a way to curb the abuses miners suffer at the hands of some members of the legal and medical profession. There must be a stringent standard for those who present "expert" testimony and the admission of possible conflicts the presenter may have for arriving at their conclusions. Finally, we must also demand that all the facts be presented in these cases in order to be certain that the ultimate settlement is correct and based on the scientific evidence.

Black Lung Trust Fund

Madam Chairman in January of 2017 the Department of Labor's Office of Workers Compensation Programs proposed major changes in regulations that determine how the Black Lung Benefits Act (BLBA or the Act) is administered. Among other things, the Act, "provides for the payment of benefits to coal miners and certain of their surviving dependents on account of total disability or death due to coal workers' pneumoconiosis. A miner who is entitled to benefits under the BLBA is also entitled to medical benefits." The funding for these benefits is generated by a federal tax assessed on each ton of coal operators produce. That funding stream has been threatened in recent months because of the inaction of Congress to extend that tax.

At the time, the Union strenuously objected to the changes proposed by DOL because of the devastating effects they would have on the overall program and the resulting benefit reductions for disabled miners. The UMWA has carefully reviewed the Proposed Rule and is deeply concerned that in an effort to unilaterally reduce costs, they have lost sight of what is important – the health and wellbeing of the miners and their families. It is unclear when you examine the proposal if the DOL is looking out for the best interest of disabled miners or trying to save money for mine operators who are ultimately responsible for paying the medical bills of these individuals. This is a bad proposal.

The Union is convinced that the Proposed Rule would damage the Black Lung Program so severely that it would eventually become even more ineffective, leaving families in these coalfield communities impoverished, and miners disabled from this deadly disease without adequate medical care. While the DOL discussed how the cuts they are proposing will have little impact on the health care industry as a whole, they ignored the fact that small communities, where these services are offered, are not reflective of large metropolitan areas of the country. The proposal appears to be aimed at reducing payment schedules to the point it forces providers in these areas to stop offering services that miners are entitled to under the BLBA.

For example, the Agency claims the average cuts to the program amount to approximately 7 percent of total benefits paid, but the decreases for some states are drastic. In Kentucky, for instance, inpatient hospital costs in 2014 were paid at 36 percent of total billing. Under the Proposed Rule those payments would be reduced to 26.5 percent of billing, a cut in benefit payments of almost $1.3 million per year. In Florida, where many UMWA Members reside, the cuts would be even more severe, from 64 percent of total billing to less than 18 percent. The most glaring example of these draconian cuts are the payments made for outpatient hospital services, cuts that would affect every state in the program. The DOL is proposing reimbursement for these services at just 20 percent of current payments; a reduction of 72 percent.

The Union would suggest that instead of trying to determine how to reduce and perhaps eliminate these Black Lung benefits, the DOL could better spend its time correcting the deficiencies in the program. The most glaring defect is placing the burden on the Black Lung Trust Fund to cover the cost of benefits owed to disabled miners by coal operators who are unwilling or unable to pay for such benefits. This is unacceptable Madam Chairman. I submit to this Committee that any operator who cannot pay or refuses to pay these mandatory benefits should not be permitted to continue to mine coal and subject future workers to the hazards that exist in the mines they operate. If they are so financially strapped or callously indifferent to the suffering they have caused, they should be run out of the industry.

Should the actions planned by DOL become effective, miners and their families would be left to suffer and die without the necessary medical treatment and financial assistance they are entitled to receive. They would, once again, bear the brunt of the mine operators' refusal to accept their responsibility for perpetuating this disease, and be subjected to the government's lack of desire to require that the owners meet their obligations. This is an intolerable situation for everyone involved and should not be permitted to occur.

The changes contemplated by the DOL are not the only threat to the benefits miners are owed from the Black Lung Trust Fund (Trust Fund). December 18, 2018, was a significant day in the lives of disabled coal miners and those who may contract Black Lung disease in the future. That date, established by Congress, as the day the excise tax placed on every ton of coal produced in the United States would be reduced by 55 percent. This tax is used by the federal government to provide the revenue necessary to operate the Trust Fund. Congress set this arbitrary deadline believing that Black Lung would be eradicated before the coal excise tax expired in 2018.

Prior to the expiration of the Coal Excise Tax, operators paid $1.10 on coal produced underground and $.55 on surface coal. According to the Congressional Budget Office (CBO), had the Tax been extended, the Trust Fund's current $6 billion debt would have been reduced to $4.5 billion by 2050. An increase of $.25 per ton of coal would have eliminated the debt altogether. The CBO has determined that allowing the tax to expire, as Congress did in December, will allow the debt to explode and require a multimillion-dollar taxpayer bailout to prop up the Trust Fund (attachment 39).

The sad fact is, no matter how far we seem to come in this country, whether it is advances in science, technology, medicine or a host of other subjects, some things never seem to change. I suppose many industries deny the problems they cause, but the people who own and operate coal mines seem to be the worst. They all argue that they should be allowed to make as much money as possible on their investment without government interference. Then, when their actions cause major economic or health problems, they want the government to force taxpayers to bail them out. That is exactly what happened in the aftermath of the recession of 2008 and that is what coal operators are asking for now. They want to keep their profits private but socialize their losses. It is time Congress told these businesses they are responsible to pay, not the American taxpayer.

When Congress failed to pass appropriations legislation at the end of 2018, it also failed to take the simple and necessary action to sustain the Federal Black Lung Disability Trust Fund by changing an arbitrary date set nearly four decades ago. This is unconscionable.

Madam Chairman, Ranking Member Byrne and the members of the Committee there is much more that I could discuss regarding the ineffectiveness of MSHA's Respirable Dust Sampling Program and the misery that failure has caused hundreds of thousands of miners and their families. However, I believe that the facts that have been laid out at this hearing and the facts that have been available in the public domain for decades are sufficient to demand action by this Committee and ultimately by the entire United States Congress. There is no longer an alternative and there can no longer be excuses. The carnage in the coalfields from this preventable disease must stop.

With that goal in mind I would like to make the following recommendations, on behalf of the nation's miners, as the starting point to correct this appalling abuse miners have faced for far too long.

1) Congress must take necessary action to require the federal Mine Safety and Health Administration assume the responsibility for conducting all respirable dust sampling used to ensure mine operators are in compliance with all aspects of the Respirable Dust Sampling Program. The standard must require that a Representative of the Secretary be present for all such sampling for the entire duration of the sampling process.
    a) This can be accomplished either through immediate Congressional legislative action or by Congress directing MSHA to issue an emergency temporary standard meeting this requirement.
    b) In an effort to pay for any additional financial burden this new sampling program would impose on MSHA, Congress must require the Agency to issue an emergency temporary standard that permits it to charge a fee for service or any other reasonable method to recover the cost associated with the program.
    c) Congress must direct MSHA to move immediately after the issuance of these emergency standards to codify them into regulation by promulgating a permanent standard that accomplishes these goals.

2) Congress must take necessary action to require the federal Mine Safety and Health Administration promulgate an emergency temporary standard that creates a separate Permissible Exposure Limit for silica. The Standard must set the PEL at the current level recommended by the National Institute for Occupational Safety and Health.
   a) This can be accomplished either through immediate Congressional legislative action or by Congress directing MSHA to issue an emergency temporary standard meeting this requirement.
   b) The emergency standard must require that the PEL for silica be separate and distinct from the Respirable Dust Standard and enforceable in accordance with all other standards established by the Agency.
   c) MSHA must implement a sampling program for silica similar to the current Respirable Dust Sampling Program. MSHA must be responsible for conducting all respirable dust sampling used to ensure mine operators are in compliance with all aspects of the silica standard.
   d) In an effort to pay for any additional financial burden this new sampling program would impose on MSHA, Congress must require the Agency to issue an emergency temporary standard that permits it to charge a fee for service or any other reasonable method to recover the cost associated with the program.
   e) Congress must direct MSHA to move immediately after the issuance of these emergency standards to codify them into regulation by promulgating a permanent standard that accomplishes these goals.
3) Congress must take necessary action to require the federal Mine Safety and Health Administration promulgate an emergency temporary standard that expands the 103(f) "walk around" rights afforded miners. The standard must permit the Representative of the Miners the right to participate in all activity conducted by a Representative of the Secretary while on mine property or in any activity that directly impacts the health and safety of miners at the operation.
   a) This can be accomplished either through immediate Congressional legislative action or by Congress directing MSHA to issue an emergency temporary standard meeting this requirement.
   b) This emergency temporary standard must require the mine operator to compensate all Representatives of the Miners who participate in such activity at their regular pay, including applicable overtime, for all such work performed.
   c) Congress must direct MSHA to move immediately after the issuance of these emergency standards to codify them into regulation by promulgating a permanent standard that accomplishes these goals.

4) Congress must take necessary action to require the federal Mine Safety and Health Administration to address the problem of miner representation and participation at mines not represented by a recognized labor organization and target such mines for compliance with all aspects of the Mine Act and all rules promulgated by the Agency to advance the safety and health of the miners. MSHA targeting should be active in nature, and include accident reporting, compliance history and patterns of noncompliance with all health and safety laws. Given the seriousness of the problem known to exist at these operations, MSHA should immediately start auditing and appropriately targeting these types of operations.
    a) This can be accomplished either through immediate Congressional legislative action or by Congress directing MSHA to issue an emergency temporary standard meeting this requirement.
    b) Congress must direct MSHA to move immediately after the issuance of these emergency standards to codify them into regulation by promulgating a permanent standard that accomplishes these goals.
5) Congress must take immediate action to restore and increase the funding stream necessary to pay for benefits owed to coal miners from the Black Lung Disability Trust Fund. The increase must be sufficient to pay all disability and medical benefits, as well as retire the debt currently incurred by the Trust Fund. Payment of the debt must be completed in a reasonable and cost-effective time frame, not to exceed 30 years from the date of the legislation.

    This legislation must contain language that does not permit companies who do not have the financial ability to pay for required benefits or refuse to pay required benefits to remain in business.

    In the event current mine operators are in arrears in payments to any beneficiary for required benefits, for any reason, the legislation must contain language that permits the Trust Fund to recover any assets it has expended to pay these benefits, either by garnishing the revenue of the mine operator or if necessary attaching the mine's assets and selling those assets to cover the debt.

Madam Chairman I would like to take this opportunity to thank you, Ranking Member Byrne and the entire Committee for allowing me the opportunity to testify at this extremely important hearing. The nation's miners are some of the hardest working, dedicated and patriotic people in this country. They have made great sacrifices to protect and energize the nation. They are willing to continue providing whatever is necessary to keep our nation strong and moving forward. They would simply request that their sacrifice be rewarded with a reasonable pension, not cut short because of Black Lung disease. Madam Chairman, the miners have waited for Congressional action far too long. Thank you.

Chairwoman ADAMS. Thank you, sir, and thank all of you for your testimony.

Under committee rule 8a, we will now question witnesses under the 5 minute rule.

I now recognize myself for 5 minutes.

Mr. Hairston, thank you again for being here, thank you for your courage.

Can you describe to us how you discovered that you had black lung and PMF?

Mr. HAIRSTON. First time I realized I was outside working on a piece of equipment and it started raining, and I ran up some steps and when I got in the bath house I couldn't breathe. I think I am getting ready to die. But I didn't pay that no attention. I just kept on working. And I was in the mine by myself one time, up on the section carrying an oxygen tank out of the mine, when I got down to where I needed to take it out on the tracks, I am sitting there, laying there, couldn't hardly breathe, trying to figure out— it seemed like I am going to have to wait to tell my—my wife, tell them I didn't make it home.

Then I got pneumonia and when I went to the hospital they seen a mass on my lung. They thought it was cancer, but they come to found out it was black lung. After they did a biopsy on it they showed it was complicated black lung.

Chairwoman ADAMS. Okay. So can you describe for us what it is like to have this disease and can you tell me a little bit about what is happening to the miners that you worked with?

Mr. HAIRSTON. When you can't do what you want to do, when you want to do something with your kids and you can't—and I am keeping one of my grandsons now that I could just watch him play ball and I can't even help him. Even when I try to do work, I have got to take—go at a pace. And looking at all the other coal miners, some of them is in worse shape than I am. Some of them, they pretty much can't even walk 10 feet before they have got to stop and start to rest.

Chairwoman ADAMS. Okay. So can you tell me, when you worked in the mines did the mine operators game the system by keeping samplers out of the dust? And what happened when MSHA inspectors arrived at that time?

Mr. HAIRSTON. Yes. At the one mine that I worked at we didn't hang the curtain until the inspector came. And most of the time, even with the dust sampler, we either covered the hole up—when the inspector was on section we covered the hole up until he come around, then we pull the tape off of it so it wouldn't take the dust up.

The boss told us not to get no bad sample, but I knew it came from the higher up than the boss.

So we did everything we could to keep from getting a better sample because if we got a better sample they recommend us or they say if we didn't do better we had to worry about them trying to get rid of us.

Chairwoman ADAMS. Thank you, sir.

Dr. Cohen, the mining industry and MSHA have argued that the alarming rise in black lung and PMF that we are seeing now is a result of exposures 10 years ago and things may have changed for the better. They caution that it might be too early to take any action.

How would you respond to that? And should we just wait 10 years or do we have enough evidence from the research that you and others have done to act today?

Dr. COHEN. I believe we have the obligation to act today. The evidence shows that the case numbers are still rising. We don't have any evidence that is plateauing or that is stopping. And I think that we would be doing a huge disservice to wait until we have another generation of miners with this disease to get data from the new rules.

And as we talked about, the new rule really doesn't address silica, which is really a huge part of this problem, in the way that we need to.

Chairwoman ADAMS. Thank you, sir.

I want to now recognize the Ranking Member for the purpose of questioning the witnesses.

Mr. BYRNE. Thank you, Madam Chairwoman.

Mr. Watzman, in your testimony you discussed the fact that MSHA does not recognize work practices of personal protection equipment as tools to reduce a miner's exposure to dust. Do you think if MSHA were able to recognize these measures today it could help to mitigate health risks, such as black lung disease? And, if so, could you explain why?

Mr. WATZMAN. Well, I do. I do believe that the traditional ways of limiting dust exposure in the mines is through air and water. And there is only so much air and water we can bring into the mines before that, in and of itself, creates unintended hazards.

If we had the ability to use personal protection there are devices that are used in other industries that provide a continuous stream of clean air over the miner's breathing zone. Those are used on occasion, voluntarily provided by operators, but they are not recognized by MSHA.

Similarly, the ability to rotate miners who are exposed to high concentrations of dust so that they are not exposed to the full shift. Again, this is a practice that is used in other industries, it is recognized in other industries, but the Mine Safety and Health Administration regulations, as they are written today, don't recognize those practices.

Mr. BYRNE. You also mentioned in your testimony that MSHA's regulations should allow for worker rotation programs you just mentioned. If you don't mind, further explain how this works and why this could help offer additional protections to miners.

Mr. WATZMAN. Sure, let us assume—let us talk about a miner who is running a continuous miner. That is a machine that is cutting the coal, one of the highly designated concentration areas in a mine. Rather than exposing that miner during a full shift, if it is an eight-hour shift, rotating provides the ability for the operator to change out two individuals during the shift so that during the second half of the shift the miner who was operating the machine during the first four hours, let us say, is then moved to a less dusty part of the mine to perform other job functions. So you are limiting the time that the miner is exposed to the areas where there may be high concentrations of dust.

Mr. BYRNE. It sounds like the NIOSH x-ray surveillance program has real potential to allow us to get a better understanding of the prevalence and severity of black lung disease. We all want to see the eradication of the disease. Should we consider making the x-ray program mandatory? Is there pushback on making this mandatory?

Mr. WATZMAN. Well, I would say it should be mandatory and that should be a priority. It should be done tomorrow. Today, only one-third of the miners participate in the x-ray surveillance program. We don't have a full understanding of the severity or the in- cidence of disease across the industry.

But more importantly—more importantly is that without participation in that program we don't know what the miners' health status is during their working career.

If we had that information and it was shared with the operators, the operators could work with the miners to help them during their working career to move them to less dusty parts of the mine. Right now, we have a pre-employment physical, there is an x-ray that is required, there is a follow-up x-ray that is required three or five years later, and then there is no requirement during the remainder of the miner's working career.

This is really a health issue. It is really having more information available to help the miner during their working career.

Mr. BYRNE. And I ask, is there pushback to this?

Mr. WATZMAN. Well, I think there are others on the panel who that question would be more appropriately addressed to, but I can tell you that on the occasions when I was working for the industry and we raised this issue, there was pushback. I couldn't understand it because we were addressing this from solely a health issue, but there was pushback.

Mr. BYRNE. Well, I will go ahead and open it up then, is there anybody on the panel that wants to push back against the suggestion Mr. Watzman made?

Mr. HAIRSTON. I do.

Mr. BYRNE. Okay. Yes, sir, please.

Mr. HAIRSTON. Reasons that coal miners don't get no x-rays is because they scared. If they go get an x-ray when the docs come around, they will fire them. So they are scared to take that test. So they won't go take them.

Mr. BYRNE. All right. Mr. Watzman, do you want to respond to that?

Mr. WATZMAN. Well, there are protections that are already written in the law. You can't discriminate against a miner, you move a miner under Part 90 to a less dusty environment, no loss of pay. There are discriminatory protections in the law. If they are not adequate then they should be looked at, but I think we need to get to the point where all miners are participating in this program so that we can address their health considerations during their working career.

Mr. BYRNE. Thank you. I appreciate your testimony. I yield back.

Chairwoman ADAMS. Thank you very much.

We will now recognize Mr. Takano from California; 5 minutes, sir.

Mr. TAKANO. Thank you, Chairwoman Adams, for this very important hearing on mine safety standards and the urgent need to protect miners from exposure to dangerous levels of silica.

Research has shown that silica dust lodges in the lungs forever— forever. And we know this. I can barely contain my anger by certain people coming before this committee. It is much more toxic than coal dust.

In 2016 OSHA updated their silica standards and lowered the permissible exposure level. And even this information, even with this information, the MSHA silica standards still have not been updated. And we know this.

Mr. Hairston, I understand why people who are desperate for their jobs, who may not know what is in the law, who may be unprotected by labor unions, wouldn't want to have those x-rays done. Miners have reported that cutting rock was like being in a room full of smoke or sitting on a cloud. We can't afford to wait another 10 years to address this epidemic. Miners would not be dying at these drastic levels if there was effective regulation and strong Federal enforcement. I am hopeful that this hearing will shed light on the issue and help us come up with effective strategies to protect miners.

Dr. Cohen, if MSHA were to require the use of end of shift monitoring equipment at all mines, what effect would that likely have on worker exposure, assuming the mine operators did not game the results?

Dr. COHEN. I think there is no doubt that it would reduce exposure. It would identify tasks that are generating huge amounts of this toxic respirable crystalline silica. You might be entering a seam that has, you know, silica within there, cutting rock, rooftop, or cutting other thing that would have—generate a lot of silica. I think it would help them change their practices and reduce exposure.

Mr. TAKANO. How would mines respond to that information?

Dr. COHEN. I think that they would then be able to use the engineering controls that are available. I think that you can with water and with ventilation. I think it is very possible to reduce dust levels. And I think that those engineering controls could be implemented and force change to organize in such a way as to reduce the exposure for these miners, or other alternatives could be done. I think that information would be very useful in a very practical time period.

Mr. TAKANO. What changes could they make if they identified higher exposures to the end of the shift?

Dr. COHEN. Then the next shifts that are working would be able to institute these ventilation changes or institute other practices that would reduce those exposures.

Mr. TAKANO. Dr. Cohen, how certain are you that silica is responsible for the spike in black lung diseases and black lung cases, particularly progressive massive fibrosis or complicated black lung? How certain are you?

Dr. COHEN. I am very certain. I think the evidence is very strong.

Mr. TAKANO. And what evidence do you have that would allow you to conclude that silica is the right culprit?

Dr. COHEN. Well, I think that we have evidence on three levels. We have the x-ray evidence that I spoke of, the pattern of disease that is associated with silica, we now have pathology case series in a larger series of pathology where we are looking at the tissue to see what is the particle in the tissue. And, finally, we are actually examining at the particle level what is the percentage and concentration of silica. So we are amassing evidence on many levels that silica is an important part of this problem.

Mr. TAKANO. Thank you, Dr. Cohen.

Mr. Hairston, thank you so much for being here and sharing your story. And I applaud you for your advocacy and the work that you do to help other miners.

Can you speak to what changes miners and mine operators could make if they have identified high silica exposure at the end of a shift? What changes could they make?

Mr. HAIRSTON. Not too much, but I am telling you, when you worked nine to ten hours a day, you don't get out of the dust exposure. If they cut back on the hours that you work and cut back on how many days you work a week, it would help, but—almost anything, because your lungs get a chance to clear out. When you work now that you don't—your lungs don't never get a chance to clear. Mr. TAKANO. What do you recommend that MSHA and Congress do to ensure that silica exposure is reduced for miners? What are your thoughts about that?

Mr. HAIRSTON. The water and the—having the air right, it would help a lot. That would be one of the things to try to get enough water and air up there to try to push the dust out. That would help a lot to try to keep from getting the exposure of it.

Mr. TAKANO. Well, thank you, Mr. Hairston. I appreciate your courage in being here today and I am sorry you are suffering from this terrible, terrible work-related disease.

Mr. HAIRSTON. Thank you.

Mr. TAKANO. I appreciate your time.

I yield back, Madam Chair.

Chairwoman ADAMS. Thank you. We are going to yield to Mr. DeSalnier of California for 5 minutes.

Ms. Stevens is recognized.

Mr. SCOTT. Are you going to recognize the Ranking Member?

Chairwoman ADAMS. She is not ready for that yet.

Ms. STEVENS. Thank you, Madam Chair. I am delighted to be at this hearing in this moment.

I am from Michigan and I ran for the seat because we wanted to stand up for the hard working men and women of this country and our labor movement. I asked to get on this committee for the very reason of what we are discussing here today. This subcommittee around workforce protections and the inalienable rights that include not dying on the job.

After declining since the 1970s, black lung disease among today's coal miners is back with a vengeance. It is affecting more than one in five miners in central Appalachia and these rates are just clearly higher than they were in the '70s. This is alarming and should immediately trigger the swift involvement of our Federal Government to allocate the resources and bring all stakeholders to the table.

Dr. Cohen, I wanted to ask you what some of the improvements that Congress can do to build upon the Obama Administration's respirable dust rule might be. And, if you don't mind, maybe kind of talking a little bit about that with the rule and why it hasn't been implemented and what we can do. We would appreciate it.

Dr. COHEN. I think that the silica standard for MSHA was sort of on the regulatory agenda towards the end of that Administration, but time ran out and they were not able to get that enacted. But I think we have an incredibly well researched and well documented OSHA standard for silica. Silica dust is the same whether it is a construction worker digging a tunnel versus a miner digging a tunnel. It is the same toxic material. There is no difference, depending on which regulatory agency is covering that worker. So it makes no sense whatsoever that we have one standard that is part of a complex formula that doesn't seem to be effective, and another standard that is very straightforward, 50 micrograms per meter cubed, action levels of 25 micrograms per meter cubed. Let us take care of this. And it was a very long 40 year process to get that standard. We should just adopt it for miners.

Ms. STEVENS. Thank you.

Mr. Roberts, thank you for your leadership. The mine workers— you are an incredible leader and we are glad that you are here.

What are some of the missed opportunities happening now that are holding us back from preventing more cases of black lung from affecting the young workers. I think Takano kind of touched on this, but if you could just dive in a little bit deeper for us, particularly from your vantage, we would appreciate that.

Mr. ROBERTS. I think it would be helpful for the committee to understand that when you have PMF, the most severe form of black lung, the cure for that is a lung transplant. That is it. It cost $1 million each. And you live about 3 years. So that is the cure. So we are now debating whether we should do something about this, right. So—and I don't mean to be overly critical, but sometimes I can't help myself after being here so many times over the years.

First of all, we have got to place in the hands of coal miners more power. They have absolutely no idea at the time they are being tested for exposure to dust, how much they are in. The new system helps with that. If you had a system that we just discussed about end of shift silica readings, there is no guarantee that they will know what that reading is. And a third thing about that is there is no standard. So until we have a standard that these companies have to meet, we are doing absolutely nothing by having the end of shift review of this because coal companies will make the decisions about whether or not they want to do something about the amount of silica that is being presented to miners who are working in the mines.

So we have to have more power to the miners, more rights to the miners, and we have got to take the system out of the hands of the people who operate the mines. And I am not here suggesting that all coal companies are bad. I am on record here in Congress that most coal companies want to do the right thing. But as I just pointed out, originally there are a lot of coal companies that do not.

Ms. STEVENS. Well, and there are certainly a lot of issues where it is easy to point the finger, but that doesn't necessarily solve the problem.

Mr. ROBERTS. That is correct.

Ms. STEVENS. And so what you are talking about with standards, as someone who also sits on the House science committee with oversight of the National Institute of Standards and Technologies, we know very well the importance of what standards will bring to this, the justice and, frankly, the health outcomes.

I do a lot of hearings. I can't think of a more important hearing around the general health outcomes and the protections of our workers.

So you mentioned you have been here a lot, that you have been having this conversation on repeat. I want to let you know it is a new day in this Congress with the leadership.

Chairwoman ADAMS. The gentlelady is out of time.

Ms. STEVENS. Thank you, Madam Chair.

Chairwoman ADAMS. Thank you.

We will now recognize Dr. Foxx from North Carolina, the Ranking Member of Ed and Labor.

Mrs. FOXX. Thank you, Dr. Adams. And I want to thank our panel members for being here today.

Mr. Watzman, mining is a vital part of the American economy and mine workers deserve a workplace that ensures their basic health and safety. One factor that is so difficult with black lung disease is the latency period between a worker being exposed to dust and the onset of the disease. In your view, are we able to know if the recent MSHA standard, the 2014 Respirable Coal Mine Dust Rule, is providing workers with the needed protection? And, based on information currently available, what actions, if any, should we be considering today?

Mr. WATZMAN. I don't think we have enough information yet. The Rule came into place in 2014, we have fully implemented across the industry the continuous personal dust monitor. That information is provided to the Mine Safety and Health Administration electronically. It is tamper-proof protected when it is shared. And based upon the information that MSHA has reported, dust levels across the industry are down dramatically. That is a step in the right direction. But I think we need to learn more over time in terms of whether this is effective or not.

You know, it is unfortunate because of the latency period that it takes so long to understand the effectiveness. And when the National Academy of Sciences recently issued their report on respirable dust, they pointed to that, that because of the latency period—and it is not my words, it was their conclusions—because of the latency period, we really don't know whether or not dust standards are effective in a short enough period of time.

So it is a problem, but I am not sure that there is much we can do to overcome that because of the 10- to 20- year latency period before disease presents itself.

Mrs. FOXX. Thank you.

Mr. Watzman, you have been actively engaged in the mining industry and worked with MSHA for over 30 years. How would you characterize the way the agency identifies priorities and addresses concerns? The title of today's hearing implies the agency has been willfully ignoring its duties. Based on your experience, is this the case?

Mr. WATZMAN. I don't think that is a fair characterization, quite honestly. I think the agency does as good a job as it can working with its stakeholders to identify priorities. They inherited a dust rule from the prior administration. They are implementing that dust rule, enforcing that dust rule from the prior administration. They have not turned their backs on that issue, they have not revised the dust rule, they have not proposed revisions, as far as I know right now, to those underlying standards. So I think that they do a good job. Could they do a better job? I am sure we could all point to organizations who could do a better job working with their stakeholders, but I don't think it is a fair characterization to say that they have turned their back on the miners.

Mrs. FOXX. Thank you again.

Mr. Watzman, we all want to see the elimination of advanced lung disease related to mining activities while preserving jobs that are vital to these workers and the communities. It is clear the mining industry has continued to evolve and improve practices over the years as new information and technologies become available.

How can we continue to encourage and facilitate the creation of additional new technology moving forward?

Mr. WATZMAN. Well, there is a barrier that needs to be overcome. There are technology providers who provide technology outside the U.S. but aren't bringing it into the U.S. This is an issue that the Assistant Secretary talked about early in his tenure. We need to come up with better procedures to get new technologies introduced, especially in the underground coal environment. MSHA has a very rigorous, time consuming, and expensive approval and certification process. We need to recognize where technology is approved by international standard setting organizations, that approval should be adequate for introduction into the U.S., and I hope that the agency is moving in that direction.

Mrs. FOXX. Thank you, Mr. Watzman. And, again, I want to thank the panelists for being here today.

I yield back, Madam Chairwoman.

Chairwoman ADAMS. Thank you very much.

I will yield now to the gentlelady from Pennsylvania, Miss Wild.

Ms. WILD. Thank you, Madam Chair.

Mr. Hairston, good morning. I am sorry that I wasn't here for the oral testimony portion, but I have read your written testimony and I appreciate it.

In a letter from November of 2018 Hal Quinn, the National Mining Association CEO, stated that the "industry is committed to ensuring that all miners who suffer from black lung receive the benefits they deserve." And in your experience, I would like to ask you, which includes working as a coal miner for 27 years before you were diagnosed and as vice president of the Fayette County Black Lung Association, would you agree or disagree with Mr. Quinn's statement that the industry is committed to ensuring that all miners who suffer from black lung receive the benefits they deserve?

Mr. HAIRSTON. I disagree.

Ms. WILD. So that hasn't been your experience?

Mr. HAIRSTON. No.

Ms. WILD. Can you tell us a little bit about your experience in terms of the benefits that you believe you should have received that you haven't?

Mr. HAIRSTON. When I filed for mine, the company waited until the last minute to even protest it. Then I think we fought mine for 2 years and Washington and Lee University wanted to help me get mine. And most coal miners, most of them try 10, 15 years before the ever get it. They always find some kind of way—at one time they were hiding the x-rays, knowing that they had it, they get these expensive hospitals to say that you ain't got it. So it ain't helping us.

Ms. WILD. Let me stop you stop you there for a second because I want to go to Dr. Cohen and ask Dr. Cohen about—well, before I get to Dr. Cohen, let me go to Mr. Watzman.

In June of 2018 there was a Reuter's article on the resurgence of black lung disease and the coal industry's opposition to maintaining the tax rate that supports the Black Lung Disability Trust Fund, and you were quoted as saying more often than not we are being called upon to provide compensation for previous or current smokers.

Mr. Watzman, can you explain that comment to Mr. Hairston or any of his work colleagues that jeopardize their health for the benefit of the coal industry? And specifically, can you provide us with any credible medical or scientific study that backs up your claim that smoking is the root cause of coal miners becoming disabled and therefore qualifying for black lung benefits?

Mr. WATZMAN. I don't have it with me, but I will provide a study for the record that I am familiar with for your benefit.

Ms. WILD. Who authored that study, Mr. Watzman?

Mr. WATZMAN. I can't recall off the top of my head.

Ms. WILD. And it is your position that study supports the claim that smoking is the root cause?

Mr. WATZMAN. I don't—I didn't say that it was the root cause.

Ms. WILD. Well, that was my question. So you don't have any evidence that it—smoking is the root cause of coal miners becoming disabled.

Mr. WATZMAN. No, I didn't—no, I don't.

Ms. WILD. Okay, thank you.

In addition, in June of last year the National Mining Association distributed a fact sheet to congressional offices that asserted that there was a "decline in medical black lung disease" and that the reduced black lung excise tax rate was more than sufficient to provide monthly disability payments.

First of all, question, did you review and approve that fact sheet before it was distributed?

Mr. WATZMAN. I didn't—I was not solely responsible for it, but I would have been involved in its development at that time.

Ms. WILD. Okay.

Dr. Cohen, I would like to turn to you. Do you care to comment on that statement that there has been—according to the National Mining Association's fact sheet to congressional offices, that there has been a decline in medical black lung disease?

Dr. COHEN. Yeah, I think that is wrong. And I think that—I think

Ms. WILD. And can you tell us what your evidence reveals?

Dr. COHEN. We have evidence from active working coal miners that is part of the NIOSH Coal Workers Health Surveillance Program that shows that the rate of disease on chest x-rays is increasing, we have evidence from former miners that are applying for black lung, including outbreaks from clinics, and then a review of national data from the Office of Workers' Compensation Programs, Black Lung Benefits Program that clearly shows that the rates of severe disease and compensated workers is increasing.

Ms. WILD. And can you give us any kind—can you quantify that at all?

Dr. COHEN. Well, I think that one of the most shocking numbers that from 1996 to the present, 2,500 miners have been compensated for disabling progressive massive fibrosis, the most severe form of the disease. And that curve I showed a bit earlier shows that it is just a very steep increase as opposed to what we would really hope for, is that under modern dust controls that we would be decreasing and eliminating this disease.

Ms. WILD. Mr. Hairston, I hope that our committee will be able to do something to help you all.

With that I yield back.

Chairwoman ADAMS. Thank you very much.

We will now yield to the gentleman from Texas, Mr. Wright. You are recognized for 5 minutes.

Mr. WRIGHT. Thank you, Madam Chairwoman.

First, Mr. Hairston, I was here earlier for your opening testimony and it was very compelling. And no one can know fully what you have been through unless they have had that disease, so God bless you and your family. I know it has been tough.

Mr. Watzman, I wanted to ask you, because this hearing kind of underscores the difficulty that Congress has in implementing any kind of new regulation or anything like that when you have this time lapse that has been discussed here. If we look at car accidents over the last 30 years, it is going to include an awful lot of accidents before cars had air bags, for example.

And, so, my first question to you is how do we get a handle on this, realizing that there has been an awful lot of improvements made in the last 25–30 years, and yet we don't have the data to know exactly what the effect of that is going to be until we are further down the road? Is there any data that is more recent that can be applied to this?

Mr. WATZMAN. Well, we have data that becomes available as the NIOSH x-ray surveillance program—as miners participate in the NIOSH x-ray surveillance program and that data becomes available. But, again, that is only a fraction of the workforce and that is the problem, that we are looking at 30–35 percent of the workforce.

And human nature, at least as it relates to me, tells me that if I am not feeling well I go see my physician. But if I am feeling well, I have no need to go to the physician. Yet, there may be an underlying disorder that I am not aware of. And that is why we feel so passionately as an industry or the industry feels so passionately, and I still feel that I am a part of it, that the x-ray surveillance program should be made mandatory so that there is a better understanding of the breadth of disease across the entirety of the industry and so that operators can work with their employees to take action to protect them during the remainder of their working career.

Mr. WRIGHT. And you hit on another point when you mentioned percentages because while percentages may be up, the total number of miners is down. And so if you are going to do an accurate comparison with the past, it needs to be an apple and apple comparison, not an apple and orange comparison.

Mr. WATZMAN. That is correct.

Mr. WRIGHT. Right. So I just want to throw that out there that if we are going to be making these comparisons over time, then they need to be relevant comparisons. You don't apply—you know, you can talk all day long about how the percentage is up, but if the total number is different, then it is going to skew the conclusion. Isn't that correct?

Mr. WATZMAN. That is correct.

Mr. WRIGHT. All right. Thank you very much.

And I yield back.

Chairwoman ADAMS. Thank you very much.

I will now yield to the Chair of Education and Labor, Chairman Scott from Virginia.

Mr. SCOTT. Thank you, Madam Chair.

President Roberts, you are aware of the reporting by Howard Berkes of National Public Radio about the epidemic of progressive massive fibrosis that really brings us here today. And your testimony calls for an emergency temporary standard for a more protective silica standard. Does your testimony call for the same standard that NIOSH has been recommending for 40 years?

Mr. ROBERTS. I think the standard that was promulgated by OSHA would be the standard that I would encourage this committee to take into consideration as they deliberate this issue.

If I could just elaborate slightly, you do not really need to wait 10 years to determine when a miner has been in the mines 5 years and he has PMF that you might want to wait another 10 years, because that miner is going to be gone.

Mr. SCOTT. The Mine Safety and Health Administration, MSHA, has the authority to issue an emergency standard when it determines that miners are exposed to a grave danger from exposure to substances or agents determined to be toxic or physically harmful. Are miners exposed today to that grave danger?

Mr. ROBERTS. Oh, absolutely, they are exposed to grave danger as we are sitting here today.

Mr. SCOTT. Thank you.

Dr. Cohen, we have heard reference to the 2014 improvement. What improvements on the silica standard were made by that 2014 standard for mine workers?

Dr. COHEN. There was no specific improvement in the silica standard in the 2014 regulations. The total dust was lowered from 2 milligrams to 1.5.

Mr. SCOTT. Well, I thought you said that silica was causing the problem of progressive massive fibrosis?

Dr. COHEN. It is.

Mr. SCOTT. And so the 2014 change didn't have anything to do with silica, is that right?

Dr. COHEN. I don't believe that it addressed it adequately, no.

Mr. SCOTT. Now, it is my understanding, Dr. Cohen, that NIOSH has been recommending a better standard, the same standard that applies now with OSHA, but not mine workers. Is that right?

Dr. COHEN. That is my understanding, yes.

Mr. SCOTT. Okay. What has happened for 40 years?

Dr. COHEN. I think that it was a long process to get the new OSHA standard through and that finally was passed. And I think that it is just absolutely nonsensical that doesn't apply to miners as well. They are workers exposed to the same dust, so I think that has to be done and should be done. And the data is there for that.

Mr. SCOTT. Mr. Hairston, you talked about the reluctance to get x-rays. Why are people afraid to get x-rays?

Mr. HAIRSTON. They scared of getting fired.

Mr. SCOTT. And why would they be fired in light of the fact that they have rights to be transferred?

Mr. HAIRSTON. I know a few guys right now, they got fired because they wouldn't work in dust. They fighting right now to try and get their jobs back.

Mr. SCOTT. And they get—they are reluctant to tell the employer because the employer—the last employer is stuck with the Workers Compensation, is that right?

Mr. HAIRSTON. Yes.

Mr. SCOTT. And so if they can get fired before they get sick, when they might be sick, maybe they will go somewhere else and somebody else will be responsible. Is that the danger?

Mr. HAIRSTON. Yes, sir. Because if you say something about it, the coal company will fire you before the government can do anything about it. You still got to wait for the government to do what they got to do to get your job back. Then you got to hire a lawyer. How many coal miners can get lawyers to fight their cases?

Mr. SCOTT. Thank you.

Now, President Roberts, you indicated that protections that union members have that non union members don't have in terms of worker protections in the contract. Can you explain what you meant?

Mr. ROBERTS. Yes. Although the law says certain things, to expect that a coal miner that doesn't have representation at the mine is going to exercise those rights knowing full well that at some point in time something could happen to him and he would be discharged, they do not exercise that right, they being the miners in non union mines. Our contract, as well as the law, says we can withdraw ourselves from any situation that we feel dangerous to our health or any situation that we feel that could injure us. And we exercise—we being our members—that on a frequent basis.

Mr. SCOTT. Thank you, Madam Chair.

I yield back.

Chairwoman ADAMS. Thank you, Mr. Scott.

I will now recognize Mr. Griffith from Virginia for 5 minutes, sir.

Mr. GRIFFITH. Thank you very much. Let me thank you, Madam Chair, and Ranking Member Byrne, and my friend, also from Virginia, the Chairman of the full committee, Mr. Scott, for inviting me to be a participant in this today. This is very important to the constituents in my district. I represent the part of the hot spot that was mentioned earlier, southwestern Virginia, and it is important.

Mr. Hairston, I believe I heard you say that you got help from Washington and Lee University School of Law. Is that correct?

Mr. HAIRSTON. Yes, sir.

Mr. GRIFFITH. And as a proud alumnus of that institution, I am glad to know they are doing some good stuff. It is a good school and they do a lot of good things.

Mr. HAIRSTON. Yes, it. They do.

Mr. GRIFFITH. And I have heard the same thing you said in your answers to Representative Scott, to Chairman Scott were the same as I have heard in the district, and that is people are afraid to go get the x-rays for fear that they will be some other reason that they lose their job.

So I am intrigued because I want to find answers to this problem. I mean I am a big supporter of coal mining, but I want to make sure that we take care of our miners.

Mr. Watzman, you indicated that we should have a universal x-ray system. Do you think that might solve this fear problem? I mean if everybody has to do it—and I will tell you, it is not an alien concept, because my mother was a school teacher, and I forget how many years it was, but every 3 or 5 years she had to go and get a chest x-ray to make sure she didn't have tuberculosis, because there was at one time a huge tuberculosis problem. So what seems to be the resistance to having everybody get an x-ray every so many years? And then that way you have got a better chance of being able to help people quicker. And it is not that somebody like Mr. Hairston be asking for the x-ray, everybody had to get it.

And, Mr. Robertson, I want your comment on that too, but Mr. Watzman?

Mr. WATZMAN. Well, that is what we believe should be the case, that every miner participates in a mandatory x-ray surveillance program. Will that address the concerns of discrimination and getting fired, I don't know the answer to that. What I do know is that will provide information to the miner and to the employer so that they can work with them during the remainder of their working career to protect their health as best as possible.

Mr. GRIFFITH. And I appreciate that.

Mr. Roberts, your thoughts? Because I don't have an opinion per se, I am just trying to learn here today.

Mr. ROBERTS. Thank you.

My view of this, and I believe that this will be the correct view, we do not necessarily have a problem with miners getting x-rays every 5, 6—whatever it might be years. Our problem is that we do not think that coal companies should be privy to that information. We have a HIPAA law that says that no one can have my medical records and we are going to say to the coal companies, who have got a less than stellar record in some instances here, here you go, here is the x-rays for the people who are working—that is going that is going to be something that miners will resist to no end. So I think we need to protect their privacy here.

Mr. GRIFFITH. And I am going to look forward to thinking about that and trying to figure it out, because I also know that sometimes a miner, even if he has a problem, won't exercise his rights for the same fears that he isn't getting the x-ray for now.

The other thing I thought was intriguing today, Mr. Watzman, was this idea of the personal—let me see if I can get it right here— the personal protective devices. I mean I have got research from Virginia Tech, and some researchers there have been working on it, they agree with the silica issue, but they think there may be other factors as well. And every mountain is a little bit different and there are different minerals in every mine, and sometimes even the mines that aren't in Appalachia have high concentrations of minerals. But if we had a personal protection device, it seems to me if that is not too heavy or burdensome, that would eliminate a lot of these concerns about whether it is coal, which we now think it is not as bad as the silica—and I think that is right, based on the science, and yet there is this research ongoing about other things. You have said that is a good idea. You think the industry would accept that?

Mr. WATZMAN. They are—in selective instances they are already being used voluntarily in the industry. These are devices—

Mr. GRIFFITH. Okay. And your answer is yes? Because I am running out of time.

Mr. WATZMAN. The answer is yes.

Mr. GRIFFITH. Mr. Roberts, what do you think? Do you think the miner would be willing to do that? Because to me that seems like a really practical solution.

Mr. ROBERTS. It really depends on your job, Congressman. And let me give you an example, if you don't mind.

Mr. GRIFFITH. Yes, sir.

Mr. ROBERTS. I ran a shuttle car in about 40 inches of coal, and you could touch the top as you ran up the—went up to the miner to get unloaded. When you came back you couldn't see anything on the other side because the coal was dragging on the top. You cannot put a shuttle car operator in an air stream helmet and expect him to operate that shuttle car safety without running over top of somebody. If you are in other occupations in the mine, you cannot wear an air stream helmet. It is impossible. There are some places you can, but in a lot of places you can't.

Mr. GRIFFITH. Well, maybe we need research to figure out how to make those devices a little bit less intrusive.

I will also tell you that one of the things that might tech folks said we might want to take a look at is—Virginia Tech folks said we might want to take a look at is the mine processing, getting the mine ready. Because apparently the dust rules don't apply until you are actually mining the product, and yet you are digging through a lot of rock to get that seam ready to be mined.

I am out of time, so I yield back.

Chairwoman ADAMS. Thank you all very much for your testimony.

And I want to thank all of the witnesses on panel one for your participation today. Certainly I learned a lot myself and certainly have a lot of compassion, Mr. Hairston, for what you have been through. And hopefully we will have an opportunity and will make a way to really provide some support.

Members of the Committee, what we have heard is very valuable. The committee may have some additional questions for you, and we ask the witnesses to please respond to the questions in writing. The hearing will be open for 14 days in order to receive the responses. I remind my colleagues that pursuant to committee practice, witness questions for the hearing record must be submitted to the majority committee staff or committee clerk within 7 days. The questions submitted must address the subject matter of the hearing.

We are going to seat the second panel. Well, let us take 5 minutes to recess to seat the second panel.

All right, thank you all very much. [Recess]

Chairwoman ADAMS. Our first witness on the second panel will be Dr. John Howard. Dr. Howard is the Director of the National Institute for Occupational Safety and Health. He has held that post since 2009. Dr. Howard previously served as director of OSHA from 2002 to 2008. Prior to coming to OSHA Dr. Howard was chief of the Division of Occupation Safety and Health of the California Department of Industrial Relations, Labor, and Workforce Development.

The next witness will be Dr.—

Mr. ZATEZALO. Zatezalo.

Chairwoman ADAMS.—Zatezalo, assistant secretary for the Mine Safety and Health Administration. Prior to leading MSHA, Dr. Zatezalo was CEO of Rhino Resources, a Kentucky coal mine operator. He also served as chair of the Kentucky and Ohio Coal Associations. He is a native West Virginian and he started his career as a coal miner.

The final witness is Miss Cindy Brown Barnes, Director of Education Workforce and Income Security for the Government Accountability Office. Miss Brown Barnes leads the GOA team that audited the Department of Labor's management of the Black Lung Disability Trust Fund. She has more than 30 years of experience performing audits of Federal agencies.

Welcome to all of our witnesses. We appreciate all of the witnesses for being here today and look forward to your testimony.

Let me remind the witnesses that we have read your written statements and they will appear in full in the hearing record.

Mr. BYRNE. Madam Chairwoman?

Chairwoman ADAMS. Yes?

Mr. BYRNE. I have a parliamentary inquiry.

Chairwoman ADAMS. Yes, sir, state your parliamentary inquiry. Mr. BYRNE. I appreciate Ms. Barnes from the GAO being here today, but it is my understanding that she will speak on issues related to the funding of the Black Lung Disability Trust Fund, and those issues are not within the jurisdiction of the committee. Do we have a responsibility to limit our hearings to subjects we can address in this committee, allowing adequate time for the other issues?

Chairwoman ADAMS. GOA was invited to testify because the Black Lung Benefits Act falls squarely in the jurisdiction of this committee and this subcommittee, including the administration of the program by the Department of Labor. This subcommittee can conduct oversight of the tax rate and the Trust Fund solvency even if we cannot legislate on the tax as that falls in Ways and Means. Indeed, Chairman Scott and Ways and Means Chairman Neal are co-requestors of the work being performed by the GAO on the Trust Fund solvency.

I want to remind everyone that the DOL secretary is one of the three trustees of the Black Lung Benefits Disability Trust Fund and GAO's testimony is addressing not only the tax but the maladministration of self-insurance, the Office of Workers' Compensation programs.

As the minority is aware, the GAO work is still underway, but when it is complete it may be timely to hold another hearing and ask OWCP to testify, however, GAO's work is not expected to be completed until the fall. And I would add that if the minority felt it was important to have testimony here today, the minority could have invited them to testify or made a request to the majority to consider an additional joint witness. However, our staff did not receive a communication in reference to that.

Mr. BYRNE. Thank you for your response.

Chairwoman ADAMS. All right. Thank you.

Our final witness—I think I just introduced her. Okay, all right.

Thank you very much. We appreciate all the witnesses for being here today and look forward to your testimony.

I do want to remind the witnesses that we have read your written statements and they will appear in full in the hearing record. Pursuant to committee rule 7d and committee practice, each of you is asked to limit your oral presentation to a 5 minute summary of your written statement.

I want to remind the witnesses that pursuant to Title 18 of the U.S. Code Section 1001, it is illegal to knowingly and willfully falsify any statement, representation, writing, document, or material fact presented to Congress, or otherwise conceal or cover up a material fact.

Before you begin your testimony, please remember to push the button on the microphone in front of you so that it will turn on and the members can hear you. And as you begin to speak the light in front of you will turn green. After 4 minutes the light will turn yellow to signal that you have 1 minute remaining. When the light turns red your 5 minutes have expired and we ask that you please wrap up.

We will let the entire panel make their presentations before we move to member questions. When answering a question please remember once again to turn your microphone on.

I will first recognize Dr. John Howard. Dr. Howard, you are recognized for 5 minutes, sir.

Testimony of John Howard, MD, Director, National Institute for Occupational Safety and Health

Dr. HOWARD. Good morning, Chairwoman Adams and Ranking Member Byrne, and distinguished members of the subcommittee.

My name is John Howard and I am the Director of the National Institute for Occupational Safety and Health, or NIOSH, which is part of the Centers for Disease Control and Prevention in the U.S. Department of Health and Human Services.

I am here today to provide two brief updates. First, I will provide an update on the science, showing how inhaling respirable crystalline silica contributes to U.S. coal miners developing a lung disease called pneumoconiosis. And, second, I will describe NIOSH's efforts to improve the technology for assessing coal miners' exposure to quartz, the form of crystalline silica found in coal mine dust.

Quartz is the most common type of crystalline silica. During coal mining activities rock that contains quartz can be disturbed, generating dust that contains respirable particles of crystalline silica which miners then can inhale.

We know that when miners in certain jobs, such as roof bolting, workers at the mine face and surface miners engage in drilling through layers of rock covering the coal seam can develop a lung disease called pneumoconiosis as a result of their inhalation. Specifically, miners can develop a type of pneumoconiosis called silicosis. Miners can also develop coal workers' pneumoconiosis, or black lung disease, mixed with silicosis.

Science tells us that quartz plays a contributing role in the current outbreak of pneumoconiosis in coal miners, particularly in the central Appalachian region, which includes eastern Kentucky, western Virginia, and in West Virginia. In these areas approximately 20 percent of active underground coal miners with 25 or more years of mining tenure have evidence of pneumoconiosis.

We know this from several lines of evidence, including, one, radiographic exams performed during coal workers' health surveillance surveys, two, Mine Safety and Health Administration inspection data, three, interviews of coal miners with progressive massive fibrosis, and, four, analysis of coal workers' lung tissue.

Timely monitoring of quartz would provide better protection for miners. As a first step, NIOSH is researching technologies to advice the science of assessing quartz exposures in the field, specifically developing and testing a prototype for a field based rapid quartz monitor, which I have with me today, a type of self assessment tool also known as an end of shift silica monitor. The rapid quartz monitoring prototype is based on three components, a sampler, an analyzer, and a quartz concentration software calculator. Concurrently, NIOSH is funding through its external contracts program the development of a stand-alone near real-time continuous quartz monitor for compliance sampling. Development and certification of the near real-time continuous quartz monitor for compliance sampling could take a decade or more, so it is not a near-term solution for assessing quartz exposure.

Between 2016 and 2018 NIOSH conducted usability tests of the field based prototype rapid quartz monitor, or end of shift silica monitor, in four coal mines in West Virginia, including three underground mines and one surface mine. The mines conducted the testing in collaboration with NIOSH, collecting more than 200 area and personal dust samples. During those tests the method used to provide only an estimate for quartz, still the mines were able to use the information from the field test prototype rapid quartz monitor to assess the efficacy of the dust control technology and were able to identify occupations and tasks characterized by exposure to high concentrations of quartz.

At this time, NIOSH is supporting MSHA evaluations of the prototype to determine how well the results correlate with the analytical results provided by the standard laboratory based MSHA P–7 approach. Sampling will be conducted in MSHA districts 2 and 3 and will be expanded to include samples from each MSHA district across the United States.

Although the field based prototype rapid quartz monitor, or end of shift silica monitor, shows promise as a self assessment tool for exposure to quartz in coal mines, it is not currently ready for use as a compliance tool.

In the meantime, more frequent quartz sampling, as opposed to dust itself, but quartz sampling, and more frequent enhanced medical surveillance would be appropriate, including retired coal miners.

Thank you, Madam Chairwoman. I would be happy to answer any questions.

[The statement of Dr. Howard follows:]

STATEMENT OF JOHN HOWARD, M.D., DIRECTOR, NATIONAL INSTITUTE FOR OCCUPATIONAL SAFETY AND HEALTH CENTERS FOR DISEASE CONTROL AND PREVENTION, U.S. DEPARTMENT OF HEALTH AND HUMAN SERVICES, SUBCOMMITTEE ON WORKFORCE PROTECTIONS, COMMITTEE ON EDUCATION AND LABOR, U.S. HOUSE OF REPRESENTATIVES, JUNE 20, 2019

Good morning, Chairwoman Adams, Ranking Member Byrne, and distinguished members of the Subcommittee. My name is John Howard and I am the Director of the National Institute for Occupational Safety and Health, or NIOSH, which is part of the Centers for Disease Control and Prevention (CDC) within the U.S. Department of Health and Human Services (HHS). I am here today to provide the Subcommittee two updates. First, I will provide an update on the science supporting the contribution that inhaling respirable crystalline silica makes to developing pneumoconiosis in U.S. coal miners. Second, I will describe NIOSH's efforts to improve the technology for assessing coal miners' exposures to quartz—the form of crystalline silica found in coal mine dust (IARC, 1997).

Science Supporting Crystalline Silica (Quartz) as a Contributing Cause of Pneumoconiosis in U.S. Coal Miners

Quartz Exposure and Pneumoconiosis in Coal Miners

As mines produce coal, a variety of activities generate dust and aerosolize it. Some airborne dust particles are small enough to remain suspended in the air for long periods of time and can be inhaled deep into the lung. The term respirable coal mine dust or "RCMD" refers to the part of coal mine dust that is composed of these small particles. RCMD is most commonly comprised of micron and submicron particles of coal, quartz, pyrite, calcite, dolomite, clay minerals, and diesel particulate matter. RCMD is generated by a number of mining activities including mining coal, loading and transporting coal, applying rock dust (i.e., a dust composed mostly of finely milled limestone), and most importantly for potential quartz exposure, mining or drilling into geologic strata overlying the coal seam or interbedded with the coal seam. The mineralogy and particle size distribution of RCMD vary both within a single mine and from mine to mine depending on the local geology, rock dusting practices, mining methods, and the use of engineering controls.

Over time, inhalation of a sufficient amount of RCMD into the lungs can lead to a spectrum of potentially disabling and sometimes fatal respiratory diseases, including pneumoconiosis—a class of interstitial lung diseases where inhalation of dust leaves the lung stiff and fibrotic, interfering with the body's ability to get oxygen to the tissues (Petsonk et al., 2013). The risk of developing these pneumoconioses is related to the cumulative amount of RCMD inhaled into the lungs over time (NIOSH, 2011). These diseases predominantly include coal workers' pneumoconiosis (CWP), silicosis (another type of pneumoconiosis), and mixed dust pneumoconiosis. Except in the setting of very intense RCMD exposure, pneumoconiosis typically presents after a latency of several decades from first exposure.

Pneumoconiosis can be detected by radiographic imaging of the chest. On plain chest radiographs, CWP and silicosis can be characterized by small opacities, more severe disease with a higher density of small opacities, and especially severe disease characterized by large opacities called progressive massive fibrosis (PMF). Since the lowest point seen in the mid-1990s, NIOSH surveillance of active coal miners for pneumoconiosis using chest radiographs has identified marked increases in the prevalence of pneumoconiosis. The most recently reported prevalence of radiographic pneumoconiosis among active underground coal miners with 25 or more years' tenure is about 20 percent in the regional areas of eastern Kentucky, western Virginia, and the state of West Virginia and 5 percent in the rest of the U.S. (Blackely, Halldin, et al., 2018). Pneumoconiosis affecting younger miners has also been reported. PMF has increased, particularly in the three states of Central Appalachia mentioned above, with a particularly large number of cases (n=416) identified as receiving care at three rural clinics in western Virginia (Blackley, Reynolds, et al., 2018). There is no medical or surgical cure for pneumoconiosis. The only approach is to prevent inhalation of respirable mineral dusts that cause pneumoconiosis such as respirable coal mine dust and respirable crystalline silica.

Quartz Exposure and Pneumoconiosis in Contemporary Coal Miners

Coal mining activities that disturb rock containing quartz can generate dust aerosols that contain respirable crystalline silica. Inhaling excessive amounts of crystalline silica causes silicosis, a type of pneumoconiosis (NIOSH 2002). It has been known for many years that coal miners, particularly miners in certain jobs such as underground coal miners engaged in roof bolting, miners at the face, and surface miners engaged in drilling through rock overburden, can develop silicosis, or CWP mixed with silicosis (Banks et al., 1983; Vallyathan et al., 2011).

Coal Workers' Health Surveillance Program Data

In a 2010 publication, NIOSH investigators thought that crystalline silica exposures were playing an important role in the increasing burden of pneumoconiosis, and rapidly progressive pneumoconiosis, in U.S. underground coal miners (Laney et al., 2010). They described an increasing occurrence of a specific type of radiographic abnormality associated with silicosis, called "r-type opacities," among underground coal miners from eastern Kentucky, western Virginia, and West Virginia. Occurrence was higher in the 2000s relative to the 1990s and 1980s and occurrence was higher in miners from those Appalachian states relative to the rest of the U.S. The same pattern of fin[illegible] was shown for PMF. Due to the nature of the data, a specific exposure mechani[illegible] their findings could not be established, but the authors noted that

> "the continuous rise in the demand for coal, coupled with increasing produ[illegible] mining equipment has led to the depletion of the largest, most easily accessible North American underground coal seams. These factors, and the increasing price of energy sources, have made mining thinner seams of coal more economically feasible" (Laney et al., 2010).

Luttrell and Honaker (2012) describe how this has led to mining large amounts of rock together with coal;

"It is not uncommon for eastern operations to experience yields under 30–35%, thereby producing only 1 t of clean coal from three or more tons of mined product. An estimate complied [*sic*] from production records supplied by coal producers suggests that the average yield is now less than 50% (i.e., 49.8% ± 3.5%) for the total USA. This situation is expected to worsen as eastern reserves become thinner and more challenging to mine…Consequently, ever increasing amounts of rock from out-of-seam dilution are being mined. …"

In a follow-up to the 2010 publication, NIOSH investigators documented that the prevalence of r-type opacities continued to increase in the 2010s in coal miners working in eastern Kentucky, western Virginia, and West Virginia relative to earlier decades, and also relative to coal miners in the rest of the U.S. (Hall et al., 2019).

MSHA Inspection Data

An evaluation of respirable dust and quartz data collected in underground coal mines by Mine Safety and Health Administration (MSHA) mine inspectors confirms underground coal miners' exposure to crystalline silica (Doney et al., 2019). Between 1982 and 2017, over two hundred thousand quartz samples were collected across the U.S. The overall respirable quartz geometric mean of these samples was 0.038 mg/m3, with 18.7 percent of samples exceeding MSHA's permissible exposure limit (PEL) that reduces allowable exposures to respirable coal mine dust to ensure exposures to no more than 0.1 mg/m3 quartz (calculated only when the percentage of quartz in respirable coal mine dust exceeded 5 percent). The percentage of samples collected for the continuous mine operator and helper occupational group, exceeding MSHA's reduced respirable coal mine dust PEL adjusted for quartz content, was 21.9 percent, and the percentage of samples exceeding the exposure limit for the roof bolter occupational group was 19.1 percent. Mean percent quartz in respirable coal mine dust samples for Central Appalachia (MSHA Districts 4, 5, and 12) were significantly higher than in the rest of the U.S.

Black Lung Clinic Data

Evaluation of coal miners with PMF seen in Appalachian clinics also supports the role for crystalline silica (quartz) in the increase of the most severe form of pneumoconiosis. In 2018, NIOSH investigators reported a group of 416 coal miners with PMF receiving care at three Black Lung clinics in western Virginia (Blackley, Reynolds, et al., 2018). Later that year, the investigators published a summary of detailed interviews with a convenience sample of 19 miners with PMF from these clinics (Reynolds et al., 2018). Nine were roof bolters, seven continuous miner operators, one shuttle car operator, and two worked a combination of jobs. Eighteen reported being in the vicinity when continuous mining machines were used to cut significant amounts of rock either to reach coal seams or in the process of extracting them. Fourteen reported that ventilation controls were not consistently maintained and 13 reported that RCMD was improperly sampled.

Lung Tissue Pathology Data

Further support for the contribution of crystalline silica (quartz) to pneumoconiosis in contemporary underground coal miners in eastern Kentucky, western Virginia, and West Virginia comes from evaluation of pathological findings in samples of lung tissue from miners in these areas. Silicosis can be clearly differentiated from CWP by microscopic examination of lung tissues.

In a 2016 report, a group of investigators sought lung tissue samples from coal miners with rapidly progressive pneumoconiosis (Cohen et al., 2016). They identified 13 miners with evaluable lung samples. The longest-held jobs for eight of these miners were operating continuous mining machines. Four miners were roof bolters, and one was a surface miner. Eleven were from West Virginia. Based on reviews of radiographs and pathological findings in lung tissue, twelve were identified as having PMF. On pathology examination, 11 miners were diagnosed as having silicosis and only four miners had classic lesions of simple CWP. Polarized light microscopy of the lung tissue samples showed the presence of large amounts of birefringent mineral dust particles consistent with crystalline silica and other minerals. Ongoing research by these investigators, with assistance from NIOSH, is comparing lung pathology in largely older lung samples held by NIOSH as part of the National Coal Workers' Autopsy Study to lung pathology findings in more recent lung samples obtained by biopsy or at the time of lung transplantation or autopsy. One aspect of the research is to use more sophisticated techniques to characterize the composition of particles found in the lung.

Conclusion

Scientific evidence to date from surveillance surveys, MSHA inspection data, clinical and radiographic examinations, and lung tissue analysis, support the conclusion that quartz, a form of crystalline silica, plays a contributing role in the current outbreak of pneumoconiosis in coal miners, particularly in eastern Kentucky, western Virginia, and in West Virginia.

Technology for Evaluating Coal Miners' Exposures to Respirable Coal Mine Dust

Continuous Personal Dust Monitor

For several decades, NIOSH has had a major ongoing research effort in the area of developing new technologies for monitoring coal miner exposure to respirable dust. This research led to the development, certification, and commercialization of the continuous personal dust monitor (CPDM) which involved close collaboration with MSHA, the mining industry, labor unions and the instrument manufacturer – Thermo Fisher Scientific.

In 2016, MSHA, under a final rule, *"Lowering Miners' Exposure to Respirable Coal Mine Dust, Including Continuous Personal Dust Monitors,"* mandated the use of a CPDM in all active U.S. underground coal mines. The Thermo Scientific PDM3700 is currently the only approved CPDM to monitor exposure to RCMD. It is jointly approved for use in coal mines by MSHA and NIOSH under criteria set forth in 30 C.F.R. part 74. The introduction of the field-based CPDM, which provides near real-time exposure data to individual miners, was a significant advancement over the traditional monitoring method, based on a gravimetric sampler whose dust collection sample must be sent to a laboratory for analysis in order to obtain results, which can take several weeks. Since its introduction into coal mines, the CPDM has significantly improved respirable coal mine dust monitoring capabilities and compliance with MSHA coal mine dust exposure regulations. The CPDM has also proven its value as a tool that enables miners and management to take proactive measures to immediately reduce exposures by quickly implementing engineering controls or modifying work tasks.

Current Methods for Evaluating Coal Miners' Exposures to Quartz

Although the introduction of the CPDM was a major step forward for monitoring miner exposure to RCMD, it measures all types of respirable dust expressed as mass concentration. The CPDM does not differentiate between the individual minerals and other components of respirable dust, and is therefore unable to assess miners' exposure to quartz (a form of crystalline silica) in near real time. Instead, quartz exposure is measured once a quarter from samples collected by MSHA for compliance purposes. Some coal mine operators also perform quartz monitoring for self-assessment and to evaluate the effectiveness of intervention strategies to reduce or eliminate exposure to quartz. Both MSHA and mine operators use a gravimetric dust sampler to perform compliance and self-assessment sampling. A compliance sample, once collected, is sent to an MSHA laboratory for analysis which can take several days to weeks before results are reported to the mine operator. A self-assessment sample is sent to a private sector laboratory for analysis which can also take several days to a week before results are reported to the mine operators.

Efforts to Improve the Technology for Measuring Coal Miners' Exposures to Crystalline Silica

Timely monitoring of quartz would provide better protection for miners. NIOSH is pursuing technologies to advance the science of rapidly assessing quartz exposures in the field through two lines of research—one involving private sector partners, and the other involving NIOSH scientists.

Academic and Private Sector Research Efforts

Funding academic and private sector companies to develop novel technologies for near real-time measurement of quartz is an important way to improve exposure assessment technology. To stimulate this type of research, NIOSH utilizes its external contracts and grants program to accelerate research in high-priority areas where there are critical knowledge gaps or commercialization challenges. In September 2018, NIOSH contracted with Thermo Fisher Scientific to develop a stand-alone, near real-time, quartz dust monitor for compliance sampling. In addition, a solicitation for New Technology Broad Agency Announcement (BAA) contracts (BAA 2019-Q-69532) invited proposals for new technologies that address non-regulatory personal measurement of coal dust or quartz. As stated in the BAA solicitation, while regulatory compliance currently requires mass-based measurement, NIOSH believes there is a market for non-mass-based units measuring coal dust, quartz, or both, that are low enough in cost that the units can be issued to every miner to provide near real-time results. This allows miners to identify elevated quartz levels and take immediate corrective action to prevent overexposure. NIOSH is currently evaluating three proposals received in response to the BAA solicitation.

NIOSH Research Efforts

At NIOSH's Pittsburgh and Spokane Mining Research Divisions, NIOSH has unique laboratory facilities and in-house research expertise that can be focused on developing a prototype for a field-based *"rapid quartz monitor"* (RQM). Starting in 2012, this NIOSH research effort has focused on developing a field-based method for rapid quartz analysis as opposed to the traditional laboratory based, MSHA P7 method (see Table 1). The field-based, RQM prototype is based on three components: (1) a *sampler*, which is composed of a pump, cyclone and sampling cassette; (2) a Fourier Transform Infrared (FTIR) *analyzer*; and (3) a software-based quartz concentration *calculator* (See Figure 1).

Specifically, the field-based RQM prototype involves a gravimetric sample collected on a filter inside a "shoot through" cassette (which has not been mine-tested as of this writing). The "shoot through" cassette is specially designed for direct insertion into any one of four commercially available portable FTIR analyzers. Once analyzed, a NIOSH-developed software program called FAST (Field Analysis of Silica Tool) automatically calculates the quartz concentration from the FTIR spectrum and sampling information provided by the mine operator. A test version of the NIOSH-developed FAST software is currently available on the NIOSH website. The analytical method used by this field-based approach—FTIR spectroscopy—is also used to conduct the laboratory-based MSHA P7 analysis for quartz compliance sampling. Compared to the laboratory-based MSHA P7 analytical method, preliminary laboratory studies show a relative difference of less than 15 percent on average for coal dust samples analyzed in the laboratory using the field-based RQM prototype.

NIOSH Field Test Evaluations

Between 2016 and 2018, NIOSH conducted usability tests of the field-based, prototype RQM at four coal mines in West Virginia, including three underground mines operating continuous miner sections and one surface mine. The traditional sampling cassette was used because the specially designed "shoot through" sampling cassette, now available, was still in development at the time of these usability tests. The mines conducted the testing in collaboration with NIOSH, collecting more than 200 area and personal dust samples with a gravimetric sampler. While the traditional sampling cassette used for this testing limited the accuracy of the analysis, and only provided an estimate for quartz, the mines were still able to use the information output from the field-based prototype RQM approach to assess the efficacy of a control technology for a continuous miner section, and to identify occupations and tasks characterized by high concentrations of quartz.

MSHA Field Test Evaluations

At the present time, NIOSH is supporting MSHA field evaluations of the field-based prototype RQM approach to determine how well the results correlate with the analytical results provided by the standard, laboratory-based, MSHA P7 approach. MSHA's Technical Support group will collect respirable coal mine dust samples on both the traditional and the "shoot through" cassette. The collected samples will be analyzed by MSHA using the field-based, prototype RQM and the standard laboratory-based MSHA P7 method. Sampling will be initially conducted in MSHA Districts 2 and 3, and will be expanded to include samples from each MSHA district across the USA.

Technological Readiness of the Field-Based, Prototype RQM for Compliance Use by MSHA

The current field-based prototype RQM monitoring approach was designed as an engineering control tool. It has the potential to be used for compliance sampling in the future, pending further validation of the prototype method in active coal mines. These technological evaluation studies are necessary to investigate whether or not specific characteristics of the dust present in the coal mining atmosphere require further refinement of the analytical technique. The timeline for completing the field testing will be influenced by the number of samples required to achieve a statistically representative dataset of underground coal mines in the USA. Analysis of the results and preparation of a paper that would document the performance of the prototype would then be completed, undergo peer and stakeholder review, and be published in a peer-reviewed scientific journal. Since the three components of the RQM are off-the-shelf components, no commercialization would be needed.

An important limitation that needs to be addressed before the prototype is considered for compliance sampling is that the field-based, prototype RQM was designed for self-assessment sampling. It was not originally conceived and designed as a compliance tool and therefore was not designed to include tamper-proof components. This means that the integrity of the sample cannot be guaranteed, which it would need to be if the prototype is to be used as a compliance tool. Another consideration is that the adoption of the field-based, prototype RQM as a compliance tool would require miners to wear two sampling devices—one for coal dust and one for quartz—which may hinder miner acceptance.

Conclusions

Science Supporting Respirable Crystalline Silica as a Contributing Cause for Pneumoconiosis in eastern Kentucky, western Virginia and West Virginia

The scientific evidence published to date demonstrates that the crystalline silica component of respirable coal mine dust contributes to the rising prevalence of pneumoconiosis in coal miners, particularly in eastern Kentucky, western Virginia and West Virginia.

Technological Readiness of the Prototype Rapid Quartz Monitor

Although showing promise as a self-assessment tool for exposure to crystalline silica in coal mines, the field-based, prototype RQM is not currently technologically ready for use as a compliance tool.

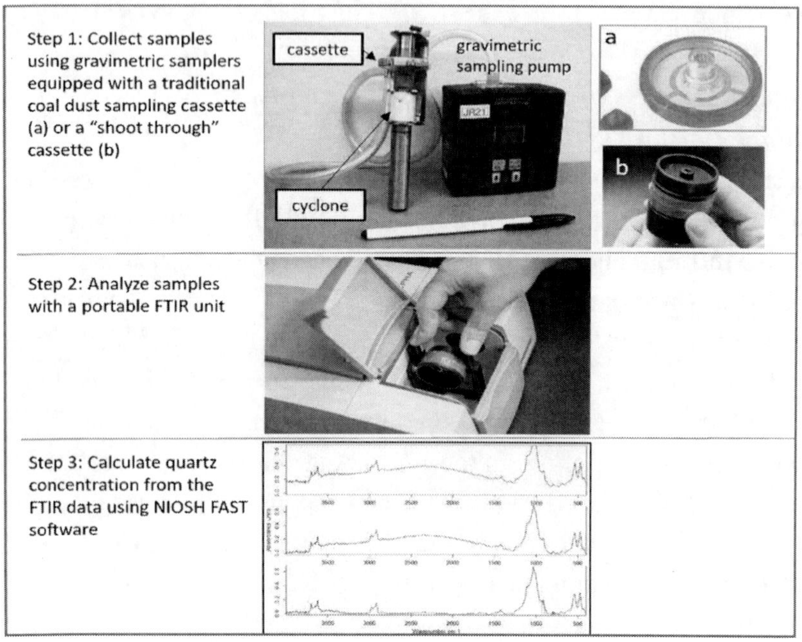

Figure 5. Process for measuring quartz exposure using the field-based prototype RQM approach.

Table 1.

	MSHA P7 method		**NIOSH Rapid Quartz Analysis**	
	Step	where	Step	where
1	Airborne respirable dust samples are collected on pre-weighed membrane filters using MSHA/NIOSH approved personal respirable dust samplers as described in 30 CFR Part 74. After collection, the filter capsules are reweighed to one thousandth of a milligram in order to determine the net sample mass.	Mine	Airborne respirable dust samples are collected on membrane filters using MSHA/NIOSH approved personal respirable dust samplers as described in 30 CFR Part 74.	Mine
2	Transporting/mailing the sample to the analytical lab		Sample remains on-site	
3	Removing the filter media from sampling cassette – The filter media containing the dust sample must be removed from the sampling cassette.	Lab	Opening the sampling cassette – The two end caps of the sampling cassette are removed while the filter media containing the dust sample remains inside the cassette.	Mine
4	Pre-treatment of the sample – The sample filters are ashed in a low-temperature radio-frequency asher to destroy the organic matrix (coal dust and collection filter).	Lab		
5	Re-deposition of the sample – Ashed samples are deposited onto an approximately 9 mm diameter area of a vinyl acrylic copolymer (VAC) (DM450) filter.	Lab		
6	Analysis of the sample using FTIR instrumentation – The sample is inserted in the FTIR analyzer (PE Model2000, GX or equivalent) and analyzed. The redeposited, ashed dust samples are scanned between wave numbers of 1,000 and 700 cm·' to determine the quartz and kaolinite content.	Lab	Analysis of the sample using FTIR instrumentation – The cassette is inserted in the portable FTIR analyzer and analyzed. The sample is scanned by FTIR between wave numbers of 4,000 and 400 cm·' to determine the quartz and kaolinite content.	Mine
7	Sample data analyzed – The mass of quartz in the deposit is determined (after correcting for the interference by kaolinite) by comparison to calibration curves for standard quartz samples and standard kaolinite samples. The percentage of quartz in the sample is calculated using the quartz mass determined from the analysis and the sample's mass of dust.	Lab	Sample data analyzed – The data generated by the FTIR analysis are processed by NIOSH FAST software to determine respirable quartz concentration and mass (after correcting for the interference by kaolinite).	Mine
8	The results are received by the mine	Mine		

References

Banks DE, Bauer MA, Castellan RM, Lapp NL. *Silicosis in surface coalmine drillers. Thorax.* 1983 Apr;38(4):275-8. PubMed PMID: 6867980; PubMed Central PMCID: PMC459535.

Blackley DJ, Halldin CN, Laney AS. Continued Increase in Prevalence of Coal Workers' Pneumoconiosis in the United States, 1970-2017. *Am J Public Health*. 2018 Sep;108(9):1220-1222. doi: 10.2105/AJPH.2018.304517. PubMed PMID: 30024799; PubMed Central PMCID: PMC6085042.

Blackley DJ, Reynolds LE, Short C, Carson R, Storey E, Halldin CN, Laney AS. Progressive Massive Fibrosis in Coal Miners From 3 Clinics in Virginia. *JAMA*. 2018 Feb 6;319(5):500-501. doi: 10.1001/jama.2017.18444. PubMed PMID: 29411024; PubMed Central PMCID: PMC5839295.

Cohen RA, Petsonk EL, Rose C, Young B, Regier M, Najmuddin A, Abraham JL, Churg A, Green FH. Lung Pathology in U.S. Coal Workers with Rapidly Progressive Pneumoconiosis Implicates Silica and Silicates. *Am J Respir Crit Care Med*. 2016 Mar 15;193(6):673-80. doi: 10.1164/rccm.201505-1014OC. PubMed PMID: 26513613; PubMed Central PMCID: PMC4824937.

Department of Defense. *Technological Readiness Assessment Deskbook.* July 2009 https://apps.dtic.mil/dtic/tr/fulltext/u2/a524200.pdf.

Doney BC, Blackley D, Hale JM, Halldin C, Kurth L, Syamlal G, Laney AS. Respirable coal mine dust in underground mines, United States, 1982-2017. *Am J Ind Med*. 2019 Jun;62(6):478-485. doi: 10.1002/ajim.22974. PubMed PMID: 31033017.

Hall NB, Blackley DJ, Halldin CN, Laney AS. Continued increase in prevalence of r-type opacities among underground coal miners in the USA. *Occup Environ Med*. 2019 Apr 25. pii: oemed-2019-105691. doi: 10.1136/oemed-2019-105691. [Epub ahead of print] PubMed PMID: 31023786.

IARC (International Agency for Research on Cancer). Coal Dust. 1. Exposure data. In: Silica, Some Silicates, Coal Dust and para-Aramid Fibrils. *IARC Monographs on the Evaluation of Carcinogenic Risks to Humans*, No. 68.

IARC Working Group on the Evaluation of Carcinogenic Risk to Humans. Lyon (FR): International Agency for Research on Cancer; 1997. Available at: https://www.ncbi.nlm.nih.gov/books/NBK410045/, Accessed 5/31/2019.

Laney AS, Petsonk EL, Attfield MD. Pneumoconiosis among underground bituminous coal miners in the United States: is silicosis becoming more frequent? *Occup Environ Med*. 2010 Oct;67(10):652-6. doi: 10.1136/oem.2009.047126. Epub 2009 Sep 22. PubMed PMID: 19773275.

Luttrell GH, Honaker RQ. "Coal preparation." In: *Encyclopedia of sustainability science and technology. 2012 edition*. Ed: RA Meyers. New York, NY: Springer, 2012. Print ISBN: 978-0-387-89469-0. Online ISBN: 978-1-4419-0851-3. https://doi.org/10.1007/978-1-4419-0851-3_431. Accessed May 31, 2019.

National Academies of Sciences, Engineering, and Medicine. 2018. *Monitoring and Sampling Approaches to Assess Underground Coal Mine Dust Exposures*. Washington, DC: The National Academies Press. https://www.nap.edu/read/25111/chapter/1.

NIOSH (National Institute for Occupational Safety and Health). 2002. *Health effects of occupational exposure to respirable crystalline silica.* DHHS (NIOSH) Publication No. 2002-129. Available at: https://www.cdc.gov/niosh/docs/2002-129/default.html.

NIOSH (National Institute for Occupational Safety and Health). 2011. Current Intelligence Bulletin 64. *Coal mine dust exposures and associated health outcomes. A review of information published since 1995.* DHHS (NIOSH) Publication No. 2011–172. Available at: https://www.cdc.gov/niosh/docs/2011-172/default.html.

Petsonk EL, Rose C, Cohen R. Coal mine dust lung disease. New lessons from old exposure. *Am J Respir Crit Care Med.* 2013 Jun 1;187(11):1178-85. doi:10.1164/rccm.201301-0042CI. PubMed PMID: 23590267.

Reynolds LE, Blackley DJ, Colinet JF, Potts JD, Storey E, Short C, Carson R, Clark KA, Laney AS, Halldin CN. Work Practices and Respiratory Health Status of Appalachian Coal Miners With Progressive Massive Fibrosis. *J Occup Environ Med.* 2018 Nov;60(11):e575-e581. doi: 10.1097/JOM.0000000000001443. PubMed PMID: 30199471.

Vallyathan V, Landsittel DP, Petsonk EL, Kahn J, Parker JE, Osiowy KT, Green FH. The influence of dust standards on the prevalence and severity of coal workers' pneumoconiosis at autopsy in the United States of America. *Arch Pathol Lab Med.* 2011 Dec;135(12):1550-6. doi: 10.5858/arpa.2010-0393-OA. PubMed PMID: 22129182.

Chairwoman ADAMS. Thank you very much.

We will recognize assistant secretary, Mr. Zatezalo. Five minutes, sir.

Testimony of David Zatezalo, Assistant Secretary of Labor for Mine Safety and Health, Department of Labor

Mr. ZATEZALO. Thank you, Madam Chairwoman Adams, Ranking Member Byrne, members of the Subcommittee. Thank you for inviting me here to testify today.

It is my honor to appear before this subcommittee and to represent President Trump, Secretary Acosta, and all 1,860 dedicated men and women of the Mine Safety and Health Administration.

What distinguishes MSHA from other federal safety agencies is our foundational mandate of inspecting every underground mine at least four times per year and every surface mine at least twice. I am pleased to report that in 2018 MSHA fulfilled that mandate with over 37,000 inspections.

Our one MSHA initiative began last year by creating the unified position of administrator for mine safety and health enforcement. We evaluated all mines for distance from MSHA offices and identified 90 mines where it made sense to cross-train inspectors. The Mine Safety and Health Academy established and revised curriculum with input from the NCFLL, which represents our field staff, and provided up to 56 hours of classroom training for those inspectors, plus 24 hours of on-the-job training with a seasoned inspector.

During the six months beginning last October, inspectors with those 90 mines spent 41 percent less travel time than previously. Clearly, this saves taxpayer dollars, but ultimately this is about more effectively achieving MSHA's core mission. Instead of spending time driving, our inspectors can spend more time on site interacting with miners and observing them.

Understand that MSHA will retain specialists in their current roles to cover specific mining conditions, such as ventilation experts for underground coal mine inspections, which are prone to special hazardous conditions. In keeping with our promise to the House of Senate Appropriations Committee, MSHA's office of accountability will audit crossover mine inspections to ensure that enforcement personnel adhere to MSHA's policies and procedures.

MSHA's injury and fatality data show the most common cause of fatalities is powered haulage accidents, accounting for half of fatalities in recent years. We launched an initiative focusing specifically on the three most common types of haulage fatalities, which are mobile equipment collisions, belt conveyers, and seat belt use. Last June, we published a request for information seeking input on these technologies, practices, and other ways to prevent such fatalities and held seven public hearings along the way. In the recently released spring unified agenda, MSHA announced our intention to issue a propose rule addressing powered haulage.

In addition to more strategically focusing on the day to day safety of miners, we are paying very close attention the "H" in MSHA, which is miners' health. MSHA continues to aggressively enforce existing standards to ensure that miners are protected from exposure to respirable dust and quartz. I am encouraged by mine operators' plus 99 percent compliance with the 2016 respirable coal dust rule in controlling coal miners exposure to quartz. The number of quartz samples collected has increased by 335 percent between 2013 and 2018. And since August of 2016 MSHA samples indicate average quartz exposures are 75 percent below the threshold limit on average.

This can further improve with real-time quartz monitoring, similar to CPDM technology, which NIOSH continues to develop, along with MSHA's collaboration. Whereas over 16 percent of quartz samples exceeded the standard in 2008, only 1.2 percent exceeded that standard in 2018, which is the lowest rate since MSHA began keeping records.

Samples that exceed the standard are reviewed in senior staff meetings. Field staff issue citations per regulations and follow up to ensure the mine addresses the cause to avoid future exceedances. And to compel compliance we have not hesitated to issue 104(b) withdrawal orders.

In addition, in the 2014 Respirable Coal Mine Dust Rule, MSHA committed to a retrospective study of the dust rule and last year we issued an RFI seeking comments on how best to structure that study.

Due to the decades-long latency period between exposure and disease manifestation, a medically valid study cannot be completed in the near-term, but MSHA anticipates the study will confirm that dramatic increases in sampling and compliance translate into reduced black lung incidents going forward.

In May of 2019 MSHA published an RFI in its regulatory agenda that includes both coal and metal, nonmetal, quartz, or silica standards.

In closing, I want to inform the Subcommittee that MSHA is more vigorously pursuing operators who refuse to pay delinquent civil penalties. Shortly after I testified last February, we launched an enhanced Scofflaw Initiative and I am pleased to report that so far it has accounted for nearly $8 million that otherwise would not have been collected.

Again, I appreciate the opportunity to discuss MSHA's important work with you. I look forward to answering any questions that members of the subcommittee may have.

[The statement of Mr. Zatezalo follows:]

Statement of David G. Zatezalo, Assistant Secretary for Mine Safety and Health, U.S. Department of Labor, before the Subcommittee on Workforce Protections, Committee on Education and Labor, United States House of Representatives, June 20, 2019

Chairwoman Adams, Ranking Member Byrne, and Members of the Subcommittee, thank you for inviting me to testify here today. It is my honor to appear before this Subcommittee and to represent President Trump, Secretary Acosta, and all 1,868 dedicated men and women of the Department of Labor's Mine Safety and Health Administration.

What primarily distinguishes MSHA from other federal safety agencies is our foundational mandate: MSHA must inspect every underground mine at least four times per year, and every surface mine at least twice. I am pleased to report that in 2018 MSHA fulfilled that mandate, conducting 37,065 total mandatory and non-mandatory inspections at 13,486 mines.

As I stated to the Subcommittee last February, I believe I could not manage effectively and wisely without first examining the entire organization from top to bottom.

I have now visited all six Metal/Nonmetal District offices, all nine Coal District offices, key Technical Support facilities, the National Mine Health and Safety Academy in West Virginia, and 49 field offices. I have met with countless field staff in person, to give them an opportunity to voice their ideas and concerns.

From my travels, I observed that the bifurcation of Coal enforcement and Metal/Nonmetal enforcement imposed artificial boundaries based on the materials mined, versus travel distances between inspectors and mines. I discovered, for instance, that enforcement staff were spending over 21% of their time traveling. To more strategically allocate MSHA's resources, we are executing a gradual reorganization that will blur but not completely erase the lines between the two main mining sectors.

Our "One MSHA" initiative began by creating the unified position of Administrator, Mine Safety & Health over all of Enforcement. We then evaluated all mines for distance from MSHA offices, and identified 90 mines where it made sense to train a coal inspector to inspect a metal/nonmetal mine, or vice versa. The Mine Academy in Beckley, WV established and revised our curriculum, with input from the National Council of Field Labor Locals (NCFLL), which represents our field staff. We provided up to 56 hours of classroom training for those inspectors, plus up to 24 hours on-the-job training with a seasoned inspector or manager.

During the six months beginning last October, inspectors for those 90 mines spent 41% less time driving than previously. Clearly this saves taxpayer dollars on vehicles, fuel, food and lodging. But ultimately this is about more effectively achieving MSHA's core mission: instead of spending time driving in a car, our inspectors can spend more time on site interacting with miners and observing safety conditions.

Based on the success of phase one, starting July 1st we are adding 117 more mines. Understand that MSHA will retain specialists in their current roles to cover specific mining conditions, such as ventilation experts inspecting underground coal mines prone to hazardous conditions like combustible coal dust and methane inundation. In keeping our promise to House and Senate Appropriations Committees, MSHA's Office of Accountability will audit crossover mine inspections to ensure that enforcement personnel adhered to MSHA's policies and procedures.

We also examined MSHA's injury and fatality data, and learned that the most common cause of fatalities is powered haulage accidents, accounting for half of fatalities in recent years. We launched an initiative focusing specifically on the three most common causes of powered haulage fatalities: mobile equipment collisions, belt conveyors, and seat belt use. Last June, we published a request for information seeking input on technologies, practices, and other ways to prevent such fatalities. In the recently released Spring Unified Agenda, MSHA announced our intention to issue a proposed rule addressing powered haulage.

As a complement to enforcement, the Trump Administration recognizes the safety and health benefits of compliance assistance. Over the past two fiscal years, MSHA has performed 8% more compliance assistance visits, half of which were for operators with 10 or fewer employees. Additionally, following three fire suppression system failures last September, with one fatality, we swiftly inspected over 4,000 pieces of mobile equipment that had such systems installed, and educated miners and operators on how to stay safe.

In addition to more strategically focusing on the day-to-day safety of miners, we are paying close attention to the "H" in MSHA: miners' health. MSHA continues to aggressively enforce existing standards to ensure that operators protect miners from exposure to respirable dust and quartz. I am encouraged by mine operators' current compliance with the respirable coal dust rule and controlling coal miners' exposure to quartz. The number of quartz samples collected increased 335% between 2013 and 2018, and since August 2016, MSHA samples indicate average quartz exposure 75% below the limit, on average. This can improve further with real-time quartz monitoring—similar to Continuous Personal Dust Monitor (CPDM) technology—which National Institute for Occupational Safety and Health (NIOSH) continues to develop with MSHA's collaboration. Whereas over 16% of quartz samples exceeded the standard in 2008, by 2018 only 1.2% exceeded the standard—the lowest rate since MSHA began keeping records. Samples that exceed the standard are reviewed in senior staff meetings. Field staff issue citations per MSHA's regulations, and follow up to ensure that the mine addresses the root cause to avoid future exceedances. To compel compliance, we have not hesitated to issue 104(b) withdrawal orders.

In addition, in the 2014 Respirable Coal Mine Dust Rule, MSHA committed to a retrospective study of the dust rule beginning February 1, 2017, and last year issued a request for information seeking comments on how best to structure that study. Due to the typically decades-long latency between exposure and disease, a medically valid study likely cannot be completed for a decade or more, but MSHA anticipates the study will confirm that dramatic improvements in sampling and compliance translate into reduced Black Lung incidence going forward. In the meantime, MSHA is currently considering appropriate next steps to address miners' exposures to quartz.

In closing, I want to inform the Subcommittee that MSHA is more vigorously pursuing operators who refuse to pay delinquent civil penalties. When the Trump administration took office, MSHA was owed $67.1 million in delinquent safety and health penalties that had accrued over decades. By not paying their fines, scofflaws gain a competitive advantage within the industry and create unsafe conditions. If not pursued, scofflaws foster an impression that violators can ignore fines with impunity. Shortly after I testified last February, we launched our enhanced Scofflaw Initiative, and I am pleased to report that so far, it has accounted for $7.2 million that otherwise would not have been collected—with $49.6 million in delinquent debt remaining, of which $14.9 is potentially collectible.

Again, I appreciate the opportunity to discuss MSHA's important work with you. I look forward to answering any questions that Members of this Subcommittee may have.

Chairwoman ADAMS. Thank you very much.

I will recognize Miss Brown Barnes for 5 minutes, ma'am.

TESTIMONY OF CINDY S. BROWN BARNES, DIRECTOR, EDUCATION, WORKFORCE, AND INCOME SECURITY, GOVERNMENT ACCOUNTABILITY OFFICE

Ms. BROWN BARNES. Chairwoman Adams, Ranking Member Byrne, and members of the subcommittee, thank you for inviting me to discuss our part in ongoing work on the Black Lung Disability Trust Fund solvency and the Department of Labor's, or DoL's, oversight of the program.

The Black Lung benefits program helps miners who have been totally disabled due to black lung disease. Coal companies found liable or the Trust Fund pays these benefits. The Trust Fund may pay if, for example, a company goes bankrupt. A domestic coal tax is the Trust Fund's primary funding source.

Today I will discuss, one, the future insolvency of the Trust Fund given the coal tax decrease and declining coal production, and, two, provide preliminary observations regarding DoL's oversight given recent coal company bankruptcies.

Last year we reported that multiple factors have challenged the finances of the Trust Fund since it was established about 40 years ago. Its expenses have consistently exceeded its revenues, interest payments have grown, and actions taken that were expected to improve Trust Fund finances did not completely address this debt. As a result the Trust Fund has borrowed from the Treasury almost every year since 1979. This caused debt and interest to accumulate. Trust fund revenue will further be challenged by the 55 percent coal tax decrease that took effect this year and by declining coal production into the future.

We did simulations that demonstrate that future Trust Fund revenue may not be sufficient to cover beneficiary payments and administrative costs through 2050. For example, we simulated that Trust Fund revenues for this year would be $187 million less than last year due to the coal tax decrease. As a result, the Trust Fund will need to continue borrowing from the Treasury to cover its expenses. When this occurs, the Federal Government is essentially borrowing from itself and from the general taxpayer to finance benefit payments to coal miners with black lung disease.

As you can see in the figure, by 2050 our simulation shows that outstanding debt could exceed $15 billion. Even if the black lung program stopped paying all beneficiaries this year, the debt could still be over $6 billion by 2050 using the current coal tax rate. However, various options, such as adjusting the coal tax and forgiving interest or debt, could reduce future borrowing and improve the Trust Fund's financial position.

Our preliminary observations indicate that Trust Fund finances have been further strained by coal operator bankruptcies. Since 2014 insolvent coal miner companies have cost the Trust Fund over $300 million. Federal law charges the DoL with ensuring that coal companies have insurance to secure their black lung benefit liabilities. To do so companies can ensure, meaning they must obtain acceptable collateral in an amount deemed adequate by DoL to secure their liability. As you can see in the table, since 2014 there have been three bankruptcies of large self-insured coal operators that have resulted in substantial losses to the Trust Fund. For example, the collateral DoL required from Alpha Natural Resources was just $12 million, although the estimated liability was about $207 million. As a result, an estimated 685 beneficiaries will be added to the Trust Fund with an estimated loss of nearly $185 million. There are 22 remaining coal operators that DoL has authorized to self-insure and many of these pose a financial risk to the Trust Fund.

Our preliminary analysis indicates that DoL did not regularly review these operators so that they could adjust collateral as needed to protect the Trust Fund. For 10 of these companies the last review occurred between 16 and 31 years ago. For 11 of these companies DoL has no estimate of their black lung liability. For companies that DoL did have liability estimates for, in some cases the collateral was tens of millions less than their estimated liability.

In 2015, DoL stopped monitoring these self-insured coal companies. Over the past 4 years, DoL has been developing new procedures for regulating self-insurance, but these procedures have not yet been put into action.

In conclusion, the future solvency of the Trust Fund remains bleak and DoL's oversight challenges have left the Trust Fund vulnerable and exposed to additional financial risks from insolvent coal mine operators without adequate collateral. Our ongoing work will present opportunities for us to further examine these issues.

Thank you. This concludes my prepared statement and I would be happy to entertain any questions.

[The statement of Ms. Brown Barnes follows:]

Black Lung Benefits Program: Financing and Oversight Challenges Are Adversely Affecting the Trust Fund, Statement of Cindy Brown Barnes, Director, Education, Workforce, and Income Security[3]

Why GAO Did This Study

Since 2009, GAO has produced a body of work on the Black Lung Benefits Program. In 2018, for instance, GAO reported that the Trust Fund, which pays benefits to certain coal miners, faced financial challenges due, in part, to the coal tax rate decrease that took effect in 2019 and declining coal production.

Trust Fund finances could be further strained by coal mine operator bankruptcies, as they can lead to benefit liabilities being transferred to the Trust Fund.

This testimony describes Trust Fund finances through 2050 and provides preliminary observations from ongoing work for this committee regarding the Department of Labor's (DOL) oversight of coal mine operator insurance.

To describe Trust Fund finances, in its 2018 report GAO developed simulations through 2050 based on various assumptions related to future coal production and the number of future black lung beneficiaries. To develop preliminary observations from its ongoing work, GAO analyzed DOL documentation and data on black lung beneficiaries and coal mine operators. GAO also reviewed relevant federal laws, regulations, policies, and guidance and interviewed DOL officials, insurance carriers, and coal mine operators, among others.

What GAO Recommends

GAO will be considering recommendations, as appropriate, when ongoing work is finished.

What GAO Found

GAO reported in 2018 that Black Lung Disability Trust Fund (Trust Fund) expenditures have consistently exceeded revenue. The Trust Fund borrowed from the

---

[3] This is an edited, reformatted and augmented version of United States Government Accountability Office, Testimony before the Committee on Education and Labor, Subcommittee on Workforce Protections, House of Representatives, Publication No. GAO-19-622T, dated June 20, 2019.

Department of the Treasury's (Treasury) general fund and hence from the taxpayer almost every year since 1979, its first complete fiscal year, causing debt and interest to accumulate. Federal law does not limit the amount the Trust Fund may borrow as needed to cover its expenditures. Trust Fund revenue will be further limited by the coal tax rate decrease of about 55 percent that took effect in 2019, and declining coal production, according to GAO's simulation. Specifically, Trust Fund revenue may not be sufficient to cover beneficiary payments and administrative costs, from fiscal years 2020 through 2050. Therefore, the Trust Fund could need to continue borrowing to cover its expenditures—including the repayment of past debt and interest—and the Trust Fund's simulated outstanding debt could exceed $15 billion by 2050 (see figure). However, as GAO reported in 2018, various options, such as adjusting the coal tax and forgiving debt, could improve the Trust Fund's financial position.

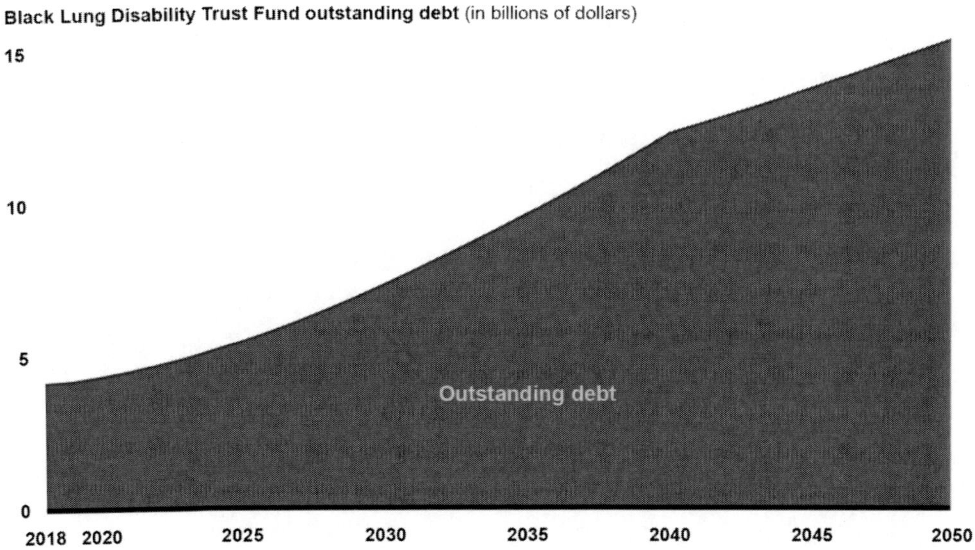

Source: GAO simulation based on data from the Departments of Labor and Treasury, the Energy Information Administration, and the Office of Management and Budget. | GAO-19-622T.

Figure 6. Trust Fund Simulated Outstanding Debt, Fiscal Years 2018 through 2050.

GAO's preliminary observations indicate that Trust Fund finances will be further strained by coal operator bankruptcies. Since 2014, an estimated black lung benefit liability of over $310 million has been transferred to the Trust Fund from insolvent self-insured coal mine operators, according to DOL data. Federal law generally requires that operators secure their black lung benefit liability. To do so, operators can self-insure if they meet certain DOL conditions. As of June 2019, there are 22 operators that are self-insured and actively mining coal, according to DOL officials. GAO's preliminary analysis indicates that DOL did not regularly review these operators so that it could adjust collateral as needed to protect the Trust Fund. As a result, the amount of collateral

DOL required from some of these operators is tens of millions less than their most recent estimated black lung benefit liability.

Chairwoman Adams, Ranking Member Byrne, and Members of the Subcommittee:

I am pleased to be here today to highlight GAO's prior and ongoing work on Black Lung Disability Trust Fund (Trust Fund) solvency, and the Department of Labor's (DOL) oversight of coal mine operator insurance given recent operator bankruptcies.[4]

The Black Lung Benefits Program provides medical and cash assistance to certain coal miners who have been totally disabled due to pneumoconiosis, also known as black lung disease.[5] Their surviving dependents may also receive assistance. Black lung benefits are generally to be paid by liable coal mine operators. However, the Trust Fund pays benefits in certain circumstances including in cases where no responsible mine operator could be identified or when the liable mine operator does not pay. The Trust Fund is financed primarily by a tax on coal produced and sold domestically, which we refer to in this statement as the coal tax.[6]

In 2018, we reported that the Trust Fund faced financial challenges and borrowed about $1.3 billion in fiscal year 2017 from the Department of the Treasury's (Treasury) general fund to cover its expenditures. Beginning in 2019, the rate of the coal tax—the Trust Fund's primary revenue source— decreased by about 55 percent. The Trust Fund may also be affected by declining future coal production, as we reported in 2018. With less revenue from the coal tax, increased federal funding will likely be needed. Under federal law the Trust Fund borrows from Treasury's general fund when necessary to cover its expenditures. Federal law does not limit the amount the Trust Fund may borrow from Treasury's general fund—and hence from the taxpayer—as needed to cover its relevant expenditures.

However, various options, such as adjusting the coal tax and forgiving interest or debt, could reduce future borrowing and improve the Trust Fund's financial position (see GAO-18-351).

In my testimony today, I will (1) discuss the future solvency of the Trust Fund given the coal tax rate decrease and declining coal production, and (2) provide preliminary observations based on ongoing work for this committee regarding DOL's oversight of coal mine operator insurance given recent operator bankruptcies.

To address our first objective we drew directly from our 2018 report. In that report we simulated, among other things, how Trust Fund debt may change through 2050 given

---

[4] GAO, *Black Lung Benefits Program: Options to Improve Trust Fund Finances*, GAO-18-351 (Washington D.C: May 30, 2018).

[5] Black lung is caused by breathing coal mine dust and the severity of the disease can range from mild—with no noticeable effects on breathing—to advanced disease, which could lead to respiratory failure and death according to the Centers for Disease Control, National Institute of Occupational Safety and Health.

[6] The coal tax is imposed on the sale of all domestic coal with two exceptions: (1) lignite coal and (2) exported coal.

the coal tax rate decrease and declining coal production.[7] Our simulations were based on various assumptions and simulated Trust Fund revenues and expenditures from fiscal years 2016 through 2050. To develop these simulations, we used actual and projection data from (1) DOL for fiscal years 2015 through 2040; (2) Treasury's Office of Tax Analysis for fiscal years 2011 through 2015; (3) the Department of Energy's Energy Information Administration (EIA) for calendar years 2015 through 2050; and (4) the Office of Management and Budget (OMB) for fiscal year 2017. We ran each simulation multiple times using different sets of assumptions about the number of future black lung beneficiaries and future coal production. Doing so provided a range of estimates about the Trust Fund's future borrowing needs and provided insight on the sensitivity of its overall financial position relative to its revenues and expenditures. In this testimony, as we did in our report, we generally present the results of a moderate set of assumptions for each simulation.[8] We assessed the reliability of the data used to develop our simulations by interviewing knowledgeable agency officials and reviewing relevant supporting documentation describing the inputs and assumptions used, if applicable. We also reviewed DOL, Treasury, EIA, and OMB data for outliers, obvious errors, or missing data. We determined that the data were sufficiently reliable for the purposes of our report.

Our preliminary observations regarding DOL's oversight of coal mine operator insurance given recent operator bankruptcies are based on ongoing work for this committee. In conducting this work, we obtained DOL documentation and data on black lung beneficiaries and coal mine operators. We also reviewed relevant federal laws, regulations, policies, and guidance and interviewed DOL officials, insurance carriers and associations, and coal mine operators, among others.[9]

We conducted the work on which this statement is based in accordance with generally accepted government auditing standards. Those standards require that we plan and perform the audit to obtain sufficient, appropriate evidence to provide a reasonable basis for our findings and conclusions based on our audit objectives. We believe that the evidence obtained provides a reasonable basis for our findings and conclusions based on our audit objectives.

Background

Black Lung Benefits

Black lung benefits include both cash assistance and medical benefits. Maximum cash assistance payments ranged from about $660 to $1,320 per month in 2018,

---

[7] Our simulations began in fiscal year 2016 because 2015 was the last complete fiscal year for which DOL data were available when we began our review. Our simulations extend through fiscal year 2050 as this is the last year of EIA coal production forecast estimates.

[8] For more information on our simulation methodology and the full range of results, see GAO-18-351.

[9] We did not conduct a legal analysis of the relevant bankruptcy court dockets. Instead, we relied on documentation provided by DOL to describe these bankruptcies.

depending on a beneficiary's number of dependents.[10] Miners receiving cash assistance are also eligible for medical benefits that cover the treatment of their black lung-related conditions, which may include hospital and nursing care, rehabilitation services, and drug and equipment charges, according to DOL documentation. DOL estimates that the average annual cost for medical treatment in fiscal year 2018 was approximately $9,667 per miner.

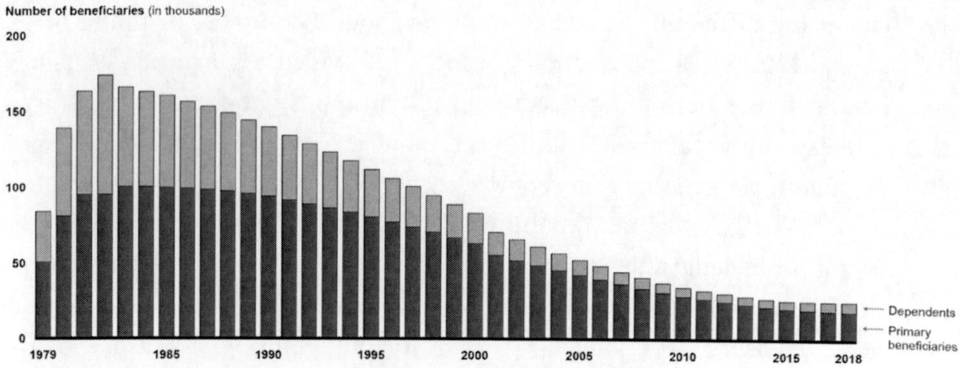

Source: GAO analysis of Department of Labor data. | GAO-19-622T.

Notes: We excluded certain black lung beneficiaries, which the Department of Labor refers to as Part B beneficiaries, whose awards are generally funded from Treasury's general fund, and not the Trust Fund.

Figure 7. Black Lung Beneficiaries, Fiscal Years 1979 through 2018.

There were about 25,600 total beneficiaries (primary and dependents) receiving black lung benefits during fiscal year 2018 (see Figure 7).[11] The number of beneficiaries has decreased over time as a result of declining coal mining employment and an aging beneficiary population, according to DOL officials. Black lung beneficiaries could increase in the near term due to the increased occurrence of black lung disease and its most severe form, progressive massive fibrosis, particularly among Appalachian coal miners, according to National Institute for Occupational Safety and Health (NIOSH) officials.[12]

---

[10] Benefit rates are set by federal law, which specifies that in the case of total disability, a miner receives 37.5 percent of the monthly pay rate of a federal employee at grade GS-2, step 1. Benefit levels are increased by 50 percent if the miner has one dependent, 75 percent if the miner has two dependents, and 100 percent if the miner has three or more dependents. If state workers' compensation benefits are less than federal black lung benefits, then the federal benefits cover the difference. Social Security Disability Insurance benefits are also reduced for recipients of black lung benefits.

[11] We excluded certain black lung beneficiaries, which DOL refers to as Part B beneficiaries, whose awards are generally funded from Treasury's general fund, and not from the Trust Fund.

[12] Recent NIOSH studies have found increases in the prevalence of black lung disease among long tenured Appalachian coal miners and have documented hundreds of miners with the most severe form of the disease, progressive massive fibrosis, receiving care at two clinics in Kentucky and Virginia. See D.J. Blackley, L.E. Reynolds, C. Short, R. Carson, E. Storey, C.N. Halldin, A.S. Laney, *Progressive Massive Fibrosis in Coal Miners From 3 Clinics in Virginia,* Journal of the American Medical Association, 319(5):500–501 February 6, 2018; and D.J. Blackley, J.B Crum, C.N. Halldin, E. Storey, A.S. Laney, *Resurgence of Progressive Massive*

Benefit Adjudication Process

Black lung claims are processed by the Division of Coal Mine Workers' Compensation in the Office of Workers' Compensation Programs (OWCP) within DOL. Contested claims are adjudicated by DOL's Office of Administrative Law Judges (OALJ), which issues decisions that can be appealed to DOL's Benefits Review Board (BRB).[13] Claimants and mine operators may further appeal these agency decisions to the federal courts. If an award is contested, claimants can receive interim benefits, which are generally paid from the Trust Fund according to DOL officials. Final awards are either funded by mine operators—who are identified as the responsible employers of claimants—or the Trust Fund, when responsible employers cannot be identified or do not pay. In fiscal year 2018, black lung claims had an approval rate of about 34 percent, according to DOL data.

In 2009, we reported on the benefits adjudication process and made several recommendations for DOL that could improve miners' ability to pursue claims.[14] An April 2015 DOL Inspector General (IG) report followed up on DOL's progress on our recommendations and found continuing problems and raised new concerns about the black lung claims and appeals process.[15] For instance, the IG reported that OALJ needed to address staff shortages, improve communication between its headquarters and district offices, and upgrade the training provided to judges and law clerks.[16] To further expedite claim adjudication, the IG recommended, among other things, that OALJ begin hearing more cases remotely using video or telephone hearings to reduce judges' travel costs and time.[17] In fiscal year 2018, OWCP reported that it took about 335 days on average to issue a decision on a claim. This is an increase from the average of 235 days that OWCP had reported to the DOL IG for fiscal year 2014.[18]

Fibrosis in Coal Miners — Eastern Kentucky, 2016, Morbidity and Mortality Weekly Report, 65:1385–1389 (December 16, 2016).

[13] For additional information on the black lung claim adjudication process see GAO, *Black Lung Benefits Program: Administrative and Structural Changes Could Improve Miners' Ability to Pursue Claims*. GAO-10-7 (Washington, D.C.: October 30, 2009).

[14] See GAO-10-7.

[15] Office of the Inspector General-Office of Audit, U.S. Department of Labor, Report to the Office of Workers' Compensation Program, Office of Administrative Law Judges, and Benefits Review Board, *Procedural Changes Could Reduce the Time Required to Adjudicate Federal Black Lung Benefits Claims*, 05-15-001-50-598 (Washington, D.C.: April 9, 2015).

[16] In September 2017, the DOL IG reported that OALJ could reduce its backlog of black lung cases by 21 percent or 28 percent by adding 3 or 6 judges. See Office of the Inspector General-Office of Audit, U.S. Department of Labor, Report to the Office of Administrative Law Judges, *Effect of OALJ Staffing Levels on the Black Lung Case Backlog*, 05-17-003-01-060 (Washington, D.C.: September 27, 2017).

[17] GAO made a related recommendation in 2009 that DOL consider shortening the time required to schedule hearings for black lung cases by examining the feasibility of using video teleconferencing technology to streamline the scheduling of hearings in remote areas, see GAO-10-7.

[18] See Office of the Inspector General-Office of Audit, U.S. Department of Labor, 05-15- 001-50-598.

Trust Fund Revenue and Expenditures

Trust Fund revenue is primarily obtained from mine operators through the coal tax. The current coal tax rates, which took effect in 2019, are $0.50 per ton of underground-mined coal and $0.25 per ton of surface-mined coal, up to 2 percent of the sales price. Coal tax revenue is collected from mine operators by Treasury's Internal Revenue Service and then transferred to the Trust Fund where it is then used by DOL to pay black lung benefits and the costs of administering the program.

Trust Fund expenditures include, among other things, black lung benefit payments, certain administrative costs incurred by DOL and Treasury to administer the black lung benefits program, and debt repayments. When necessary for the Trust Fund to make relevant expenditures under federal law, the Trust Fund borrows from the Treasury's general fund. When this occurs, the federal government is essentially borrowing from itself—and hence from the taxpayer—to fund its benefit payments and other expenditures.

Trust Fund Borrowing Will Likely Continue to Increase through 2050

As we reported in 2018, Trust Fund expenditures have consistently exceeded revenue. The Trust Fund borrowed from Treasury's general fund almost every year since 1979, its first complete fiscal year.[19] We noted in our 2018 report that Trust Fund borrowing would continue to increase through 2050 due, in part, to the planned coal tax rate decrease of about 55 percent that took effect in 2019 and declining coal production.

We simulated the effects of the tax rate decrease on Trust Fund finances through 2050, and reported the results of a moderate case set of assumptions related to future coal production and prices and the number of new black lung beneficiaries.[20] These simulations were not predictions of what will happen, but rather models of what could happen given certain assumptions.

Our moderate case simulation suggested that Trust Fund revenue may decrease from about $485 million in fiscal year 2018 to about $298 million in fiscal year 2019, due, in part, to the approximate 55 percent decrease in the coal tax rate.[21] Our simulation, which

---

[19] When necessary for the Trust Fund to make relevant expenditures, funds are appropriated to the Trust Fund as "repayable advances," and then those advances must be repaid with interest to the general fund of the U.S. Treasury. We refer to this process as annual borrowing from Treasury's general fund because, for reporting purposes, we often refer to the total amount of the repayable advances made in a particular fiscal year. According to the Department of the Treasury, the general fund includes assets and liabilities used to finance the daily and long-term operations of the U.S. government as a whole.

[20] Our simulations began in fiscal year 2016 because fiscal year 2015 was the last complete fiscal year for which DOL data were available when we began our review. Our simulations extend through fiscal year 2050 because that is as far as the EIA produces coal production forecasts which we relied on in developing our simulations relative to future coal tax revenue. For more information on our simulation methodology, see GAO-18-351.

[21] The simulated values for Trust Fund revenue and expenditures through 2050 are presented in nominal dollars, meaning they are not adjusted for inflation.

incorporated EIA data on future expected coal production, also showed that annual Trust Fund revenue would likely continue to decrease beyond fiscal year 2019 due, in part, to declining coal production. Domestic coal production declined from about 1.2 billion tons in 2008 to about 775 million tons in 2017, according to EIA.[22] Based on these projections, our moderate simulation showed that Trust Fund annual revenue may continue to decrease from about $298 million in fiscal year 2019 to about $197 million in fiscal year 2050.[23]

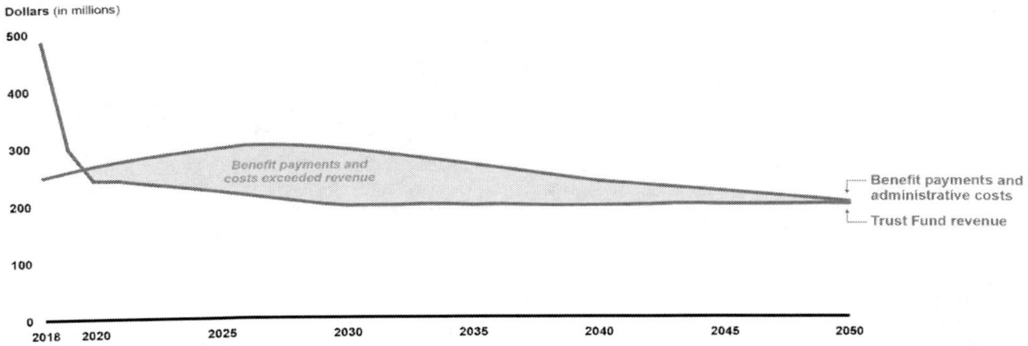

Source: GAO simulation based on data from the Departments of Labor and Treasury, the Energy Information Administration, and the Office of Management and Budget. | GAO-19-622T.

Notes: Trust Fund revenue and black lung benefit payments and administrative costs are simulated from fiscal years 2018 through 2050 and presented in nominal dollars. Moderate case simulations assumed that future coal production is consistent with the Energy Information Administration's reference case, which generally assumes trend improvement in known technologies, a view of economic and demographic trends that reflects the current central views of economic forecasters and demographers, and that current laws and regulations affecting the energy sector are unchanged through 2050. Moderate case simulations also assumed that future numbers of new black lung beneficiaries evolve over time based on the average growth rate for the period from fiscal years 2003 to 2015. Given the complexities of estimating future coal production and prices and new black lung beneficiaries, our simulations are subject to considerable uncertainty, and simulated Trust Fund revenues and expenditures are unlikely to be precise. For more information on our simulation methodology and the full range of results, see GAO-18-351.

Figure 8. Black Lung Disability Trust Fund Simulated Revenue and Black Lung Benefit Payments and Administrative Costs Based on Moderate Case Assumptions, Fiscal Years 2018 through 2050.

Future simulated Trust Fund revenue would likely be insufficient to cover combined black lung benefit payments and administrative costs, according to our moderate case simulation. Specifically, revenue may not be sufficient to cover beneficiary payments and administrative costs from fiscal years 2020 through 2050 (see Figure 8). For instance, in fiscal year 2029, simulated benefit payments and administrative costs would likely

[22] U.S. Department of Energy, Energy Information Administration: *Annual Coal Report 2017* (Washington, D.C.: November 2018).

[23] These are equivalent to about $290 million and $100 million in 2018 after adjusting for inflation.

exceed simulated revenue by about $99 million.[24] These annual deficits could decrease over time to about $4 million by fiscal year 2050 due, in part, to the assumed continued net decline in total black lung beneficiaries.[25]

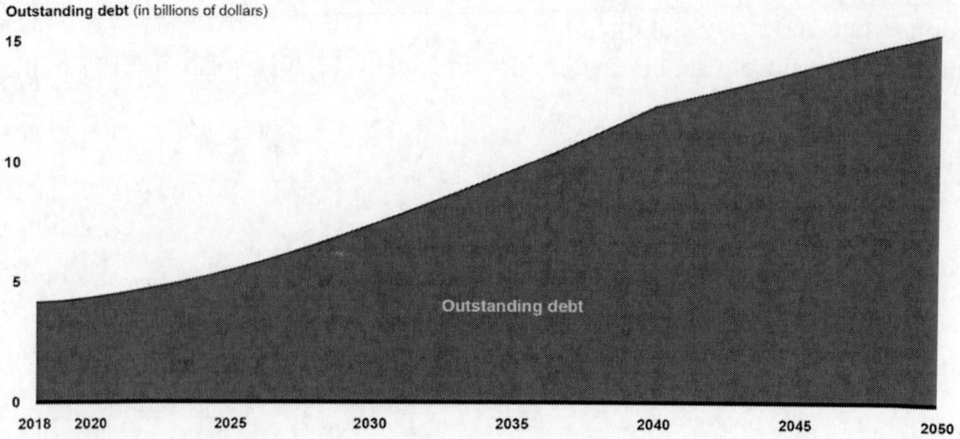

Source: GAO simulation based on data from the Departments of Labor and Treasury, the Energy Information Administration, and the Office of Management and Budget. | GAO-19-622T.

Notes: The principal amount of the Trust Fund's outstanding debt includes the principal amount of the Trust Fund's legacy debt—which was refinanced following the Energy Improvement and Extension Act of 2008 with repayment to be complete by fiscal year 2040—and the Trust Fund's annual borrowing from Treasury's general fund through 2050, which is simulated from fiscal years 2018 through 2050 and presented in nominal dollars. Moderate case simulations assumed that future coal production is consistent with the Energy Information Administration's reference case, which generally assumes trend improvement in known technologies, a view of economic and demographic trends that reflects the current central views of economic forecasters and demographers, and that current laws and regulations affecting the energy sector are unchanged through 2050. Moderate case simulations also assumed that future numbers of new black lung beneficiaries evolve over time based on the average growth rate for the period from fiscal years 2003 to 2015. Given the complexities of estimating future coal production and prices and new black lung beneficiaries, our simulations are subject to considerable uncertainty and simulated annual borrowing is unlikely to be precise. For more information on our simulations methodology and the full range of results, see GAO-18-351.

Figure 9. Black Lung Disability Trust Fund Simulated Principal Amount of Outstanding Debt to Treasury's General Fund Based on Moderate Case Assumptions, Fiscal Years 2018 through 2050.

If Trust Fund spending on benefit payments and administrative costs continues to exceed revenues each year, then the Trust Fund would need to continue borrowing from Treasury's general fund to cover those costs, as well as borrowing to cover debt repayment. Our moderate simulation suggested that the Trust Fund's outstanding debt could increase from about $4.2 billion in fiscal year 2019 to about $15.4 billion in fiscal

[24] This is equivalent to about $78 million in 2018 after adjusting for inflation.
[25] This is equivalent to about $2 million in 2018 after adjusting for inflation.

year 2050 (see Figure 9). While our moderate case simulated a $15.4 billion Trust Fund debt in 2050, the amount could vary from about $6 billion to about $27 billion depending, in part, on future coal production and the number of new beneficiaries. Even if the Congress were to completely eliminate black lung benefits as of fiscal year 2019, the Trust Fund's outstanding debt in fiscal year 2050 could still exceed $6.4 billion, according to our simulation.[26] Eliminating black lung benefits, however, would generally mean that coal tax revenue would be collected solely to fund the repayment of Trust Fund debt. As we reported in 2018, other options such as adjusting the coal tax and forgiving interest or debt, could also reduce future borrowing and improve the Trust Fund's financial position (see GAO-18-351).

Preliminary Observations Raise Concerns About DOL's Oversight of Coal Mine Operator Insurance

Federal law generally requires that coal operators secure their black lung benefit liability. Operators can purchase commercial insurance for this purpose or may self-insure if they meet certain DOL conditions. For example, self-insurers must obtain collateral in the form of an indemnity bond, deposit or trust, or letter of credit in an amount deemed necessary and sufficient by DOL to secure their liability.[27]

DOL officials said that the collateral they required from the five self-insured operators that filed for bankruptcy between 2014 and 2016 was inadequate to cover their benefit liabilities. For example, the collateral DOL required from Alpha Natural Resources was about 6 percent of its estimated benefit liability. As a result, approximately $185 million of estimated benefit liability was transferred to the Trust Fund, according to DOL data. We reviewed DOL documentation related to the five operator bankruptcies.[28] Table 2 shows the bankrupt operators; the amount of collateral each operator had at the time of bankruptcy; estimated benefit liability at the time of bankruptcy; and estimated benefit liability and number of beneficiaries that transferred to the Trust Fund, if applicable. Overall, three of these bankruptcies affected the Trust Fund, and two did not according to DOL. DOL officials told us that the bankruptcies of Arch Coal and Peabody Energy did not affect the Trust Fund because their benefit liabilities were assumed by the reorganized companies after emerging from bankruptcy.

---

[26] This includes eliminating all cash assistance and medical benefits.

[27] A letter of credit may only be used in conjunction with another acceptable form of collateral.

[28] We did not conduct a legal analysis of the relevant bankruptcy court dockets. Instead, we relied on documentation provided by DOL to describe these bankruptcies. DOL officials said that these were the self-insured operator bankruptcies that occurred from 2014 through 2016 that had the potential to affect the Trust Fund most in terms of total benefit liabilities that could be transferred to the Trust Fund, depending on the outcome of bankruptcy proceedings. DOL officials also included Walter Energy, but we excluded this company from our review because at the time of our review its bankruptcy proceeding had not progressed enough for us to assess the potential effect on the Trust Fund.

Table 2. Self-insured coal operator bankruptcies reviewed, filed from 2014 through 2016

Coal operator	Collateral at time of bankruptcy	Black lung benefit liability at time of bankruptcy	Estimated transfer of liability to Trust Fund	Estimated number of beneficiaries transferred to the Trust Fund
Alpha Natural Resources	$12 million	$206.6 million	$184.7 million	685
Arch Coal	$6.9 million	$90 million	$0	0
James River Coal Company	$0.4 million	$63.7 million to $75.9 milliona	$62.8.million to $75 million	212
Patriot Coal	$15 million	$80 million	$65.1 million	687
Peabody Energy	$20 million	$68.4 million	$0	0

Source: DOL data, as confirmed by DOL officials. | GAO-19-622T.

Notes: In addition to collateral, DOL also in some cases received other funds, such as through a settlement agreement. Therefore, DOL's estimated loss to the Trust Fund may not equal estimated black lung benefit liability minus collateral. Estimates of operator liability and Trust Fund losses are based on projected payments over ensuing decades on existing and future claims, according to DOL officials.

[a]DOL and operator actuaries disputed James River Coal Company's estimated benefit liabilities and therefore DOL developed an estimated range of liability instead of an exact estimate.

As of June 2019, there are 22 operators that are self-insured and actively mining coal, according to DOL officials.[29] To ensure that the collateral they required from these operators was adequate to protect the Trust Fund, DOL officials said that they periodically reauthorized them which entailed, among other things, reviewing their most recent audited financial statements and claims information. DOL officials said that they prepared memos documenting these reviews and communicated with coal operators about whether their financial circumstances warranted increasing or decreasing their collateral. Table 3 provides information on the 22 self-insured operators including the date of each operator's most recent DOL reauthorization; the amount of DOL required collateral; and the operator's most recent estimated black lung benefit liability. Should any of these operators file for bankruptcy, they could also affect the Trust Fund because the amount of an operators' benefit liability that is not covered by collateral could also become the responsibility of the Trust Fund.

Preliminary analysis from our ongoing work indicates that DOL did not regularly monitor self-insured operators. Agency regulations state that DOL may adjust the amount of collateral required from self-insured operators when experience or changed conditions warrant. We reviewed DOL's most recent reauthorization memos for each of the 22 operators. While some of these operators had been reauthorized more recently, we found that others had not been reauthorized by DOL in decades. One operator in particular had not been reauthorized by DOL since 1988. Additionally, for most of these operators, DOL either did not have estimates of their benefit liabilities, or the estimates were out of date (see Table 3).

[29] These include parent operators only. Subsidiaries of these operators may also be covered.

Table 3. Self-insured operator reauthorization date, collateral, and estimated benefit liability

Self-insured coal operator (from most recently reviewed by the Department of Labor (DOL), to least recently reviewed)	Date of most recent reauthorization	Collateral required by DOL to self-insure, as of September 2018	Most recent estimated black lung benefit liability
Coal operator 1	2018	$3.6 million	$18.4 million, as of 12/31/2017
Coal operator 2	2015	$1.1 million	No estimate available
Coal operator 3	2015	$2.5 million	$206 million, as of 8/03/2015
Coal operator 4	2014	$29.5 million	$109 million, as of 12/31/2016
Coal operator 5	2013	$8 million	No estimate available
Coal operator 6	2013	$1 million	No estimate available
Coal operator 7	2012	$8.4 million	$668,000, as of 1/1/1992
Coal operator 8	2012	$20.3 million	$68.4 million, as of 4/13/2016
Coal operator 9	2012	$1 million	No estimate available
Coal operator 10	2012	$15 million	No estimate available
Coal operator 11	2012	$21 million	$21.8 million, as of 12/31/2014
Coal operator 12	2011	$5.5 million	$47 million, as of 12/31/1984
Coal operator 13	2003	$0.4 million	No estimate available
Coal operator 14	2001	$0.8 million	$7.8 million, as of 01/01/1993
Coal operator 15	2000	$0.4 million	No estimate available
Coal operator 16	2000	$1.5 million	No estimate available[a]
Coal operator 17	1999	$1.4 million	No estimate available
Coal operator 18	1999	$29.2 million	No estimate available
Coal operator 19	1998	$6.9 million	$90 million, as of 12/31/2015
Coal operator 20	1997	$1.4 million	No estimate available
Coal operator 21	1994	$7.7 million	No estimate available
Coal operator 22	1988	$24.8 million	$15.1 million, as of 1/31/2005

Source: DOL data. | GAO-19-622T.

[a]According to DOL officials, this operator was acquired by another self-insured operator who assumed their benefit liability.

Beginning in summer 2015, DOL officials said that they stopped permitting any new coal mine operators to self-insure as the agency worked with auditors, economists, and actuaries to develop new procedures for self-insurance. At the same time, DOL generally stopped reauthorizing the 22 self-insured operators.[30] Earlier this year, two of these operators have filed for bankruptcy—Westmoreland Coal Company and Cloud Peak Energy—according to DOL officials. Additionally, due to deteriorating financial conditions, DOL recommended revoking another operator's self-insurance authority (Murray Energy).[31] However, Murray appealed this decision and DOL postponed responding to the appeal until their new self-insurance procedures are implemented, according to DOL officials.

---

[30] DOL officials said that they reauthorized one of the 22 self-insured operators in 2018 to allow it to self-insure the legacy benefit liabilities of another operator that it had purchased.

[31] DOL regulations state that the agency, with good cause shown, may revoke the authorization of any self-insurer.

DOL's new self-insurance procedures are currently being reviewed by OMB, and DOL officials said they did not know when they would likely be implemented. Until such procedures are implemented, DOL cannot ensure that the collateral it has required from self-insured operators is adequate to protect the Trust Fund should these operators become insolvent.

Chairwoman Adams, Ranking Member Byrne, and Members of the Subcommittee, this concludes my prepared statement. I would be happy to respond to any questions you may have at this time.

If you or your staff has any questions concerning this testimony, please contact me at (202) 512-7215. Contact points for our Offices of Congressional Relations and Public Affairs may be found on the last page of this statement. In addition to the contact named above, Blake Ainsworth (Assistant Director), Justin Dunleavy (Analyst in Charge), Angeline Bickner, Alex Galuten, Courtney LaFountain, Rosemary Torres Lerma, Kate van Gelder, Catherine Roark, and Almeta Spencer made key contributions to the testimony. Other staff who made key contributions to the reports cited in the testimony are identified in the source products.

Chairwoman ADAMS. Thank you very much.

Under Committee Rule 8, we will now question witnesses under the 5 minute rule.

I now recognize myself for 5 minutes.

Dr. Howard, in 1974 NIOSH recommended reducing the permissible exposure limit for silica to 50 milligrams per cubic meter from 100 milligrams. Is that still the position?

Dr. HOWARD. Yes.

Chairwoman ADAMS. So are there any credible policy justifications for reducing the standard at OSHA, as was done in 2016? What is your response to that?

Dr. HOWARD. We stand by our recommendations that were made many years ago. We were very fortunate that OSHA finally accepted our recommendations and issued a silica rule. And we work closely with MSHA if they so choose to develop a silica rule.

Chairwoman ADAMS. So is there excessive risk to miners at and below the current 100 micrograms per cubic meter threshold?

Dr. HOWARD. We certainly believe that any exposure to quartz is not a healthful thing.

Chairwoman ADAMS. So what about 50?

Dr. HOWARD. Yes, ma'am. Yes.

Chairwoman ADAMS. Okay.

Mr. Secretary, what about that? Is there any good reason why OSHA should have one silica standard and MSHA should have another that is half as protective?

Mr. ZATEZALO. Well, Madam Chairman, the laws are very different. While OSHA's silica standard, for those of you that are familiar with it, recognizes the use of personal protective equipment, or PPE, MSHA's specifically does not allow it for any terms of compliance. And additionally, the average micrograms per cubic meter has been at just slightly over 25 micrograms. The standard is at 100 as it has been from the inception of this legislation. The biggest issue in here is the prohibition against counting personal protective equipment.

Chairwoman ADAMS. So are miners—

Mr. ZATEZALO. So OSHA—what I am trying to say is that OSHA's standard, while it is lower, is achieved through the use of PPE. MSHA's standard is not allowed to count PPE.

Chairwoman ADAMS. Okay. So are miners somehow less susceptible to silica related disease than construction workers?

Mr. ZATEZALO. I am sorry?

Chairwoman ADAMS. Are miners less susceptible to silica related disease than construction workers?

Mr. ZATEZALO. They are not, and that is exactly why we enforce that law very regularly, very rigidly. We are up 80 percent on quartz inspections and quartz sampling in the last 10 years. And I will tell you that every quartz sample is taken by MSHA, not by the industry.

Chairwoman ADAMS. Okay. You have been quoted in the past as saying that PMF cases are clearly silica problems, and other times you said that you don't think the science of causation is well-defined. Which is it?

Mr. ZATEZALO. I think PMF problems are largely contributed to by quartz, of which silica is a component. Silica is a component of quartz. What we actually measure is quartz.

Chairwoman ADAMS. So, okay.

Dr. Howard, do you agree with the Assistant Secretary's statement? What is your view?

Dr. HOWARD. Well, I have said that in my testimony that quartz is the most common form of crystalline silica.

Chairwoman ADAMS. Okay. Well, thank you very much.

I am going to now recognize the Ranking Member for the purpose of questioning the witnesses.

You are recognized, Mr. Byrne.

Mr. BYRNE. Thank you, Madam Chairwoman.

Secretary Zatezalo, I am glad to see you are moving forward with a formal request for information on respirable crystalline silica. As we have discussed here today, the National Institute of Occupational Safety and Health is working on an end of shift measuring device, and there is additional research under way, on advanced lung diseases related to mine activities. What type of information from the public do you hope to gain in the request for information?

Mr. ZATEZALO. What I hope to gain from the public in this RFI is some alternative means of using PPE to achieve a lower compliance rate. Or, I am sorry, a lower threshold rate. The people who make air stream helmets have now discontinued that. I can tell you of mines today that are using air stream helmets voluntarily that in the future will not be able to. There are a number of different PPE providers, some of which we have been aware of, some of which we have not.

So it is really the science of PPE and its current state is very critical to achieving a lower standard as we go forward in the future. As Cecil Roberts stated, not all miners can easily wear PPE, depending on their job. So it is important that we actually have some good definition around that.

What I hope to achieve in that is the segregation of a quartz standard, as well as current information to enable us to make informed decisions. And we have released that on May 22.

Mr. BYRNE. As we heard from Mr. Roberts earlier, there is real concern about the issue of tampering with dust samples. As MSHA is tasked with enforcing the laws and regulations impacting mining operations, how does MSHA currently ensure there is no tampering with the data collected from continuous personal dust monitors?

Mr. ZATEZALO. CPTMs offer a lot of tamper-proof improvements. For example, if the unit sits still too long, if it is hung somewhere its functionality is obviated. It immediately voids the sample. So it is very good from that aspect. It can’t be moved out of the way completely.

The second thing that we do is that data is transmitted electronically from the unit directly to MSHA. So there is no interpretation, there is no interference.

And, thirdly, one of the more important things is that those units give people, machine operators, and miners real-time data on what they are actually exposed to. And this is critical to them being able to make adjustments in how they cut and how they work throughout the shift.

Mr. BYRNE. You note in your testimony that the agency recently examined injury and fatality data to determine the most common causes of mining fatalities. Can you expand on the findings in this area and the ongoing initiatives MSHA has launched as a result?

Mr. ZATEZALO. Certainly, sir. The most common cause of mining fatalities has been power haulage for the past several years. Power haulage is especially onerous and it is one of those events that whereas it is very low probability, it is very high consequence. These large pieces of equipment are very unforgiving when you collide with them or when you have an interaction with them.

So we did an RFI to make sure that we knew what all the best technologies were out there, because our laws are very archaic in this regard, in that we essentially require when a big truck goes into reverse that it emits a beep, beep, beep sound and that is it. And that has not I don’t think changed since 1974-ish. And I could be wrong on that. Maybe it was ’72, but I think it was ’74.

There are new technologies out there today, such as proximity detection, such as alarms, sensors on your vehicles, such as cameras, that enable operators to actually see what is going on around them. That is the largest single cause and that is what we are addressing.

Some other things that we had last year, we had a very severe rash of fire incidents on large pieces of equipment. Those incidents provoked us to go ahead and do a complete inspection of all trucks in the mining industry. We inspected over 4,000 trucks and went through all the fire suppression on those, worked with operators to make sure that they were up to speed. Several of them had been installed incorrectly. So we are trying to do that in a lot of ways. There is a compliance assistance program to make sure that people actually can benefit from what we are doing rather than just receive citations.

Mr. BYRNE. Thank you.

I yield back, Madam Chairwoman.

Chairwoman ADAMS. Thank you very much.

I will now yield to the gentleman from California, Mr. Takano for 5 minutes, sir.

Mr. TAKANO. Thank you, Madam Chair, and thank you to our witnesses for coming to this hearing today as we work towards ensuring safety standards for miners.

As we all know, progressive massive fibrosis is a debilitating and deadly disease. The levels of this disease have increased over the past 25 years and do not show signs of abating. This is a health epidemic and we need to act now. We have got convincing scientific evidence to indicate that. The lives of miners are at stake. We cannot wait another decade to address silica exposure. We already have the data and information available to us now.

Assistant Secretary Zatezalo, when you were before this committee in 2018 you stated that you were waiting for a report from the National Academy of Sciences and that report was released a year ago. Please explain to members of this committee and to the miners that MSHA is charged with protecting why you have not updated the standards.

Mr. ZATEZALO. We have not updated the standards, sir, because when I took this oath of office to come in here, I promised that I would obey the laws, and part of them include the Administrative Procedures Act, sir.

Mr. TAKANO. What does that have to do—you said that you would—you would—after receiving the National Academy of Sciences report—that was the key thing you were waiting for.

Mr. ZATEZALO. We—we are—we are—

Mr. TAKANO. What is this—

Mr. TAKANO.—working on the National Academy of Sciences report, along with NIOSH and we have worked tirelessly on it since we began. We have increased our sampling, we have lowered the average exposure, and we continue to do that every day. However, sir, I do have—

Mr. TAKANO. Well, we will get more—

Mr. ZATEZALO.—procedures I have to—

Mr. TAKANO.—into what that report says. I am reclaiming my time, sir.

You know, you said that you were collecting data on quartz and not silica. Dr. Howard, explain the difference between quartz and silica to me.

Dr. HOWARD. Well, I am not a mineralogist, but silica, crystalline silica is the most common form of quartz we find in a coal mine.

Mr. TAKANO. So saying that he was collecting silica quartz samples and not silica seems to me a distinction that doesn't make a difference.

Dr. HOWARD. Potato, Potato.

Mr. TAKANO. Thank you. Thank you.

I find that testimony, you know, highly, highly deceptive Mr. Zatezalo.

Mr. ZATEZALO. It is not deceptive at all, sir.

Mr. TAKANO. You think there is a difference between quartz and silica?

Mr. ZATEZALO. There is a difference between quartz and silica. Quartz is made up of—quartz is made up of anywhere from 60–98 percent silica. Quartz and silica are two different things.

Mr. TAKANO. I see, I see. Okay.

Mr. ZATEZALO. We use—we use measuring quartz—

Mr. TAKANO. Reclaiming my time, reclaiming my time. Sir, let me ask my next question.

You know, the Mine and Safety and Health Administration is failing miners. Inspecting underground mines only four times a year does not help miners. I mean you talk about how you are inspecting mines. Refusing to implement new technology does not help miners. The slow walking and delaying of updating standards does absolutely nothing to help miners. We are out of time. MSHA needs to address the standards now.

Over a year ago the National Academy of Sciences recommended the use of end of shift silica monitoring technology, and Dr. Howard just described their development of affordable technology that enables mines to conduct end of shift monitoring of miners' silica exposure. What are your plans to require that this technology be used?

Mr. ZATEZALO. Sir, that technology is not for compliance and it will not withstand the scrutiny of a system that has to be used for compliance and enforcement. It is an engineering tool, not a compliance tool.

Mr. TAKANO. Okay. Well, let us switch—I want to know—

Mr. ZATEZALO. We do not prevent anyone from using it.

Mr. TAKANO. I want to know if you can explain with all the work that NIOSH, OSHA, and the National Academy of Sciences and MSHA have done regarding the hazards of silica over the last 40 years why you are starting the process with a request for information, the RFI, the earliest baby step of the regulatory process, rather than going directly to a formal proposal.

Mr. ZATEZALO. It is the process that I understand I am required to follow, sir.

Mr. TAKANO. It is my understanding that you don't have to start with an RFI, that you could go directly to a formal proposal given all the information we already have.

Mr. ZATEZALO. Given that the average exposure is already half of what OSHA's limit is, it would seem to me that an emergency standard would be uncalled for.

Mr. TAKANO. Okay. All right. Well, I—it is a—I think that we have an ample amount of information already as I cited.

Should Congress amend the Act to make a knowing violation of mandatory safety and health standard, which recklessly endangers the health of a—or safety of a miner a felony?

Mr. ZATEZALO. I do not understand your question.

Mr. TAKANO. Should Congress amend the Mine Act to make a knowing violation of a mandatory safety and health standard, which recklessly endangers the health or safety of a miner, a felony?

Mr. ZATEZALO. As I have said to you last year, sir, that is Congress' discretion.

Mr. TAKANO. Today, as you know, it is a mere misdemeanor. Would that deter such conduct as we saw in the Upper Big Branch mine where 29 miners were killed on April 5, 2010.

Mr. ZATEZALO. Difficult for me to say that, sir.

Mr. TAKANO. All right.

Well, thank you very much for your testimony. I yield back.

Chairwoman ADAMS. Thank you very much.

The gentleman from Virginia, Mr. Cline is recognized for 5 minutes.

Mr. CLINE. Thank you, Madam Chair. I thank the witnesses for being here.

The mining industry contributes greatly to our economy and to our energy security, and as we know, miners have made many sacrifices and it is important that we support them. Industry has been making changes to better protect and monitor the health of their miners and we should be looking for ways to further encourage this.

In my home district, Washington and Lee School of Law has an advanced administrative litigation clinic for black lung. This clinic assists coal miners and survivors who are pursuing Federal Black Lung benefits. The clinic has represented roughly 200 clients since being established in 1996 and has a success rate of five times the national average. I am glad my district and this committee are putting a focus on ways to better protect miners.

I would first begin by asking Mr. Watzman, can you speak to the technologies that are being used to better monitor dust? Oh, I am sorry. Assistant secretary Zatezalo.

Mr. ZATEZALO. Zatezalo.

Mr. CLINE. I apologize.

Mr. ZATEZALO. It is all right.

Mr. CLINE. Can you please speak to the cross-training and consolidation efforts on the coal mine safety and health inspectors and the metal and nonmetal mine safety and health inspectors? As this number of active mines has decreased over the years, do these changes keep pace with what is needed and has there been any input from industry on this consolidation?

Mr. ZATEZALO. The crossover inspections that we started last year, sir, were entered into as a way to allow inspectors—at inspectors' suggestion—allow inspectors to spend more time at mines and less traveling in their vehicles. I told you in my opening testimony that in the first 6 months it has now saved about 41 percent of the time.

The question with it was really the crossover training. All of these people who are inspectors in the classic sense, they are experienced, they know what they are doing, but they need to brush up on the laws and differences in them. So with that regard, we put them through a 56 hour program. We went through it with the union, we did a 24-hour site on site, boots on the ground together transfers, and it seems to be going very smoothly from an inspector standpoint and from the operator standpoint.

Now, we have revised our training, we have taken some points on board from our crossover inspectors and from our NCFLL union folks. We have revised that. We are very fortunate that we have our own Mine Safety and Health Academy, and we put that training on ourselves. And I think it is going fairly well right now. We are probably going to do a little wider swath on that in the future. I will point out to you that we will not reduce the role of specialists, and we have not crossed over underground hazardous mines at all. We will not jeopardize those. What we cross over on is primarily sand and gravel operations, stone pits, that sort of stuff.

Mr. CLINE. You have gotten a pretty good—as you say, you have gotten a pretty good feedback on that from the inspectors?

Mr. ZATEZALO. We have good feedback from the inspectors and we have—I have specifically asked a number of operators about it. We have had fair to medium impact. I will put it that way. I am actually going to speak to a group in Indiana in a few weeks and I am going to ask them those questions again.

Mr. CLINE. Great. Thank you very much.

Mr. ZATEZALO. Thank you.

Mr. CLINE. Madam Chair, I yield back.

Chairwoman ADAMS. Thank you very much.

We will now yield 5 minutes to the gentlelady from Pennsylvania, Miss Wild.

Ms. WILD. Thank you, Madam Chair.

Greetings and thank you for being here on this, what I consider to be a very, very important issue.

By way of background, I represent a district in Pennsylvania and I practiced law for 30-some years and often saw clients who were victimized by lack of insurance by a party on the other side or inadequate insurance. So this is something that causes me a great deal of concern.

Ms. Barnes, you noted that many mine operators are underinsured for black lung liability. And we know that a group of mine operators recently filed for bankruptcy and were able to shift over $300 million of liability to the Black Lung Trust Fund. All of this is happening while the excise tax rate on coal that funds the Black Lung Trust Fund was reduced.

In order to avoid purchasing workers' compensation insurance, mine operators may self-insure if they demonstrate to the Department of Labor that they have the necessary assets to cover their black lung liabilities. Am I right about that?

Ms. BROWN BARNES. Yes, that is correct.

Ms. WILD. What documentation does the Department of Labor require to confirm that mine operators have sufficient assets to cover such liabilities so that they can self-insure?

Ms. BROWN BARNES. Well, this is what we have been trying to get a clear answer on as part of our ongoing work. And they are in the process now of revising those procedures, so we will have a better answer once we complete our assessment.

Ms. WILD. Well, to date, what kind of documentation has been required by the Department in order to ensure that a mine operator can properly cover its liabilities in the event it chooses to self-insure?

Ms. BROWN BARNES. Yeah, it is—it is varied and it has been rather sketchy and there has been some difficulty obtaining that documentation.

Ms. WILD. Okay. Are there any kind of audits done of the documentation that is provided?

Ms. BROWN BARNES. That is part of what they are trying to implement currently, to do some audits of that.

Ms. WILD. Okay. Well, as I said, this is—the self-insured situation has caused me a great deal of concern. In the context of the recent bankruptcies, particularly Alpha Natural Resources, do you think the Department of Labor was unaware of the disproportionate lack of reserves before approving it to self-insure?

Ms. BROWN BARNES. In terms of whether they were aware or unaware, one thing that we have noticed is that they have not been overseeing it and that has been part of the problem, monitoring it and looking—checking on it periodically to see what is going on there.

Ms. WILD. So let me just shift to the Assistant Secretary, if I may, on this same area.

Was the Department of Labor unaware of the disproportionate lack of reserves before approving Alpha Natural to self-insure?

Mr. ZATEZALO. Ma'am, MSHA has no role in the Federal Black Lung Trust Fund. It is my understanding that is guaranteed by the U.S. Treasury. But MSHA actually has no role in the Federal Black Lung Trust Fund.

Ms. WILD. So if we refuse to raise the excise tax rate back to its 2008–2018 levels, and if the Black Lung Trust Fund goes insolvent, the Department of Labor is going to have to borrow money from the U.S. Treasury. Is that right? Either one of you.

Mr. ZATEZALO. That is the way I understand it.

Ms. WILD. And, Ms. Barnes, is that your understanding?

Ms. BROWN BARNES. Yes, that is correct.

Ms. WILD. So in effect, we would be shifting the cost of the Black Lung Trust Fund away from the coal operators and to the taxpayers, right?

Ms. BROWN BARNES. Yes.

Ms. WILD. It is my understanding also that according to SEC filings, Alpha Natural Resources' CEO pocketed over $20 million in the 3 years leading up to their bankruptcy. And after the company exited bankruptcy in 2016 he was paid another $1.8 million in compensation. Is that your understanding as well?

Mr. ZATEZALO. I have no involvement in that, no knowledge of it.

Ms. WILD. Are you aware of that, Ms. Barnes?

Ms. BROWN BARNES. I was not.

Ms. WILD. That is a pretty outrageous situation, wouldn't you say?

Ms. BROWN BARNES. That—that is a cause for concern.

Ms. WILD. Thank you. That is all I have.

I yield back.

Chairwoman ADAMS. Thank you.

I want to now recognize the Chair of the Education and Labor Committee, Mr. Scott, from Virginia. Mr. Scott, you are recognized.

Mr. SCOTT. Thank you.

Mr. Zatezalo, we sent you several oversight letters about the situation where Affinity Mine had been put on a pattern of violation sanctions and even after for serious violations, including some that involved miners' deaths. And that sanction was lifted. Our concern was it didn't appear to be consistent with the statutory requirements that they have complete inspections without serious violations.

Now, we sent you letters to kind of follow up to see what had happened and we got responses, and I want to thank you for the responses, but it didn't address the point we were trying to get to, and that is how Affinity Mines could have been relieved from sanctions.

And so I am asking you if we can get emails, memos, leading up to the decision to remove Affinity Mine from the POV, communications with external parties leading up to the decision, and a list of meetings and copies of meetings or memos summarizing meetings between MSHA and Pocahontas Coal, the owner of Affinity Mines, regarding that decision.

Would that be a problem in getting that information from you?

Mr. ZATEZALO. Sir, I believe that you are aware that has been—that is the subject of a lawsuit between—that the UMWA filed on us that is currently open in the fourth—in the District Court in southern West Virginia.

We have sent to you, I believe, a 52 page response and I think a 32—I am not completely—

Mr. SCOTT. I appreciate the response, but—

Mr. ZATEZALO. And further information—I will be happy to make available to you any information that we file with the Court. As such, sir, we are represented by the Department of Justice and we will be happy to provide you everything that we file with the Court.

Mr. SCOTT. And that is what we got was just court filings and now copies of emails and other things that could have helped us understand how they got relieved of those sanctions.

Mr. ZATEZALO. It is under litigation, sir. I am sorry that I can't speak to you more frankly about it.

Mr. SCOTT. I understand. But we would like to get that information.

Mr. Howard, we have heard about the difference between OSHA and MSHA on the silica standard. When was the silica standard first recommended by NIOSH?

Dr. HOWARD. Oh, I think it was 42 or 43 years ago, sometime in the early '70s.

Mr. SCOTT. And finally in 2016 OSHA adopted that standard?

Dr. HOWARD. Yes. As the former secretary of labor said, better late than never.

Mr. SCOTT. Well, is there any reason why MSHA cannot implement the same standard?

Dr. HOWARD. Well, I don't speak for MSHA, sir.

Mr. SCOTT. Well, you have recommended it to—for MSHA?

Dr. HOWARD. Sir, I have made a recommendation to that effect.

Mr. SCOTT. And you mentioned a monitor of retired mine workers?

Dr. HOWARD. I did.

Mr. SCOTT. What did you mean there?

Dr. HOWARD. Sir, as you well know—and it is not just the mining industry, but in any hazardous industry where there are exposures that occur that could result in adverse health effects, often times the workers will leave the workforce and we lose the ability—although if we do a special study of retired workers—but we often lose the ability to follow up in these long latency diseases in which the manifestations or the severity of the manifestations may not occur while the individual is employed. And then they go and they leave and we lose track of following the full picture, characteristics of the disease.

So I think one of the recommendations that we think is appropriate is to look at the medical surveillance, not just of the worker who is working, but rather to follow them in retirement, or in an abrupt type of retirement where they have to leave because of illness.

Mr. SCOTT. Thank you.

Ms. Brown Barnes, the Ranking Member had expressed concerns about the jurisdictional matters and whether we have jurisdiction over the tax, but the fact of the matter is, if the foreign trust fund goes broke or doesn't have sufficient funds, that the general fund of the U.S. government will pay the benefits. Is that right?

Ms. BROWN BARNES. Yes, that is correct.

Mr. SCOTT. And the problem is if the money is not there and we don't—and we stop appropriating the money, then the workers may be without benefits.

Who estimates the amount that the mine owners have to put up as collateral?

Ms. BROWN BARNES. The Department of Labor does that, the OWCP.

Mr. SCOTT. And as your written testimony points out, several of those businesses are putting up way under 10 percent of what the expected liability is. Is that right?

Ms. BROWN BARNES. Yes.

Mr. SCOTT. Do you have an estimate about how much potential underfunding there is?

Ms. BROWN BARNES. I don't have a complete estimate because the Department doesn't have an estimate. But we know from at least our preliminary work that it is at least tens of millions of dollars.

Mr. SCOTT. Tens of?

Ms. BROWN BARNES. Millions.

Mr. SCOTT. Millions or billions?

Ms. BROWN BARNES. Millions.

Mr. SCOTT. Okay. Now, but there are a lot of businesses, many businesses for which you had no estimate at all for their potential liability. Is that right?

Ms. BROWN BARNES. Yes.

Mr. SCOTT. Thank you, Madam Chair.

Chairwoman ADAMS. Thank you very much.

Okay. We are going to hear now from Mr. Griffin of Virginia. You have 5 minutes, sir.

Mr. GRIFFIN. Thank you very much; appreciate it. And as I indicated earlier, I am not normally on this committee and I am very appreciative of the committee for allowing me to participate.

Let us pick up with the Fund, since that is where Chairman Scott ended.

You indicated in your testimony that if we had no more claims, the debt would continue to rise on this, and that is because of old debt and interest payments. Is that correct?

Ms. BROWN BARNES. Yes, that is correct.

Mr. GRIFFIN. And you also said that one of the things we might be able to do—because a lot of the companies that were responsible did go bankrupt—one of the things you indicated we might be able to do would be to forgive interest or part of the debt. That might help stabilize the Fund as well. Is that correct?

Ms. BROWN BARNES. Yeah. We did present options in our work from last year and it did have some of those considerations that we laid out.

Mr. GRIFFIN. Because one of the things that my current coal operators tell me is that if they just had to pay for the responsibilities of what they had now, as opposed to paying for the mining companies that are no longer around, they believe that a reasonable number could be achieved and reached without a whole lot of gnashing of teeth and wailing going on. Do you concur in that opinion, or do you have no opinion?

Ms. BROWN BARNES. It depends. And it depends on the underlying assumptions that is based on.

Mr. GRIFFIN. Okay. And I appreciate that, but I do think it is something we should continue to work on.

Assistant Secretary, we heard earlier from one of our miners, and he is still here, and he said something about tape at one point in his testimony. And I am wondering, you indicated that the machines measuring the dust and so forth were better today, but I have had miners tell me, even if they were not asked to by the company, because they were afraid the mine might go out of business, they would put tape over the sensors on the monitors. Does the new equipment have the ability to thwart those types of efforts?

Mr. ZATEZALO. Yes, sir. The new equipment senses any kind of tampering, lack of movement, lower than expected dust, and it will void the sample and communicate that electronically to the end of the shift.

Mr. GRIFFIN. So if it was lower than expected, would that be— how is that measured? Is that measured real-time or is over like every hour?

Mr. ZATEZALO. Well, if you put—it is in real-time, it is a continuous monitor. It provides, you know—and I am going to tell you, NIOSH did a great job getting this developed and out there and I hope they're successful with the quartz monitor.

But—

Mr. GRIFFIN. All right.

Mr. ZATEZALO.—the machine senses when somebody is trying to tamper with it and it will void itself if it senses that.

Mr. GRIFFIN. All right.

Mr. ZATEZALO. And we also sample with a parallel system, sir, that is a gravimetric system. Our samples are not tampered with by anybody, they are under the supervision of MSHA.

Mr. GRIFFIN. All right. So we have gotten into this whole controversy over OSHA standards, NIOSH, and MSHA. And you indicated earlier that you all could not count the same way as OSHA does because you weren't allowed to count PPEs as being equipment that could be used. Why is that and how do I fix it?

Mr. ZATEZALO. It is a nuance, sir, of the mining law. PPE is not allowed to count towards compliance.

Mr. GRIFFIN. So what you are saying to me is get a bill. Am I correct in that?

Mr. ZATEZALO. Yes, sir.

Mr. GRIFFIN. All right.

Mr. ZATEZALO. There are people that use PPE, but it does not count towards their compliance.

Mr. GRIFFIN. All right. And then is there something we need to do to get more technology on the PPEs? Because if it is too cumbersome to wear in certain parts of the mine, got to be ways that we can make it less cumbersome with our space age technology.

Mr. ZATEZALO. I think there is and that is why we are out for an RFI on that very subject.

Mr. GRIFFIN. Okay. And explain that to me, what are you doing in the RFI on that subject?

Mr. ZATEZALO. An RFI is just a request for information—

Mr. GRIFFIN. Yes, sir, I know, but what are you doing on it?

What—

Mr. ZATEZALO.—from all the providers. We are gathering information from all the providers and we will see if there are acceptable ways we can go about this.

Mr. GRIFFIN. Because it would seem to me we ought to be able to make that a much simpler process. And, as I said before, you know, we have got the silica problem we know about, we have got the coal we know about, but there is also—every mountain is a little different and we have got different substances out there. And instead of trying to chase the different substances, it seems to me if we give clean air to the miners, we are solving a lot of problems and maybe even reducing costs over time. Do you agree?

Mr. ZATEZALO. I think that is correct and I think that it has been a wonderful thing that has been shown about CPDM is that when you get that information on their actual exposures into the hands of the operators and the people that are actually there running machinery and doing the work, they will manage that correctly. That is why we are plus 99 percent compliant, sir.

So I think anytime, to the extent that people are educated on that and that people have the immediacy of feedback, I think they will manage that process very well.

Mr. GRIFFIN. Thank you very much. I yield back.

Chairwoman ADAMS. Thank you.

I want to yield now 5 minutes to Dr. Foxx of North Carolina, who is Ranking Member from the committee.

Mrs. FOXX. Thank you, Madam Chairwoman.

I want to thank all of our witnesses for being here today.

Assistant Secretary Zatezalo, can you explain the difference between the primary functions and mission of your agency, the Mine Safety and Health Administration, and the National Institute for Occupational Safety and Health? Additionally, how do the agencies currently collaborate? And how do you think they could better work together in the future on eliminating black lung disease?

Mr. ZATEZALO. Yes, ma'am, thank you.

We are two disparate agencies. The MSHA agency is primarily enforcement, education. Those are our primary goals. We also have a tech support arm that does a lot of our laboratory work.

NIOSH, on the other hand—and Dr. Howard may wish to clarify this—NIOSH is sort of the R&D side. MSHA does not do R&D. We do not develop technologies. That is all done through NIOSH. And we collaborate very well together. I have been to NIOSH's facilities, they have been to ours, we meet frequently. Several of his people are here with us today. I think our working relationship is very good and I think we share a lot of commonality in goals.

So I will ask Dr. Howard if he would care to add anything to that.

Dr. HOWARD. Certainly I would echo that. I think our collaboration is excellent, I thank the Assistant Secretary for his enthusiasm to work with us. I think we work really well together, both on the leadership level as well as the staff level.

Mrs. FOXX. Well, thank you both.

Again, Assistant Secretary Zatezalo, the last time you appeared before the Committee you indicated you were working on visiting all of your agency's field offices, and it is good to hear today that you were able to accomplish this goal.

What was your biggest takeaway from those visits?

Mr. ZATEZALO. My biggest takeaway is what a great group of people that we have, what a great bunch we have at MSHA. We have an—you know, these lung issues are things that we very much care about. Almost all of MSHA's employees, inspectors and people in the field, they are all miners, ex-miners. They live this every day and they live in these communities. And I think we have a really great group of people. A lot of them would like to see more frequent communication. Several of them have complained to me about specific things and I have tried to alleviate those where we could.

But I guess the—you know, what I was most impressed with was what a great group of serious people we have, how dedicated they are.

Mrs. FOXX. Thank you for that.

One more question. I am glad to hear you recognize the importance and benefits of compliance assistance visits, especially for smaller mine operators. Under your leadership, how are you encouraging more operators to take advantage of this opportunity?

Mr. ZATEZALO. Well, what we are doing is building up our program in certain areas. Unfortunately, over the years mining tends to shift around to different parts of the country, and so we found ourselves with areas where there were a lot of miners and not enough EFSMS, or our field people on the education side. We are moving some people in there. We have put some more people in there and we will—our compliance visits and compliance sessions last year were up over 8 percent. We conduct a lot of training, especially on the CPDM. We conduct all the training for certification on CPDM throughout the industry. And we just have a lot of people that are out there hustling, trying to get around as much as they can. The small mine services group subset has been especially effective and I am very pleased with what we are seeing out of those groups.

Mrs. FOXX. Thank you, and thank you all again. And thank you, Madam Chairwoman.

I yield back. Or, Mr. Chairman, I yield back.

Mr. SCOTT. Thank you. Thank you, Dr. Foxx.

The Chair head was called to vote in the Financial Services Committee, and so I will close up.

I remind our colleagues that pursuant to committee practice, materials for submission for the hearing must be submitted to the committee clerk within 14 days following the last day of the hearing, preferably in Microsoft Word format. Materials must address the subject matter of the hearing. Only a member of the committee or an invited witness may submit materials for inclusion in the hearing record.

Documents have to be in the form—the record set form.

So I want to thank the witnesses for your participation today. What we have heard today is extremely valuable. The members of the committee may have some additional questions for you and we ask the witnesses to please respond to those in writing. The hearing record will be held open for 14 days in order to receive those responses.

I remind my colleagues that pursuant to committee practice, witness questions for the hearing must be submitted to the majority committee staff within seven days. The questions submitted must address the subject matter of the hearing.

I now recognize the distinguished Ranking Member for his closing statement.

Mr. BYRNE. Thank you, Mr. Chairman. I thank you for being an adequate substitute for Chairwoman Adams.

Mr. SCOTT. Thank you.

Mr. BYRNE. And I want to thank everybody on this panel and the prior panel. I think we have had an excellent day discussing these very, very important issues and the information that you and the previous panel have supplied to us will be very valuable as the committee makes its decisions about what, if any, actions we need to take.

But what I would really like to do is address the miners that are here today and perhaps miners that are looking at us from other places.

Mining is a very important part of the American economy, but mining doesn't happen without the people that do it. And miners are important people because you help drive the American economy. Now, it is a dangerous thing to mine. We know that. And what we have been talking about today are things that perhaps we can do, all of us working together, to make things safer and healthier for our miners who are so important to our economy and to our country.

I think everybody up here, regardless of party designation, cares deeply for what we can do to make sure that we can make people safe and keep them safe and healthy. That is in everybody's interest.

I am also worried about preserving jobs in mining. We have had a real downturn in jobs in mining. In the previous Administration we almost had a war in a certain area of mining, in coal mining. And we need to be all about trying to preserve jobs, not kill jobs.

So I hope that we will be concerned about that too, and understand just how valuable mining is and has been to America for generations.

So I take our responsibility very seriously, our responsibility to you and to future generations of miners. You will continue to do what you do so very well, and that is a big part of what makes America great.

So thank you for what you do. We are going to continue to look out for you and those that follow you, because you are the most important part of mining.

And with that, Mr. Chairman, I yield back.

Mr. SCOTT. Thank you. And I want to thank the witnesses for providing us with their valuable expertise. I want to thank the members of the subcommittee for your participation. And I note the presence and interest of my colleague from Virginia, Mr. Griffith. Thank you for being with us today.

I think I can speak for all of them and say we have learned an enormous amount of valuable information from the witnesses today. We have heard compelling evidence that the most serious forms of black lung disease are again on the rise. We know what can be done about it and we know that MSHA should be doing more to save the lives of our Nation's miners from this terrible, preventable disease.

We have also heard strong evidence about the growing indebtedness of the Black Lung Disability Trust Fund and the Labor Department's failure to oversee the self-insurance program, shifting more and more of the liability for black lung disease from the companies that cause the problem to the taxpayers.

I think we can all agree that the work performed by our Nation's courageous coal miners should not be cursed by the scourge of this dreaded occupational disease that we know can be prevented. They deserve safe working conditions and a long, healthy retirement.

I finally ask unanimous consent to insert into the record a letter from the United Mine Workers of America and the United Steel Workers of America to the Assistant Secretary of Labor, and correspondence to and from the Assistant Secretary in request to information about the Pocahontas Coal Company Affinity Mine being relieved of its sanction under the—relieved of their sanctions. We will pursue that, Mr. Zatezalo, and to get better answers than we have gotten. If there is no further business, without objection, the committee stands adjourned.

June 19, 2019

Mr. David G. Zatezalo, Assistant Secretary
Mine Safety and Health Administration
Room 5C330
201 12th Street South
Arlington, VA 22202-5452

Dear Mr. Zatezalo:

We are writing to request that the Mine Safety and Health Administration immediately initiate a rulemaking to establish a new mandatory standard for respirable crystalline silica, and take certain other steps to protect miner health. The specific impetus for this request is the recent rise in diagnosed cases of coal workers' pneumoconiosis (Black Lung) and progressive massive fibrosis (PMF) amongst our nation's coal miners. However, the risk of silicosis has not been eliminated in metal and non-metal mines, and the standard should apply in all mines under MSHA's jurisdiction, both underground and surface, no matter what the commodity.

As we are all aware, numerous reports over the past several years have shown a disturbing trend in black lung cases, most notability in central Appalachia. These studies have shown that one in five miners with 25 years or more of experience are suffering from black lung. In many of these miners, the disease has advanced to PMF, the worst stage of black lung, caused by the inhalation of coal and silica dust. The only option for an improved quality of life for these miners is a lung transplant, and that is only possible when the miner is healthy enough to qualify for the surgery.

National Public Radio (NPR) first broke the story on the increase in December 2016. They obtained data from eleven black lung clinics and found 962 cases of PMF from the past decade. This was a much higher number than the National Institute for Occupational Safety and Health (NIOSH) had found. NIOSH's records showed only 99 cases from 2012 to 2016.

On December 16, 2016, NIOSH released a report published in the Morbidity and Mortality Weekly Report that showed one clinic in Kentucky reported 60 cases of PMF within twenty months. It noted a resurgence of this debilitating and deadly disease in central Appalachia. The report stated that these numbers show "an urgent need for effective dust control in coal mines to prevent coal workers' pneumoconiosis" and "is a strong signal that action is needed in the area to identify existing cases at an earlier stage and prevent future cases."

The report also pointed to new or modified mining practices that might be causing this resurgence. Slope mining is one potential source of exposure. This requires miners to cut through hundreds of feet of mostly sandstone to reach the coal seam being mined. This causes miners to be exposed to extremely high concentrations of respirable crystalline silica. The report also noted mining thinner seams of coal requires cutting more rock to obtain the height needed.

NPR continued its research and released a report in July 2017 finding an additional 1,000 cases, bringing the count to nearly 2,000 cases since 2010, twenty times the amount found by NIOSH during the same period. Even more disturbing is the fact that the true number is likely higher because many of the clinics in the area either could not provide data, or had incomplete data.

On February 6, 2018, NIOSH reported finding what they believe is the largest cluster of PMF reported in scientific literature. NIOSH observed 11,200 miners and found 416 cases of PMF. Miners as young as 38 years old and some with as little as eight years of mining experience were diagnosed with PMF. The report also noted the fact that we have gone from nearly having eliminated the disease in the 1990s to the highest concentration of cases anyone has ever seen. Also, in the 1990s, PMF clinics were primarily treating miners ranging in age from their 60s to 80s. Now, they are seeing miners in their 30s to 50s. These numbers are both disturbing and unacceptable.

May 2018 brought two additional studies that documented the rise in PMF cases as well as an increase in lung transplants for miners with the deadly disease. The first study, by Dr. Kirsten Almberg and her colleague Dr. Robert Cohen at the University of Chicago, identified more than 4,600 cases of PMF. Half of the cases identified occurred within the last sixteen years. The study also found sharp increases in PMF year after year in central Appalachian mining states, including thirty percent in West Virginia and sixteen percent in Kentucky and Virginia. The second study found a threefold increase in the rate of lung transplants due to black lung. Eighty percent of lung transplants that have occurred due to PMF have occurred in the past decade alone. An additional 27 miners were put on waiting lists and either died before they received the transplant or became too sick for the surgery and no longer qualified. These transplants cost upwards of $1 million dollars each and most are paid for through federal black lung programs.

In June 2018, the National Academies of Science, Engineering, and Medicine (NAS) released their review of MSHA's new Coal Mine Dust Rule that took effect in 2014 and was fully implemented in 2016. The review referenced MSHA data showing compliance rates above 99 percent. However, the review noted, "these approaches may not guarantee that exposures will be controlled adequately or that future disease rates will decline." The NAS report also found that "a fundamental shift is needed in the way mine operators approach exposure control," including "beyond compliance" efforts that exceed current MSHA regulations. The report pointed to the fact that dust readings may not be representative of the exposure of miners who are not wearing a dust monitor. The report also called for the development of a real-time silica monitor. While it may be some time before real-time silica monitors are available, NIOSH has created an end of shift silica monitor that can give silica readings much faster than the current process of sending the samples off to a laboratory and waiting for the results to return.

While the rise of black lung and PMF among coal miners is an immediate public health crisis, the risk of silicosis among other miners has not been eliminated. A 2008 NIOSH study found 134 deaths from silicosis among metal and nonmetal miners in selected states between 1990 and 1999. A more recent survey by MSHA found 94 cases of silicosis among 3395 metal and nonmetal miners surveyed between 2000 and 2016.

The state of New Jersey requires the reporting of silicosis cases. The New Jersey Department of Health Silicosis Surveillance Project recorded 561 cases of silicosis between 1979 and 2011. Of these, 81, or 14.4%, were in the mining sector, with a high concentration among surface miners of non-metallic minerals. While the number of cases in New Jersey has declined with each succeeding decade, the decline is largely due to the general decline in mining employment, including the closure of all underground mines in the state. All these numbers are likely to be underestimates, since silicosis is frequently misdiagnosed as other respiratory diseases.

Clearly, we are facing an epidemic of black lung and PMF caused or exacerbated by silica exposure in coal mines. The risk of silicosis still exists in metal and nonmetal mines. What can MSHA do? While MSHA's new Coal Mine Dust Rule closed many loopholes, increased sampling, provided real-time coal mine dust exposure results, and lowered concentration limits for coal mine dust, improvements can be made. Of course, that rule does not apply to metal and nonmetal mines. We therefore request that MSHA take the following actions to protect all miners.

Lower the allowable concentration limit of silica: MSHA's current silica standards are simply inadequate to protect miners from developing silicosis and PMF. MSHA's current standard has not been updated since 1985 and is in desperate need of revision. The undersigned believe that MSHA must promulgate a new silica standard to protect miners from PMF and silicosis. OSHA has recently promulgated a new standard, effectively cutting the allowable concentration from 100 to 50 micrograms of silica per cubic meter of air, averaged over an eight-hour shift. MSHA should consider the OSHA silica rule and then promulgate a new rule that is as, if not more, protective of miners. Currently, our nation provides less protection from silica to miners than to any other group of workers. That is unacceptable.

We believe this is the single most effective step that MSHA can take. On the coal side, the current Coal Mine Dust Rule measures all respirable dust in a coal mine, lumping coal dust with silica. Judging by their respective permissible exposure limits, silica is fifteen to thirty times more fibrogenic than coal dust. A doubling of the silica content in coal mine dust will have a small impact on the measurement of coal mine dust, but a large impact on the health of an exposed miner. And, of course, the Coal Mine Dust Rule only applies to coal mines. A strongly protective silica regulation, reflecting the latest scientific evidence, is essential in metal and nonmetal mines as well.

Fortunately, much of the work on a new standard has already been done by OSHA. The record of the OSHA rulemaking contains a massive amount of evidence and analysis on the health effects of silica and the need for the 50 microgram standard. Of course, MSHA must always be open to new evidence, and the agency will have to do its own determination of feasibility and control measures, but miners are biologically no different from other workers. Much of OSHA's work should be directly transferable to MSHA.

Require the Use of NIOSH's new end-of-shift silica sampler: While real-time silica monitoring is the ultimate goal, such technology will take some time to develop. In the meantime, MSHA and operators should make use of the newly developed end-of-shift sampler that will produce results the same day. Current laboratory delays make it extremely difficult, if not impossible, for employers to adjust operations quickly if miners are being exposed to high silica concentrations. The end-of-shift samplers are also cost-effective for operators because they eliminate laboratory costs. As a result, an end-of-shift sampler pays for itself within 200 samples. End of shift samplers should be required in all mines with potential silica exposure.

Sample more miners: While operator compliance with the new Coal Mine Dust Rule is over 99 percent, this is only true for miners who are wearing the continuous personal dust monitor. The level of coal and silica dust exposure experienced by miners who are not sampled is unknown. The amount of dust exposure permitted by MSHA's regulations is meaningless without adequate sampling. The alarming rate at which black lung and PMF are rising is not consistent with a 99 percent compliance rate. It is reasonable to assume that miners who are not sampled could be exposed to dangerously high amounts of respirable dust. MSHA should require the monitoring of more miners on more shifts. Although the problem is most acute in coal mines, adequate monitoring should be required in all mines.

Address high silica cutting situations: Special attention needs to be given to situations when miners are exposed to particularly high concentrations of silica. In coal mines, these include cutting overcasts, slopes, and unusually high amounts of rock within coal seams. These extremely hazardous conditions can be addressed through the mine's ventilation and dust control plans. Requiring the operator to sample for silica during these situations as well as mandating additional ventilation requirements could help dramatically decrease miners exposure to silica. Although the precise measures may differ in different commodities, plans addressing high silica concentrations should be required in all mines.

Work closely with the medical community: Access to data and statistics from those who treat miners diagnosed with deadly dust diseases is key to understanding the extent and severity of those diseases. While dust sampling data is valuable, the true indicator of success is whether or not miners are contracting black lung, PMF or silicosis and at what rate. MSHA has the opportunity to work closely with other groups and agencies that possess valuable knowledge on this subject, including NIOSH, the National Black Lung Association, the National Coalition of Black Lung and Respiratory Disease Clinics, the Office of Workers' Compensation Programs, the Health Resources and Services Administration, and medical programs for respiratory disease such as that at National Jewish Hospital. MSHA should embrace the opportunity to share valuable information with these stakeholders. MSHA could use this information to spot trends in the data, while protecting the confidentiality of miners. By monitoring trends, MSHA could quickly and accurately identify mines where a large number of miners have been diagnosed with dust diseases. MSHA could then take action to limit exposure at these problematic mines.

The time for action is now. We stand ready to work with all stakeholders to do everything we can to protect our nation's miners from these debilitating and deadly diseases. We anxiously await MSHA's plan to address one of the worst occupational health crises of our time.

Respectfully,

Cecil E. Roberts, President,
United Mine Workers of America

Leo W. Gerard, President,
United Steel, Paper and Forestry, Rubber, Manufacturing, Energy, Allied Industrial and Service Workers International Union

COMMITTEE ON EDUCATION
AND THE WORKFORCE
U.S. HOUSE OF REPRESENTATIVES
2176 RAYBURN HOUSE OFFICE BUILDING
WASHINGTON, DC 20515–6100

September 21, 2018

The Honorable David Zatezalo
Assistant Secretary for Mine Safety
Mine Safety and Health Administration
U.S. Department of Labor
201 12th Street South, Suite 401
Arlington, VA 22202-5450

Dear Mr. Zatezalo:

We are writing to inquire into the legal basis for the Mine Safety and Health Administration's (MSHA) decision to enter into a settlement agreement to terminate the Pattern of Violations (POV) Notice regarding the Affinity Mine operated by Pocahontas Coal located in Raleigh County, West Virginia. Specifically, this letter requests information necessary for the Committee to assess whether MSHA's actions to terminate the POV exceeded its statutory authority and whether the Department of Labor (DOL) acted properly in this matter.

As provided by Section 104(e) of the Federal Mine Safety and Health Act of 1977 (Mine Act), a POV Notice will terminate if, upon an inspection of the entire mine, MSHA finds no significant and substantial (S&S) violations of mandatory safety and health standards.[1] According to MSHA data, that precondition has not been met, as there have been numerous S&S violations at the Affinity Mine this year and those violations have persisted right up to the date the settlement was finalized on August 28, 2018.

In particular, a dissent included in the Federal Mine Safety and Health Review Commission's (FMSHRC) August 28, 2018 Order vacating a Petition for Discretionary Review by Pocahontas Coal states, in part:

> Although Pocahontas Coal Company's motion to the Commission nominally seeks merely to withdraw the operator's appeal of this matter and gain dismissal of the proceedings, the parties' filings make clear that Pocahontas's request is part of a broader agreement in which the Secretary of Labor seeks to unilaterally relieve Pocahontas's Affinity Mine of its pattern of violations designation. Such a settlement is directly contrary to the express language of the Mine Act and the Secretary's own regulations, and approving the settlement only provides cover for an unlawful agreement by the current administration.[2] (emphasis added)

Legislative History and Intent of the Pattern of Violations Provision in the Mine Act

In enacting the POV provisions in the Mine Act, Congress provided MSHA with its most powerful "tool to protect miners when the operator demonstrates [its] disregard for the health and safety of miners through an established pattern of violations."[3] Congress directed that when a mine is in POV status, "a withdrawal order shall be issued" and miners removed from the area of the hazardous area of the mine until the violation is abated for "any violation of a mandatory health or safety standard" that is S&S.[4] Congress intended the POV provision to be used for mine operators who have not responded to the Agency's other enforcement efforts. The legislative history states that Congress believed that the existence of a pattern would signal to both the mine operator and the Secretary that "there is a need to restore the mine to effective safe and healthful conditions and that the mere abatement of violations as they are cited is insufficient."[5] Following Congress' intent, MSHA's regulations implementing the POV provision are geared to "protecting miners working in mines operated by habitual offenders whose chronic S&S violations have not been deterred by the Secretary's other enforcement tools."[6]

MSHA Lacks Authority to Terminate POV due to Affinity's Chronic S&S Violations

Since the issuance of the POV Notice on October 24, 2013, MSHA has cited the Affinity Mine 265 times for S&S violations.[7] Although this mine operator has made progress in reducing its reported injury rates below the national average since 2013, there has not been a complete mine inspection free from S&S violations reflected in the public record. Indeed, MSHA issued 36 S&S violations so far this year, including one for the failure to maintain mobile and stationary machinery and equipment "in safe operating condition" a mere six days *before* this settlement was approved. Even more noteworthy, only eight days *after* FMSHRC approved the settlement, MSHA issued an S&S violation on September 5 for failure to provide protection from falls of roof, face and ribs—the same hazards that underpinned the basis for MSHA issuing the POV Notice in 2013.[8] Two days later on September 10, another S&S citation was issued for failure to

---

[1] An "S&S" violation is a serious violation which is "of such nature as could significantly and substantially contribute to the cause and effect of a coal or other mine safety or health hazard." 30 U.S.C. § 814(d)(1).

[2] *The Mine Safety and Health Administration et al v. Pocahontas Coal*, Federal Mine Safety and Health Review Commission, Order vacating Petition for Discretionary Review by Pocahontas Coal for cases WEVA 2014-395-R, WEVA 2014-1028, WEVA 2015-854, Dissent of Commissioner Robert F. Cohen, Jr. (August 28, 2018).

[3] Report of the Senate Committee on Human Resources, Subcommittee on Labor, Federal Mine Safety and Health Act of 1977, Report No. 95-181 (May 16, 1977)

[4] Under Section 104(e)(1), a "withdrawal order" is an order issued by the MSHA inspector "requiring the operator to cause all persons in the area affected by such violation, except those persons referred to in subsection (c), to be withdrawn from, and to be prohibited from entering, such area until an authorized representative of the Secretary determines that such violation has been abated."

[5] Ibid.

[6] Preamble to Final Rule on Pattern of Violations, Federal Register, Vol. 78, No. 15 , January 23, 2013, pp. 5060

[7] Since the POV Notice was issued, MSHA has cited the Affinity Mine for 263 S&S violations and issued withdrawal orders under Section 104(e) as follows: 10 in 2013, 63 in 2014, 42 in 2015, 59 in 2016, 56 in 2017, and 33 through August 28, 2018. Source: Mine Data Retrieval System (accessed September 9, 2018).

[8] Mine Data Retrieval System, Violations History for the Affinity Mine (accessed September 8, 2018)

provide protection from falls of roof, face and ribs. And a third S&S violation was written on September 18 for failure to maintain machinery in safe operating condition.

Once a POV Notice has been issued, MSHA's authority to withdraw a Notice is constrained by the prerequisites set in the Mine Act: Section 104(e)(3) states that before a POV Notice can be terminated, there must be an inspection of the entire coal mine where MSHA finds no S&S violations.[9] MSHA's POV regulations mirror this requirement.[10] Hence, under the Mine Act and MSHA's regulations, a mine cannot be removed from POV absent compliance with this statutory requirement. MSHA's prosecutorial discretion is unequivocally cabined by federal law and its own regulations.

The FMSHRC dissent further states:

> The Secretary's response in support of Pocahontas's motion is similarly silent toward the law's plain requirement that Pocahontas pass an inspection free of any S&S citations before it can be relieved of the POV designation. There is no indication that Pocahontas's Affinity Mine has received such a clean inspection. Rather than providing a clear indication to the Commission that the parties are proceeding within the framework of the Mine Act, the parties attempted to shield their actions from the public by initially filing pleadings before us in secret (i.e., "under seal").

Secrecy in Efforts to Terminate POV Raises Red Flags

Although the pleadings in this case were subsequently unsealed following a FMSHRC demand that MSHA and Pocahontas show cause, it begs a number of questions: What justification was there for MSHA to file its motion under seal when there is no national security or business confidential information at issue? What is the purpose of shielding the settlement agreement from the public in a cloak of secrecy? Was there an effort to evade public scrutiny of what may be an unlawful arrangement with this operator by making its initial filing under seal?

Despite a history of repeated S&S violations—which persisted in each and every year since the POV Notice was issued in 2013--and the Mine Act's unambiguous requirement under Section 104(e)(3) that a mine may not be removed from a POV absent a complete MSHA inspection free from S&S violations, MSHA has inexplicably terminated the POV Notice. For that reason, we are seeking information to better understand the legal basis for this decision and what transpired inside the DOL that led MSHA to take this unprecedented action.

Request for Information

Pursuant to Rule X of the Rules of the House of Representatives, we request the following information and documents to be provided no later than October 5th, 2018:

1) A copy of the settlement agreement, and any attachments to such agreement or memorandum of agreement or side letters between MSHA and Pocahontas Coal, (including its controlling entities United Coal Company (UCC), and Metinvest AB) regarding the termination of the POV Notice at the Affinity Mine.
2) The date(s) of a complete inspection of the Affinity Mine that yielded no S&S violations since the issuance of the POV Notice in October 2013.
3) If there has not been a complete inspection that yielded no S&S violations, then please provide the legal basis for removing the Affinity Mine from POV in light of the fact that MSHA continued to cite S&S violations during each complete inspection of the Affinity Mine since MSHA issued the POV notice.
4) All written communications between MSHA (and the DOL Solicitor's office) and Pocahontas Coal, UCC or Metinvest AB (and its counsel) regarding the removal of the Affinity mine from POV, including letters, e-mails and memos.
5) A list of all meetings and copies of minutes or memos summarizing such meetings between MSHA (and the DOL Solicitor's office) and Pocahontas Coal, UCC or Metinvest AB (and its counsel) regarding the removal of the Affinity Mine from POV between January 20, 2017 and the date of this letter.

---

[9] Section 104(e)(3) states: "If, upon an inspection of the <u>entire</u> coal or other mine, an authorized representative of the Secretary finds no violations of mandatory health or safety standards that could significantly and substantially contribute to the cause and effect of a coal or other mine health and safety hazard, the pattern of violations that resulted in the issuance of a notice under paragraph (1) shall be deemed to be terminated and the provisions of paragraphs (1) and (2) shall no longer apply." (emphasis added)

[10] 30 CFR 104.4 states: "Termination of notice. (a) Termination of a section 104(e)(1) pattern of violations notice shall occur when an MSHA inspection of the <u>entire</u> mine finds no S&S violations or if MSHA does not issue a withdrawal order in accordance with section 104(e)(1) of the Mine Act within 90 days after the issuance of the pattern of violations notice." (emphasis added)

6) A copy of all communications between MSHA (and its Solicitor) and Pocahontas Coal, UCC or Metinvest AB (and its counsel) regarding the decision to initially file pleadings with FMSHRC under seal with respect to terminating the POV at the Affinity Mine.
7) Who in the DOL's Solicitor's office authorized the filing of the government's pleadings under seal in this matter? Who reversed this decision?
8) A copy of internal DOL communications regarding the removal of the Affinity Mine from POV, including communications between personnel in the Office of the Secretary of Labor and MSHA, and communications between the MSHA District 4 Office and MSHA headquarters, for the time period between January 20, 2017 and the date of this letter.

We look forward to receiving this information within the time frame set forth above. Please contact Richard Miller, Labor Policy Director for the Committee on Education and the Workforce Democrats, at 202-225-3725 or richard.miller@mail.house.gov.

Sincerely,

ROBERT C. "BOBBY" SCOTT
Ranking Member

MARK TAKANO
Ranking Member
Subcommittee on Workforce Protections

cc: Nicholas Geale, Chief of Staff to the Secretary
Hon. Scott Dahl, Inspector General
Hon. Michael G. Young, Acting Chair, Federal Mine Safety and Health Review Commission
Hon. Virginia Foxx, Chair, Committee on Education and the Workforce
Hon. Bradley Byrne, Chair, Subcommittee on Workforce Protections

COMMITTEE ON EDUCATION AND LABOR
U.S. HOUSE OF REPRESENTATIVES
2176 RAYBURN HOUSE OFFICE BUILDING
WASHINGTON, DC 20515-6100

April 2, 2019

The Honorable David Zatezalo
Assistant Secretary for Mine Safety
Mine Safety and Health Administration
U.S. Department of Labor
201 12th Street South, Suite 401
Arlington, VA 22202-5450

Dear Mr. Zatezalo:

On September 21, 2018, we wrote to you to request information about the Mine Safety and Health Administration's (MSHA) decision to enter into a settlement agreement to terminate the Pattern of Violations (POV) Notice regarding the Affinity Mine operated by Pocahontas Coal located in Raleigh County, West Virginia. That September 21, 2018, request asked for the following information and any related documents:

1) A copy of the settlement agreement, and any attachments to such agreement or memorandum of agreement or side letters between MSHA and Pocahontas Coal, (including its controlling entities United Coal Company (UCC) and Metinvest AB) regarding the termination of the POV Notice at the Affinity Mine.
2) The date(s) of a complete inspection of the Affinity Mine that yielded no S&S violations since the issuance of the POV Notice in October 2013.
3) If there has not been a complete inspection that yielded no S&S violations, then please provide the legal basis for removing the Affinity Mine from POV in light of the fact that MSHA continued to cite S&S violations during each complete inspection of the Affinity Mine since MSHA issued the POV notice.
4) All written communications between MSHA (and the DOL Solicitor's office) and Pocahontas Coal, UCC or Metinvest AB (and its counsel) regarding the removal of the Affinity mine from POV, including letters, e-mails and memos.
5) A list of all meetings and copies of minutes or memos summarizing such meetings between MSHA (and the DOL Solicitor's office) and Pocahontas Coal, UCC or Metinvest AB (and its counsel) regarding the removal of the Affinity Mine from POV between January 20, 2017, and the date of that letter.
6) A copy of all communications between MSHA (and its Solicitor) and Pocahontas Coal, UCC or Metinvest AB (and its counsel) regarding the decision to initially file pleadings with Federal Mine Safety and Health Review Commission (FMSHRC) under seal with respect to terminating the POV at the Affinity Mine.
7) Who in the DOL's Solicitor's office authorized the filing of the government's pleadings under seal in this matter? Who reversed this decision?
8) A copy of internal DOL communications regarding the removal of the Affinity Mine from POV, including communications between personnel in the Office of the Secretary of Labor and MSHA, and communications between the MSHA District 4 Office and MSHA headquarters, for the time period between January 20, 2017, and the date of that letter.

As of the date of *this* letter, MSHA has partially responded to Request 1 above by providing a copy of the settlement agreement and a copy of documents filed with the FMSHRC relating to the settlement but has not provided letters between MSHA and Pocahontas Coal (including its controlling entities UCC and Metinvest AB) regarding the termination of the POV Notice at the Affinity Mine.

MSHA has also failed to respond to Requests 2-8. This is particularly concerning because in your October 1, 2018, response you claimed that "the Department exercised its broad discretion to reach a settlement" in terminating the POV Notice for a mine that has not met the necessary statutory preconditions, and yet, you failed to answer the request that asks for the legal basis for this broad discretion that does not appear in either statute and or legislative history.[1]

MSHA's failure to respond in full to these requests is interfering with the Committee's constitutional authority and duty to conduct oversight, and MSHA's lack of responsiveness is particularly disconcerting given the unprecedented termination of a POV Notice in apparent violation of the strictures within the Mine Act. We reiterate the requests above and request that you provide the information and documents as soon as possible, but in no case later than April 16, 2019.

---

[1] Section 104(e)(3) of the Federal Mine Safety and Health Act of 1997 (Mine Act) states that in order for a POV Notice to be terminated, there must be "no violations of mandatory health or safety standards that could significantly and substantially contribute to the cause and effect of a coal or other mine health and safety hazard" and does not provide any discretion for the Department to do otherwise. Furthermore, the Senate Committee report for the Mine Act elaborates that, "Both Sections 105(c) [codified at 104(d) Unwarrantable Failure] and 105(d) [codified at 104(e) Pattern of Violations] require an inspection of the mine in its entirety in order to break the sequence of the issuance of orders. However, Section 105(c) requires that the inspection must reveal no unwarranted "violations", and under Section 105(d) the inspection must reveal no violations of a "significant and substantial" nature" (emphasis added).

Please contact Cathy Yu with the Committee at cathy.yu@mail.house.gov with any questions. Please send all official correspondence relating to this request to tylease.alli@mail.house.gov.

Sincerely,

ROBERT C. "BOBBY" SCOTT
Chairman

ALMA S. ADAMS
Chairwoman
Subcommittee on Workforce Protections

U.S. Department of Labor

Office of the Assistant Secretary for
Congressional and Intergovernmental Affairs
Washington, D.C. 20210

APR 2 6 2019

The Honorable Robert C. "Bobby" Scott
Chairman
Committee on Education and Labor
U.S. House of Representatives
Washington, DC 20515

Dear Chairman Scott:

The Department of Labor (the Department) has received your letter regarding the Mine Safety and Health Administration's (MSHA) authority to enter into settlement with Affinity Mine (Affinity) operated by Pocahontas Coal Company. As you acknowledged in your letter, the Department provided a response to your initial inquiry of September 21, 2018. The Department's 52-page response was sent October 1, 2018, and provided responses to the questions you raised. This letter and its attachments provide an additional 39 pages in further response to your inquiry on this matter.

The United Mine Workers of America has challenged MSHA's authority to enter into settlement with Affinity in federal district court. The Department of Justice represents the Secretary of Labor in this matter and the case remains in litigation. Due to this pending litigation, the Department is unable to provide further comment. However, attached please find the government's filings explaining its authority to enter into settlement with Affinity, which address the underlying concerns raised in your April 2, 2019, letter.

If you have further questions regarding this issue, please contact the Office of Congressional and Intergovernmental Affairs at (202) 693-4600.

Sincerely,

Joe Wheeler
Acting Assistant Secretary

Enclosures

CC: The Honorable Virginia Foxx, Ranking Member, Committee on Education and Labor

Case 5:18-cv-01478 Document 8 Filed 03/11/19 Page 1 of 2 PageID #: 97

IN THE UNITED STATES DISTRICT COURT
FOR THE SOUTHERN DISTRICT OF WEST VIRGINIA

UNITED MINE WORKERS OF AMERICA, INTERNATIONAL UNION	:	
Plaintiff,	:	
v.	:	Civil Action No. 5:18-cv-1478
DAVID G. ZATAZELO, et al.	:	
Defendants.	:	

DEFENDANTS' MOTION TO DISMISS

Defendants by and through their undersigned counsel file this Motion to Dismiss pursuant Federal Rule of Civil Procedure 12(b)(1) and 12(b)(6). A Memorandum in Support of their Motion is attached for the Court's review.

Respectfully submitted,

JOSEPH H. HUNT
Assistant Attorney General

BRAD P. ROSENBERG
Assistant Branch Director

DANIELLE W. YOUNG
/s/ Danielle W. Young
Danielle W. Young (TX Bar No. 24098649)
Trial Attorney, Federal Programs Branch
U.S. Department of Justice, Civil Division
1100 L Street, NW Room 12312
Washington, DC 20005
(202) 616-2035
Email: Danielle.Young2@usdoj.gov

/s/ Fred B. Westfall, Jr.
FRED B. WESTFALL, JR., AUSA (W.Va. Bar No. 3992)
Office of the United States Attorney for the Southern District of West Virginia
300 Virginia Street East, Room 4000
Charleston, WV 25301
(304) 345-2200

Case 5:18-cv-01478 Document 8 Filed 03/11/19 Page 2 of 2 PageID #: 98

(304) 347-5443 (fax)

Counsel for Defendants

IN THE UNITED STATES DISTRICT COURT
FOR THE SOUTHERN DISTRICT OF WEST VIRGINIA

UNITED MINE WORKERS OF AMERICA, INTERNATIONAL UNION	:	
Plaintiff,	:	
v.	:	Civil Action No. 5:18-cv-1478
DAVID G. ZATAZELO, et al.	:	
Defendants.	:	

MEMORANDUM IN SUPPORT OF DEFENDANTS' MOTION TO DISMISS

INTRODUCTION

For five years, the Mine Safety and Health Administration ("MSHA") imposed and kept in place a Pattern of Violations ("POV") notice at Affinity Mine, which is owned by Pocahontas Coal Company, LLC ("Pocahontas"). During this time period, Pocahontas took significant steps to improve the Mine's safety. Pocahontas also challenged the POV Notice before the Federal Mine Safety and Health Review Commission ("Commission"). Recognizing the important safety improvements Pocahontas made at Affinity Mine—which is now indisputably one of the safest mines in the entire region—MSHA exercised its enforcement discretion under the Mine Act and agreed to remove the POV Notice in exchange for Pocahontas withdrawing its challenge before the Commission, which was on an administrative appeal at the time. The Commission dismissed the appeal. Now, the United Mine Workers of America International Union ("the Union") seeks to challenge the termination of the POV Notice, even though none of its members work in Affinity Mine.

The Complaint suffers from two incurable jurisdictional defects. To begin with, the Union asks this Court to set aside the Commission's order dismissing Pocahontas's appeal, which triggered the termination of the POV Notice pursuant to the settlement agreement. But the plain text of the statute provides that circuit courts shall have "exclusive jurisdiction" when "[a]ny person adversely affected or aggrieved by an order of the Commission [seeks to] obtain a review of such order." 30 U.S.C. § 816(a)(1). The same provision also requires that review be obtained in the appropriate circuit court within 30 days of the Commission's decision—a time period that has long since lapsed. *Id.*

This Court also lacks jurisdiction because the Complaint fails to identify any member of the Union that has standing in his own right, as is required for associational standing. Because none of the Union's members work in the Mine they cannot be affected by MSHA's actions with respect to it. And to the extent the Union is alleging that the termination of the POV Notice at Affinity Mine risks the safety of its members working in *other* mines by diminishing the deterrent effect of that enforcement mechanism, that allegation falls short of identifying an injury that is imminent and non-speculative. To the contrary, documents attached to the Complaint suggest that MSHA's treatment of Affinity Mine was effective in improving safety conditions for mineworkers. The Union thus lacks Article III standing.

The Complaint also suffers from additional defects warranting dismissal. The Complaint alleges that the Secretary lacks the authority to remove POV notices outside of the statutory provision requiring termination when a mine receives an inspection free of any significant violations. That provision provides that if upon inspection "no violations of mandatory health or safety standards [are found] that could significantly and substantially contribute to the cause and effect of a coal or other mine health and safety hazard, the [POV] . . . notice . . . shall be deemed to be terminated." 30 U.S.C. § 814(e)(3). But nothing in this provision or elsewhere in the statute limits the Secretary's enforcement discretion to *only* being able to remove POV notices under such circumstances. In short, although the statute mandates the termination of a POV notice when there is a clean inspection, it does not set forth the exclusive means for termination of such notices. Indeed, the Secretary's enforcement decisions are not otherwise subject to judicial review because they are committed to agency discretion by law. But even if they were not, the APA claims should still be dismissed because the Secretary acted lawfully and in accordance with his discretion. For similar reasons, the Union's mandamus claim should also be dismissed because it cannot show that any clear duty exists or that the Union has any clear and indisputable right to enforce the POV Notice at Affinity Mine. And, in any event, the mandamus relief the Union seeks is duplicative of the relief it seeks under the APA, which is itself a sufficient reason for dismissal. Finally, without any viable claims remaining, the Union's claim for relief under the Declaratory Judgment Act should likewise be dismissed because there is no independent basis for jurisdiction.

BACKGROUND

A. Statutory Background

In ratifying the Mine Act, Congress strengthened and streamlined MSHA's enforcement proceedings of mandatory health and safety standards. *Thunder Basin Coal Co. v. Reich,* 510 U.S. 200, 211 (1994). The Secretary, through MSHA, is authorized to issue citations and orders to mine operators for violations of mandatory health and safety standards. 30 U.S.C. § 814. A mine operator has thirty days to challenge an enforcement action before the Commission, after which it becomes final and not subject to review. 30 U.S.C. § 815(a) and (d). If an operator files a notice of contest within thirty days, it is provided with the opportunity for a full hearing before an administrative law judge, as well as potential review of the judge's decision by the Commission. 30 U.S.C. §§ 823(d)(1), (2). Operators may challenge adverse Commission decisions in the respective court of appeals, and appeal the circuit court decisions to the Supreme Court. 30 U.S.C. § 816(a)(1).

Section 104(e)(1) of the Mine Act requires that "[i]f an operator has a pattern of violations of mandatory health or safety standards in the coal or other mine which are of such nature as could have significantly and substantially contributed to the cause and effect of coal or other mine health or safety hazards, he shall be given written notice that such pattern exists." 30 U.S.C. § 814(e)(1); *see* 30 C.F.R. §§ 104.1-104.4. If, within 90 days after the notice is issued, an MSHA inspector finds a significant and substantial (S&S) violation at the mine, MSHA is directed to issue a withdrawal order under section 104(e) of the Act requiring all miners to leave the area of the mine where the violation occurred. *Id.*; 30

C.F.R. § 104.3(c). The Mine Act further states that as long as a mine is in POV status, the mine will be subject to a withdrawal order for any subsequent S&S violation until an inspection of the entire mine reveals no further S&S violations. 30 U.S.C. § 814(e)(3).

B. Factual Background[1]

The facts are not in dispute. On October 24, 2013, MSHA determined that a Pattern of Violations existed at Pocahontas' Affinity Mine under Section 104(e)(1) of the Mine Act. Compl. Attach. No. 1 (Notice). Pocahontas timely contested the POV notice. On November 3, 2015, the Administrative Law Judge affirmed the POV notice in response to cross motions for summary decision filed by the parties. *Sec'y of Labor, MSHA v. Pocahontas Coal Co., LLC,* Docket No. WEVA 2014-1028, 37 FMSHRC 2654 (ALJ Miller, Nov. 3, 2015); Ex. No. 2. Pocahontas timely appealed.

MSHA's POV Notice against the Mine remained in effect while on appeal at the Commission. During that period, officials at the Mine and MSHA worked together to improve the mine's safety record, which included instituting a Corrective Action Program and changing the mine's management team. Compl. Attach. No. 9 (Oct. 3, 2018 Letter). The mine noticeably improved its safety record, and although the mine did not receive an inspection completely free of S&S violations, it became one of the safest mines within MSHA's jurisdiction, achieving one of the lowest rates of S&S citations and lost time accidents for any mine within its MSHA District, as well as mines throughout the nation that employ roughly the same number of miners. *Id.* The mine also improved its All-Injuries Incident Rate, reducing it from 9.91 in 2012 to 3.85 in 2018. *Id.*

Consequently, in mid-2018–approximately 5 years after the POV Notice first went into effect— MSHA agreed to remove the POV Notice at the Mine, provided that Pocahontas withdraw its appeal to the Commission. *See* Compl. Attach. No. 7 (Settlement Agreement). Pocahontas subsequently moved to

[1] Documents attached to the complaint as exhibits are properly considered in a Rule 12 motion. *Goines v. Valley Cmty. Servs. Bd.*, 822 F.3d 159, 166 (4th Cir. 2016) (citing Fed. R. Civ. Pro. 10(c)).

withdraw its appeal before the Commission and attached the Settlement Agreement. *See* Compl. Attach. 3. The Commission approved the appeal's dismissal by a vote of 3 to 1. *See* Compl. Attach. No. 6 (Aug. 28, 2018 Order). Exercising his enforcement discretion, the Secretary removed the POV Notice.

The Union did not intervene in the Commission's proceedings or file suit in the appropriate circuit court challenging the Commission's order. Instead, several months after the Commission's decision, the Union filed this action alleging that the only way for the Mine to be released from its POV status is through receiving an inspection without any S&S violations under Section 104(e)(3) of the Mine Act, which states that if upon inspection "no violations of mandatory health or safety standards [are found] that could significantly and substantially contribute to the cause and effect of a . . . mine health and safety hazard, the [POV] . . . notice . . . shall be deemed to be terminated." 30 U.S.C. § 814(e)(3).

STANDARD OF REVIEW

The Defendants move to dismiss the Complaint for lack of subject matter jurisdiction. Fed. R. Civ. P. 12(b)(1). The plaintiff bears the burden of establishing the court's subject-matter jurisdiction. *Strawn v. AT&T Mobility*, 530 F.3d 293, 296 (4th Cir. 2008); *Richmond, Fredericksburg & Potomac R.R. Co. v. United States*, 945 F.2d 765, 768 (4th Cir.1991). Where, as here, there is a facial challenge to subject matter jurisdiction, the Court accepts only the well-pleaded factual allegations of the complaint as true, and determines whether those factual allegations are sufficient to establish jurisdiction. *Adams v. Bain*, 697 F.2d 1213, 1219 (4th Cir. 1982).

Defendants also move to dismiss for failure to state a claim upon which relief can be granted. Fed. R. Civ. P. 12(b)(6). Rule 12(b)(6) authorizes a court to dismiss a claim on the basis of a dispositive issue of law. *Neitzke v. Williams*, 490 U.S. 319, 326 (1989). To survive a motion to dismiss under Rule 12(b)(6), a complaint must contain sufficient factual allegations, accepted as true, to state a claim for relief that is "plausible on its face." *Bell Atl. Corp. v. Twombly*, 550 U.S. 544, 570 (2007). The facts alleged "must be enough to raise a right to relief above the speculative level." *Id.* at 555. While a court must treat the complaint's factual allegations as true, it need not accept as true "legal conclusions," *Ashcroft v. Iqbal*, 556 U.S. 662, 678 (2009), nor "allegations that are merely conclusory, unwarranted deductions of fact, or unreasonable inferences," *Veney v. Wyche*, 293 F.3d 726, 730 (4th Cir. 2002) (citation omitted). In assessing a Rule 12(b)(6) motion, a court may consider documents of which it may take judicial notice, without converting a Rule 12(b)(6) motion into one for summary judgment. *Sec'y of State for Def. v. Trimble Navigation Ltd.*, 484 F.3d 700, 705 (4th Cir. 2007).

ARGUMENT

I. The Mine Act Precludes Jurisdiction Over Plaintiff's Claims

Because the Union seeks to have this Court overturn an order of the Commission, the Mine Act precludes jurisdiction in this Court. The Mine Act provides that:

> Any person adversely affected or aggrieved by an order of the Commission issued under this chapter may obtain a review of such order in any United States court of appeals for the circuit in which the violation is alleged to have occurred or in the United States Court of Appeals for the District of Columbia Circuit, by filing in such court within 30 days following the issuance of such order a written petition praying that the order be modified or set aside. . . . Upon such filing, the court shall have *exclusive jurisdiction* of the proceeding.

30 U.S.C. § 816(a)(1) (emphasis added). Seeking to avoid this provision of the Act, the Union alleges that it does not apply because it is not challenging any order of the Commission. *See* Compl. ¶¶ 9, 35. Yet the relief sought by the Union belies this conclusory allegation: The Union asks this Court to "set aside" MSHA's "terminati[on of] the POV Notice at Affinity Mine" and compel MSHA to "enforc[e] the POV Notice at Affinity Mine." Compl. Prayer, ¶¶ 2-3. That proposed relief, however, would undercut the Commission's order. In contrast to the dissenting opinion, the majority's order implicitly recognized that the Secretary's authority to terminate a POV notice was not reviewable. The order also permitted Affinity Mine to withdraw its petition for discretionary review of the POV Notice *in exchange for* MSHA's termination of the POV Notice pursuant to the express terms of the settlement agreement.[2]

---

[2] Although the Commission received a copy of the settlement agreement, Commission lacks jurisdiction to review settlements that do not involve contested penalties. As MSHA explained in its submission to

See Compl. Attachs. 5-7. What the Union is really seeking then is for this Court to strike down the Commission's order. *See* Compl., Attach. 6 (Aug. 28, 2018 Order). But for the Commission's decision, the POV Notice would still be in place. *See* Compl. Attach. ¶¶4-5 (providing that MSHA would only terminate the POV Notice if the Commission issued "a full, clear, and unambiguous dismissal of the Proceeding" and that without such a dismissal the agreement would be "null and void"). Indeed, the Union now seeks to rely on the arguments raised by the dissenting panel member's opinion, which argued that the Secretary lacked the discretion to remove the POV Notice—even though those very arguments were implicitly rejected by the majority of the Commission in issuing its decision. *See* Compl. ¶¶ 24-25. It is thus plain from the allegations in the Complaint and the relief sought that the Union is, in fact, seeking to have this Court review and, ultimately, overturn an order of the Commission.

The Mine Act, however, clearly limits "review of such order[s] [to the] United States court of appeals for the circuit in which the violation is alleged to have occurred," providing those courts alone with "exclusive jurisdiction of [such] proceeding[s]." 30 U.S.C. § 816(a)(1). The Supreme Court has affirmed as much, recognizing that the Mine Act "establishes that the Commission and the courts of appeals have exclusive jurisdiction over challenges to agency enforcement proceedings . . . [and that] the Act expressly authorizes district court jurisdiction in only two provisions, §§ 818(a) and 820(j), which respectively empower the *Secretary* to enjoin habitual violations of health and safety standards and to coerce payment of civil penalties," but does not provide such a right to any others. *Thunder Basin Coal Co.*, 510 U.S. at 208–09. The Mine Act thus precludes jurisdiction over Plaintiff's claims in this Court and should be dismissed under Rule 12(b)(1).[3]

---

the Commission, because MSHA retains enforcement discretion in the issuance of POV notices, it likewise retains the same enforcement discretion to remove such notices under the Commission's decision in *Sec'y of Labor, MSHA v. Pocahontas Coal Company*, 38 FMSHRC 176 (2016).

[3] The Union had notice of the Commission's decision within the statutory deadline to file in the appropriate Circuit court, yet failed to do so. *See* Compl. Attach. 8 (Sept. 14, 2018 Letter). The Union also could have intervened in the proceedings before the Commission, but it chose not to do so. *See* 29

II. Plaintiff Lacks Standing because None of its Members Work at Affinity Mine.

Even if this Court concludes that the Union properly brought suit here rather than in a court of appeals, this case should still be dismissed for lack of jurisdiction because the Union lacks standing. Article III standing is one of the justiciability doctrines emanating from the case-or-controversy requirement in Article III of the Constitution. *See Friends of the Earth, Inc. v. Laidlaw Envtl. Servs. (TOC), Inc.*, 528 U.S. 167, 180 (2000) (explaining that the underpinning of standing jurisprudence is "[t]he Constitution's case-or-controversy limitation on federal judicial authority, Art. III, § 2"). The "irreducible constitutional minimum" for Article III standing consists of three elements: (i) an injury in fact; (ii) a fairly traceable causal connection; and (iii) redressability. *Lujan v. Defs. of Wildlife*, 504 U.S. 555, 560-61 (1992) (plurality opinion).

An organization may have standing solely on behalf of its members, commonly referred to as "representational" or "associational" standing, when three elements are satisfied: (i) at least one of its members has standing to sue in his own right; (ii) the interests that the association seeks to protect are germane to its purpose; and (iii) the adjudication of the association's claims and relief sought does not require the participation of any individual member of the association.[4] *See Hunt v. Wash. State Apple Advert. Comm'n*, 432 U.S. 333, 343 (1977); *S. Walk at Broadlands Homeowner's Ass'n, Inc. v. OpenBand at Broadlands, LLC*, 713 F.3d 175, 184 (4th Cir. 2013). Plaintiff attempts to bring this action, not in it is own right, but solely on behalf of its members, *see* Compl. ¶ 34, but it fails to satisfy the first element for associational standing.

C.F.R. § 2700.4 (permitting intervention by affected miners and their representatives).

[4] An organization can also bring suit directly on its own behalf, as opposed to on behalf of its members, which is known as "organizational standing." *See Havens Realty Corp. v. Coleman*, 455 U.S. 363, 378 (1982). This sort of standing requires the organization to show that it has suffered "a concrete and demonstrable injury to the organization's activities" *id.* at 379; *see also Lane v. Holder*, 703 F.3d 668, 674 (4th Cir. 2012). Absent from the Complaint, however, is any factual allegation that the Union's own activities are being harmed by Defendants' actions with respect to Affinity Mine. Instead, the Complaint alleges only associational standing. *See* Compl. ¶ 34.

A. Plaintiff fails to identify any member with standing.

The first requirement for associational standing is that the organization must identify at least one member with standing. As the Supreme Court explained, the law of associational standing requires "plaintiff-organizations to make *specific allegations* establishing that at least one *identified* member had suffered or would suffer harm." *Summers v. Earth Island Inst.*, 555 U.S. 488, 498 (2009) (emphasis added). In contravention of that fundamental requirement, the Complaint does not contain any allegations that identify any member of the Union who has suffered any actual specific harm because of the termination of the POV Notice at Affinity Mine. *See* Compl. ¶ 34 (failing to identify any specific members as having standing). Instead, the Complaint merely makes a generalized conclusory allegation that its "members are adversely affected and aggrieved" because the termination of the POV notice at Affinity mine has "decreas[ed] safety in the nation's mines . . . all over the country" thus creating an "injur[y] in fact." *Id.* Even if such an injury were non-speculative, which it is not, *see infra* Part II(B), this allegation falls short of meeting Plaintiff's obligation to establish associational standing by *identifying members* who can satisfy the elements of Article III standing. *Id.* at ¶ 34. As the Fourth Circuit explained, "although it is possible that each . . . member is being harmed . . . —without specific mention of any *individual* member's injury—[such allegation] surely stops short of the line between possibility and plausibility." *S. Walk at Broadlands Homeowner's Ass'n.*, 713 F.3d at 185 (holding that there generalized allegation that "all members of organization were harmed by Defendants' actions" was insufficient to confer associational standing). Here, as in *South Walk*, there is only a generalized allegation that every member is being harmed without specific mention of any individual member's injury. *See id.* And absent from the Complaint is any allegation that even a single member of the Union works in Affinity Mine—where the POV notice was actually removed. Without any "specific mention of any individual member's injury," *id.*, the Union cannot qualify for associational standing, and the Complaint should be dismissed on that ground alone.

B. Plaintiff's members lack an injury-in-fact.

The Complaint is also deficient because it fails to allege an injury in fact, which is the "[f]irst and foremost" of the three elements of Article III standing. *Steel Co. v. Citizens for a Better Env't*, 523 U.S. 83, 103 (1998). To establish an injury-in-fact requires "an invasion of a legally protected interest" that is "concrete and particularized," and "actual or imminent, not conjectural or hypothetical." *Spokeo, Inc. v. Robins*, 136 S. Ct. 1540, 1548 (2016) (quoting *Lujan*, 504 U.S. at 560); *see also Sprint Commc'ns. Co. v. APCC Servs., Inc.*, 554 U.S. 269, 273-74 (2008). It is well understood that speculation or the identification of an injury that is remote, abstract, or otherwise not "certainly impending" will not suffice for an injury in fact. *See Clapper v. Amnesty Int'l USA*, 133 S. Ct. 1138, 1148 (2013) (rejecting the idea that an "objectively reasonable likelihood" of injury suffices as "certainly impending" injury); *Beck v. McDonald*, 848 F.3d 262, 271 (4th Cir. 2017), *cert. denied sub nom. Beck v. Shulkin*, 137 S. Ct. 2307 (2017) (emphasizing the same).

The Complaint seeks to allege a novel theory that the Union has standing, even though none of its members work at Affinity Mine, because the termination of the POV Notice at Affinity Mine will diminish the deterrent effect of the regulatory scheme at *other mines* in which its members actually work. Compl. ¶ 34. But this alleged injury is far too speculative and remote to constitute an injury in fact. It depends on other mine operators viewing a one-time settlement agreement between MSHA and Pocahontas with regard to Affinity Mine's POV status, that only took place after MSHA kept in place the POV Notice for *five years*—the longest in history—and after Pocahontas significantly improved its safety rating at Affinity Mine, as indicating that the Secretary will not be fully exercising his enforcement authority at other mines. *See* Compl. Attach. 9 at 1-3 (Oct. 3, 2018 Letter). It also depends on those mine operators in turn deciding that it is in their own interest to violate the Mine Act and its safety regulations, thus decreasing their mine's safety, because there is a possibility that MSHA will ultimately settle POV notices against them too, even though part of the reason MSHA settled with Pocahontas was to ensure it retained its enforcement ability—not to weaken it. *See id.* at 2. In short, the Union's alleged "injury" depends on the mental states of third-party operators of other mines, and it is entirely speculative that a one-time settlement agreement will make those operators take MSHA's enforcement authority less seriously and thereby reduce safety for the Union's members.

In fact, undisputed evidence attached to the Complaint shows that Affinity Mine is safer than it was five years ago; indeed, it is one of the safest mines in the entire region. *See id.* at 1-3. MSHA's enforcement of the POV scheme has been remarkably successful and the settlement of this particular notice was done, in part, to ensure continued success in improving safety across the nation's mines. *Id.* at 3 (noting "the dramatic reduction in the number of mines meeting the screening criteria to be considered for POV"); *see also* 30 C.F.R. § 104.1 (noting that the purpose of the POV scheme is "restoration of effective safe and healthful conditions at such mines"). Plaintiff's conclusory allegation that a one-time settlement with Pocahontas, which is meant to ensure MSHA's continued successful enforcement of the POV scheme, will reduce the safety of all other mines, is too speculative to qualify as an injury that is "certainly impending." *See Clapper*, 133 S. Ct. at 1148; *Beck*, 848 F.3d at 271.

III. <u>Plaintiff Fails to State a Claim Against the Defendants because MSHA Has Enforcement Discretion to Remove Mines from POV Status.</u>

Even if this Court had jurisdiction, this case should still be dismissed. The basis for the relief Plaintiff seeks under the Administrative Procedures Act ("APA"), Mandamus Statute, and the Declaratory Judgment Act ("DJA") is a pure legal issue: whether the Secretary has enforcement discretion under the Mine Act to remove POV notices. He does.

A. Plaintiff's claims under the APA are Unreviewable.

Under the APA, courts cannot review an "agency action [that] is committed to agency discretion by law." 5 U.S.C. § 701(a)(1)-(2). An action is committed to agency discretion when "the statute is drawn so that a court would have no meaningful standard against which to judge the agency's exercise of discretion." *Heckler v. Chaney*, 470 U.S. 821, 830 (1985). "In determining whether a meaningful standard for reviewing agency discretion exists, courts consider the particular language and overall structure of the statute in question, as well as the nature of the administrative action at issue." *Speed Mining, Inc. v. Fed. Mine Safety & Health Review Comm'n*, 528 F.3d 310, 317 (4th Cir. 2008).

The Fourth Circuit has already recognized in a similar context that "there are no manageable standards in the Mine Act that enable [courts] to review the Secretary's discretionary exercise of [his] enforcement authority." *Id.* at 311. In *Speed Mining*, an owner of a mine contended that the Secretary lacked the authority to cite owners for violations of the Mine Act committed by their independent contractors, arguing that only the independent contractor should have been cited. *Id.* at 314. The court first addressed the Mine Act's language, which provided that if the Secretary "believes that an operator . . . has violated [the Mine Act]," the Secretary shall "issue a citation to the operator." 30 U.S.C. § 814(a) (2000). But because that provision gave the Secretary "no direction as to which operator or operators to cite" for a mine with multiple operators, the court concluded that the statute's language did not provide a manageable standard to apply to the Secretary's discretionary enforcement decision of who to cite for a particular violation. *Speed Mining*, 528 F.3d at 317.

The Fourth Circuit next examined the nature of the administrative action at issue—enforcement discretion—and determined that only "further support[ed] [its] conclusion that the Secretary's actions are unreviewable." *Id.* at 318. The court began its analysis by emphasizing that this is "an area in which the courts have traditionally been most reluctant to interfere." *Id.* at 318. Enforcement discretion depends on a "'number of factors which are peculiarly within' the Secretary's expertise," such as "'determining whether a violation has occurred, . . . whether agency resources are best spent on this violation another, whether the agency is likely to succeed if it acts, [and] whether a particular enforcement action [] best fits the agency's overall policies.'" *Id.* (quoting *Heckler*, 470 U.S. at 831). The court recognized that the Secretary is "far better equipped than the courts to balance [competing] factors and determine its enforcement priorities." *Id.* at 18-19. It further likened enforcement discretion to prosecutorial discretion, which is an area which "[c]ourts have long held . . . is 'particularly ill-suited to judicial review," because both require the balancing of numerous, complicated factors. *Id.* (quoting *Wayte v. United States*, 470 U.S. 598, 607 (1985)). The Fourth Circuit thus reasoned that although "the Commission plays a vital role in ensuring that the Secretary's enforcement actions are supported by fact and consistent with the Mine Act's text, it does not have the authority to second-guess the Secretary's policy-based choice of defendant." *Id.* at 319. Given the discretionary nature of the Secretary's enforcement decisions, and the lack of a meaningful standard to review such decisions, the Fourth Circuit held that such decisions were "committed to agency discretion by law, and therefore, unreviewable" under the APA or otherwise.[5] *Id.* (internal quotation marks omitted).

As in *Speed Mining*, the Mine Act here provides no meaningful standard for review of the Secretary's decision of whether to issue, maintain, or to terminate a POV notice apart from one mandatory circumstance in which the Secretary must terminate such notices. The Mine Act's POV provision states that, "[i]f an operator has a pattern of violations of mandatory health or safety standards in the coal or other mine which are of such nature as could have significantly and substantially contributed to the cause and effect of coal or other mine health or safety hazards, he shall be given written notice that such pattern exists." 30 U.S.C. § 814(e)(1). Yet just as in *Speed Mining* the Act provided no guidance on who to cite for a particular violation, the Act here provides no guidance on what constitutes a "pattern," leaving such decisions up to the enforcement discretion of the Secretary who "shall make such rules as he deems necessary to establish criteria for determining when a pattern of violations of mandatory health or safety standards exists." 30 U.S.C. § 814(e)(4). And the Secretary's rule for determining when a pattern exists merely sets forth balancing factors that guide his discretionary decision. *See* 30 C.F.R. §104.2 (listing eight different criteria MSHA will consider in determining whether

---

[5] The court noted that, although the APA does not apply to the "making of any order, notice, or decision made pursuant to [the Mine Act], or to any proceeding for the review thereof," 30 U.S.C. § 956, the principles of unreviewability pursuant to the "committed to agency discretion" doctrine nonetheless apply. *Id.* at 316 n.*.

to issue a notice including "mitigating circumstances"). These factors, like those at issue in *Speed Mining*, require the Secretary to engage in a "complicated balancing of a number of factors which are peculiarly within" the Secretary's expertise. *Speed Mining*, 528 F.3d at 318.

To show that the Secretary's discretion is subject to judicial review, the Union cites section 814(e)(3) of the Act and its mirroring regulation. That provision requires that "[i]f, upon an inspection of the entire coal or other mine, an authorized representative of the Secretary finds no violations of mandatory health or safety standards that could significantly and substantially contribute to the cause and effect of a coal or other mine health and safety hazard, the pattern of violations that resulted in the issuance of a [POV] . . . notice shall be deemed to be terminated." *See* 30 U.S.C. § 814(e)(3); *see also* 30 C.F.R. 104.4.[6] But this provision of the Act does not set forth any meaningful standard to review the Secretary's decisions to terminate POV notices under circumstances apart a mine receiving a clean inspection. Simply put, it provides a mandatory condition under which the Secretary *must* terminate a POV notice (after a mine receives a clean inspection free from S&S violations), but it does not provide the *exclusive* means for terminating such a notice. *See, e.g.*, "Shall", Black's Law Dictionary (defining "shall" as generally "imperative or mandatory," but also recognizing that it may merely denote a permissive "may" depending on the context, and that as against the Government it must be construed as merely permissive unless another intent is manifest), *available at* https://thelawdictionary.org/shall/; *see also* Scalia, Reading Law, at 114 (citing *Railroad Co. v. Hecht*, 95 U.S. 168, 170 (1877) (the same)).

Absent from the provision is any word of exclusion, such as "only." *See* Scalia at 93-100. To read the Act as foreclosing the Secretary from exercising his enforcement discretion to terminate such notices in other circumstances would contradict its plain language. Congress is well aware of how to connote

[6] MSHA's implementing regulation for termination of POV Notices, 30 C.F.R. § 104.4, mirrors the provisions of 30 U.S.C. § 814e(3). Like its statutory counterpart, the regulation sets forth circumstances under which the Secretary must terminate a POV notice. The same analysis set forth in this section thus also applies to the mirroring regulation.

exclusivity and used the word "only" and the phrase "shall only" elsewhere in the Act to connote exclusivity 29 times. *See generally* Federal Mine Safety & Health Act of 1977 (Mine Act), Pub. L. No. 95-164 (Nov. 9, 1977), as amended 30 U.S.C. §§ 801 *et seq.* In enacting subsection 814(e)(3), Congress sought to ensure that mines would not be placed on POV indefinitely, and provided a bright line at which such notices are terminated automatically. But there is nothing in the language of this provision, nor in any other provision of the Mine Act, that limits the Secretary from otherwise rescinding a mine's POV notice if he deems it warranted. In short, apart from requiring the termination of a notice when a mine receives a clean inspection, Congress has committed the enforcement of POV notices entirely to the Secretary's discretion, with no meaningful standards by which to judge his discretion.

This result is confirmed by the nature of the administrative action at issue: enforcement discretion. As the Fourth Circuit stated, "It is difficult to think of a category of administrative action less prone to review than the Secretary's exercise of [his] exclusive authority to enforce the Mine Act." *Speed Mining*, 528 F.3d at 318. As with the decision of who to cite for a violation, *see id.*, the decision of whether to issue or to terminate a POV notice is likewise subject to the Secretary's discretion because it involves the complicated balancing of numerous factors based on the Secretary's expertise, *see* 30 C.F.R. §104.2 (listing eight different criteria MSHA will consider in deciding whether to issue a notice including "mitigating circumstances"). Indeed, the federal courts have repeatedly emphasized the Secretary's enforcement discretion in a number of similar contexts. *E.g.*, *Sec'y of Labor v. Twentymile Coal Co.*, 456 F.3d 151, 157 (D.C. Cir. 2006) ("Under the Act, the Secretary's charging discretion is as uncabined as that of a United States Attorney under the Criminal Code."); *Brock v. Cathedral Bluffs Shale Oil Co.*, 796 F.2d 533, 538 (D.C. Cir. 1986) ("The language of the guidelines is replete with indications that the Secretary retained his discretion to cite production-operators as he s[ees] fit."). The Commission has likewise recognized MSHA's discretion in designating a violation as "significant and substantial," *Sec'y of Labor, MSHA v. Mechanicsville Concrete, Inc.*, 18 FMSHRC 877 (1996), in vacating a violation, *Sec'y of Labor,*

MSHA v. RBK Construction, Inc., 15 FMSHRC 2099, 2101 (1993), and in deciding whether to place a mine in POV status, *Sec'y of Labor, MSHA v. Brody Mining*, 36 FMSHRC 2027, 2048 (2014).

Moreover, it would make little sense for Congress to give MSHA the discretionary authority to decline to issue a POV notice, but then to deny MSHA the discretion to remove such a notice when it deems it appropriate given its enforcement priorities. Just as a prosecutor may choose to indict, but later opt to dismiss the indictment, the balancing of the competing factors that may have resulted in an initial POV notice may change over time, *see* 30 C.F.R. §104.2, and the Secretary has the enforcement discretion under the Mine Act to remove the notice as he sees fit outside of one mandatory requirement for automatic termination. *See* 30 U.S.C. § 814(e)(3); *Speed Mining*, 528 F.3d at 318 (recognizing the similarities between the Secretary's enforcement discretion under the Mine Act and prosecutorial discretion). In fact, decisions *not* to enforce, such as the decision to remove the POV Notice at Affinity Mine, are "presumptively unreviewable." *See Heckler* , 470 U.S. at 832; *Speed Mining*, 528 F.3d at 318.

In sum, to give section 814(e)(3) the constrained reading Plaintiff asserts would be contrary to the notion of enforcement discretion and would ignore the provision's plain language, which contains no words of exclusion that would limit the Secretary's enforcement discretion. The enforcement decision to remove a POV notice is "committed to agency discretion by law and therefore unreviewable." *Speed Mining*, 528 F.3d at 317 (internal quotation marks omitted).

B. Even assuming reviewability, the Union's APA claims should nevertheless be dismissed.

Even if the decision of whether to remove a POV notice is not committed to agency discretion by law, the Union's APA claims would still fail because the Union has failed to allege a violation of the Mine Act, much less that MSHA acted in an arbitrary and capricious manner.

The Secretary has the discretion to terminate POV notices, and the only limit on that discretion is that if upon inspection of an entire mine an inspector "finds no violations of mandatory health or safety standards that could significantly and substantially contribute to the cause and effect of a coal or other mine health and safety hazard, the pattern of violations that resulted in the issuance of a [POV] . . . notice shall be deemed to be terminated." *See* 30 U.S.C. § 814(e)(3); *see also* 30 C.F.R. 104.4 (mirroring regulation). As explained above, this provision merely requires that the Secretary terminate a POV notice if a mine receives a clean inspection free from S&S violations, so that it is not stuck on the POV enforcement scheme in perpetuity, which has escalating enforcement consequences. *See Supra* Part III(A); 30 U.S.C. § 814(e)(1)-(2) & 30 C.F.R. 104.3 (listing enforcement consequences). It does not, however, preclude the Secretary from exercising his authority to terminate such notices in other circumstances apart from a clean inspection. *See Supra* Part III(A).

Here, the Union does not allege that MSHA has failed to terminate a POV notice at Affinity Mine upon a clean inspection, which *would* violate the Act. *See* 30 U.S.C. § 814(e)(1); 30 C.F.R. 104.4. Instead, the Union is alleging that MSHA's termination of a POV notice at the Mine violates this provision, and thus that MSHA is "unlawfully with[holding] . . . [e]nforcement of the POV notice," "exceed[ing] the agency's statutory authority," and acting in an "arbitrary and capricious" manner by relying on factors other than a "clean inspection" to terminate a POV notice. Compl. ¶¶ 36-42. Put differently, the Union's argument for each of its APA claims hinges on the Court adopting the Union's unduly narrow interpretation of section 814(e)(3) and its mirroring regulation, i.e., that the provision sets forth both the mandatory and the exclusive means for terminating POV notices. As noted above, that interpretation of section 814(e)(3) is contrary not only to the statute's plain language, but also the very notion of enforcement discretion. *See Supra* Part III(A). At most, Congress has placed an outer limit on the Secretary's discretion by requiring termination of a POV notice upon a mine receiving a clean inspection, thereby ensuring that mines are not stuck in the POV enforcement scheme for perpetuity, which has serious, escalating consequences, including withdrawal orders. 30 U.S.C. § 814(e)(1)-(2). But Congress has not limited the Secretary's discretion to otherwise terminate such notices apart from such circumstances—indeed, the provision contains no words of exclusion that would limit the Secretary from exercising his discretion in circumstances apart from the mine receiving a clean inspection. *See supra* Part III(A). Consequently, the Union's claims under the APA should all be dismissed because MSHA has acted in accordance with its enforcement discretion.

IV. The Union's Mandamus Claim Should Be Dismissed.

"Mandamus is a 'drastic' remedy that must be reserved for 'extraordinary situations' involving the performance of official acts or duties." *Cumberland Cty. Hosp. Sys., Inc. v. Burwell*, 816 F.3d 48, 52 (4th Cir. 2016) (quoting *Kerr v. U.S. Dist. Court for N. Dist. of Cal.*, 426 U.S. 394, 402 (1976)). "[T]o establish the conditions necessary for issuance of a writ of mandamus, the party seeking the writ must demonstrate that (1) [it] has a clear and indisputable right to the relief sought; (2) the responding party has a clear duty to do the specific act requested; (3) the act requested is an official act or duty; (4) there are no other adequate means to attain the relief [it] desires; and (5) the issuance of the writ will effect right and justice in the circumstances." *United States ex rel. Rahman v. Oncology Assoc., P.C.*, 198 F.3d 502, 511 (4th Cir. 1999) (citing *Kerr*, 426 U.S. at 403).

The Union's mandamus claim should be dismissed for several reasons. As explained in Part II, the Union has no "clear and indisputable right" to force MSHA to take any action at Affinity Mine because none of its members even work at that mine. *See* Compl. ¶¶ 34 (not identifying any members who work in Affinity Mine). For the same reason, MSHA owes no "clear duty" to the Union or its members. And even if the Union did have members at Affinity Mine, the decision to terminate a POV notice is a discretionary enforcement decision, *see supra* Part III, and is therefore not subject to mandamus because there is no "clear duty" to take any specific action. *Cf. Heckler*, 470 U.S. at 828-32 (explaining that decisions not to enforce are presumptively committed to agency discretion); *Drew v. Lawrimore*, 380 F.2d 479, 483 (4th Cir. 1967) (recognizing that mandamus should generally not "interfere with the exercise of [officials'] discretion"). Because the Union has failed to meet the first two requirements of the mandamus test, its mandamus claim must be dismissed.

Even if the Court disagrees regarding these first two requirements by finding that the Union has a "clear and indisputable right to the relief sought" and that MSHA has a "clear duty" to take the actions that the Union seeks, mandamus would still be barred because—under that scenario—the APA would provide an adequate means to attain the relief the Union desires. Although the Fourth Circuit has not directly addressed the issue, it is well-established that "the availability of judicial review for challenged agency conduct under the APA precludes review of, and issuance of mandamus for, the same conduct under § 1361." *See South Carolina v. United States*, 243 F. Supp. 3d 673, 683 (D.S.C. 2017), *aff'd*, 907 F.3d 742 (4th Cir. 2018); *see also, e.g., Callaway Golf Co. v. Kappos*, 802 F.Supp.2d 678, 690 (E.D. Va. 2011); *Syngenta Crop Prot., Inc. v. E.P.A.*, 444 F. Supp. 2d 435, 452-53 (M.D.N.C. 2006). In fact, every court of appeals to address the issue has concluded that the availability of relief under the APA forecloses the issuance of mandamus under § 1361. *See, e.g., Serrano v. U.S. Attorney Gen.*, 655 F.3d 1260, 1264 (11th Cir. 2011); *Sharkey v. Quarantillo*, 541 F.3d 75, 93 (2d Cir. 2008); *Mt. Emmons Mining Co. v. Babbitt*, 117 F.3d 1167, 1170 (10th Cir. 1997); *Stehney v. Perry*, 101 F.3d 925, 934 (3d Cir. 1996); *Seiden v. United States*, 537 F.2d 867, 870 (6th Cir. 1976); *see also Indep. Mining Co. v. Babbitt*, 105 F.3d 502, 507 n.6 (9th Cir. 1997) (questioning the applicability of a mandamus remedy where there is an APA remedy).

The Union seeks the exact same relief under the Mandamus Act as it does under section 706(1) of the APA, that MSHA be compelled to enforce the POV Notice at Affinity Mine. *Compare* Compl. ¶ 38, *with* Compl. ¶ 45. In short, the Union has—and is currently seeking—other adequate judicial remedies to obtain the same relief. Because the requested writ of mandamus would add nothing beyond the relief the Union is already seeking under the APA, the "extraordinary circumstances for which mandamus is reserved are not present." *Syngenta*, 444 F. Supp. 2d at 453 (citation omitted). For these reasons then, the Union's mandamus claim should also be dismissed.

V. The Union's Declaratory Judgment Act Claim Should also be Dismissed.

"[I]t is elementary that a federal court may properly exercise jurisdiction in a declaratory judgment proceeding when three essentials are met: (1) the complaint alleges an "actual controversy" between the parties "of sufficient immediacy and reality to warrant issuance of a declaratory judgment;" (2) the court possesses an independent basis for jurisdiction over the parties and (3) the court does not abuse its discretion in its exercise of jurisdiction." 28 U.S.C. § 2201; *Volvo Const. Equip. N. Am., Inc. v. CLM Equip. Co., Inc.*, 386 F.3d 581, 592 (4th Cir. 2004). But here the first two requirements are missing. First, as explained in Part I, there is no actual controversy because the Union cannot meet the requirements for standing as none of its members actually work in Affinity Mine. Second, because the Union lacks any viable claim under the APA or the Mandamus Act, its claim under the Declaratory Judgment Act should likewise be dismissed because there is no independent basis for jurisdiction. *See Volvo Const.*, 386 F.3d 592; *Clear Sky Car Wash. LLC v. City of Chesapeake, Va.*, 910 F.Supp.2d 861, 871 n. 8 (E.D.Va.2012), *aff'd*, 743 F.3d 438 (4th Cir. 2014) (affirming decision stating "the Court must have before it a properly pled claim over which it has an independent basis for exercising original jurisdiction before it may act pursuant to the Declaratory Judgment Act."). Indeed, the Declaratory Judgment Act provides only for a remedy, declaratory relief, not an independent cause of action. *E.g.*, *Campbell ex rel. Equity Units Holders v. Am. Int'l Grp., Inc.*, 86 F. Supp. 3d 464, 471 (E.D. Va.), *aff'd sub nom.* 616 F. App'x 74 (4th Cir. 2015) (dismissing claim for declaratory relief on the grounds that there was no independent cause of action); *Pohutsky v. Pella Corp.*, No. 2:14-MN-00001-DCN, 2015 WL 2379496, at *7 (D.S.C. May 19, 2015) (the same). Because the Union has no independent cause of action, this Court lacks jurisdiction, and its Declaratory Judgment Act claim for relief should be dismissed.

CONCLUSION

For the reasons set forth above, this action should be dismissed.

Respectfully submitted,

JOSEPH H. HUNT
Assistant Attorney General

BRAD P. ROSENBERG
Assistant Branch Director

DANIELLE W. YOUNG
/s/ Danielle W. Young
Danielle W. Young (TX Bar No. 24098649)
Trial Attorney, Federal Programs Branch
U.S. Department of Justice, Civil Division

1100 L Street, NW Room 12312
Washington, DC 20005
(202) 616-2035
Email: Danielle.Young2@usdoj.gov

/s/ Fred B. Westfall, Jr.
FRED B. WESTFALL, JR., AUSA (W.Va. Bar No. 3992)
Office of the United States Attorney for the Southern District of West Virginia
300 Virginia Street East, Room 4000
Charleston, WV 25301
(304) 345-2200
(304) 347-5443 (fax)

Counsel for Defendants

Case 5:18-cv-01478 Document 18 Filed 04/01/19 Page 1 of 15 PageID #: 201

IN THE UNITED STATES DISTRICT COURT
FOR THE SOUTHERN DISTRICT OF WEST VIRGINIA

UNITED MINE WORKERS OF AMERICA, INTERNATIONAL UNION	:	
Plaintiff,	:	
v.	:	Civil Action No. 5:18-cv-1478
DAVID G. ZATEZALO, et al.	:	
Defendants.	:	

REPLY IN SUPPORT OF DEFENDANTS' MOTION TO DISMISS

As is now clear from Plaintiff's opposition brief, the United Mine Workers of America does not have any members working at Affinity Mine. Undaunted by its total lack of connection to any of the events being challenged in this litigation, including its failure to intervene in enforcement proceedings before the Commission, the Union attempts to salvage this Court's jurisdiction by casting its challenge as focusing on agency action rather than an order of the Commission. But for the Commission's order, however, the Pattern of Violations (POV) Notice at Affinity Mine would still be in place. That makes the Commission's order the cause of any alleged harm to the Union. As such, the Union's lawsuit would have belonged in a court of appeals, if it had been filed on time. The Union's lawsuit simply does not belong in this Court.

Even if this is the correct court to be adjudicating the Union's claims, this case should still be dismissed because the Union lacks standing. Simply put, because none of its members actually work at Affinity Mine, the Union is a Plaintiff in search of a controversy. The Union nonetheless claims that the one-time settlement of the POV Notice at Affinity Mine, after the Mine had been in POV status for five years, could diminish the deterrent effect of the enforcement scheme as a whole, thus impacting Union members at other, unidentified mines. Those allegations, however, are far too speculative and remote to cross the threshold from mere possibility into plausibility. They certainly do not rise to the level of a "certainly impending" injury or demonstrate a "substantial risk" of future injury.

Finally, even if this court were to find that it has jurisdiction, this case should still be dismissed for failure to state a claim because Congress afforded the Secretary the enforcement discretion to determine whether to issue, maintain, or terminate a POV Notice. Because the Secretary acted in accordance with his discretion under the Mine Act, the Union cannot state a claim under the Administrative Procedures Act (APA), Mandamus, or Declaratory Judgment Acts.

ARGUMENT

I. Plaintiff's Collateral Attack on the Commission's Order in District Court is Barred by the Mine Act.

The Union failed to intervene in the administrative proceedings to challenge the settlement agreement between Pocahontas and the Secretary and then missed its statutory deadline to challenge the Commission's order in the appropriate circuit court under section 106(a)(1). Recognizing that it has otherwise lost its opportunity to challenge the removal of the POV Notice at Affinity Mine, the Union now tries to reframe its lawsuit as one merely about agency action that does not involve the Commission. *See* Pl.'s Opp'n to Defs.' Mot. to Dismiss (Pl.'s Opp'n), at 4-5, ECF No. 17. That attempt fails.

First, the Union argues that the Commission's order was not the actual cause of any alleged harm because the order, in the Union's view, merely made the Administrative Law Judge's finding that the POV Notice was validly issued final and unappealable. *See id.* at 5. But that characterization of the Commission's order is less than fulsome. As Defendants explained in their opening brief, the Commission's decision also dismissed Pocahontas's petition for review and implicitly recognized that the Secretary's authority to terminate a POV notice was not reviewable. *See* Defs.' Mot. to Dismiss (Defs.' Mem.), at 6-7, ECF No. 9. The Union does not dispute in its opposition that the Commission received a copy of the settlement agreement as part of Pocahontas's motion to withdraw its petition. *See* Compl. Attachs. 5-7, ECF No. 1-1. Nor does the Union dispute that the settlement agreement was expressly conditioned upon the Commission granting the dismissal of the petition. *See* Compl. at ¶ 24; *see also id.* Attach. 7, ¶¶ 4-5 (providing that Mine Safety and Health Administration (MSHA) would only terminate the POV Notice if the Commission issued "a full, clear, and unambiguous dismissal of the Proceeding" and that without such a dismissal the agreement would be "null and void"). Thus, but for the Commission's order, the settlement agreement would not have gone into effect, the POV Notice would likely still be in place at Affinity Mine today,[1] and the Union would not be "adversely affected or aggrieved by an order of the Commission." 30 U.S.C. § 816(a)(1); *See also* Defs.' Mem. at 6-7.

The Union next complains that, because it was not a party to the administrative proceedings, it had no reason to know it should intervene in those proceedings or challenge the Commission's order. *See* Pl.'s Opp'n at 5-6. If true, that argument would prove Defendants' point that the Union is a mere bystander that has no real connection to Affinity Mine because none of its members work there. *See id.* at 11. In fact, however, the Union admits it had actual notice: Although Pocahontas, without the Secretary's concurrence, initially filed the settlement agreement and its motion to withdraw its petition under seal, that seal was later removed and the filings were made public. *See id.* at 5.

The Union next argues that because the Commission had no authority to review the Secretary's discretionary removal of the POV Notice by settlement, the Commission is not the cause of the Union's alleged injury. *See id.* at 5-6. Just because the Commission implicitly recognized that it lacked authority to review the termination of the POV Notice does not mean that the Union could not have

[1] It is possible that the POV notice could have been terminated in other ways, of course. For example, the Commission could have invalidated it. It nevertheless remains the case that but for the Commission's decision, the settlement agreement that terminated the POV Notice at Affinity Mine would not have gone into effect.

challenged that jurisdictional determination either before the Commission or in circuit court. Indeed, the dissenting Commissioner raised this very point, arguing that the Commission did have jurisdiction and "should not assent" to the settlement agreement by dismissing Pocahontas's petition. *See* Compl. Attach. 6 at 8. Simply put, the Union is challenging the settlement of an enforcement proceeding, but the Mine Act "establishes that the Commission and the courts of appeals have exclusive jurisdiction over challenges to agency enforcement proceedings . . . ." *Thunder Basin Coal Co. v. Reich,* 510 U.S. 200, 208–09 (1994). It bears repeating that but for the Commission's order, the settlement agreement would not have gone into effect and the POV Notice would still be in place at Affinity Mine. If the Union wanted to challenge the Commission's order, it should have intervened in the proceedings to try to prevent the settlement or it could have attempted to bring suit in circuit court challenging the Commission's decision, which, as the dissenting panel member pointed out, "assent[ed]" to the settlement agreement. *See* Compl. Attach. 6 at 8. But it cannot now collaterally attack the administrative proceedings in district court. *See* 30 U.S.C. § 816(a)(1).

II. Plaintiff's Alleged Diminished Deterrence Injury is Too Speculative to Confer Standing.

The Union has failed to identify any member who could establish the elements of Article III standing. The Union admits as much, but argues that it need not show that any member has suffered an injury in fact because it is relying on the narrow exception set forth in *Summers v. Earth Island Inst.*, 555 U.S. 488, 498-99 (2009), that an association need not identify a member who has suffered an injury when all of its members are harmed by the same action. *See* Pl.'s Opp'n at 7-8.

First, completely absent from the Union's complaint is an allegation that "all" of its members are being harmed; instead, the complaint merely states that "Plaintiff, its members, and other miners" are being harmed. *See* Compl. ¶ 34. Second, even if the Union had pleaded differently, the *Summers* exception only applies when an association has identified a concrete injury that applies to each or all of its members. *E.g.*, *NAACP v. State of Ala. ex rel. Patterson*, 357 U.S. 449, 465 (1958) (showing that all organization members suffered identified harm from release of membership lists). By contrast, where an organization makes only a "terse allegation" that all of its members are being harmed "without specific mention of any individual member's injury[,]" that allegation "surely stops short of the line between possibility and plausibility, *for purposes of the limited 'all members' exception to the Summers identification requirement*."[2] *S. Walk at Broadlands Homeowner's Ass'n, Inc. v. OpenBand at Broadlands, LLC*, 713 F.3d 175, 185 (4th Cir. 2013) (internal citations omitted) (emphasis added). For example, in *Southern Walk*, the court addressed whether an exclusive broadband arrangement was harming all of the homeowner's association's members. *Id.* The court reasoned that there was "no indication" that *every* association member desired different broadband services and thus concluded that the *Summers* exception did not apply. *Id.* In so holding, the court recognized that even when a substantial number of an association's members suffers the same harm, that does not excuse the requirement that the association either identify a specific member's harm or clearly identify a specific concrete injury that applies to *all* of its members under the *Summers* exception. *See id.* at 184-85.

Like the association in *Southern Walk*, the Union here has made only a terse allegation that all of its members are being harmed by the settlement agreement. *See* Compl. ¶ 34. And, as in *Southern Walk*, the allegations in the complaint provide "no indication" that *each* of the Union's tens of thousands of members is facing an imminent injury of being rendered less safe as a result of the removal of the POV Notice at Affinity Mine (where they do not even work).[3] In fact, it is not possible that *all* of the Union's members could be harmed as the Union's own website shows that its "diverse"

---

[2] The Union argues in a footnote that the Fourth Circuit did not address the *Summers* exception in *Southern Walk*, but as clearly set forth in this quote, the Fourth Circuit did address the issue.

[3] In fact, given that none of the mineworkers at Affinity Mine have challenged the removal of the POV Notice, it seems unlikely that every member of the Union, none of whom works at Affinity Mine, is nevertheless suffering a concrete injury.

membership includes many individuals outside of the mining industry who could not possibly be affected by the removal of the POV Notice at Affinity Mine, such as "public employees," "health care workers," and the "Navajo Nation". *See* United Mine Workers of America, About, http://umwa.org/about/.[4] In short then, without a "specific mention of any individual member's injury[,]" Plaintiff's conclusory allegation "surely stops short of the line between possibility and plausibility, for purposes of the limited 'all members' exception to the *Summers* identification requirement." *S. Walk*, 713 F.3d at 185 (internal citation omitted).

The problem with the applicability of the *Summers* exception here highlights an even more fundamental problem with the Union's standing argument: the Union has failed to allege an actual or imminent injury. The Union says otherwise, claiming—for the first time—that because this case involves a future injury, it merely needs to allege that Defendants' actions in removing the POV Notice at Affinity Mine "creates a 'substantial risk of harm.'"[5] Pl.'s Opp'n at 8-9. In support of this position, the Union cites *Kenny v. Wilson*, 885 F.3d 280, 287 (4th Cir. 2018). But that case is both inapposite and taken out of context.

In *Kenny*, the Fourth Circuit was confronted with the issue of whether student–members of an organization, "all of whom ha[d] previously been charged under one of the two statutes" prohibiting certain expressive conduct, faced a "substantial risk" of "future arrest if, while on or around the grounds of a school, their actions are interpreted to fall under any of the broad terms of the statutes." 885 F.3d at 286-87. The court noted that under the governing case law involving future

---

[4] At the motion to dismiss stage, "[a] court may take judicial notice of information publicly announced on a party's web site, so long as the web site's authenticity is not in dispute and 'it is capable of accurate and ready determination.'" *Jeandron v. Bd. of Regents of Univ. Sys. of Maryland*, 510 F. App'x 223, 227 (4th Cir. 2013) (quoting Fed. R. Evid. 201(b)).

[5] Nowhere in the Union's complaint does the word "risk" or "future injury" appear, instead it makes pure conclusory allegations that it has been injured without any supporting factual allegations. *See, e.g.*, Compl. ¶ 34.

arrest there were two ways to show a "substantial risk" of injury: by establishing "an intention to engage in a course of conduct arguably affected with a constitutional interest, but proscribed by a statute, and there exists a credible threat of prosecution thereunder[,]" or by making a "sufficient showing of self-censorship, which occurs when a claimant is chilled from exercising his right to free expression." *Id.* at 288 (citation omitted). Obviously, neither of these constitutional criteria are applicable here.

More instructive is the Fourth Circuit's decision in *Beck v. McDonald*, which addressed whether a data breach of plaintiffs' personal information held by the Veterans Affairs was sufficient (1) to create a "certainly impending" threat of identity theft or (2) "substantial risk" that identify theft would occur, thereby "prompt[ing] a party to reasonably incur costs to mitigate or avoid that harm." 848 F.3d 262, 275-76 (4th Cir.), *cert. denied sub nom. Beck v. Shulkin*, 137 S. Ct. 2307 (2017). The Fourth Circuit first rejected plaintiffs' argument that because the laptop containing plaintiffs' data was stolen, the threat of identity theft was certainly impending, reasoning that the conclusion plaintiffs would suffer identity theft rested on the assumption that the thief stole the laptop for the personal information it contained and that the thief would select plaintiffs' information instead of thousands of others' information to engage in identity theft. *Id.* at 275. The court recognized that this "attenuated chain of possibilities" based on the "actions by third parties independent of the defendants" was insufficient to establish a certainly impending injury—even if there was an "objectively reasonable likelihood" of injury. *Id.* at 268, 275-76 (quoting *Clapper v. Amnesty Int'l USA*, 133 S. Ct. 1138, 1147-48 (2013)). The court also rejected plaintiffs' argument that plaintiffs had established a "substantial risk" of injury, holding that neither the 33% increase in likelihood of identity theft, nor the defendant's decision to pay for credit monitoring, indicated a substantial risk, even if the plaintiffs had taken affirmative steps to mitigate the harm themselves. *Id.* at 276. Finally, the court noted that the more time that lapses without a report from plaintiffs of an actual injury, the alleged "threatened injuries become more and more speculative." *Id.* at 275.

As in *Beck*, the Union's harm rests on an "attenuated chain of possibilities." It depends on a one-time settlement between Pocahontas and the Secretary regarding the POV Notice at Affinity Mine, after the Mine had been on POV status for five years, "undermin[ing] the POV . . . deterrent effect[,]" which will in turn cause third-party mine operators at mines *other than* Affinity Mine to "no longer [be] deterred from unlawful action," thus "decreasing safety in the nation's mines" and creating an "injur[y] in fact." Compl. ¶ 34. As in *Beck*, when the threatened injury is dependent on the actions of third parties (here, mine operators at other mines) independent from Defendants, the alleged harm is too speculative to constitute a certainly impending injury. It is, at best, unlikely that mine operators at other mines where the Union's members work will start violating the Mine Act to the extent they would be put on POV status, based on the remote possibility of a settlement agreement several years later after hundreds of withdrawal orders likely affecting production are issued. This is especially true given MSHA's undisputed continued commitment to "maintain[ing] the Department's existing and highly effective enforcement ability" through the POV scheme. *See* Compl. Attach. 9 at 2-3. For the same reason then, the Union's allegations do not rise to the level of a "substantial risk" of injury: There is no substantial risk that *all* of the Union's members will be rendered less safe as a result of a one-time settlement at a mine where none of the Union's members actually work. *See* Pl.'s Opp'n at 11 (admitting it has no members at Affinity Mine). And the fact that the Union has not identified any increase in safety hazards at other mines where its members have been working the past seven months since the settlement agreement took effect at Affinity Mine underscores that the Union has no real interest at stake. *See Beck*, 848 F.3d at 275.

Despite the lack of connection between the Union's members and Affinity Mine, the Union nevertheless argues that its allegations establish the plausibility of its alleged injury. *See* Pl.'s Opp'n at

10. In support, the Union cites injury data prior to the issuance of the POV Rule six years ago. *Id.* at 10-11. True enough that prior to the POV Rule, mines across the country were significantly less safe, but that data is not relevant here because it shows nothing about the post-settlement safety conditions at mines during the past seven months. The Secretary has not removed the entire POV scheme; he merely exercised his discretion as part of a settlement agreement to remove the POV Notice at one mine, which had significantly improved its safety rating, to ensure the continued success of the POV enforcement scheme and avoid an adverse ruling from the Commission. Compl. Attach. 9 at 2-3. In fact, the Secretary continues to vigorously defend the POV enforcement scheme in other litigation. *See Ohio Coal Ass'n et al. v. Sec'y of Labor et al.*, 2:14-cv-02646 (S.D. Ohio). Tellingly, the Union has not made a single factual allegation about post-settlement safety conditions at mines across the country; 2018 was actually the second safest year on record in terms of fatalities. U.S. Dep't of Labor, *U.S. Mining Fatalities in 2018 Were Second Lowest on Record* (Jan. 5, 2019), https://www.msha.gov/news-media/press-releases/2019/01/09/us-mining-fatalities-2018-were-second-lowest-record.

In a last-ditch effort to bolster its standing argument the Union argues that, "[i]f the UMWA lacks standing, then no party exists which could bring this case." Pl.'s Opp'n at 11 n.9. That argument is a non-starter: As the Supreme Court has repeatedly held, "the assumption that if [plaintiffs] have no standing to sue, no one would have standing, is not a reason to find standing." *Clapper*, 568 U.S. at 420 (citing cases). In any event, the Union misses the mark because the mineworkers who actually work at Affinity Mine *would* have standing to sue if they could identify an injury-in-fact as to them; tellingly, none chose to do so. And while it is possible that the Union could have standing if a POV notice was removed at a mine where its members worked, the Secretary has not removed any other POV notices by settlement. The fact that the Union has to search for a case involving a mine where none of its members work further undercuts its injury argument because it shows that the POV scheme has retained its enforcement strength.[6]

III. The Union has failed to State a Claim under the APA because the Decision to Remove a POV Notice is a Discretionary Enforcement Decision of the Secretary.

The Union argues that its APA claims are reviewable. It points to the statutory language to show that there is a clear standard for determining when a POV notice must be terminated, but that provision merely states the following:

> If, upon an inspection of the entire coal or other mine, an authorized representative of the Secretary finds no violations of mandatory health or safety standards that could significantly and substantially contribute to the cause and effect of a coal or other mine health and safety hazard, the pattern of violations that resulted in the issuance of a notice under paragraph (1) shall be deemed to be terminated . . . .

30 U.S.C. § 814(e)(3). Contrary to the Union's unduly narrow reading that the statute only permits the termination of a POV notice if there is a clean inspection, *see* Pl.'s Opp'n at 13-19, this provision merely sets forth a *sufficient* condition under which a POV notice must be terminated; it does not set forth the exclusive means, that is, a necessary condition for termination. *See, e.g.*, *Twp. of Tinicum v. U.S. Dep't of Transp.*, 582 F.3d 482, 489 (3d Cir. 2009) (collecting cases explaining the difference between "if" sufficient conditional statements and "only if" necessary conditional statements).

The Union's handwashing analogy, *see* Pl.'s Opp'n at 15-16 n.12, is instructive here when properly reframed to an "if" conditional statement like the provision at issue here (rather than a necessary conditional statement containing words of exclusion such as "only if" or "if and only if"). *See Tinicum*, 582 F.3d at 489. The termination provision is similar to a sign in a restaurant that says: "If

---

[6] Although the Union notes that the Defendants did not raise the issue of prudential standing, *see* Pl.'s Opp'n at 6 n.4, there is no need for the Court to reach this issue, because the Union cannot meet the requirements for Article III standing. *Doe v. Virginia Dep't of State Police*, 713 F.3d 745, 753 (4th Cir. 2013) (recognizing that when a plaintiff is "unable to meet the requirements for Article III standing . . . [the court] need not engage in prudential standing analysis.").

employees use the restroom, then they must wash their hands." Such a sign clearly sets forth a sufficient condition (using the restroom) under which employees *must* wash their hands. Yet it does not prevent employees from washing their hands under other circumstances apart from using the restroom—after all, using the restroom is not a necessary condition for handwashing. Employees are free to wash their hands if their hands get greasy, if they handle money, etc. The same is true here: Like the handwashing sign, the statutory provision merely states a sufficient condition (a clean inspection) for the termination of a POV notice. But it does not set forth any necessary conditions, nor does it make the converse true (i.e., that if the POV notice is terminated then there must have been a clean inspection).[7]

At most then, section 814(e)(3) sets forth only one limited standard by which to judge the Secretary's discretion: if there is a clean inspection then the Secretary must terminate the POV notice. But there is no allegation here that the Secretary failed to remove a POV notice after a clean inspection, which *would* violate the Act. And there are no other standards set forth in the statute or its implementing regulations to guide the Secretary's decision to terminate POV notices in other circumstances. *Speed Mining, Inc. v. Fed. Mine Safety & Health Review Comm'n*, 528 F.3d 310, 317 (4th Cir. 2008). Although the Union claims that Defendants' plain reading of the statute would give the

[7] The Union has committed a logical fallacy known as "affirming the consequent." The Union assumes because the statute essentially says, "If there's a clean inspection, then the POV notice is terminated" that the converse is true, i.e., "That if the POV notice is terminated, then there must have been a clean inspection." But that is not correct, only the contrapositive is necessarily true, and different antecedents can lead to the same consequent. *See, e.g.*, *In re Stewart Foods, Inc.*, 64 F.3d 141, 145 n.3 (4th Cir. 1995) (explaining the logical fallacy of "affirming the consequent"); *Indem. Ins. Co. of N. Am. v. W & T Offshore, Inc.*, 756 F.3d 347, 355 n.5 (5th Cir. 2014) (same); *Gilliam v. Nevada Power Co.*, 488 F.3d 1189, 1196-97 n.7 (9th Cir. 2007) (same); *United Tel. Co. of Carolinas v. FCC*, 559 F.2d 720, 726 (D.C. Cir. 1977) (same); *Zen42 LLC v. Washington & Lee Univ.*, No. 6:17-CV-00053, 2017 WL 4532580, at *3 n. 2 (W.D. Va. Oct. 10, 2017); *see also* Wikipedia, https://en.wikipedia.org/wiki/Affirming_the_consequent.

Secretary unfettered discretion, the real issue is whether the Secretary has the same discretion to remove a POV notice as he does to issue it in the first place. He does.

Further, the Union fails entirely to address the second prong of the test for reviewability—the nature of the administrative action at issue. *Id.* at 318. As set forth in Defendants' Memorandum, the nature of the administrative action at issue is enforcement discretion, an area long held to be ill prone to judicial review. *See* Defs.' Mem. at 15-16. The Union apparently concedes that the statute gives the Secretary the enforcement discretion to determine whether to issue a POV notice in the first place, but nevertheless argues that the administrative action at issue here, removal of the notice, does not allow for enforcement discretion. *See* Pl.'s Opp'n at 16. That argument, as explained above, is inconsistent with the plain language of the statutory text, and it is also incompatible with the notion of enforcement discretion. It would make little sense for Congress to permit the Secretary the discretion to determine that a POV notice is not warranted in the first instance, yet deny him the discretion to terminate a POV notice once issued. *See* Defs.' Mem. at 15-16. After all, the careful calculations that warranted the issuance of a POV notice may change over time. *Id.* (citing 30 C.F.R. § 104.2 (listing eight different criteria MSHA will consider in determining whether to issue a notice including "mitigating circumstances")). Sensibly, Congress gave the Secretary the discretion to determine whether to issue, maintain, or terminate a POV notice, and the only limit on that discretion is the safe harbor provision of section 814(e)(3), which protects mine operators by requiring termination of a POV notice after a clean inspection. In sum, both the provision's plain language and the nature of the administrative action at issue make clear that the enforcement decision to remove a POV notice is "committed to agency discretion by law, and therefore unreviewable." *Speed Mining*, 528 F.3d at 317.

Even if the decision of whether to remove a POV notice is not committed to agency discretion by law, the Union's APA claims would still fail. All of the Union's APA claims hinge on the Court adopting the Union's unduly narrow interpretation of section 814(e)(3) and its mirroring regulation, i.e., that the provision sets forth a necessary condition for terminating POV notices. *See* Compl. ¶¶ 36-42. But as Defendants explained above, the only action by the Secretary that would violate that section is if the Secretary *failed to remove* a POV notice after a mine received a clean inspection. There is no allegation of such a failure here, accordingly, there is no violation of the Mine Act, and the Union's APA claims must be dismissed.

IV. The Union's Claims for Relief Under the Mandamus Statute and the Declaratory Judgment Act Should Also Be Dismissed.

The Union has not met its burden to establish that it has a claim under the Mandamus Statute or the Declaratory Judgment Act. As Defendants explained in their memorandum, *see* Defs.' Mem. at 18-19, the Union has failed to state a claim for mandamus relief. To begin with, the Union is not a real party in interest in this matter; it did not even attempt to participate in the underlying administrative proceedings. *See* Pl.'s Opp'n at 5. The Union is a third party looking for violations at mines where none of its members even work. *See* Compl. ¶ 34 (not identifying any members who work at Affinity Mine); Pl.'s Opp'n at 11 (admitting none of it members work at Affinity Mine). Consequently, the Defendants owe no "clear duty" to the Union, nor does the Union have "a clear and indisputable right to the relief sought" as it has no real connection to Defendants' discretionary enforcement actions at Affinity Mine. *See South Carolina v. United States*, 907 F.3d 742, 754 (4th Cir. 2018) (citation omitted).

An even more fundamental problem is that the Union seeks the exact same relief under the Mandamus Statute as it does under the APA. The Fourth Circuit recently affirmed that eligibility for relief under the APA's "§ 706(1) [], in turn, preclude[s] an award of mandamus relief."[8] *Id.* at 755. Although the Union cites three older cases from courts outside of this circuit, none of those decisions are binding on this Court and they are all contrary to the well-established rule that mandamus is an extraordinary remedy that is available only when "'no other adequate means to attain the relief sought" exists. *Id.* at 754 (quoting *Kerr v. U.S. Dist. Court for N. Dist. of Cal.*, 426 U.S. 394, 403 (1976)). This Court should follow the Fourth Circuit's recent decision in *South Carolina* and dismiss the Union's claim for mandamus relief.

The Union's claim for additional relief under the Declaratory Judgment Act must likewise be dismissed. To recap, the Union cannot meet the first two requirements for declaratory judgment to issue. *See* Defs.' Mem. at 19-20. There is no "actual controversy" because the Union lacks standing. *See id.*; *see also supra* Part II. And there is no independent basis for this court to exercise jurisdiction over the claim for relief under the Declaratory Judgment Act because the Union's APA and mandamus claims should be dismissed. *See* Defs.' Mem. at 19-20; *see also supra* Parts III-IV. Moreover, the Act is not an independent cause of action, but instead is only an additional form of relief. *See* Defs.' Mem. at 20. For these reasons, the Union's claim for additional relief under the Declaratory Judgment Act should also be dismissed. *See* Defs.' Mem. at 19-20.

CONCLUSION

The Court should dismiss this lawsuit.

Respectfully submitted,

JOSEPH H. HUNT
Assistant Attorney General
BRAD P. ROSENBERG
Assistant Branch Director

DANIELLE W. YOUNG
/s/ Danielle W. Young
Danielle W. Young (TX Bar No. 24098649)
Trial Attorney, Federal Programs Branch
U.S. Department of Justice, Civil Division
1100 L Street, NW Room 12312
Washington, DC 20005
(202) 616-2035
Email: Danielle.Young2@usdoj.gov

/s/ Fred B. Westfall, Jr.
FRED B. WESTFALL, JR., AUSA (W.Va. Bar No. 3992)
Office of the United States Attorney for the Southern District of West Virginia
300 Virginia Street East, Room 4000
Charleston, WV 25301
(304) 345-2200
(304) 347-5443 (fax)

Counsel for Defendants

[8] Defendants' memorandum incorrectly stated that the Fourth Circuit had not yet addressed the issue, even though Defendants had quoted the underlying district court decision and noted the Fourth Circuit's affirmance of it.

Mine Safety and Health Administration: https://www.govinfo.gov/content/pkg/CPRT-116HPRT40937/pdf/CPRT-116HPRT40937.pdf

[Questions submitted for the record and their responses follow:]

**COMMITTEE ON
EDUCATION AND LABOR**

U.S. HOUSE OF REPRESENTATIVES
2176 RAYBURN HOUSE OFFICE BUILDING
WASHINGTON, DC 20515-6100

August 13, 2019

Ms. Cindy S. Brown Barnes
Director
Education, Workforce and Income Security (EWIS)
Government Accountability Office
441 G Street, NW
Washington, DC 20548

Dear Ms. Brown Barnes:

I would like to thank you for testifying at the June 20, 2019, Subcommittee on Workforce Protections hearing entitled *"Breathless and Betrayed: What is MSHA Doing to Protect Miners from the Resurgence of Black Lung Disease?"*

Please find enclosed additional questions submitted by Committee members following the hearing. Please provide a written response no later than Tuesday, August 20, 2019, for inclusion in the official hearing record. Your responses should be sent to Jordan Barab of the Committee staff. He can be contacted at 202-225-3725 should you have any questions.

I appreciate your time and continued contribution to the work of the Committee.

Sincerely,

ROBERT C. "BOBBY" SCOTT
Chairman

Committee on Education and Labor
Workforce Protections Subcommittee Hearing
"Breathless and Betrayed: What is MSHA Doing to Protect Miners from the Resurgence of Black Lung Disease?"
Thursday, June 20, 2019
10:15 a.m.

Representative Alma Adams (D-NC)

- What should the Department of Labor do to ensure that self-insured coal operators have enough assets committed as collateral in the event there is a bankruptcy?

- Should Congress consider rescinding the option for coal mine operators to self-insure for their black lung liability? What are the pros and cons of this option?

COMMITTEE ON
EDUCATION AND LABOR
U.S. HOUSE OF REPRESENTATIVES
2176 RAYBURN HOUSE OFFICE BUILDING
WASHINGTON, DC 20515-6100

August 13, 2019

Mr. Robert Cohen, MD, FCCP
Clinical Professor
Environmental and Occupational Health Sciences
University of Illinois
School of Public Health, 1068 SPHPI, MC-923
1603 W. Taylor Street
Chicago, Illinois 60612

Dear Professor Cohen:

I would like to thank you for testifying at the June 20, 2019, Subcommittee on Workforce Protections hearing entitled *"Breathless and Betrayed: What is MSHA Doing to Protect Miners from the Resurgence of Black Lung Disease?"*

Please find enclosed additional questions submitted by Committee members following the hearing. Please provide a written response no later than Tuesday, August 20, 2019, for inclusion in the official hearing record. Your responses should be sent to Jordan Barab of the Committee staff. He can be contacted at 202-225-3725 should you have any questions.

I appreciate your time and continued contribution to the work of the Committee.

Sincerely,

ROBERT C. "BOBBY" SCOTT
Chairman

Committee on Education and Labor
Workforce Protections Subcommittee Hearing
"Breathless and Betrayed: What is MSHA Doing to Protect Miners from the Resurgence of Black Lung Disease?"
Thursday, June 20, 2019
10:15 a.m.

<u>Representative Alma Adams (D-NC)</u>

- If MSHA were to require the use of end-of-shift silica monitoring equipment in all underground coal mines and such information was posted in the mine, what effect would that likely have on worker exposure, assuming the mine operators did not game the collection of silica monitoring results? How could mines respond to that information? What changes could they make if they identified high exposures at the end of a shift?

COMMITTEE ON
EDUCATION AND LABOR
U.S. HOUSE OF REPRESENTATIVES
2176 RAYBURN HOUSE OFFICE BUILDING
WASHINGTON, DC 20515-6100

August 13, 2019

Mr. Gary Hairston
Vice President
Fayette County Black Lung Association
214 Maplewood Lane
Beckley, WV 25801

Dear Mr. Hairston:

I would like to thank you for testifying at the June 20, 2019, Subcommittee on Workforce Protections hearing entitled *"Breathless and Betrayed: What is MSHA Doing to Protect Miners from the Resurgence of Black Lung Disease?"*

Please find enclosed additional questions submitted by Committee members following the hearing. Please provide a written response no later than Tuesday, August 20, 2019, for inclusion in the official hearing record. Your responses should be sent to Jordan Barab of the Committee staff. He can be contacted at 202-225-3725 should you have any questions.

I appreciate your time and continued contribution to the work of the Committee.

Sincerely,

ROBERT C. "BOBBY" SCOTT
Chairman

Enclosure

Committee on Education and Labor
Workforce Protections Subcommittee Hearing
"Breathless and Betrayed: What is MSHA Doing to Protect Miners from the Resurgence of Black Lung Disease?"
Thursday, June 20, 2019
10:15 a.m.

Representative Alma Adams (D-NC)

- What will be the effect on miners if the group of state attorneys general and this Administration succeed in their quest to completely invalidate the Affordable Care Act through the Courts (which includes the Byrd Amendments)?

COMMITTEE ON
EDUCATION AND LABOR
U.S. HOUSE OF REPRESENTATIVES
2176 RAYBURN HOUSE OFFICE BUILDING
WASHINGTON, DC 20515-6100

August 13, 2019

Mr. John Howard, MD
Director
National Institute for Occupational Safety and Health
Patriots Plaza 1
395 E Street, SW, Suite 9200
Washington, DC 20201

Dear Dr. Howard:

I would like to thank you for testifying at the June 20, 2019, Subcommittee on Workforce Protections hearing entitled *"Breathless and Betrayed: What is MSHA Doing to Protect Miners from the Resurgence of Black Lung Disease?"*

Please find enclosed additional questions submitted by Committee members following the hearing. Please provide a written response no later than Tuesday, August 20, 2019, for inclusion in the official hearing record. Your responses should be sent to Jordan Barab of the Committee staff. He can be contacted at 202-225-3725 should you have any questions.

I appreciate your time and continued contribution to the work of the Committee.

Sincerely,

ROBERT C. "BOBBY" SCOTT
Chairman

Committee on Education and Labor
Workforce Protections Subcommittee Hearing
"Breathless and Betrayed: What is MSHA Doing to Protect Miners from the Resurgence of Black Lung Disease?"
Wednesday, June 20, 2019
10:15 a.m.

Representative Alma Adams (D-NC)

- Your testimony notes several reasons that the newly developed end-of-shift sampling technology is not yet appropriate to be used as an enforcement tool, but you state that the technology can be used "to assess the efficacy of a control technology for a continuous miner section, and to identify occupations and tasks characterized by high concentrations of quartz."
    - Is new technology ready to be used for those functions today?
    - Is there any reason this technology cannot be used by all mine operators to sample miners with potential silica exposure and to record and share this information with miners, their union, MSHA and NIOSH as a way to identify the levels of silica exposure—even though it cannot be used for enforcement?
- Can the information gathered then be used to determine whether engineering controls are being used adequately to control silica dust, and what improvements need to be made on the next shift?

COMMITTEE ON
EDUCATION AND LABOR
U.S. HOUSE OF REPRESENTATIVES
2176 RAYBURN HOUSE OFFICE BUILDING
WASHINGTON, DC 20515-6100

August 13, 2019

Mr. Cecil Roberts
President
United Mine Workers of America (UMWA)
18354 Quantico Gateway Drive, Suite 200
Triangle, VA 22172

Dear Mr. Roberts:

I would like to thank you for testifying at the June 20, 2019, Subcommittee on Workforce Protections hearing entitled *"Breathless and Betrayed: What is MSHA Doing to Protect Miners from the Resurgence of Black Lung Disease?"*

Please find enclosed additional questions submitted by Committee members following the hearing. Please provide a written response no later than Tuesday, August 20, 2019, for inclusion in the official hearing record. Your responses should be sent to Jordan Barab of the Committee staff. He can be contacted at 202-225-3725 should you have any questions.

I appreciate your time and continued contribution to the work of the Committee.

Sincerely,

ROBERT C. "BOBBY" SCOTT
Chairman

Committee on Education and Labor
Workforce Protections Subcommittee Hearing
"Breathless and Betrayed: What is MSHA Doing to Protect Miners from the Resurgence of Black Lung Disease?"
Wednesday, June 20, 2019
10:15 a.m.

Representative Alma Adams (D-NC)

- MSHA's FY 2020 budget proposes the merger of metal and non-metal mining divisions. What is your view regarding this merger and its effect on miners' safety?

- Mr. Zatezalo's testimony states that as part of the merger of the two divisions, MSHA "identified 90 mines where it made sense to train a coal inspector to inspect a metal/nonmetal mine, or vice versa." His testimony states MSHA is providing "up to 56 hours of classroom training for those inspectors, plus up to 24 hours on-the-job training with a seasoned inspector or manager." How long does it take to train an underground coal mine inspector? Is "up to 56 hours" and 24 hours on-the-job training that you are now requiring enough for miners to be assured that an MSHA inspector who inspects metal/non-metal mines is competent in all facets of underground coal mines?

- Did MSHA consult the UMWA before making this proposal?

- What is MSHA's ultimate objective in this merger?

- Would you support a requirement for MSHA to delay this action until the Government Accountability Office can conduct a study on the effects of this merger on mine safety?

COMMITTEE ON
EDUCATION AND LABOR
U.S. HOUSE OF REPRESENTATIVES
2176 RAYBURN HOUSE OFFICE BUILDING
WASHINGTON, DC 20515-6100

August 13, 2019

Mr. Bruce Watzman
8219 Varenna Drive
Sarasota, FL 34231

Dear Mr. Watzman:

I would like to thank you for testifying at the June 20, 2019, Subcommittee on Workforce Protections hearing entitled *"Breathless and Betrayed: What is MSHA Doing to Protect Miners from the Resurgence of Black Lung Disease?"*

Please find enclosed additional questions submitted by Committee members following the hearing. Please provide a written response no later than Tuesday, August 20, 2019, for inclusion in the official hearing record. Your responses should be sent to Jordan Barab of the Committee staff. He can be contacted at 202-225-3725 should you have any questions.

I appreciate your time and continued contribution to the work of the Committee.

Sincerely,

ROBERT C. "BOBBY" SCOTT
Chairman

Enclosure

Committee on Education and Labor
Workforce Protections Subcommittee Hearing
"Breathless and Betrayed: What is MSHA Doing to Protect Miners from the Resurgence of Black Lung Disease?"
Thursday, June 20, 2019
10:15 a.m.

Representative Alma Adams (D-NC)

- Mr. Watzman, who paid for your travel to this hearing?

COMMITTEE ON EDUCATION
AND LABOR
U.S. HOUSE OF REPRESENTATIVES
2176 RAYBURN HOUSE OFFICE BUILDING
WASHINGTON, DC 20515-6100

August 13, 2019

Mr. David Zatezalo
Assistant Secretary
Mine Safety and Health Administration
U.S. Department of Labor
201 12th Street S.
Arlington, VA 22202

Dear Assistant Secretary Zatezalo:

I would like to thank you for testifying at the June 20, 2019, Subcommittee on Workforce Protections hearing entitled "*Breathless and Betrayed: What is MSHA Doing to Protect Miners from the Resurgence of Black Lung Disease?"*

Please find enclosed additional questions submitted by Committee members following the hearing. Please provide a written response no later Tuesday, September 3, 2019, for inclusion in the official hearing record. Your responses should be sent to Jordan Barab of the Committee staff. He can be contacted at 202-225-3725 should you have any questions.

I appreciate your time and continued contribution to the work of the Committee.

Sincerely,

ROBERT C. "BOBBY" SCOTT
Chairman

Committee on Education and Labor
Workforce Protections Subcommittee Hearing
"Breathless and Betrayed: What is MSHA Doing to Protect Miners from the Resurgence of Black Lung Disease?"
Thursday, June 20, 2019
10:15 a.m.

<u>Representative Alma Adams (D-NC)</u>

SILICA SAMPLING

- Your testimony stated there was a high compliance rate in 2018 for quartz (silica) samples. It indicated that nearly 99% of all samples recorded readings below the current Permissible Exposure Limit (PEL) of 100 micrograms per cubic meter (ug/m3), and only 1.2% exceeded the PEL.

    - Was this 99% compliance rate exclusively for underground coal mines?
    - What percentage of quartz (silica) samples taken in underground coal mines in 2018 exceeded 50 ug/m3 (which is the standard recommended by NIOSH and adopted by OSHA)?
- MSHA conducts quartz (silica) sampling for underground coal mines 4 times per year (one per quarter). Is this frequency sufficient to assure the sampling is representative of routine miner exposure to quartz (silica)? If not, what frequency of sampling is necessary to be representative of typical miner exposure?
- How many valid consecutive coal mine dust samples are required each quarter under MSHA's respirable dust rule?
- Your testimony indicated that MSHA reviewed mines with quartz (silica) samples which exceeded the PEL. In the past 12 months, has MSHA placed any mines on the reduced standard due to excessive levels of quartz (silica) in the coal mine dust? Please provide a list of mines placed on the reduced standard and the new standard set for each mine?
- In 2018, how many operating coal mines were on a reduced standard due to excessive levels of quartz (silica)?
- What occupations and areas does MSHA sample when it is sampling for quartz (silica)?
    - When MSHA takes samples for quartz, does this include sampling miners engaged in slope mining, where miners are driving through rock to reach coal seams?
    - When MSHA takes samples for quartz (silica), does it sample miners engaged in cutting overcasts through rock bearing strata?
    - When MSHA takes samples for quartz (silica), does it include miners engaged in development work? If so, what percentage of such miners are sampled?
    -

SILICA STANDARD

- You testified that MSHA is required by the Administrative Procedures Act to issue a Request For Information for a silica standard instead of going straight to a proposal. Can you cite where in the APA or any specific mine safety legislation that MSHA is required to start the regulatory process with an RFI?
- Do you believe as a matter of policy or a matter of occupational health that two agencies within the Department of Labor should have radically different permissible exposure limits for a carcinogen?

END OF SHIFT SAMPLING TECHNOLOGY

- Does MSHA support the issuance of a new Standard to require mine operators to use recently developed technology to sample and report miners' exposure to quartz (silica) for surveillance and engineering purposes at the end of every shift?
    - If not, why not?
    - what criteria would the new technology have to meet in order for MSHA to support or require its use for end-of-shift sampling?
    - Does MSHA have a process underway to move toward use of this technology? If not, why not?
    - How many mines are currently using end-of-shift monitoring for silica with the new technology developed by NIOSH?

ADJUSTED MINING CONDITIONS

- Do you have evidence that some mine operators adjust mining conditions when MSHA inspectors conduct monitoring activities, including monitoring for quartz (silica)?
    - Please provide any evidence MSHA has collected over the past five years where some mine operators have adjusted mining conditions when MSHA inspectors conduct monitoring activities, including monitoring for quartz (silica).

AIRSTREAM HELMETS

- You indicated in testimony that air stream helmets are no longer produced. Was CONSOL funding development of these?
- What is the name of the company that produced the air stream helmets? When did this stop? Who purchased these air stream helmets?
- Are there activities in a coal mine where air stream helmets cannot be used?
- Do air stream helmets impair the ability to communicate with other miners?

UNPAID FINES

- Your testimony discussed unpaid civil penalties for Violations of the Federal Mine Safety and Health Act. It stated "By not paying their fines, scofflaws gain a competitive advantage within the industry and create unsafe conditions. If not pursued, scofflaws foster an impression that violators can ignore fines with impunity."
    - Has MSHA recovered overdue fines by issuing citations for non-payment under Section 104(a) of the Mine Act and, when payment is not made, issued withdrawal orders under Section 104(b)?
    - How many overdue fines have been collected this way under the initiative launched by MSHA?
- In May 2018, the U.S. Department of Justice brought a civil action for non-payment of civil penalties exceeding $4.7 million against 23 mine operations controlled by West Virginia Governor Jim Justice and his family. These mines are operating in Virginia, West Virginia, Tennessee, Alabama, and Kentucky. Is there a reason that MSHA did not use withdrawal orders under Section 104(b) of the Mine Act to encourage the Justice mine operators to make payment on overdue fines?
- The Robert C. Byrd Mine Safety Protection Act (H.R. 1903) introduced in the 115th Congress included a provision in Section 305 which expressly authorizes MSHA to issue a withdrawal order for mines that are more than 6 months overdue on payment of a fine or penalty following issuance of a final order. This provision also authorized a payment plan and consequences for failure to abide by that plan. Would this proposed change to the Mine Act provide MSHA with a useful tool that would enable timely administrative enforcement against scofflaws without the necessity for judicial proceedings?

MERGER OF COAL AND METAL/NON-METAL DIVISIONS

- Your FY 2020 budget proposes the merger of metal and non-metal mining divisions in MSHA. Is that a sound decision? Expecting MSHA inspectors to do both jobs would seem to require a lot more training.
- How long does it take for an MSHA underground coal inspector to be fully trained?
- Can you explain how "up to" 56 hours of classroom training and "up to" 24 hours of on-the-job training will be adequate for miners to be assured that the inspector understands all of the hazards in a mine and how to correct them?
- Did you consult with the United Mineworkers about this change to MSHA?
- We can't really be sure of the effect of this merger on the safety of miners. Would you be willing to delay this action until the Government Accountability Office can conduct a study on the effects of this merger on the safety of miners?

Questions for the Record – "Breathless and Betrayed: What is MSHA Doing to Protect Miners from the Resurgence of Black Lung Disease?"
Black Lung Testimony—6/2019

What should the Department of Labor do to ensure that self-insured coal operators have enough assets committed as collateral in the event there is a bankruptcy?

Our June 20, 2019 testimony[1] stated that Trust Fund finances are being further strained by coal operator bankruptcies. Since 2014, insolvent self-insured coal mine operators transferred over $310 million in estimated black lung benefits liabilities to the Trust Fund, according to Department of Labor (DOL) data. Our preliminary analysis indicates that DOL did not regularly review self-insured coal operators so that it could adjust collateral as needed to protect the Trust Fund from bankruptcies. DOL officials said that the collateral they required from self-insured operators has been inadequate to fully cover the benefit liabilities of coal companies that have defaulted on black lung benefit payments.

In July 2019, DOL implemented new self-insurance procedures. We are evaluating DOL's new procedures, along with their corresponding internal controls. We plan to provide you a report of our evaluation in January 2020.

Should Congress consider rescinding the option for coal mine operators to self-insure for their black lung liability? What are the pros and cons of this option?

We are concerned about the solvency of the Black Lung Disability Trust Fund, and our prior work has presented options[2] for Congress to consider to improve the Fund's financial stability. Because the collateral DOL required from self-insured operators was inadequate to cover the benefit liabilities of bankrupt coal operators (as stated by DOL officials), rescinding self-insurance could begin mitigating the risk that bankruptcies have on the Trust Fund. However, if self-insurance is rescinded, the legacy cost of self-insurance will likely persist for many years. For example, if a mine operator becomes insolvent, the Trust Fund may still be responsible for paying benefits to miners covered by the legacy self-insurance of an operator, depending on the outcome of bankruptcy. This is why it is important that DOL obtain sufficient collateral before bankruptcy occurs. We are evaluating these issues and plan to provide you a report of our findings in January 2020.

---

[1] GAO, *Black Lung Benefits Program: Financing and Oversight Challenges Are Adversely Affecting the Trust Fund*, GAO-19-622T (Washington, D.C.: June 20, 2019).
[2] GAO, *Black Lung Benefits Program: Options for Improving Trust Fund Finances*, GAO-18-351 (Washington D.C: May 30, 2018).

Response to Additional Questions by Robert Cohen, MD, FCCP

Mining Education and Research Center
University of Illinois at Chicago, School of Public Health

Subcommittee on Workforce Protections
Committee on Education and Labor
U.S. House of Representatives
Breathless and Betrayed: What is MSHA Doing to Protect Miners from the Resurgence of Black Lung Disease?
June 20, 2019

Dear Chairwoman Adams,

Thank you for your question, "If MSHA were to require the use of end-of-shift silica monitoring equipment in all underground coal mines and such information was posted in the mine, what effect would that likely have on worker exposure, assuming the mine operators did not game the collection of silica monitoring results? How could mines respond to that information? What changes could they make if they identified high exposures at the end of a shift?"

I believe that this information would be extremely useful and could be used immediately by workers in the mine. If, for example, workers noted that there were high silica levels in an area of development, they could bring to bear more intense engineering controls.

1) Increase ventilation on the affected unit by the use of ventilation curtain and tubing and other modalities.
2) Increase the use of water suppression
3) Other administrative controls such as changing the pace of production or development in order to reduce the generation of dust.

These changes could be brought to bear rapidly and in time so that the subsequent shifts of miners would not be exposed to those same high levels. This would be of great value and could significantly reduce miners' exposures.

Please feel free to contact me if you have any further questions.

Sincerely,

Robert A. Cohen, MD

Committee on Education and Labor
Workforce Protections Subcommittee Hearing
"Breathless and Betrayed: What is MSHA Doing to Protect Miners from the Resurgence of Black Lung Disease?"
Thursday, June 20, 2019
10:15 a.m.

Representative Alma Adams (D-NC)

- What will be the effect on miners if the group of state attorneys general and this Administration succeed in their quest to completely invalidate the Affordable Care Act through the Courts (which includes the Byrd Amendments)?

It would be harder for the coal miner to get his black lung without the 15-year presumption. Because he would have to do all the proving and the coal companies wouldn't have to. And the widows would have to reapply for their black lung in a time when they just lost their husband. Then they will lose the money they were getting and they will have to reapply and they will have to prove that black lung helped cause their husband's death and it may take years.

Gary Hairston

Gary Hairston

10-15-19

Committee on Education and Labor
Workforce Protections Subcommittee Hearing
"Breathless and Betrayed: What is MSHA Doing to Protect Miners from the Resurgence of Black Lung Disease?"
Wednesday, June 20, 2019
10:15 a.m.

Questions for the Record

Representative Alma Adams (D-NC)

Question 1:
Your testimony notes several reasons that the newly developed end-of-shift sampling technology is not yet appropriate to be used as an enforcement tool, but you state that the technology can be used "to assess the efficacy of a control technology for a continuous miner section, and to identify occupations and tasks characterized by high concentrations of quartz."

Is new technology ready to be used for those functions today?

The National Institute for Occupational Safety and Health (NIOSH) technology has not been fully validated as a quantitative method in the field. However, preliminary field testing has shown that the NIOSH technology has utility as a semi-quantitative method that can be used as a self-assessment tool to measure relative changes in quartz concentration within a single mine. NIOSH is working with the Mine Safety and Health Administration (MSHA) to complete this field testing.

Question 2:
Is there any reason this technology cannot be used by all mine operators to sample miners with potential silica exposure and to record and share this information with miners, their union, MSHA and NIOSH as a way to identify the levels of silica exposure—even though it cannot be used for enforcement?

Until the technology has been fully validated in the field it is premature to use it to quantify levels of quartz exposure.

Question 3:

Can the information gathered then be used to determine whether engineering controls are being used adequately to control silica dust, and what improvements need to be made on the next shift?

Limited field data indicate that the method can be used to assess the effectiveness of engineering controls and changes made to those engineering controls to reduce exposure to quartz.

United Mine Workers of America

CECIL E. ROBERTS
INTERNATIONAL PRESIDENT

TELEPHONE
(703) 291-2420
FAX (703) 291-2451

UNITED MINE WORKERS HEADQUARTERS
18354 QUANTICO GATEWAY DRIVE, SUITE 200
Triangle, VA
22172-1779

August 20, 2019

Robert C. "Bobby" Scott, Chairman
Committee on Education and Labor
U.S. House of Representatives
2176 Rayburn House Office Building
Washington D.C. 20515-6100

Dear Chairman Scott:

Thank you for the questions you have submitted on behalf of Representative Adams for the record from the June 20, 2019 Hearing titled: "Breathless and Burdened". Per your request, attached are the answers for the record to those questions.

I would also like to thank you for the opportunity to testify before the committee as well as your hard work, dedication, and support. If there is anything else we can do to help, or if you have any additional questions, please feel free to contact my office at, (703) 291-2440.

Sincerely,

Cecil E. Roberts

Cecil E. Roberts

Q: MSHA's FY 2020 budget proposes the merger of metal and non-metal mining divisions. What is your view regarding this merger and its effect on miners' safety?

A: There is no need or justification for the two divisions to merge their budgets. We are forced to ask if the underlying reason is to give the Agency the ability to hide how it is allocating enforcement spending, for example, taking money from coal enforcement and using it in metal/non-metal. Miners in both types of mines deserve to know just how much money their government is spending on preserving their health and safety.

Q: Mr. Zatezalo's testimony states that as part of the merger of the two divisions, MSHA "identified 90 mines where it made sense to train a coal inspector to inspect a metal/nonmetal mine or vice versa." His testimony states MSHA is providing "up to 56 hours of classroom training for those inspectors, plus up to 24 hours on-the-job training with a seasoned inspector or manager." How long does it take to train an underground coal mine inspector? Is "up to 56 hours" and 24 hours on-the-job training that you are now requiring enough for miners to be assured that an MSHA inspector who inspects metal/non-metal mines is competent in all facets of underground coal mines?

A: There are no metal/non-metal inspectors being trained to inspect underground coal mines at this time. However, we believe MSHA intends to do so in the future.

A newly hired coal inspector is required to have 21 weeks of classroom training at the MSHA Mine Academy along with on-the-job training in between his or her classroom training. In most cases, a new inspector will receive three weeks of classroom training, then three weeks of on-the-job training, then be back in the classroom for three weeks, and so on. The overall training process takes about one year.

If MSHA were to decide in the future to cross-train some metal/non-metal inspectors so that they may inspect underground coal mines, it is our position that they would have to start from scratch due to the unique hazards associated with coal mines. The current 56 hours of classroom training and 24 hours of on-the-job training would in no way be sufficient.

Q: Did MSHA consult the UMWA before making this proposal?

A: No. We were notified, but only after a plan had been internally adopted by the Agency. We had no opportunity to provide input into the plan's development.

Q: What is MSHA's ultimate objective in this merger?

A: MSHA argues that this merger will save money administratively, but at what ultimate cost? Miners' lives are at risk every day they go to work. This merger will mean that both coal and metal/non-metal miners will suffer reductions in the health and safety protections MSHA is required to provide. This is about reducing enforcement activity and nothing else.

Metal non-metal mines can certainly be operated in a dangerous manner absent proper oversight by the Agency. However, they do not have the same inherent dangers as underground coal mines, where the entire environment is combustible and the atmosphere is toxic without constant and proper ventilation. Metal non-metal inspectors are simply not equipped to inspect coal mines, and the training MSHA proposes is woefully inadequate to make them so.

Q: Would you support a requirement for MSHA to delay this action until the Government Accountability Office can conduct a study on the effects of this merger on mine safety?

A: Yes. An assessment of how this will affect not only the Agency but more importantly the miners it is required to protect, should have been done before this plan was ever put into motion.

Bruce Watzman
8219 Varenna Drive
Sarasota, FL 34231

August 20, 2019

The Honorable Robert C. "Bobby" Scott
Chairman
Committee on Education and Labor
U.S. House of Representatives
2176 Rayburn House Office Building
Washington, D.C. 20515

Dear Mr. Chairman:

Below is my response to the Question for the Record submitted by Representative Alma Adams following my appearance before the Workforce Protections Subcommittee on June 20, 2019.

Question:

Mr. Watzman, who paid for your travel to the hearing?

Response:

My travel expenses were reimbursed by my previous employer, the National Mining Association.

Please let me know if you have any additional questions.

Sincerely,

Bruce Watzman

Responses of David G. Zatezalo, Assistant Secretary for Mine Safety and Health, U.S. Department of Labor, to Questions for the Record stemming from June 20, 2019, hearing of the Subcommittee on Workforce Protections, Committee on Education and Labor, U.S. House of Representatives

QUESTIONS SUBMITTED by Representative Alma Adams

SILICA SAMPLING

Ms. Adams: Your testimony stated there was a high compliance rate in 2018 for quartz (silica) samples. It indicated that nearly 99% of all samples recorded readings below the current Permissible Exposure Limit (PEL) of 100 micrograms per cubic meter (ug/m3), and only 1.2% exceeded the PEL.

Was this 99% compliance rate exclusively for underground coal mines?

Mr. Zatezalo. Yes, 98.9% of all underground coal mine samples were below the PEL with 1.1% above the PEL of 100 micrograms per cubic meter (μg/m3) in 2018.

Ms. Adams. What percentage of quartz samples taken in underground coal mines in 2018 exceeded 50 ug/m3 (which is the standard recommended by NIOSH and adopted by OSHA)?

Mr. Zatezalo. 2.5% of quartz samples taken in underground coal mines exceeded 50 μg/m3 for the 2018 calendar year.

Ms. Adams: MSHA conducts quartz (silica) sampling for underground coal mines 4 times per year (one per quarter).

Is this frequency sufficient to assure the sampling is representative of routine miner exposure to quartz (silica)? If not, what frequency of sampling is necessary to be representative of typical miner exposure?

Mr. Zatezalo. MSHA believes the Agency's sampling frequency for quartz, along with other protections, such as reducing miners' exposure to respirable dust, more frequent operator sampling, and expansion of medical surveillance, is sufficient to assure that the sampling is representative of miners' exposure to quartz.

Ms. Adams: How many valid consecutive coal mine dust samples are required each quarter under MSHA's respirable dust rule?

Mr. Zatezalo. For underground mechanized mining units, operators must conduct consecutive shift sampling until 15 valid representative samples are taken. The Designated Occupation (DO) must be completed first and then each Other Designated Occupation (ODO) sequentially during separate time frames. The DO is the occupation at the greatest risk of respirable dust exposure. MSHA requires an additional group of 15 for the DO when information indicates that the operator is not following the approved ventilation plan. The mine operator is also required to sample consecutive shifts until five valid representative samples are taken on each Part 90 miner (miners with evidence of pneumoconiosis) each quarter. In addition, the mine operator is also required to sample consecutive shifts until five valid representative samples are taken on each Designated Area (DA) each quarter. The DA is an area in the mine established by the mine operator in the approved ventilation plan that represent dust generation sources, *e.g.*, belt transfer points.

For surface coal mines and the surface areas of underground coal mines, the mine operator is also required to sample consecutive shifts until one valid representative sample is taken for each Designated Work Position (DWP) each quarter. The DWP is the occupation at the greatest risk of respirable dust exposure at surface coal mines. When this sample exceeds the standard the mine operator is required to sample consecutive shifts on that DWP until five valid representative samples are taken during the same quarter that are in compliance.

Ms. Adams: Your testimony indicated that MSHA reviewed mines with quartz (silica) samples which exceeded the PEL.

In the past 12 months, has MSHA placed any mines on the reduced standard due to excessive levels of quartz (silica) in the coal mine dust?

Mr. Zatezalo. MSHA places occupations and areas of the mine, not the entirety of a mine, on reduced standards based on samples with excessive levels of quartz. The attached list contains 81 mines that had occupations placed on a reduced standard during the past 12 months.

Note: Some mines may have multiple areas or occupations on a reduced standard. The attached list contains the new standard established at the mine from 6-20-2018 through 6-19-2019.

Ms. Adams: Please provide a list of mines placed on the reduced standard and the new standard set for each mine?

Mr. Zatezalo. Both lists are included in response to the previous question.

Ms. Adams: In 2018, how many operating coal mines were on a reduced standard due to excessive levels of quartz (silica)?

Mr. Zatezalo. In calendar year 2018, MSHA established a reduced standard based on excessive levels of quartz at 95 mines.

Ms. Adams: What occupations and areas does MSHA sample when it is sampling for quartz (silica)?

Mr. Zatezalo. MSHA usually samples 5 to 7 occupations on each mechanized mining unit each quarter, *e.g.*:

Designated Occupations (highest risk occupations)– such as, continuous mining machine operator, tailgate shearer operator, jack setter operator;

Other Designated Occupations (2nd highest risk occupations)–such as, roof bolter operator, shuttle car operator; and

Part 90 miners (miners with evidence of pneumoconiosis).

Ms. Adams. When MSHA takes samples for quartz, does this include sampling miners engaged in slope mining, where miners are driving through rock to reach coal seams?

Mr. Zatezalo. Yes, MSHA samples shaft and slope construction.

Ms. Adams: When MSHA takes samples for quartz (silica), does it sample miners engaged in cutting overcasts through rock bearing strata?

Mr. Zatezalo. Yes.

Ms. Adams. When MSHA takes samples for quartz (silica), does it include miners engaged in development work? If so, what percentage of such miners are sampled?

Mr. Zatezalo. MSHA's sampling program includes sampling miners engaged in development work. MSHA samples are analyzed for respirable coal mine dust and quartz. During production, which is development, all Designated Occupations, Other Designated Occupations, and Designated Work Positions are sampled. Part 90 Miners (miners with evidence of pneumoconiosis) are also sampled. The percentage of miners sampled varies depending on the number of miners present during the sampling.

SILICA STANDARD

Ms. Adams: You testified that MSHA is required by the Administrative Procedures Act to issue a Request For Information for a silica standard instead of going straight to a proposal.

Can you cite where in the APA or any specific mine safety legislation that MSHA is required to start the regulatory process with an RFI?

Mr. Zatezalo. To clarify, the APA encourages early public participation in rulemaking. Consistent with this, Agencies can publish RFIs or Advance Notices of Proposed Rulemaking (ANPRMs) in the Federal Register to request data, comments, or other information on regulatory issues before proceeding with a specific regulatory proposal. In the interest of transparency and to solicit public engagement at the earliest stage, MSHA chose to publish an RFI. Receiving stakeholders' input will help inform the Agency in making decisions and issuing a meaningful and defensible Notice of Proposed Rulemaking.

Ms. Adams: Do you believe as a matter of policy or a matter of occupational health that two agencies within the Department of Labor should have radically different permissible exposure limits for a carcinogen?

Mr. Zatezalo. No. It should be noted, however, that the basis of the comparison between OSHA and MSHA's PEL is in fact different. OSHA's PEL is lower, but its silica standards explicitly permit employers to continue performing silica-generating activities where exposures exceed the PEL, provided that the employer (1) can demonstrate that it is not feasible to reduce and maintain employee exposures to or below the PEL using engineering and work practice controls, (2) has used such controls to reduce employee exposure to the lowest feasible level, and (3) has supplemented the controls with the use of appropriate respiratory protection. *See, e.g.*, 29 CFR 29 CFR 1910.1053(f)(1). Although MSHA's PEL is higher, MSHA's standards require engineering and administrative controls sufficient to assure that miners work in environoments in which airbourne silica concentrations remain, at all times, at or below the PEL during each 8-hour shift. MSHA will issue an RFI to solicit information and data on feasible best practices to protect miners' health from exposure to quartz in respirable dust, including an examination of the PEL, potential new or developing protective technologies, and/or technical and educational assistance.

END OF SHIFT SAMPLING TECHNOLOGY

Ms. Adams: Does MSHA support the issuance of a new Standard to require mine operators to use recently developed technology to sample and report miners' exposure to quartz (silica) for surveillance and engineering purposes at the end of every shift?

If not, why not?

what criteria would the new technology have to meet in order for MSHA to support or require its use for end-of-shift sampling?

Does MSHA have a process underway to move toward use of this technology?

If not, why not?

How many mines are currently using end-of-shift monitoring for silica with the new technology developed by NIOSH?

Mr. Zatezalo. MSHA does not support at this time a new standard requiring the use of the end-of-shift monitoring technology for surveillance and engineering purposes unless and until it is shown to be scientifically sound, accurate, repeatable, and capable of producing and providing results that are defensible. MSHA is assisting the National Institute for Occupational Safety and Health (NIOSH) in field testing this technology. End-of-shift monitoring technology, including its method of measurement, needs further refinement before MSHA can support the issuance of a new standard. According to NIOSH, numerous interferences can affect the performance of this new technology. As Dr. John Howard, Director of NIOSH and Administrator of the World Trade Center Health Program at the Department of Health and Human Services, discussed at the June 20 hearing, "Although the field based prototype rapid quartz monitor or end of shift silica monitor shows promise as a self-assessment tool for exposure to quartz [in] coal mines, it is not currently ready for use as a compliance tool."

MSHA does support mines using the end-of-shift monitor for self-assessment. MSHA also supports mines with overexposure problems adding this technology to their mine ventilation plan as an engineering tool to provide mine operators with additional information. However, in order for MSHA to support or require its use for end-of-shift sampling, the new technology should be scientifically sound, accurate, repeatable, and capable of producing and providing results that are defensible. MSHA has several concerns with this recently developed technology, many of which NIOSH has already identified. One of MSHA's immediate concerns is that the tamper-resistant sample cassette traditionally used for compliance sampling is not appropriate for the analyzer. Additional testing of the compliance cassette is needed to determine if its use might affect the quartz analyses and under report exposures. Analytic accuracy depends on a uniform particle distribution on the filter, and there is currently no established uniform particle distribution for sample cassettes using backing plates. Also, the analysis and method of reporting the results may create chain of custody issues.

MSHA is currently working with NIOSH to evaluate the use of this technology, including field testing in underground coal mines. As Dr. Howard and I discussed, neither NIOSH nor MSHA believes that this technology is currently ready for use as a compliance tool. MSHA is not aware of any coal mine operators using this technology.

ADJUSTED MINING CONDITIONS

Ms. Adams: Do you have evidence that some mine operators adjust mining conditions when MSHA inspectors conduct monitoring activities, including monitoring for quartz (silica)?

Mr. Zatezalo. No.

Ms. Adams: Please provide any evidence MSHA has collected over the past five years where some mine operators have adjusted mining conditions when MSHA inspectors conduct monitoring activities, including monitoring for quartz.

Mr. Zatezalo. See response above.

AIRSTREAM HELMETS

Ms. Adams: You indicated in testimony that air stream helmets are no longer produced.

Was CONSOL funding development of these?

Mr. Zatezalo. The Airstream Helmet is a powered air purifying respirator (PAPR) helmet. RACAL Health and Safety developed the Airstream helmet and MSHA first approved it in 1979. RACAL transferred the MSHA Approvals to 3M in 1998. 3M notified its customers that they will discontinue the product by June 1, 2020. MSHA has no knowledge of the funding source for the development of the Airstream helmet.

Ms. Adams: What is the name of the company that produced the air stream helmets?

Mr. Zatezalo. RACAL Health and Safety produced and sold the first MSHA-approved Airstream helmet model AH 5.

Ms. Adams: When did this stop?

Mr. Zatezalo. RACAL transferred the MSHA Approvals to 3M effective on May 19, 1998. On June 27, 2019, 3M notified its customers they would discontinue the product by June 1, 2020.

Ms. Adams. Who purchased these air stream helmets?

Mr. Zatezalo. MSHA believes the purchasers were primarily coal mine operators.

Ms. Adams: Are there activities in a coal mine where air stream helmets cannot be used?

Mr. Zatezalo. There are activities and mines where the Airstream helmets would be difficult to use due to the helmet's size and bulk. Miners working in low coal or other confined areas may find the Airstream helmet more challenging. Miners operating equipment from an on-board cab also may have difficulty wearing the Airstream helmet. In a survey of miners who wore the RACAL Airstream helmet, MSHA learned that face shield fogging, the translucent visor support, and the temple seals impacted the miners' visibility. Temple seals also made it difficult to wear prescription glasses.

Ms. Adams: Do air stream helmets impair the ability to communicate with other miners?

Mr. Zatezalo. Any respirator covering the mouth will impair communications. Because the Airstream helmet provides positive pressure within the mask, its design allows for an opening near the wearer's mouth that facilitates verbal communication better than a half-mask or similar respirator.

UNPAID FINES

Ms. Adams: Your testimony discussed unpaid civil penalties for Violations of the Federal Mine Safety and Health Act. It stated "By not paying their fines, scofflaws gain a competitive advantage within the industry and create unsafe conditions. If not pursued, scofflaws foster an impression that violators can ignore fines with impunity."

Has MSHA recovered overdue fines by issuing citations for non-payment under Section 104(a) of the Mine Act and, when payment is not made, issued withdrawal orders under Section 104(b)?

Mr. Zatezalo. Yes. MSHA has issued 51 104(a) citations and 24 104(b) withdrawal orders.

Ms. Adams: How many overdue fines have been collected this way under the initiative launched by MSHA?

Mr. Zatezalo. MSHA has collected $3.6 million in delinquent debt under its Scofflaw Program.

Ms. Adams: In May 2018, the U.S. Department of Justice brought a civil action for non-payment of civil penalties exceeding $4.7 million against 23 mine operations controlled by West Virginia Governor Jim Justice and his family. These mines are operating in Virginia, West Virginia, Tennessee, Alabama, and Kentucky.

Is there a reason that MSHA did not use withdrawal orders under Section 104(b) of the Mine Act to encourage the Justice mine operators to make payment on overdue fines?

Mr. Zatezalo. The debt over which the Department of Justice filed in May 2019 included debt properly forwarded from MSHA to the Department of the Treasury in accordance with the law in addition to debt that MSHA had not yet forwarded. MSHA actively pursued and continues to pursue debt that falls under MSHA's Scofflaw Program at Jim Justice-controlled entities, including issuing 30-day letters (demanding payment or the establishment of a payment plan), citations, and withdrawal orders where necessary. MSHA has issued three 104(a) citations and two 104(b) withdrawal orders to mines owned by this group for non-payment of this debt. MSHA remains committed to working with the Departments of Treasury and Justice and taking action where appropriate under its Scofflaw Program to address health and safety concerns and enforce final orders of the Federal Mine Safety and Health Review Commission.

Ms. Adams: The Robert C. Byrd Mine Safety Protection Act (H.R. 1903) introduced in the 115th Congress included a provision in Section 305 which expressly authorizes MSHA to issue a withdrawal order for mines that are more than 6 months overdue on payment of a fine or penalty following issuance of a final order. This provision also authorized a payment plan and consequences for failure to abide by that plan.

Would this proposed change to the Mine Act provide MSHA with a useful tool that would enable timely administrative enforcement against scofflaws without the necessity for judicial proceedings?

Mr. Zatezalo. MSHA is currently issuing citations under Mine Act Section 104(a) and withdrawal orders under Section 104(b) to operators when they do not comply with the requirements in the demand letter and pay or enter into a payment plan.

MERGER OF COAL AND METAL/NON-METAL DIVISIONS

Ms. Adams: Your FY 2020 budget proposes the merger of metal and non-metal mining divisions in MSHA.

Is that a sound decision? Expecting MSHA inspectors to do both jobs would seem to require a lot more training.

Mr. Zatezalo. Yes, it is a sound decision. MSHA's initiative to combine the coal and metal/nonmetal enforcement programs is designed to increase efficiency by reducing the time inspectors spend in vehicles traveling to mines and increasing the time at mines improving the health and safety conditions for the miners.

Most MSHA inspectors have at least five years of experience in the mining industry before becoming inspectors. They go through extensive classroom training at the National Mine Health and Safety Academy and required on-the-job training to become Authorized Representatives (ARs). Further, inspectors are required to attend journeymen training and other specialty training courses, such as electrical, ventilation, impoundments, etc. throughout their careers.

The mines transferred as part of the merger are primarily smaller, surface mines and/or mines with lower risk profiles. Underground coal mines will continue to be inspected by underground coal inspectors. Unique metal/nonmetal mines will continue to be inspected by metal/nonmetal inspectors. That is, specialized hazards will have specialized enforcement. MSHA designed additional merger training for inspectors focusing on the differences between coal and metal/nonmetal standards and requirements, and inspectors will have additional on-the-job training at crossover mines. MSHA is also incorporating this merger training in its new and journeyman inspector courses moving forward.

Ms. Adams: How long does it take for an MSHA underground coal inspector to be fully trained?

Mr. Zatezalo. Underground coal inspectors are required to attend six training modules, which include multiple courses, at the National Mine Health and Safety Academy, spread out over approximately 18 months. Inspectors return to their field office between each module for additional on-the-job training. Generally, inspectors receive their Authorized Representative (AR) card after completing the six modules, but based on a District Manager's discretion, a trainee may be prepared to independently inspect less complicated coal mines after completing four modules. In total, it takes aproximately 1 ½ to 2 years for a new inspector to be fully trained and ready to inspect coal mines as an AR. It should be noted, however, that underground coal mines are not part of the merger and will continue to be inspected by underground coal inspectors.

Ms. Adams: Can you explain how "up to" 56 hours of classroom training and "up to" 24 hours of on-the-job training will be adequate for miners to be assured that the inspector understands all of the hazards in a mine and how to correct them?

Mr. Zatezalo. The 56 and 24 hours of training is in addition to the training that all inspectors receive as trainees and journeymen. As stated in my testimony, the mines affected by the merger are primarily surface mines, such as sand, stone, and gravel (aggregate mines), and/or are determined to be lower-risk mines. These operations have similar processes, equipment, and related hazards, regardless of commodity, and are already familiar to inspectors. Small aggregate mines and small surface coal mines consist of very few pieces of mining equipment. Most have a small crusher, a small conveyor belt system, a front-end loader, and a small truck. The additional training is targeted to focus on differences in regulations and requirements between coal and metal/nonmetal operations. In addition, consistent with our longstanding policy, if an inspector is assigned a mine where they believe that additional training is required for them to effectively inspect the mine, then we provide additional hands-on, on-the-job training for the inspector.

Ms. Adams: Did you consult with the United Mineworkers about this change to MSHA?

Mr. Zatezalo. Yes, I met with the United Mine Workers on several occasions, as well as stakeholders, industry, and state associations, to discuss the plan to combine the enforcement program areas.

Ms. Adams: We can't really be sure of the effect of this merger on the safety of miners.

Would you be willing to delay this action until the Government Accountability Office can conduct a study on the effects of this merger on the safety of miners?

Mr. Zatezalo. MSHA implemented the first phase of the merger in October 2018 and the second in July 2019. MSHA generally has received positive feedback from industry and inspectors, as well as demonstrated travel efficiencies (savings) and effectiveness as inspectors can spend more of their time at mine sites helping to improve the health and safety conditions for miners. MSHA will fully participate in any study or audit by the GAO, but does not feel it is appropriate to stop or delay this needed consolidation.

Mines Placed on Reduced Dust Standards
6/20/2018 thru 6/19/2019

	District	Mine ID	State	Mine Name	Mine Type	New Dust Standard (mg/m^3)
1	C02	3608248	PA	Shawver Operation	Surface	1.0
2	C02	3608398	PA	EPB Strip	Surface	0.9
3	C02	3608489	PA	West Spring Energy	Surface	0.3
4	C02	3609843	PA	Atlas Anthracite Coal Corporation	Facility	0.3
5	C02	3610150	PA	MAST MINE	Surface	0.2
6	C02	3610233	PA	Broad Mountain Slope	Underground	0.2
7	C02	3610252	PA	Day Mine	Surface	0.2
8	C02	3610263	PA	Gurdish Mine	Surface	0.4
9	C03	1800529	MD	Cobra No 1	Surface	1.2
10	C03	1800780	MD	Casselman Mine	Underground	0.6
11	C03	3300968	OH	Hopedale Mine	Underground	1.0
12	C03	3301925	OH	Orange Strip	Surface	0.3
13	C03	4608656	WV	Morgan Camp Mine	Underground	1.0
14	C03	4608864	WV	Tunnel Ridge Mine	Underground	1.4
15	C03	4609028	WV	Mountain View Mine	Underground	0.8
16	C03	4609546	WV	Beech Mountain Mine	Underground	1.0
17	C04	4605437	WV	American Eagle Mine	Underground	0.6
18	C04	4607491	WV	S-7 Surface Mine	Surface	0.4
19	C04	4607938	WV	Black Castle Mining Company, LLC	Surface	0.3
20	C04	4608315	WV	Brushy Eagle	Underground	0.7
21	C04	4608818	WV	Callisto Mine	Surface	0.3
22	C04	4609036	WV	Seven Pines	Surface	0.4
23	C04	4609048	WV	Slip Ridge Cedar Grove Mine	Underground	0.5
24	C04	4609070	WV	Boone North No. 2 Surface Mine	Surface	0.3
25	C04	4609092	WV	Allen Powellton Mine	Underground	0.6
26	C04	4609152	WV	Black Oak Mine	Underground	1.0
27	C04	4609212	WV	Panther Eagle Mine	Underground	0.6
28	C04	4609297	WV	Blue Creek No. 1 UG Mine	Underground	0.3
29	C04	4609538	WV	Grassy #1 Surface	Surface	0.2
30	C04	4609540	WV	Hominy #1 Surface Mine	Surface	0.3
31	C04	4609550	WV	Black Eagle	Underground	0.6
32	C05	1518050	KY	No. 2	Underground	0.5
33	C05	1519396	KY	Persimmon #1	Surface	0.6
34	C05	1519515	KY	Mine #4	Underground	0.9
35	C05	1519532	KY	Access Energy	Underground	1.3
36	C05	1519622	KY	Job 51	Surface	0.5
37	C05	1519712	KY	Cheyenne Enterprises 9E	Underground	1.2
38	C05	1519847	KY	2	Underground	0.4
39	C05	4407087	VA	D-6 North Fork	Underground	1.0
40	C05	4407160	VA	Preacher Creek Strip	Surface	0.2

(Continued)

Mines Placed on Reduced Dust Standards
6/20/2018 thru 6/19/2019

	District	Mine ID	State	Mine Name	Mine Type	New Dust Standard (mg/m^3)
41	C05	4407220	VA	D-17	Underground	0.7
42	C05	4407290	VA	Kilgore Creek	Surface	0.4
43	C05	4407326	VA	Louis Lowe Surface Mine	Surface	0.3
44	C07	1518361	KY	D-21	Underground	0.4
45	C07	1518426	KY	Mine #5	Underground	1.0
46	C07	1519419	KY	Noble Mine #2	Surface	0.6
47	C07	1519459	KY	Right Oakley Surface	Surface	0.5
48	C07	1519609	KY	Kentucky Energy LLC Job #2	Surface	0.8
49	C08	1102664	IL	Viper Mine	Underground	0.9
50	C08	1103203	IL	Mine No. 1	Underground	1.2
51	C09	0503505	CO	Deserado Mine	Underground	0.5
52	C09	0503836	CO	Foidel Creek Mine	Underground	0.7
53	C09	0504864	CO	King II	Underground	0.7
54	C09	2401950	MT	Bull Mountains Mine No 1	Underground	0.7
55	C09	2902170	NM	San Juan Mine 1	Underground	1.0
56	C09	4201566	UT	Skyline Mine #3	Underground	0.4
57	C09	4202241	UT	Lila Canyon	Underground	0.9
58	C09	4202335	UT	Castle Valley Mine #4	Underground	1.1
59	C10	1519806	KY	Poplar Grove Mine	Underground	0.6
60	C12	4601544	WV	Road Fork #51 Mine	Underground	0.7
61	C12	4606578	WV	Red Fox Surface Mine	Surface	0.4
62	C12	4608647	WV	Eckman Surface Mine	Surface	0.3
63	C12	4608663	WV	Stonecoal Branch Mine No. 2	Underground	1.3
64	C12	4608786	WV	No 57 Mine	Underground	0.4
65	C12	4608884	WV	No 58	Underground	0.6
66	C12	4609029	WV	Mountaineer II Mine	Underground	1.1
67	C12	4609217	WV	Powellton #1 Mine	Underground	1.1
68	C12	4609294	WV	Washington Mine	Underground	0.6
69	C12	4609395	WV	Dry Branch Surface Mine	Surface	0.4
70	C12	4609442	WV	Apollo Surface Mine	Surface	0.5
71	C12	4609522	WV	Road Fork # 52 Mine	Underground	0.5
72	C12	4609533	WV	Berwind Deep Mine	Underground	0.3
73	C12	4609564	WV	Elklick Surface Mine	Surface	0.4
74	C12	4609566	WV	#1 Mine	Surface	0.2
75	M3	0100851	AL	Oak Grove Mine	Underground	0.7
76	M3	0101247	AL	No 4 Mine	Underground	1.3
77	M3	0101401	AL	No 7 Mine	Underground	0.4
78	M3	0102996	AL	Jap Creek Mine	Surface	1.4
79	M3	0103172	AL	Searles Mine No. 2, 3, 4, 5, 6, 7, 8 & 9	Surface	1.1
80	M3	0103455	AL	Weller Mine	Surface	0.4

	District	Mine ID	State	Mine Name	Mine Type	New Dust Standard (mg/m^3)
81	M3	0103503	AL	Lolley Mine No. 1	Underground	0.3

If there is no further business, without objection, the committee stands adjourned.
[Whereupon, at 12:53 p.m., the subcommittee was adjourned.]

In: Black Lung Programs: MSHA, Benefits and Challenges ISBN: 978-1-53619-388-6
Editor: Ross D. Blodgett

Chapter 2

Black Lung Benefits Program: Improved Oversight of Coal Mine Operator Insurance Is Needed*

United States Government Accountability Office

Abbreviations

BRB	Benefits Review Board
DOL	U.S. Department of Labor
Treasury	U.S. Department of the Treasury
NCCI	National Council on Compensation Insurance
NIOSH	National Institute for Occupational Safety and Health
OALJ	Office of Administrative Law Judges
OWCP	Office of Workers' Compensation Programs
EIA	U.S. Energy Information Administration

Why GAO Did This Study

In May 2018, GAO reported that the Trust Fund, which pays benefits to certain coal miners, faced financial challenges. The Trust Fund has borrowed from the U.S. Treasury's general fund almost every year since 1979 to make needed expenditures.

* This is an edited, reformatted and augmented version of the United States Government Accountability Office Report to Congressional Requesters, Publication No. GAO-20-21, dated February 2020.

GAO's June 2019 testimony included preliminary observations that coal operator bankruptcies were further straining Trust Fund finances because, in some cases, benefit responsibility was transferred to the Trust Fund.

This chapter examines (1) how coal mine operator bankruptcies have affected the Trust Fund, and (2) how DOL managed coal mine operator insurance to limit financial risk to the Trust Fund. GAO identified coal operators that filed for bankruptcy from 2014 through 2016 using Bloomberg data. GAO selected these years, in part, because bankruptcies were more likely to be resolved so that their effects on the Trust Fund could be assessed. GAO analyzed information on commercially- insured and self-insured coal operators, and examined workers' compensation insurance practices in four of the nation's top five coal producing states. GAO also interviewed DOL officials, coal mine operators, and insurance company representatives, among others.

What GAO Recommends

GAO is making three recommendations to DOL to establish procedures for self-insurance renewals and coal operator appeals, and to develop a process to monitor whether commercially-insured operators maintain adequate and continuous coverage. DOL agreed with our recommendations.

What GAO Found

Coal mine operator bankruptcies have led to the transfer of about $865 million in estimated benefit responsibility to the federal government's Black Lung Disability Trust Fund (Trust Fund), according to DOL estimates. The Trust Fund pays benefits when no responsible operator is identified, or when the liable operator does not pay. GAO previously testified in June 2019 that it had identified three bankrupt, self-insured operators for which benefit responsibility was transferred to the Trust Fund. Since that time, DOL's estimate of the transferred benefit responsibility has grown—from a prior range of $313 million to $325 million to the more recent $865 million estimate provided to GAO in January 2020. According to DOL, this escalation was due, in part, to recent increases in black lung benefit award rates and higher medical treatment costs, and to an underestimate of Patriot Coal's future benefit claims.

DOL's limited oversight of coal mine operator insurance has exposed the Trust Fund to financial risk, though recent changes, if implemented effectively, can help address these risks. In overseeing self-insurance in the past, DOL did not estimate future benefit liability when setting the amount of collateral required to self-insure; regularly review operators to assess whether the required amount of collateral should change; or always take action to protect the Trust Fund by revoking an operator's ability to self-insure as appropriate. In July 2019, DOL began implementing a new self-insurance process that could help address past deficiencies in estimating collateral and regularly reviewing self-insured operators. However, DOL's new process still lacks procedures for its planned annual renewal of self-insured operators and for resolving coal operator appeals should operators dispute DOL collateral requirements. This could hinder DOL from revoking an operator's ability to self-insure should they not comply with DOL requirements. Further, for those operators that do not self-insure, DOL does not monitor them to ensure they maintain adequate and continuous commercial coverage as appropriate. As a result, the Trust Fund may in some instances assume responsibility for paying benefits that otherwise would have been paid by an insurer.

February 21, 2020

The Honorable Robert C. "Bobby" Scott
Chairman
Committee on Education and Labor
House of Representatives

The Honorable Richard E. Neal
Chairman
Committee on Ways and Means
House of Representatives

The federal government's Black Lung Disability Trust Fund (Trust Fund) finances medical and cash assistance to certain coal miners who have been totally disabled due to pneumoconiosis (also known as black lung disease).[1] Black lung benefits are generally to be paid by responsible coal mine operators. However, the Trust Fund pays benefits in certain circumstances, including in cases where no responsible mine operator can be identified or when the liable mine operator does not pay.

[1] A miner's surviving dependents can also receive compensation. Black lung is caused by breathing coal mine dust, and the severity of the disease can range from mild—with no noticeable effects on breathing—to advanced disease, which could lead to respiratory failure and death according to the Department of Health and Human Service's Centers for Disease Control, National Institute for Occupational Safety and Health. See https://www.cdc.gov/niosh/docs/2019-130/default.html.

As we reported in May 2018, the Trust Fund faces financial challenges.[2]

Its expenditures have consistently exceeded revenue and the Trust Fund has essentially borrowed with interest from the Department of the Treasury's (Treasury) general fund almost every year since 1979, which was its first complete fiscal year.[3] In fiscal year 2019, the Trust Fund borrowed about $1.9 billion to cover its expenditures, according to Department of Labor (DOL) officials.

Trust Fund revenue is primarily obtained through a tax on coal produced and sold domestically, which we refer to in this chapter as the coal tax.[4]

The coal tax rate has varied over the years. From 1986 through 2018, the coal tax rate was $1.10 per ton of underground-mined coal and $0.55 per ton of surface-mined coal, up to 4.4 percent of the sales price. In 2019, the rate of the coal tax decreased to $0.50 cents and $0.25 cents per ton of underground-mined and surface-mined coal, respectively, up to 2 percent of the sales price. In 2020, the rate of the coal tax increased to pre-2019 levels. However, it is scheduled to decrease again beginning in 2021. With less revenue from the coal tax, the Trust Fund will likely need to borrow more from Treasury's general fund, and taxpayers will ultimately be responsible for repaying this accumulating debt.

In June 2019, we reported preliminary observations that coal operator bankruptcies were further straining Trust Fund finances because, in some cases, responsibility for benefit payments was transferred from the bankrupt operator to the Trust Fund.[5] This may occur, for instance, when the amount of collateral DOL requires from a self-insured coal operator does not fully cover the operator's benefit responsibility should the operator become insolvent.

This chapter examines (1) how coal mine operator bankruptcies have affected the Trust Fund, and (2) how DOL managed coal mine operator insurance to limit financial risk to the Trust Fund. To address both objectives, we reviewed relevant federal laws, regulations, and DOL procedures. We also interviewed DOL officials, coal mine operators, and insurance company representatives. Additionally, we interviewed officials from the National Mining Association, National Council on Compensation Insurance (NCCI), National Council of Self-Insurers, and the American Academy of Actuaries, among others.

---

[2] GAO, *Black Lung Benefits Program: Options for Improving Trust Fund Finances*, GAO-18-351 (Washington D.C.: May 30, 2018).

[3] Under federal law, when necessary for the Trust Fund to make relevant expenditures, funds are appropriated to the Trust Fund as "repayable advances," and then those advances must be repaid with interest to the general fund of the Treasury. 26 U.S.C. §9501(c). For reporting purposes, we refer to this process as "borrowing" from Treasury's general fund, which is distinct from the borrowing authority provided by law to some agencies. According to the Treasury, the general fund includes assets and liabilities used to finance the daily and long-term operations of the U.S. government as a whole.

[4] The coal tax is imposed on the sale of all domestically produced coal with two exceptions: (1) lignite coal and (2) exported coal.

[5] GAO, *Black Lung Benefits Program: Financing and Oversight Challenges Are Adversely Affecting the Trust Fund*, GAO-19-622T (Washington D.C.: June 20, 2019).

To assess how coal mine operator bankruptcies affected the Trust Fund, we analyzed Bloomberg Terminal (Bloomberg) data and consulted DOL to identify coal operators that filed for bankruptcy from 2014 through 2016, and whose cases had progressed far enough such that the outcome (or likely outcome) was known. During these years, domestic coal production declined from about 1 billion tons in 2014 to about 728 million tons in 2016, which was the lowest annual production level since 1978, according to U.S. Energy Information Administration (EIA) data.[6]

Additionally, bankruptcies filed during these years were more likely to be resolved at the time we conducted our work than more recently filed bankruptcies, so their effects on the Trust Fund could be assessed.[7] We identified eight coal mine companies that filed for bankruptcy during our selected years.[8] To assess the reliability of the Bloomberg data, we interviewed Bloomberg officials and reviewed relevant system documentation. In addition, to assess the completeness of the Bloomberg data, we conducted a limited legal search for bankruptcy filings and verified our results with DOL. We determined that the data were sufficiently reliable for the purposes of this chapter. To examine how each of the eight coal mine operator bankruptcies affected the Trust Fund, we interviewed DOL officials and reviewed DOL-provided documentation. For instance, we reviewed bankruptcy settlement agreements and reorganization plans, where applicable. We did not conduct a legal analysis of the relevant bankruptcy court dockets, and relied solely on documentation DOL provided to describe these bankruptcies.

To examine how DOL managed coal mine operator insurance to limit financial risk to the Trust Fund, we analyzed data and documentation on commercially-insured and self-insured coal mine operators. Specifically, we reviewed NCCI data on the commercial workers' compensation insurance policies purchased by coal mine operators to secure their black lung benefit liability from 2016 through 2018, the most recent three complete years of data available.[9] We reviewed the data to identify, among other things, whether operators had lapses in coverage.

Specifically, we verified whether the 13 largest coal producers that were not authorized to self-insure maintained adequate and continuous commercial coverage during these years.[10] We also reviewed DOL documentation on each of the 22 coal mine operators that were self- insured at the time we conducted our work.[11] For instance, we

---

[6] EIA, *Annual Coal Report 2018* (Washington D.C.: October 2019).

[7] Bankruptcies proceedings can vary in duration. We identified coal mine operator bankruptcies that were filed from 2014 through 2016 because they were more likely to be resolved. Bankruptcies filed more recently may still be ongoing and their effects on the Trust Fund may not yet be known.

[8] Our search focused on the bankruptcies of parent operators rather than individual subsidiaries.

[9] NCCI officials said that once they transmit data to DOL it effectively becomes DOL data. Therefore, for reporting purposes, we will refer to this data as DOL data.

[10] The coal operators represented approximately 25 percent of all coal produced in 2017. See EIA, *Annual Coal Report 2017* (Washington D.C.: November 2018).

[11] The self-insured arrangements can include those that cover legacy federal black lung liabilities (e.g., formerly employed miners only). This may arise when an operator no longer actively mines coal, owns subsidiaries that no longer actively mine coal, or is using commercial insurance for its current mining operations and self-

identified the amount of collateral DOL required from these operators to self-insure and DOL's most recent reauthorization memo that documented its periodic review of these operators.

We assessed the reliability of the NCCI data in several ways. Specifically, we interviewed DOL and NCCI officials on how policy data is obtained, processed, stored, and shared; reviewed documentation including a data dictionary and users guide; reviewed DOL's procedures and error checks for validating that the NCCI data conforms to established parameters; and reviewed the data for obvious errors, outliers, or missing information and for logical connections between policy and endorsement data. We determined that the data were sufficiently reliable for the purposes of this chapter. However, we concluded that the beneficiary data we reviewed in an attempt to determine the extent to which the Trust Fund paid benefits during fiscal year 2018 on behalf of uninsured operators were not sufficiently complete and consistently recorded. Thus, we were unable to assess the effect on the Trust Fund of DOL not monitoring coal operator compliance with commercial insurance requirements. This condition and its causes are further described in the report, which form the basis for one of our recommendations.

We also examined workers' compensation insurance practices in four states—Kentucky, Pennsylvania, West Virginia, and Wyoming—to identify relevant practices that could inform DOL's administration of coal operator insurance at the federal level. Such practices may be informative because both workers' compensation and federal black lung disability payments generally support workers with conditions, such as black lung, that were contracted as a result of their employment. Workers' compensation is generally mandated by state law and employers are typically required to purchase workers' compensation insurance to secure these liabilities, or may self-insure.[12] Thus, state practices in monitoring and overseeing workers' compensation insurance may provide informative context for examining DOL's practices in overseeing federal black lung insurance.

To review state practices for monitoring and overseeing workers' compensation insurance, we interviewed state insurance commissioners and reviewed selected workers' compensation laws, regulations, and guidance in the four states we contacted. We selected Kentucky, Pennsylvania, West Virginia, and Wyoming because they were among the top five coal producing states in 2017, according to EIA data, and therefore may be most familiar with workers' compensation insurance that covers black lung. Additionally, these states provided geographic variation covering EIA's three main domestic coal producing regions: the Appalachian coal region, the Interior coal region, and the Western coal region. Kentucky is divided between EIA's Appalachian and

insurance for its past operations. Self-insured operators and their subsidiaries may use a combination of self-insurance and commercial insurance to cover their liabilities, according to DOL.

[12] National Academy of Social Insurance, *Workers' Compensation: Benefits, Costs, and Coverage* (Washington, D.C.: October 2019). Also see Congressional Research Service (CRS), *Workers' Compensation: Overview and Issues,* R44580 (Washington D.C.: Sept. 6, 2019).

Interior coal regions. These states also provided variation in terms of the options available to coal mine operators to secure their workers' compensation benefit liability. For instance, with the exception of Wyoming, all selected states allowed operators to self-insure. In Wyoming, coal mining is considered an "extra-hazardous" occupation and mine operators must purchase workers' compensation insurance from a state-provided option. In our selected states, we obtained information on, among other things, state practices for determining the amount of collateral required from coal mine operators to self-insure their workers' compensation benefit liabilities, if applicable. We also obtained information about the extent to which state officials reviewed self-insured coal mine operators to assess whether the amount of collateral they required changed based on an operator's changing financial condition.

We conducted this performance audit from May 2018 through February 2020 in accordance with generally accepted government auditing standards. Those standards require that we plan and perform the audit to obtain sufficient, appropriate evidence to provide a reasonable basis for our findings and conclusions based on our audit objectives. We believe that the evidence obtained provides a reasonable basis for our findings and conclusions based on our audit objectives.

BACKGROUND

Black lung benefit payments include both cash assistance and medical care. Maximum cash assistance payments ranged from about $670 to $1,340 per month in 2019, depending on a beneficiary's number of dependents.[13] Miners receiving cash assistance are also eligible for medical treatment of their black lung-related conditions, which may include hospital and nursing care, rehabilitation services, and reimbursement for drug and equipment expenses, according to DOL documentation. DOL estimates that the average annual cost for medical care in fiscal year 2019 was approximately $8,225 per miner.

During fiscal year 2019, about 25,700 beneficiaries received black lung benefits (see Figure 1).[14] The number of beneficiaries has decreased from about 174,000 in 1982 as a result of declining coal mining employment and an aging beneficiary population, according to DOL. Black lung beneficiaries could increase in the near term due to the rise

---

[13] Benefit rates are set by federal law, which specifies that in the case of total disability, a miner receives 37.5 percent of the monthly pay rate of a federal employee at grade GS-2, step 1. Benefit levels are increased by 50 percent if the miner has one dependent, 75 percent if the miner has two dependents, and 100 percent if the miner has three or more dependents. If state workers' compensation benefits are less than federal black lung benefits, then the federal benefits cover the difference. Social Security Disability Insurance benefits are also reduced for recipients of black lung benefits.

[14] This number excludes black lung beneficiaries whose claims were filed on or before December 31, 1973, as these awards are generally funded from Treasury's general fund, and not the Trust Fund. It also excludes beneficiaries that receive medical-benefits only.

in the occurrence of the disease in its most severe form, progressive massive fibrosis, particularly among Appalachian coal miners, according to the National Institute for Occupational Safety and Health (NIOSH).[15] NIOSH reported that coal miners in central Appalachia are disproportionately affected; as many as 1 in 5 show evidence of black lung, which is the highest level recorded in 25 years.[16] NIOSH has attributed the rise in occurrence of black lung to multiple factors, including increased exposure to silica.[17]

Black lung claims are processed by the Office of Workers' Compensation Programs within DOL. Contested claims are adjudicated by DOL's Office of Administrative Law Judges, which issues decisions that can be appealed to DOL's Benefits Review Board.[18] Claimants and mine operators may further appeal these DOL decisions to the federal courts. If an award is contested, claimants can receive interim benefits until their case is resolved, which are generally paid from the Trust Fund, according to DOL. In fiscal year 2019, about 33 percent of black lung claims were approved, according to DOL data. Final awards are either funded by mine operators—who are identified as the responsible employers of claimants—or the Trust Fund, when responsible employers cannot be identified or do not pay. Of the approximately 25,700 beneficiaries receiving black lung benefits in 2019, 13,335 were paid from the Trust Fund; 7,985 were paid by responsible mine operators; and 4,380 were receiving interim benefits, according to DOL data. DOL officials told us that the more common reasons that beneficiary claims are paid from the Trust Fund include operator insolvency and unclear employment history of miners, among other reasons (see Figure 2). The operator responsible for the payment of benefits is generally the operator that most recently employed the miner.[19]

---

[15] Recent NIOSH studies found increases in the prevalence of black lung disease among long-tenured Appalachian coal miners and have documented hundreds of miners with the most severe form of the disease, progressive massive fibrosis, receiving care at two clinics in Kentucky and Virginia. See D.J. Blackley, L.E. Reynolds, C. Short, R. Carson, E. Storey, C.N. Halldin, and A.S. Laney, "Progressive Massive Fibrosis in Coal Miners From 3 Clinics in Virginia," *Journal of the American Medical Association*, 319(5):500–501 (February 6, 2018); and D.J. Blackley, J.B. Crum, C.N. Halldin, E. Storey, and A.S. Laney, "Resurgence of Progressive Massive Fibrosis in Coal Miners — Eastern Kentucky, 2016," *Morbidity and Mortality Weekly Report*, 65:1385–1389 (December 16, 2016).

[16] David J. Blackley, Cara N. Halldin, and A. Scott Laney, "Continued Increase in Prevalence of Coal Workers' Pneumoconiosis in the United States, 1970–2017," *American Journal of Public Health* 108, no. 9 (September 1, 2018).

[17] NIOSH reported that there has been a transition in the coal industry to mine thinner coal seams, which increases a miners' potential exposure to crystalline silica. Department of Health and Human Services, *Current Intelligence Bulletin #64, Coal Mine Dust Exposures and Associated Health Outcomes: A Review of Information Published Since 1995*, NIOSH Publication No. 2011–172 (April 2011).

[18] For additional information on the black lung claim adjudication process, see GAO, *Black Lung Benefits Program: Administrative and Structural Changes Could Improve Miners' Ability to Pursue Claims*, GAO-10-7 (Washington, D.C.: Oct. 30, 2009).

[19] In cases where the operator that most recently employed the miner is no longer in business or otherwise unable to pay the claim, the responsible operator generally becomes the one that next most recently employed the miner. 20 C.F.R. § 725.495(a).

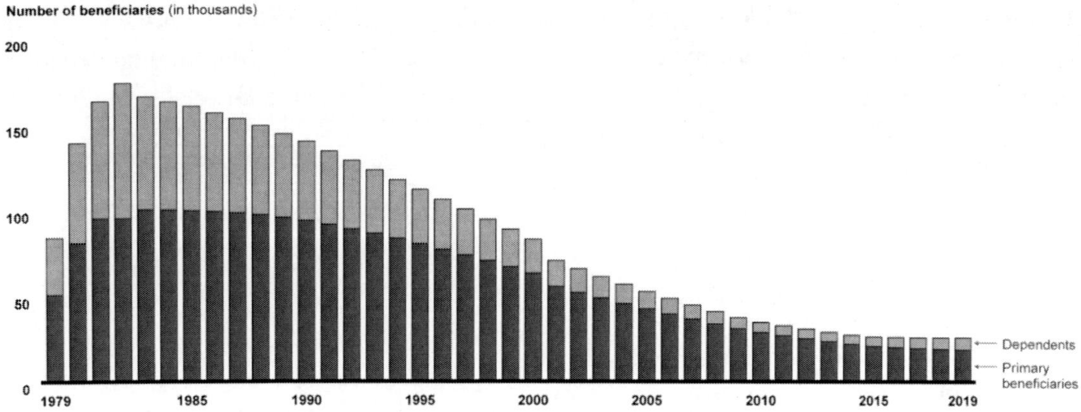

Source: GAO analysis of Department of Labor data. | GAO-20-21.

Notes: We excluded black lung beneficiaries whose claims were filed on or before December 31, 1973, as these awards are generally funded from Treasury's general fund, and not the Trust Fund. For reporting purposes, we refer to a coal miner or their spouse (if the miner is deceased) as a primary beneficiary. If there is no surviving spouse, benefits can be awarded to certain dependents, such as surviving children, which we refer to as dependent beneficiaries.

Figure 1. Black Lung Beneficiaries, Fiscal Years 1979 through 2019.

Black Lung Insurance

Federal law generally requires coal mine operators to secure their black lung benefit liability.[20] A self-insured coal mine operator assumes the financial responsibility for providing black lung benefits to its eligible employees by paying claims as they are incurred. Operators are allowed to self-insure if they meet certain DOL conditions. For instance, operators applying to self-insure must obtain collateral in the form of an indemnity bond, deposit or trust, or letter of credit in an amount deemed necessary and sufficient by DOL to secure their liability.[21]

Operators that do not self-insure are generally required to purchase coverage from commercial insurance companies, state workers' compensation insurance funds, or other entities authorized under state law to insure workers' compensation.[22] DOL regulations require commercial insurers to report each policy and federal black lung endorsement issued, canceled, or renewed in a form determined by DOL.[23] DOL accepts electronic

[20] 30 U.S.C. § 933(a). Employers that are not coal mine operators are not required to secure their liability with respect to employees engaged in the transportation of coal or in coal mine construction. 30 U.S.C. § 932(b).

[21] A letter of credit may only be used in conjunction with another acceptable form of collateral.

[22] According to DOL regulations, an endorsement affording coverage under the Federal Coal Mine Health and Safety Act of 1969, as amended, shall be attached and applicable to the standard workers' compensation and employer's liability policy prepared by NCCI. See 20 C.F.R. § 726.203(a). An endorsement, sometimes called a rider, amends a policy's coverages, terms, or conditions.

[23] 20 C.F.R. § 726.208.

reporting of this information from insurers via their respective rating bureaus.[24] DOL retains this information— insured company name, address, federal employer identification number, and policy and endorsement data—so that DOL staff can later research claims to determine which operator and insurer may be liable.

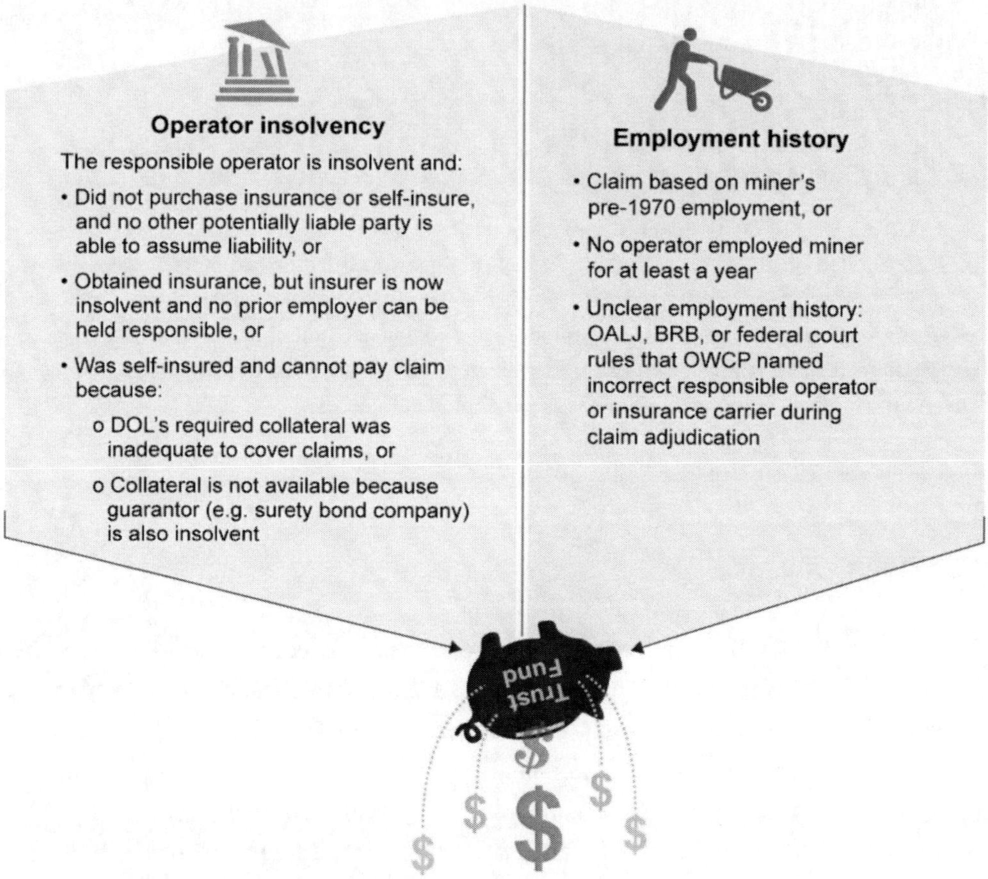

Source: Department of Labor (DOL) officials.| GAO-20-21.

Notes: This figure depicts the most common reasons why a black lung claim may be paid by the Black Lung Disability Trust Fund (Trust Fund) instead of by a responsible mine operator, according to DOL officials. It is not intended to be an exhaustive list of all reasons why a claim may be paid by the Trust Fund. The Office of Administrative Law Judges (OALJ), Benefits Review Board (BRB), and the Office of Workers' Compensation Programs (OWCP) are part of DOL.

Figure 2. Most Common Reasons Black Lung Benefits May Be Paid from the Black Lung Disability Trust Fund.

---

[24] Rating bureaus collect statistical data for the purpose of developing rating information that is filed with state insurance regulators and that is used by insurers to develop premium rates. Beginning in 2012, NCCI began providing a daily file of policy and endorsement information reported to it by insurers domiciled in states that require this type of reporting to their respective rating bureaus. In addition to the data it collects as the rating bureau for various states, NCCI collects similar information from states with independent state rating bureaus and submits it to DOL as part of the daily data file. These electronic file submissions replaced a process wherein insurers submitted paper reports to DOL for issued, renewed, and cancelled policy and endorsement transactions.

As we have noted in prior reports, insurance companies are regulated primarily by the states with state law providing state regulators with the authority and funding to regulate insurance.[25] State insurance regulation is designed to, among other things, help insurers remain solvent and able to pay claims when due. Effective insurer underwriting[26] and risk management practices—such as reinsurance[27]–serve a similar function. While insurer insolvency occurs infrequently, when it does state insurance commissioners are typically appointed as receiver and supervise the rehabilitation or liquidation of these insurers, and state guaranty funds may assume liability for paying covered claims of insolvent insurers that have liquidated.[28]

SOME SELF-INSURED OPERATOR BANKRUPTCIES SHIFTED LIABILITY TO THE TRUST FUND, BUT COMMERCIAL INSURANCE COVERAGE CAN HELP LIMIT TRUST FUND EXPOSURE

Self-Insured Operators Transferred About $865 Million in Estimated Liability to the Trust Fund, More than Double DOL's Previous Estimate

Of the eight coal mine operator bankruptcies we identified, three resulted in a transfer of estimated benefit liability from the coal operator to the Trust Fund and five did not, according to DOL. Using Bloomberg data, we identified coal mine operators that filed for bankruptcy from 2014 through 2016.[29] Figure 3 shows how many operators were self-insured or commercially-insured at the time of bankruptcy, and if responsibility for benefits was shifted from the bankrupt operator to the Trust Fund.

---

[25] GAO, International Insurance Capital Standards: Collaboration Among U.S. Stakeholders Has Improved but Could Be Enhanced, GAO-15-534 (Washington, D.C.: June 25, 2015); and Insurance Markets: Impacts of and Regulatory Response to 2007-2009 Financial Crisis, GAO-13-583 (Washington D.C.: June 27, 2013).

[26] Underwriting is the process by which an insurer examines the risks posed by a prospective policyholder to determine whether the insurer will accept the risk and, if so, establishes the appropriate rate for the coverage provided.

[27] Reinsurance is a risk-management practice that involves one insurer transferring, or "ceding," all or part of a risk to another insurer who assumes responsibility for sharing in the cost of benefits under an insurance contract.

[28] Property and casualty insurers, which provide black lung coverage, generally pay assessments to state guaranty funds based on the amount of premium written to finance the cost of resolving insolvent insurers.

[29] Our search focused on the bankruptcies of parent operators rather than individual subsidiaries. Bankruptcy proceedings can vary in duration. We identified coal mine operator bankruptcies that were filed from 2014 through 2016, in part, because they were more likely to be resolved. Bankruptcies filed more recently may still be ongoing and their effects on the Trust Fund may not yet be known.

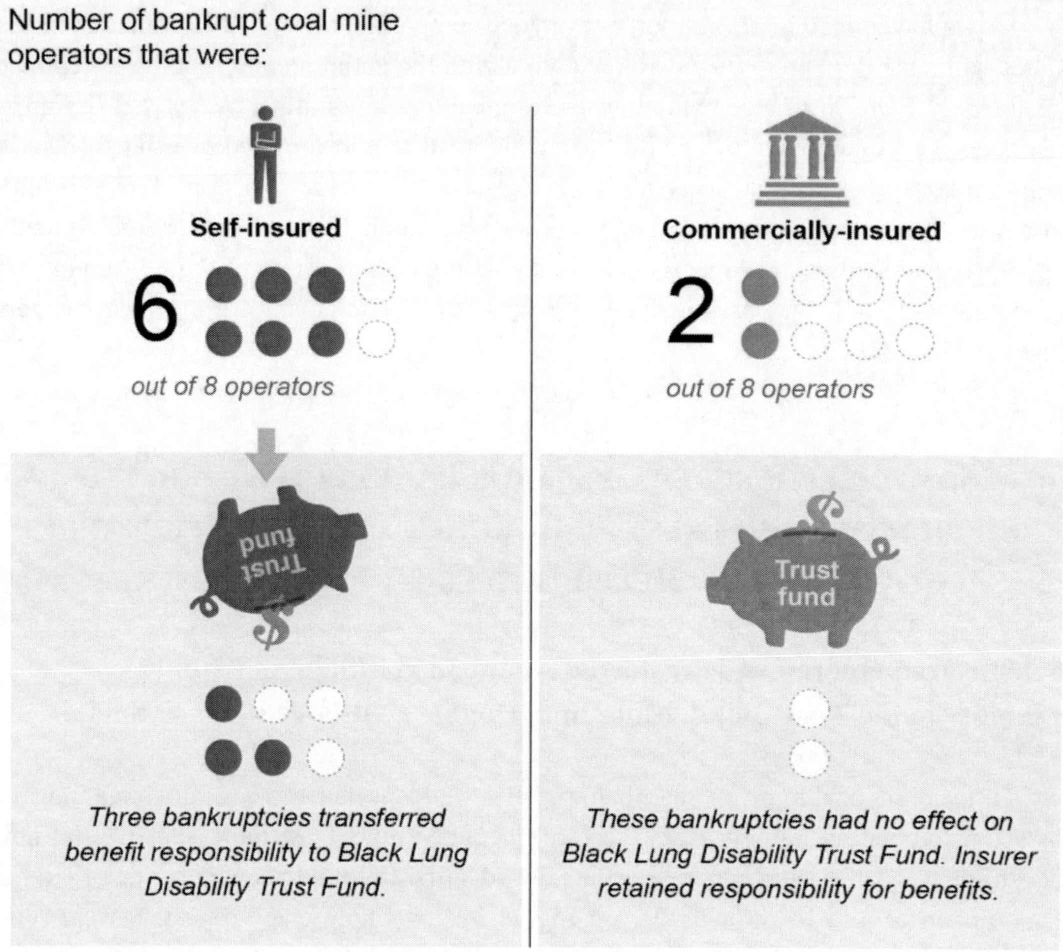

Source: Department of Labor (DOL)officials.| GAO-20-21.

Figure 3. Coal Mine Operator Bankruptcies Filed from 2014 through 2016.

Three self-insured coal mine operator bankruptcies affected the Trust Fund. Specifically, the bankruptcies of Alpha Natural Resources (Alpha), James River Coal (James River), and Patriot Coal (Patriot) resulted in a transfer of benefit liability to the Trust Fund of an estimated $865 million, according to DOL.[30] DOL officials said that the amount of collateral they required from these three operators to self-insure was inadequate to fully cover their estimated benefit liability. When this occurs, benefit liability in excess of the collateral can be transferred to the Trust Fund. For example, the collateral DOL required from Alpha was about $12 million and approximately $494 million of estimated benefit liability transferred to the Trust Fund, according to DOL's estimate (see Table 1).

[30] DOL officials said benefit liability transfers to the Trust Fund over time as claims accrue and are paid over future decades.

Table 1. Self-insured coal mine operator bankruptcies that affected the Black Lung Disability Trust Fund, filed from 2014 through 2016

Coal operator	Amount of collateral at time of bankruptcy	Estimated benefit liability transferred to the Trust Fund	Estimated number of beneficiaries for whom liability has been transferred to the Trust Fund[a]
Alpha Natural Resources	$12 million	$494 million	1,839
James River Coal	$0.4 million	$141 million	490
Patriot Coal	$15 million	$230 million	993
Total	$27.4 million	$865 million	3,322

Source: Department of Labor (DOL). | GAO-20-21.

[a] These totals include claims in active pay status as of September 2019, and estimates of newly awarded claims in fiscal year 2020 and into the future, according to DOL.

DOL estimates for how these three operator bankruptcies will affect the Trust Fund have more than doubled from what DOL had previously reported.[31] In June 2019, we reported that DOL estimated that between $313 million to $325 million in benefit liabilities would transfer to the Trust Fund as a result of these bankruptcies.[32] In January 2020, however, DOL provided updated estimates stating that $865 million in benefit liabilities would transfer to the Trust Fund as a result of these bankruptcies. According to DOL, their estimates increased to account for higher black lung benefit award rates that occurred from fiscal years 2016 through 2019; higher medical treatment cost inflation in recent years; and different discount rate assumptions.[33] Additionally, DOL's prior estimate for the Patriot bankruptcy did not account for future claims and the effect of those claims on the Trust Fund.

The three other self-insured coal mine operator bankruptcies we identified did not affect the Trust Fund. Specifically, Arch Coal, Peabody Energy, and Walter Energy were also self-insured operators, but DOL officials said that their federal black lung benefit liabilities were assumed by a reorganized company or by a purchaser, and therefore did not transfer to the Trust Fund.

DOL officials said that they take three key actions, as appropriate, to protect the financial interests of the Trust Fund during self-insured operator bankruptcies.

---

[31] Fiscal Year 2020 Congressional Budget Justification, Black Lung Disability Trust Fund.

[32] GAO-19-622T.

[33] Discount rates are interest rates used to determine the current value of estimated future benefit payments.

1. DOL officials said that they file a claim in every case with the bankruptcy court for the reimbursement of an operator's full estimated federal black lung benefit liability.[34]
2. If an operator plans to reorganize or if it is acquired by a purchaser, DOL officials said that they negotiate with the company or the purchaser, as appropriate, to help ensure benefit responsibility will be "passed through" to a reorganized operator or purchaser, rather than be discharged and become the responsibility of the Trust Fund.
3. If benefit liabilities are not "passed-through" to an operator, DOL officials said that they seek settlement agreements, whereby the Trust Fund receives an allowed general unsecured claim in an amount based on an operator's estimated benefit liability.

DOL officials said that during the bankruptcy of James River they negotiated a settlement agreement providing DOL with a general unsecured claim in an amount commensurate with its estimate of the operator's benefit liability at the time of bankruptcy. However, these officials said that given the low priority under bankruptcy law for their general unsecured claim, the payout they received was only about $400,000, which was just a small portion of the estimated benefit liability that transferred to the Trust Fund.[35]

DOL officials said that during the bankruptcy of Alpha they negotiated both a "pass through" and a settlement agreement in which certain liabilities would be transferred to the Trust Fund, while other liabilities would be retained by Alpha. DOL officials said that they received a payout from Alpha of $7.4 million, although $494 million in estimated benefit liability transferred to the Trust Fund. Further, as a condition of the agreement, DOL officials said that they agreed to let Alpha self-insure after it emerged from bankruptcy.

Since 2016, several other self-insured operators have also filed for bankruptcy, according to DOL officials, including Cambrian Coal, Cloud Peak Energy, Murray Energy, and Westmoreland Coal. DOL officials said that $17.4 million in estimated black lung benefit liability will transfer to the Trust Fund as a result of Westmoreland Coal's bankruptcy. Given the uncertainty of the bankruptcy process in terms of whether liabilities will or will not transfer to the Trust Fund, however, DOL officials said that they could not speculate on how the other bankruptcies may affect the Trust Fund.

---

[34] The claim DOL submitted for the reimbursement of Patriot's estimated black lung benefit liability at the time of its bankruptcy in May 2015 did not include future claims for which the operator may be named liable for as claims accrue and are paid over future decades, according to DOL.

[35] According to DOL officials, the settlement agreement of about $400,000 they received was in addition to the $400,000 that James River had in collateral.

State Insurance Regulation and Insurer Practices Help to Protect the Trust Fund from Assuming Responsibility for Paying Benefits of Commercially-Insured Operators

Insurance contracts or policies to secure operators' benefit liabilities are required by law to include a provision that insolvency or bankruptcy of an operator does not release the insurer from the obligation to make benefit payments.[36] As previously discussed, state insurance regulation, insurer underwriting and risk management practices, and state guaranty funds also help to protect the Trust Fund from having to assume responsibility for paying black lung benefits on behalf of bankrupt coal operators. Thus, by being commercially insured, the two operator bankruptcies we identified that filed for bankruptcy between 2014 and 2016—Energy Future Holdings and Xinergy Ltd—did not affect the Trust Fund, according to DOL (see Figure 3).

State insurance commissioners monitor the financial health of insurers, including performing periodic examination of insurer financial statements. Further, rating agencies, such as Standard & Poor's, Moody's, and AM Best, issue insurer financial strength ratings, which represent the agencies' opinions on insurers' financial strength and ability to pay policy and contract obligations. Eight of the nine insurers that issued approximately 90 percent of the workers' compensation policies with federal black lung coverage from 2016 through 2018, according to our review of DOL data,[37] had at least an "A-" financial strength rating from AM Best (with the one remaining being a state insurer that was not rated).[38]

In deciding whether to provide federal black lung coverage, insurers we interviewed said they consider an operator's historical black lung claim losses, financial condition, and mine location among other factors.[39]

However, insurance company officials identified various challenges in writing and pricing black lung coverage that produces an appropriate amount of premiums to cover expected losses. The challenges cited by these officials included the long latency period of black lung disease; changes in law regarding benefit eligibility and how the disease is defined; the ability of miners to refile claims indefinitely; and the inability of insurers and

---

[36] 30 U.S.C. § 933(b)(2).

[37] The DOL data included policies with federal black lung endorsements as reported by insurers in the 36 states, and the District of Columbia, for which NCCI collects data. The data also includes information from the Pennsylvania Compensation Rating Bureau and the Coal Mine Compensation Rating Bureau of Pennsylvania. These data did not include coverage provided to employers through the North Dakota, Ohio, Washington, or Wyoming state workers' compensation funds or the nine states other than Pennsylvania with independent rating bureaus.

[38] AM Best is a worldwide provider of insurance ratings that help the financial industry and consumers assess an insurer's financial strength, creditworthiness, and ability to honor obligations to policyholders.

[39] Insurers we interviewed also said that they inspect every coal mine before they provide coverage, including reviewing ventilation plans, dust sampling results from DOL's Mine Safety and Health Administration, and other workplace safety measures.

operators to settle claims.[40] One official noted that there is much risk and little profit in black lung coverage.

Insurance companies can use reinsurance to protect themselves from catastrophic losses that could threaten their solvency and ability to pay claims, and to reduce wide fluctuations in their annual losses. For example, workers' compensation claims can take years to fully develop after premiums have been set, which in turn can adversely affect an insurer's financial position if premiums have underestimated actual claims. Insurance company officials said that they reinsure their workers' compensation coverage, but some said that their reinsurance policies either explicitly excluded occupational disease claims, including black lung, or cover black lung but have conditions and loss thresholds that would generally result in the exclusion of such claims. However, reinsurance, even if it does not explicitly cover federal black lung claims, can help manage the risk of workers' compensation losses and losses in other lines of insurance that an insurer writes, thereby indirectly helping to ensure that the insurer can pay all types of claims, including federal black lung.

If an insurer becomes insolvent, state guaranty funds reduce the potential for the Trust Fund to assume responsibility for paying claims. States have different rules for guaranty fund benefit coverage and limits. In the states we reviewed, state guaranty funds generally pay federal black lung benefits, although there may be certain limitations on the claims they will pay.[41] For example, in West Virginia, there is no maximum claim limit that the state guaranty fund will pay on standard workers' compensation claims; but in Kentucky, a state guaranty fund official told us that, in the guaranty fund's opinion, state law limits federal black lung claims to $300,000.[42] Also, a guaranty fund could reject a federal black lung claim, which could result in the Trust Fund having to assume responsibility for paying the claim. An official from one state guaranty fund that maintained data on rejected black lung claims said that the most common reason for rejection is that claims are filed after the date set by the bankruptcy court for receiving claims. DOL officials said it is very uncommon for the Trust Fund to assume responsibility for federal black lung claims of insolvent insurers. However, DOL does not maintain data to readily determine the extent to which this actually occurs, as discussed later in this chapter.

---

[40] For example, a miner may file a claim many years after working for a mine operator because of the extended latency between exposure to dust and identification of black lung disease.

[41] Wyoming requires employers in extra-hazardous industries to obtain workers' compensation coverage from a state insurance fund rather than from a commercial insurer. Therefore, a state guaranty fund would not be applicable for these claims.

[42] The official noted, however, that no federal black lung claim handled by the association has reached the maximum per claim threshold.

DOL's Limited Oversight Has Exposed the Trust Fund to Financial Risk, and Its New Self-Insurance Process Lacks Enforcement Procedures

In overseeing coal mine operator self-insurance in the past, DOL did not estimate future benefit liability when setting collateral; regularly review operators to monitor their changing financial conditions; or always use enforcement tools available to protect the financial interests of the Trust Fund, such as by revoking an operator's ability to self-insure, if warranted. In July 2019, DOL began implementing a new self-insurance process that, if implemented effectively, should help to address some of these past deficiencies. Specifically, DOL plans to consider an operator's future benefit liability when setting collateral and to review self-insured operators more frequently. However, the new process still lacks procedures for self- insurance renewals and coal operator appeals, which could hinder DOL from taking enforcement actions to protect the Trust Fund as needed. Additionally, DOL does not monitor whether operators that do not self-insure maintain adequate and continuous commercial insurance coverage as required by law.

DOL Did Not Estimate Future Benefit Claims When Setting Collateral and Regularly Review Self-Insured Operators

Agency regulations require DOL to obtain collateral from coal mine operators applying to self-insure in an amount deemed by DOL to be necessary and sufficient to secure the payment of the operators' liability.[43]

To determine collateral amounts under the former process, agency procedures stated that DOL first assess an operator's net worth by reviewing, among other factors, the operator's audited financial statement and black lung claims information. DOL then determined the amount of collateral equal to 3, 5, or 10 years of the operator's annual black lung benefit payments made at the time of the operator's self-insurance application, depending on its net worth. Specifically, if net worth was $1 billion or greater, agency procedures stated that DOL set collateral equal to 3 years of benefit payments. If net worth ranged from $500 million to $1 billion, DOL set collateral equal to 5 years of benefit payments. If net worth ranged from $10 million to $500 million, DOL set collateral equal to 10 years of benefit payments. Agency procedures did not permit operators with net worth less than $10 million to self-insure.

[43] 20 C.F.R. § 726.105.

DOL's former process for determining collateral did not routinely consider potential future claims for which an operator could be responsible. DOL had periodically reauthorized coal operators to self-insure, by reviewing an operator's most recent audited financial statement and claims information, among other things. DOL prepared memos documenting these reviews and communicated with coal operators about whether their financial circumstances warranted increasing or decreasing their collateral. Estimating future costs based on sound actuarial practice is essential to the integrity of the insurance and the risk financing system and is key to fulfilling the promises embodied in insurance contracts, according to Actuarial Standards Board standards.[44] Additionally, in three of the four states we contacted, state insurance officials said that they used actuarial methods to assess an operator's future estimated benefit liability when considering how much collateral should be required to self- insure.[45] The remaining state, Wyoming, did not allow coal mine operators to self-insure.

Table 2 provides information on the 22 operators that were self-insured under DOL's former process, including the date of each operator's last DOL reauthorization; the amount of DOL-required collateral; and the operator's estimated black lung benefit liability, if available.

Agency regulations state that DOL may adjust the amount of collateral required from self-insured operators when experience or changed conditions so warrant,[46] but DOL did not regularly monitor these operators to reauthorize their ability to self-insure. In reviewing DOL's most recent reauthorization memos for each of the 22 self-insured operators, we found that while some of these operators had been reauthorized more recently, others had not been reauthorized by DOL in decades. One operator in particular had not been reauthorized by DOL since 1988.

DOL officials stated that from 2009 to 2012, six employees handled coal operator reauthorizations and associated work actions. Due to attrition, however, this number dropped at times to three employees, according to DOL officials. Additionally, DOL had no written procedures that specified how often reauthorizations should occur after an operator's initial 18- month reauthorization. In contrast, in two of the four states we contacted, state insurance officials were required to review self-insured employers at least annually.[47]

---

[44] Actuarial Standards Board, Actuarial Standard of Practice, No. 53, Do. No. 190: Estimating Future Costs for Prospective Property/Casualty Risk Transfer and Risk Retention.

[45] Kentucky state officials noted that they generally use the term "security" rather than "collateral". For reporting purposes, however, we use the term collateral both for DOL and for the states we contacted.

[46] 20 C.F.R. § 726.105.

[47] Wyoming does not allow coal mine operators to self-insure, as previously mentioned.

Table 2. Self-insured coal mine operator reauthorization date, collateral, and estimated benefit liability under DOL's former self-insurance process

Self-insured coal operator	Date of last reauthorization	Amount of collateral required by DOL to self-insure under its former process	Estimated black lung benefit liability
Coal operator 1	2018	$3.6 million	$18.4 million, as of 12/31/2017
Coal operator 2	2015	$1.1 million	No estimate available
Coal operator 3	2015	$2.5 million	$206 million, as of 8/03/2015
Coal operator 4	2014	$29.5 million	$109 million, as of 12/31/2016
Coal operator 5	2013	$8 million	No estimate available
Coal operator 6	2013	$1 million	No estimate available
Coal operator 7	2012	$8.4 million	$668,000, as of 1/1/1992
Coal operator 8	2012	$20.3 million	$68.4 million, as of 4/13/2016
Coal operator 9	2012	$1 million	No estimate available
Coal operator 10	2012	$15 million	No estimate available
Coal operator 11	2012	$21 million	$21.8 million, as of 12/31/2014
Coal operator 12	2011	$5.5 million	$47 million, as of 12/31/1984
Coal operator 13	2003	$0.4 million	No estimate available
Coal operator 14	2001	$0.8 million	$7.8 million, as of 01/01/1993
Coal operator 15	2000	$0.4 million	No estimate available
Coal operator 16	2000	$1.5 million	No estimate available[a]
Coal operator 17	1999	$1.4 million	No estimate available
Coal operator 18	1999	$29.2 million	No estimate available
Coal operator 19	1998	$6.9 million	$90 million, as of 12/31/2015
Coal operator 20	1997	$1.4 million	No estimate available
Coal operator 21	1994	$7.7 million	No estimate available
Coal operator 22	1988	$24.8 million	$15.1 million, as of 1/31/2005

Source: Department of Labor (DOL) data. | GAO-20-21.

[a] According to DOL officials, this operator was acquired by another self-insured operator who assumed their benefit liability.

DOL Did Not Always Use Enforcement Tools to Protect the Trust Fund

Revoking an operator's ability to self-insure, fining mine operators for operating without insurance, and placing liens on operator assets are tools DOL has available to mitigate financial losses to the Trust Fund.[48]

[48] DOL regulations state that the agency, with good cause shown, may revoke the authority of any coal operator to self-insure. 20 C.F.R. § 726.115. Additionally, the Black Lung Benefits Act states that DOL can fine mine operators up to $1,000 a day for operating without insurance. 30 U.S.C. § 933(d)(1). However, DOL officials said that, per the Inflation Adjustment Act, they can actually charge operators up to $2,924. DOL officials said the last time they fined a coal operator for operating without insurance was in 2007, and that they do not have

Based on our review of DOL documentation, however, we found instances when DOL did not use these tools to protect the Trust Fund, or was hindered from doing so because of an operator's ongoing appeal or bankruptcy.

- In September 2001, DOL required $5 million in additional collateral from James River, which would have increased its collateral from $0.4 million to $5.4 million. Although DOL did not receive the additional collateral, it did not revoke the operator's authority to self-insure, which is a potential option under agency regulations. Further, DOL had not reauthorized James River at any point from August 2001 until it filed for bankruptcy in April 2014. If DOL had revoked James River's ability to self-insure, it could have potentially prevented the Trust Fund from being responsible for claims based on a miner's employment from 2001 through 2016, when James River liquidated. Additionally, if the operator had been unable to obtain commercial insurance, DOL could have potentially fined the operator for each day it operated without insurance. Instead, DOL took no action during these years and estimated benefit liability of $141 million was shifted to the Trust Fund, according to DOL. DOL officials stated that they do not have records explaining why James River did not provide the additional collateral or why they did not revoke its authority to self-insure.
- In August 2014, DOL required $65 million in collateral from Patriot, increasing its collateral from $15 million to $80 million. Patriot appealed this decision and, in the 8 months that followed before Patriot filed for bankruptcy in May 2015, DOL did not obtain additional collateral, or revoke Patriot's ability to self-insure because the appeal was still pending. DOL officials said they would not typically revoke an operator's authority to self-insure during an ongoing appeal. As a result, DOL was hindered from using this enforcement tool.

Liens on operator assets can be an effective tool to protect the Trust Fund if an operator defaults on its benefit liabilities, but DOL officials said that they are hindered from using this tool if an operator files for bankruptcy. DOL can place a lien on a coal operator's assets under federal law if they refuse the demand to pay the black lung benefit payments for which they are liable. In the event of bankruptcy or insolvency, federal law states that the lien imposed shall be treated in the same manner as a lien for taxes due and owing to the United States under certain laws.[49] However, DOL officials said that operators rarely stop paying benefits until after they file for bankruptcy. Once a bankruptcy occurs, DOL officials said that they are generally prevented by the court from

records of whether fines were used prior to 2007. If an operator is uninsured and is a corporation, the president, secretary, and treasurer of the operator can be liable for the assessed penalties and for benefit claims for the period in which the operator was uninsured. However, DOL officials said that they do not maintain records of those instances when DOL sought to hold company officials liable.

[49] 30 U.S.C. § 934(b).

placing a lien and taking an operator's assets in lieu of payment of current and future benefit liabilities. Under bankruptcy law, DOL officials said that they have no special status over other creditors with outstanding financial claims. Instead, DOL officials said that obtaining sufficient collateral is a better way to protect the Trust Fund.

DOL Has Implemented a New Self-Insurance Process, but It Lacks Procedures to Help Ensure Enforcement Actions

In July 2019, DOL began implementing a new process for coal mine operator self-insurance that should help to address some past deficiencies if implemented effectively. Specifically, DOL is to consider an operator's future benefit liability when setting collateral and plans to more frequently review self-insured operators (see text boxes). Under the new process, DOL officials plan to assess the risk of operator bankruptcy using various financial metrics related to profitability and solvency.

DOL's New Self-Insurance Process Will Include Estimates of Future Benefit Liability

Coal mine operators applying to DOL to self-insure will be required to submit:

- a completed application;
- a certified consolidated financial statement for each of the 3 years prior to its application;
- recent black lung claims information; and
- a certified actuarial report on the operator's existing and future black lung benefit liabilities.

DOL plans to use the information submitted by coal mine operators to assess the insolvency risk of each operator using various financial metrics related to profitability and solvency. Depending on the results of their analysis, DOL plans to categorize the risk-level of each applicant as low, medium, or high. DOL will then set the amount of collateral required to self-insure by linking the operator's risk category to a corresponding percentage of the operator's actuarial estimated benefit liability. DOL policies state that they would require a high-risk operator to secure with collateral 90 percent of estimated benefit liability, a medium-risk operator to secure 45 percent, and a low-risk operator to secure 15 percent. However, in February 2020, DOL officials said they plan to revise these percentages to 100 percent, 85 percent, and 70 percent for high-risk, medium-risk, and low-risk operators, respectively.

Source: Department of Labor (DOL) officials and coal mine operator self-insurance policies. | GAO-20-21.

DOL's New Self-Insurance Process Will Require More Frequent Coal Mine Operator Reviews

Coal mine operators that are already authorized to self-insure will be required to submit:

- a self-insurance renewal application (annually);
- a financial summary (quarterly);
- a certified consolidated financial statement (annually);
- black lung claims information (annually); and
- actuarial estimate of benefit liability (to be submitted every three years).

DOL plans to use the information self-insured operators submit to update their insolvency risk analysis. If an operator's risk category changes (e.g., from low-to medium-risk), DOL plans to send a form to the operator requiring an additional amount or type of collateral. Upon receiving the completed form, and proof that the collateral has been obtained, DOL stated that they will notify the operator that its authority to self-insure has been reauthorized.

Source: Department of Labor (DOL) coal mine operator self-insurance policies. | GAO-20-21.

As a result, DOL officials said that the amount of collateral they will require from operators to self-insure going forward will be based on both an estimate of an operator's current and future black lung liability and the risk of default due to insolvency. As of October 2019, DOL officials said that most self-insured operators had submitted their application and supporting documentation and that they were reviewing this information to decide whether these operators should continue to be self-insured.[50] DOL's new self-insurance process made important changes, but overlooked other key internal control improvements that are needed to protect the financial interests of the Trust Fund. DOL's new requirements for setting collateral and for the annual and quarterly review of self-insured operators are key components of internal controls, which call for agency management to implement control activities through policy.[51]

However, DOL's new self-insurance process lacks procedures that could help to prevent past oversight deficiencies from reoccurring. Among other things, DOL's procedures do not specify (1) the duration of an operator's self-insurance authority, (2) the time frames for submitting renewal applications and supporting documentation, and (3) the conditions under which an operator's self-insurance authority would not be renewed. Without such procedures, DOL has no basis to take enforcement action should an operator not submit its self-insurance renewal application and supporting documentation.

---

[50] DOL officials said 18 of the 22 self-insured coal mine operators would be required to renew their self-insurance authority under the new process. These officials said that they did not ask Cambrian Coal, Cloud Peak Energy, or Westmoreland Coal to renew their self- insurance authority given their ongoing bankruptcies. Additionally, DOL officials said that they did not require one other operator to renew its self-insurance authority because it was acquired by a purchaser, and is now covered under the purchaser's self-insurance authority.

[51] GAO, *Standards for Internal Control in the Federal Government*, GAO-14-704G (Washington D.C., September 2014).

DOL staff are also hindered from taking enforcement action during an operator's ongoing appeal, as previously mentioned. DOL policies state that an operator may request reconsideration if its self-insurance application has been denied or if it believes the collateral required by DOL is too high to secure its benefit liabilities. However, DOL lacks procedures that specify, among other things, the length of time that operators have to submit supporting information. Further, DOL does not specify a goal for how much time DOL appeals decisions should take. For example, in October 2015, DOL recommended revoking Murray Energy's (Murray) authority to self-insure due to deteriorating financial conditions. Murray appealed this decision, and DOL officials said they postponed responding to the appeal until their new self-insurance process was implemented so that they could evaluate Murray under its new process along with the other self-insured operators. However, Murray filed for bankruptcy in October 2019 and DOL had not revoked its authority to self-insure or requested additional collateral because Murray's appeal was still pending and DOL was still evaluating how much collateral it would require from the operator under its new self-insurance process.

DOL Does Not Monitor Whether Coal Mine Operators Maintain Commercial Insurance Coverage

DOL does not monitor coal mine operators that do not self-insure and, thus, must commercially insure their federal black lung liabilities to make certain they maintain adequate and continuous coverage as required by law. DOL previously monitored operators' compliance with the program's insurance requirements by annually sending letters to a selection of operators seeking confirmation that they had maintained adequate coverage, but discontinued the process once the agency began receiving NCCI policy data. In order to use the policy data for the purpose of identifying operators that have not maintained coverage, DOL would, as a starting point, have to maintain a record of all employers that operate a coal mine. However, DOL officials explained that they do not currently maintain such a record.

In the absence of effective DOL monitoring of operator compliance, we evaluated the potential risk that uninsured operators could pose to the Trust Fund. Specifically, in examining the 13 largest coal operators that were not approved to self-insure their federal black lung liabilities and, therefore, had to obtain commercial coverage, we found that some insurers erred in reporting endorsements and in one instance an operator did not have adequate coverage.

- We found six operators (parent or subsidiary) that were not insured for the entire 3 year period from 2016 through 2018, according to our review of DOL data. When we discussed our findings with DOL, agency officials had to research each operator individually and in some cases contact the operator or their insurer to find out whether or not they had been covered. DOL concluded that these entities were insured. However, the insurers had not properly reported the federal black lung endorsement on new policies or subsequent renewals, in addition to other reporting issues.[52]

- One of these six operators also had, inadvertently, not maintained adequate commercial coverage for its mining operations in Texas, and had not self-insured those operations. In this instance, the operator obtained an excess loss policy that only pays claims once they exceed a high threshold and, therefore, is not sufficient by itself to secure the payment of the operator's benefit liabilities.[53] DOL data does not include information on excess loss policies and, while the data NCCI provides on standard workers' compensation policies with federal black lung endorsements lists operators' addresses, they do not provide the specific states for which endorsements apply.

Designing processes to achieve agency objectives and respond to risks is a principle of effective internal controls.[54] Without a process to monitor operator compliance with program insurance requirements, DOL risks not identifying a lapse or cancellation of operator coverage. This could result in the Trust Fund having to assume responsibility for paying benefits that would otherwise have been paid by an insurer.[55]

DOL officials said the Trust Fund infrequently pays claims on behalf of uninsured operators due to the civil penalties that it can impose on operators and certain company officers. These officials also said that operators that do not maintain insurance coverage typically employ few miners and are out of business by the time a claim is filed and, thus, cannot be held liable for benefit claims. However, DOL officials acknowledged that they do not track how often claims are paid by the Trust Fund on behalf of uninsured operators that should have been insured.

We attempted to examine the extent to which claims were paid by the Trust Fund in fiscal year 2018 on behalf of uninsured operators that should have been insured.[56] We found that DOL's black lung claimant and payment system does not identify whether potentially responsible operators should have had commercial insurance coverage. The

---

[52] We found similar reporting issues with two self-insured coal operators that had subsidiaries that were commercially insured or insured by a state workers' compensation insurance fund.

[53] When we raised the issue with the operator's insurer, they said they had inadvertently omitted Texas from the list of states covered by the federal black lung endorsement on the operator's standard workers' compensation policy. According to the insurer, they have corrected the error and made the changes retroactive to the endorsement's original effective date to ensure the operator's Texas operations will be covered.

[54] GAO-14-704G.

[55] Another potential consequence of DOL's failure to monitor operator compliance with program insurance requirements is that responsibility for the payment of benefits can shift from operators that most recently employed a miner and are uninsured to other operators that previously employed the miner and are insured.

[56] Such a figure, had we been able to calculate it, would have represented the losses the Trust Fund could have avoided that year had operators complied with the program's insurance requirements.

data on responsible operators and insurers, as well as the basis on which an operator was determined to be responsible, were not consistently recorded. DOL officials said that the data fields that identify responsible operators and their insurers should reflect the information collected from DOL's initial determination. DOL officials said that in some cases, after an adjudication decision determined the Trust Fund was responsible for paying benefits, claim examiners may have deleted the previously recorded responsible operator and insurer data, creating potential inconsistencies in the data.

DOL officials acknowledged that its processes and guidance for recording information on responsible operators and the basis for those decisions resulted in inconsistent and potentially inaccurate recording of claim and benefit data. As a result, DOL issued preliminary guidance in February 2019 to field supervisors and claims examiners. However, the revised guidance does not include how to identify potentially responsible operators that should have had commercial coverage but did not.

Monitoring agency internal control systems and evaluating the results of those activities is a principle of effective internal control.[57] Without complete and consistently recorded information on potentially responsible operators and insurers, and the basis for determination decisions, DOL is not able to effectively evaluate the financial impact claims paid on behalf of uninsured operators have on the Trust Fund. Determining the financial impact of these claims would be important to DOL's evaluation of the effectiveness of a process for monitoring operator compliance with black lung program insurance requirements.

CONCLUSION

The Black Lung Disability Trust Fund faces financial challenges, and DOL's limited oversight of coal mine operator insurance has further strained Trust Fund finances by allowing operator liabilities to transfer to the federal government. DOL's new self-insurance process may help to address past deficiencies in setting collateral and reviewing self-insured operators if implemented effectively. However, DOL still lacks procedures on self-insurance renewals and coal operator appeals that could help to ensure that DOL staff will take enforcement actions when needed. Establishing clear self-insurance renewal procedures could better position DOL to take action to protect the Trust Fund should an operator not submit its renewal application and supporting documentation, or comply with DOL's collateral requirements.

[57] GAO-14-704G.

Procedures that identify time lines for self-insured operators to submit documentation supporting their appeals, and that identify a goal for how much time DOL should take to make appeals decisions could help to ensure that DOL is able to revoke an operator's ability to self-insure, when warranted Commercially-insured federal black lung liabilities can limit the Trust Fund's exposure to financial risk, but only if operators maintain adequate and continuous coverage as required. Currently, DOL does not identify lapses or cancellations in coverage among commercially-insured operators until after a claim is filed. Establishing a process to identify lapses and cancellations in coverage before claims get filed could help prevent the Trust Fund from becoming responsible for these claims.

RECOMMENDATIONS FOR EXECUTIVE ACTION

We are making the following three recommendations to the Department of Labor:

- The Director of the Office of Workers' Compensation Programs should develop and implement procedures for coal mine operator self- insurance renewal that clarifies how long an operator is authorized to self-insure; when an operator must submit its renewal application and supporting documentation; and the conditions under which an operator's self-insurance authority would not be renewed. (Recommendation 1)
- The Director of the Office of Workers' Compensation Programs should develop and implement procedures for self-insured coal mine operator appeals that identify time lines for self-insured operators to submit documentation supporting their appeals and that identify a goal for how much time DOL should take to make appeals decisions. (Recommendation 2)
- The Director of the Office of Workers' Compensation Programs should develop and implement a process to monitor operator compliance with commercial insurance requirements and periodically evaluate the effectiveness of this process. This process should be designed to detect errors and omissions in reporting insurance coverage using complete, accurate, and consistently recorded data. (Recommendation 3)

AGENCY COMMENTS AND OUR EVALUATION

We provided a draft of this chapter to the Department of Labor (DOL) for review and comment. Their written comments are reproduced in appendix I. DOL also provided technical comments and clarifications, which we have incorporated, as appropriate. DOL agreed with our three recommendations and said it is acting to implement them to achieve further improvements in ensuring the effective oversight of coal mine operator insurance.

DOL acknowledged the importance of improving oversight of coal mine operator insurance and commented that it made major oversight improvements in recent years. DOL commented that it began developing a new coal mine operator self-insurance process in 2015, before GAO began its review, and DOL formally approved this process in 2017. In July 2019, DOL stated that its new process was finalized when the Office of Management and Budget (OMB) approved the forms to collect financial and other information from coal mine operators. DOL stated that it is now reviewing information obtained from coal mine operators, and expects to set the amount of collateral required to self-insure under its new process in the first half of 2020. We commend DOL's efforts to address the deficiencies of its past self-insurance process. However, we remain concerned about continuing coal operator bankruptcies and the looming unsecured black lung benefit liabilities that still threaten the Trust Fund.

DOL commented that adopting GAO's recommendations would further improve its oversight of coal mine operator insurance going forward. Specifically, DOL reported that it will (1) ensure letters granting or renewing self-insurance authority will inform operators that their authorization expires in one year and that they must submit renewal information three months in advance of the expiration date, (2) ensure letters denying self-insurance will inform operators that they have a 30- day appeal period (limited to one extension) and that DOL has set a goal of resolving all appeals within 90 days of the denial letter, and (3) modify existing computer systems to identify lapses or cancellations of commercial insurance coverage, and require operators identified as having lapsed or cancelled coverage to obtain or provide proof of coverage within 30 days.

As agreed with your offices, unless you publicly announce the contents of this chapter earlier, we plan no further distribution until 30 days from the report date. At that time, we will send copies of this chapter to the appropriate congressional committees, the Secretary of Labor, and other interested parties.

Cindy Brown Barnes
Director, Education, Workforce, and Income Security Issues

Alicia Puente Cackley
Director, Financial Markets and Community Investment

APPENDIX I: COMMENTS FROM THE U.S. DEPARTMENT OF LABOR

U.S. Department of Labor Office of Workers' Compensation Programs
Washington, DC 20210

Cindy Brown Barnes
Director, Education, Workforce, and Income Security
U.S. Government Accountability Office
441 G Street, NW
Washington, DC 20548

Via email

Dear Ms. Brown Barnes:

Thank you for the opportunity to review and comment on the U.S. Government Accountability Office (GAO) draft report entitled "Black Lung Benefits Program: Improved Oversight of Coal Mine Operator Insurance Is Needed" (GAO-20-21). The Department of Labor (DOL), Office of Workers' Compensation Programs (OWCP), administers the coal mine operator insurance provisions of the Black Lung Benefits Act (BLBA). OWCP agrees with GAO on the importance of improving oversight of coal mine operator insurance and, as GAO acknowledges, has made major oversight improvements in recent years. OWCP also agrees with GAO's three recommendations to achieve further improvement, is acting to implement them, and is committed to ensuring effective oversight of coal mine operator insurance.

The BLBA requires coal mine operators to compensate coal miners and eligible survivors if the miner becomes totally disabled or dies as a result of pneumoconiosis (commonly referred to as "black lung disease"). Coal mine operators are required to secure the payment of their potential benefits liability either by qualifying as a self-insurer or by purchasing a commercial insurance policy. OWCP has the authority to authorize operators to self-insure and set security deposit amounts. Securing benefits liability helps protect the government's Black Lung Disability Trust Fund (the Trust Fund), which pays benefits when operators fail to make benefits payments due to bankruptcy or other reasons. Federal law requires the U.S. Treasury to make repayable advances to the Trust Fund to meet all benefit obligations; so, benefit payments to miners and survivors are never in jeopardy, even when operators do not pay them.

We appreciate that GAO has recognized the significant improvements OWCP has made in recent years to its process for authorizing self-insurers. Prior to these improvements, OWCP did not always consider potential future benefits claims in setting operators' security amounts, or regularly review operators to assess their continued eligibility to self-insure. Bankruptcies of several self-insured coal mine operators transferred benefits liability to the Trust Fund because inadequate security was required from them. OWCP has replaced that process with one that incorporates major improvements designed to address past deficiencies. *Report p. 16; see also report pp. 20, 25 (same).* Under the new process, OWCP will set security amounts based on operators' actuarial-estimated liabilities and financial health/risk of default. The actuarial estimates used in the new process are based on OWCP's latest and most refined approaches for estimating black lung liability – the same updated information and revised assumptions that recently led DOL, as GAO observes, to increase its estimate of Trust Fund liability resulting from several bankruptcies. *See report p. 12.* The improvements in the new self-insurance process allow OWCP to estimate operator liability more accurately, require adequate initial security, recalculate security amounts as necessary in response to emerging developments, and better protect the Trust Fund from any future defaults by operators on benefits payments.

OWCP began developing the new self-insurance process in 2015, long before GAO issued its report or even initiated its engagement on this matter. Over a two-year period, OWCP staff worked with outside experts (actuaries and financial analysts) to review existing self-insurance practices and devise changes to them. The new self-insurance process that emerged from this work was formally approved by OWCP in 2017. OWCP then proceeded to develop, and secure Office of Management and Budget (OMB) approval of, forms to collect financial and other information from coal mine operators for the new process. In July 2019, OMB approved the forms, and OWCP began implementing the new process. The agency is now reviewing information obtained from coal mine operators, and expects to set security amounts under the new process in the first half of this year.

Adopting GAO's recommendations will further improve OWCP's oversight of coal mine operator insurance arrangements. To implement GAO's first recommendation (clarification of self-insurance procedures), OWCP's letters granting or renewing self-insurance authority will inform operators their authorization expires in one year and that they must submit renewal information three months in advance of the expiration date. For the second recommendation (procedures for self-insured coal mine operator appeals), OWCP letters denying self-insurance will inform operators that they have a 30-day appeal period (limited to one extension); also, OWCP has set a goal of resolving all appeals within 90 days of the denial letter. For the third recommendation (procedures to monitor commercial insurance compliance), OWCP will modify existing computer systems to identify lapses or cancellations of commercial insurance coverage, and will require operators identified as having lapsed or cancelled coverage to obtain or provide proof of coverage within 30 days.

Finally, as noted by GAO, the Trust Fund is currently $5.8 billion in debt, and that debt is projected to exceed $12.6 billion (in today's dollars) by 2044. Coal mine operator bankruptcies are not the major driver of Trust Fund debt: only $1.0 billion of the projected 2044 debt of $12.6 billion is due to recent bankruptcies; almost all of the remainder ($11.4 billion) is due to accrued interest on the advances from the U.S. Treasury to ensure benefits payments. Nevertheless, effective oversight of coal mine operator insurance is essential for ensuring that bankruptcies do not add further to the Trust Fund's already sizeable debt.

Thank you again for the opportunity to review and comment on the draft report. GAO's engagement has been helpful and productive. OWCP has appreciated the opportunity to continue its critical review and improvement of oversight practices.

Sincerely,

Julia K. Hearthway
Director

In: Black Lung Programs: MSHA, Benefits and Challenges ISBN: 978-1-53619-388-6
Editor: Ross D. Blodgett

Chapter 3

BLACK LUNG BENEFITS PROGRAM: OPTIONS FOR IMPROVING TRUST FUND FINANCES*

United States Government Accountability Office

ABBREVIATIONS

DOL	Department of Labor
EIA	Energy Information Administration
EIEA	Energy Improvement and Extension Act of 2008
HHS	Department of Health and Human Services
OMB	Office of Management and Budget
Treasury	Department of the Treasury

WHY GAO DID THIS STUDY

With revenue of about $450 million in fiscal year 2017, the Trust Fund paid about $184 million in benefits to more than 25,000 coal miners and eligible dependents. However, the Trust Fund also borrowed about $1.3 billion from the Treasury's general fund in fiscal year 2017 to cover its debt repayment expenditures. Adding to this financial challenge, the coal tax that supports the Trust Fund is scheduled to decrease by about 55

* This is an edited, reformatted and augmented version of the United States Government Accountability Office Report to Congressional Requesters, Publication No. GAO-18-351, dated May 2018.

percent beginning in 2019. GAO was asked to review the financial positon of the Trust Fund and identify options to improve it.

This chapter examines (1) factors that have challenged the financial position of the Trust Fund since its inception and (2) the extent to which Trust Fund debt may change through 2050, and selected options that could improve its future financial position. GAO reviewed Trust Fund financial data from fiscal years 1979 through 2017. GAO also interviewed officials from the Departments of Labor, Treasury, Health and Human Services (HHS) and representatives of coal industry and union groups. Using assumptions, such as the about 55 percent coal tax decrease and moderately declining coal production, GAO simulated the extent to which Trust Fund debt may change through 2050. GAO also simulated how selected options, such as forgiveness of debt, could improve finances. The options simulated are not intended to be exhaustive. Further, GAO is not endorsing any particular option or combination of options.

GAO provided a draft of this chapter to DOL, Treasury, and HHS. The agencies provided technical comments, which were incorporated as appropriate.

WHAT GAO FOUND

Multiple factors have challenged Black Lung Disability Trust Fund (Trust Fund) finances since it was established about 40 years ago. Its expenditures have consistently exceeded its revenues, interest payments have grown, and actions taken that were expected to improve Trust Fund finances did not completely address its debt. When necessary to make expenditures, the Trust Fund borrows with interest from the Department of the Treasury's (Treasury) general fund. Because Trust Fund expenditures have consistently exceeded revenue, it has borrowed almost every year since 1979, its first complete fiscal year, and as a result debt and interest payments increased. Legislative actions were taken over the years including (1) raising the rate of the coal tax that provides Trust Fund revenues and (2) forgiving debt. For example, the Energy Improvement and Extension Act of 2008 provided an appropriation toward Trust Fund debt forgiveness; about \$6.5 billion was forgiven, according to Department of Labor (DOL) data (see figure). However, coal tax revenues were less than expected due, in part, to the 2008 recession and increased competition from other energy sources, according to DOL and Treasury officials. As a result, the Trust Fund continued to borrow from Treasury's general fund from fiscal years 2010 through 2017 to cover debt repayment expenditures.

GAO's simulation suggests that Trust Fund borrowing will likely increase from fiscal years 2019 through 2050 due, in part, to the coal tax rate decrease of about 55 percent that will take effect in 2019 and declining coal production. The simulation estimates that Trust Fund borrowing may exceed $15 billion by 2050 (see figure). However, various options, such as adjusting the coal tax and forgiving interest or debt, could reduce future borrowing and improve the Trust Fund's financial position. For example, maintaining the current coal tax rates and forgiving debt of $2.4 billion could, under certain circumstances, balance the Trust Fund by 2050, whereby revenue would be sufficient to cover expenditures. However, a coal industry representative said that maintaining or increasing the coal tax would burden the coal industry, particularly at a time when coal production has been declining. Further, Treasury officials noted that the costs associated with forgiving Trust Fund interest or debt would be paid by taxpayers.

May 30, 2018

The Honorable Robert C. "Bobby" Scott
Ranking Member Committee on Education and the Workforce
House of Representatives

The Honorable Richard E. Neal
Ranking Member Committee on Ways and Means
House of Representatives

The Honorable Sander M. Levin
House of Representatives

The Black Lung Disability Trust Fund (Trust Fund), established in 1978 by the Black Lung Benefits Revenue Act of 1977, funds benefits to certain coal miners who have been totally disabled due to pneumoconiosis, also known as black lung disease. Their surviving dependents may also receive compensation. That Act authorized the Trust Fund to pay benefits in certain circumstances including in cases where no responsible mine operator could be identified or when the liable mine operator does not pay. The Trust Fund is financed primarily by a tax on coal produced and sold domestically, which we refer to in this chapter as the coal tax.[1]

The Trust Fund faces financial challenges and borrowed about $1.3 billion in fiscal year 2017 from the Department of the Treasury's (Treasury) general fund to cover its

---

[1] The coal tax is imposed on the sale of all domestic coal with two exceptions: (1) lignite coal and (2) exported coal.

total expenditures, according to Department of Labor (DOL) officials who administer the Trust Fund.[2]

Beginning in calendar year 2019, the coal tax will decrease by approximately 55 percent which, in turn, will increase borrowing, according to DOL projections. Additionally, coal production has been declining as the coal industry faces challenges from increased competition from other energy sources, which may further affect future Trust Fund revenue.[3] With less revenue contributed by mine operators through the coal tax, increased federal funding may be needed because under federal law the Trust Fund borrows from Treasury's general fund to cover its expenditures.

Given the potential for increased federal funding of Trust Fund expenditures as a result of the decreasing tax rate, you asked us to review the financial positon of the Trust Fund and to identify options that could improve its future financial position. This chapter examines (1) factors that have challenged the financial position of the Trust Fund since its inception; and (2) the extent to which the Trust Fund's debt may change through 2050, and selected options that could improve its future financial position.

To address our first objective, we reviewed relevant federal laws, regulations, policy, and guidance as well as agency documentation. We primarily focused on changes to the coal tax rates and other legislative actions taken that were expected to improve the financial position of the Trust Fund, such as debt refinancing and forgiveness provisions contained in the Energy Improvement and Extension Act of 2008 (EIEA). We also reviewed publicly available Trust Fund financial data obtained from the DOL Office of Workers' Compensation Programs' Annual Reports to Congress and annual bulletins issued by the Treasury. We examined information on Trust Fund revenue and expenditures from 1979 (the Trust Fund's first complete fiscal year) through 2017, the most recent year data were available at the time of our review.[4] For example, we reviewed the annual amounts of coal tax revenue collected and the annual amounts paid by the Trust Fund in black lung benefits, administrative costs, and debt servicing. We assessed the reliability of the data by discussing it with relevant agency officials and reviewing it for missing data, outliers, or obvious errors. We determined that the data were sufficiently reliable for the purposes of our review. Additionally, we interviewed officials from DOL's Office of Workers' Compensation Programs and Mine Safety and Health Administration; the Department of the Treasury's Offices of Federal Program Finance and Tax Analysis; the Department of Health and Human Services' (HHS)

---

[2] When necessary for the Trust Fund to make relevant expenditures, funds are appropriated to the Trust Fund as "repayable advances," and then those advances must be repaid with interest to the general fund of the U.S. Treasury. We refer to this process as annual borrowing from Treasury's general fund because, for reporting purposes, we often refer to the total amount of the repayable advances made in a particular fiscal year. According to the Department of the Treasury, the general fund includes assets and liabilities used to finance the daily and long-term operations of the U.S. government as a whole.

[3] U.S. Department of Energy, Energy Information Administration, *Annual Coal Report 2016* (Washington, D.C.: November 2017).

[4] We received fiscal year 2017 Trust Fund financial data from DOL officials which we incorporated, as appropriate.

National Institute for Occupational Safety and Health and the Health Resources and Services Administration, which funds black-lung-related grant programs; the National Mining Association (an organization that represents the mining industry); and the United Mine Workers of America (an organization that represents coal miners).

To address our second objective, we simulated the extent to which Trust Fund debt may change through 2050 and how various options may affect future Trust Fund finances. Our simulations are based on various assumptions and simulate Trust Fund revenues and expenditures from fiscal years 2016 through 2050.[5] To develop these simulations, we used actual and projection data from (1) DOL for fiscal years 2015 through 2040; (2) Treasury's Office of Tax Analysis for fiscal years 2011 through 2015; (3) the Department of Energy's Energy Information Administration (EIA) for calendar years 2015 through 2050; and (4) the Office of Management and Budget (OMB) for fiscal year 2017. We ran each simulation multiple times using different sets of assumptions about the number of future black lung beneficiaries and future coal production. Doing so provided a range of estimates about the Trust Fund's future borrowing needs and provided insight on the sensitivity of its overall financial position relative to its various revenues and expenditures. In this chapter, we generally present the results of a moderate set of assumptions for each simulation. For more information on our simulation methodology and the full range of results, see appendixes I and II. We assessed the reliability of the data used to develop our simulations by interviewing knowledgeable agency officials and reviewing relevant supporting documentation describing the various inputs and assumptions used, if applicable. We also reviewed DOL, Treasury, EIA, and OMB data for outliers, obvious errors, or missing data. We determined that the data were sufficiently reliable for the purposes of this chapter.

To identify options that may improve future Trust Fund finances, we interviewed officials from DOL, Treasury, HHS, the National Mining Association, and the United Mine Workers of America. We then selected options to simulate based, in part, on these interviews and the availability of DOL and other data. These options included adjusting the coal tax, forgiving interest on some or all Trust Fund debt, forgiving some or all Trust Fund debt, or various combinations of these options. The options we simulated are not intended to be exhaustive and we are not endorsing any particular option or combination of options.

We conducted this performance audit from February 2017 through May 2018 in accordance with generally accepted government auditing standards. Those standards require that we plan and perform the audit to obtain sufficient, appropriate evidence to provide a reasonable basis for our findings and conclusions based on our audit objectives.

---

[5] Our simulations began in fiscal year 2016 because fiscal year 2015 was the last complete fiscal year for which DOL data were available when we began our review. Our simulations extend through fiscal year 2050 because that is as far as the EIA produces coal production forecasts which we relied on in developing our simulations relative to future coal tax revenue.

We believe that the evidence obtained provides a reasonable basis for our findings and conclusions based on our audit objectives.

BACKGROUND

Black lung benefits include both cash assistance and medical benefits. Maximum cash assistance payments generally ranged from about $650 to $1,300 per month in fiscal year 2017, depending on the number of dependents the miner has.[6] Miners receiving cash assistance are also eligible for medical benefits that cover the treatment of their black-lung- related conditions, which may include hospital and nursing care, rehabilitation services, and drug and equipment charges, according to DOL documentation. DOL estimates that the average annual cost for medical treatment in fiscal year 2017 was approximately $6,980 per miner.

There were about 25,700 total beneficiaries (primary and dependents) receiving black lung benefits during fiscal year 2017 (see figure 1).[7] The decrease in the number of beneficiaries over time has resulted from a combination of declining coal mining employment and an aging beneficiary population, according to DOL officials. Further, black lung beneficiaries could increase in the near term due to the increased occurrence of black lung disease and its most severe form, progressive massive fibrosis, particularly among Appalachian coal miners, according to HHS officials.[8]

Black lung claims are processed by DOL's Office of Workers' Compensation Programs. Contested claims are adjudicated by DOL's Office of Administrative Law Judges, which issues decisions that can be appealed to the Benefits Review Board.[9] Claimants and mine operators may further appeal these agency decisions to the federal courts. If an award is contested, claimants can receive interim benefits, which are generally paid from the Trust Fund according to DOL officials, while their claims are in

---

[6] Benefit rates are set by federal law, which specifies that in the case of total disability, a miner receives 37.5 percent of the monthly pay rate of a federal employee at grade GS-2, step 1. Benefit levels are increased by 50 percent if the miner has one dependent, 75 percent if the miner has two dependents, and 100 percent if the miner has three or more dependents. If state workers' compensation benefits are less than federal black lung benefits, then the federal benefits cover the difference. Social Security Disability Insurance benefits are also reduced for recipients of black lung benefits.

[7] We excluded black lung beneficiaries whose claims were filed on or before December 31, 1973, as these awards are generally funded from Treasury's general fund, and not from the Trust Fund.

[8] Recent HHS National Institute for Occupational Safety and Health studies have found increases in the prevalence of black lung disease among long tenured Appalachian coal miners and have documented hundreds of miners with the most severe form of the disease, progressive massive fibrosis, receiving care at two clinics in Kentucky and Virginia—see D.J. Blackley, L.E. Reynolds, C. Short, R. Carson, E. Storey, C.N. Halldin, A.S. Laney, "Progressive Massive Fibrosis in Coal Miners From 3 Clinics in Virginia," *Journal of the American Medical Association*, February 6, 2018 (319(5):500–501); and D.J. Blackley, J.B. Crum, C.N. Halldin, E. Storey, A.S. Laney, "Resurgence of Progressive Massive Fibrosis in Coal Miners — Eastern Kentucky, 2016," *Morbidity and Mortality Weekly Report*, December 16, 2016 (65:1385–1389).

[9] For additional information on the black lung claim adjudication process see GAO, *Black Lung Benefits Program: Administrative and Structural Changes Could Improve Miners' Ability to Pursue Claims*, GAO-10-7 (Washington, D.C.: October 30, 2009).

the appeals process. Final awards are either funded by mine operators—who are identified as the responsible employers of claimants—or the Trust Fund, when responsible employers cannot be identified or do not pay.[10] In fiscal year 2017, black lung claims had an approval rate of about 29 percent, according to DOL data. Of the 19,430 primary black lung beneficiaries receiving benefits during fiscal year 2017, 64 percent (12,464) were paid from the Trust Fund, 25 percent (4,798) were paid by liable mine operators, and 11 percent (2,168) were receiving interim benefits, according to DOL officials.

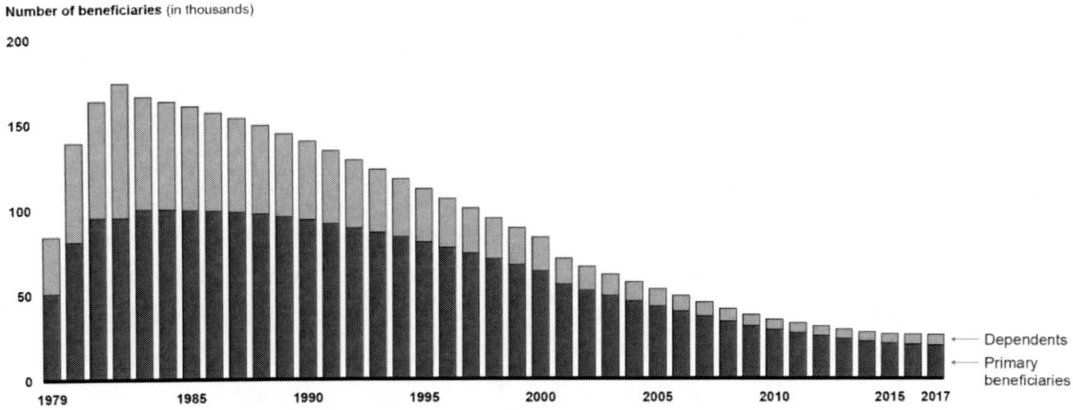

Source: GAO analysis of Department of Labor data. | GAO-18-351.

Notes: We excluded black lung beneficiaries whose claims were filed on or before December 31, 1973, as these awards are generally funded from Treasury's general fund, and not the Trust Fund.

Figure 1. Black Lung Beneficiaries, Fiscal Years 1979 through 2017.

Black Lung Disability Trust Fund revenue is primarily obtained from mine operators through the coal tax. The coal tax is imposed at two rates, depending on whether the coal is extracted from underground or surface mines. The current tax rates are $1.10 per ton of underground-mined coal and $0.55 per ton of surface-mined coal, up to 4.4 percent of the sales price. Therefore, if a ton of underground-mined coal is sold for less than $25, than the tax paid would be less than $1.10. For instance, if a ton of underground-mined coal sold for $20, than it would be taxed at 4.4 percent of the sales price, or $0.88.[11] To a lesser extent, the Trust Fund also receives other miscellaneous revenue from interest payments, and various fines and penalties paid by mine operators, among other sources, according to DOL documentation. Coal tax revenue is collected from mine operators by Treasury's Internal Revenue Service and then transferred to the Trust Fund where it is

[10] Mine operators liable for black lung awards must secure the payment of their benefits liability by either qualifying as a self-insurer or by purchasing and maintaining a commercial insurance contract (including a policy or contract procured from a state agency).

[11] For more information on coal production and prices, see U.S. Department of Energy, Energy Information Administration, *Annual Coal Report 2016* (Washington, D.C.: November 2017).

then used by DOL officials to pay black lung benefits and the costs of administering the program.

Trust Fund expenditures include, among other things, black lung benefit payments, certain administrative costs incurred by DOL and Treasury to administer the black lung benefits program, and debt repayments. When necessary for the Trust Fund to make relevant expenditures under federal law, the Trust Fund borrows from the Treasury's general fund. When this occurs, the federal government is essentially borrowing from itself—and hence from the general taxpayer—to fund its benefit payments and other expenditures.

Multiple Factors Have Challenged Trust Fund Finances Resulting in Growing Debt

Multiple factors have challenged Trust Fund finances since it was established about 40 years ago. Its expenditures have consistently exceeded its revenue, interest payments have grown, and legislative actions taken that were expected to improve Trust Fund finances did not completely address its debt.[12] Combined black lung benefit payments and program administrative costs exceeded Trust Fund revenue every year for the program's first decade (fiscal years 1979 through 1989), resulting in the accrual of debt.[13] During the Trust Fund's first three fiscal years in particular, revenue covered less than 40 percent of the Trust Fund's combined benefit payments and administrative costs.[14] For instance, in fiscal year 1980, the Trust Fund received about $251 million in revenue and paid about $726 million in black lung benefits and administrative costs.[15]

Beginning in 1982, revenue increased as a result of the Black Lung Benefits Revenue Act of 1981 that doubled the coal tax rates from $0.50 to $1 per ton of underground-mined coal and from $0.25 to $0.50 per ton of surface-mined coal, up to 4 percent of the sales price.[16] Even with the tax rate increase, combined benefit payments and administrative costs continued to exceed revenue throughout the 1980s (see Figure 2). As

---

[12] For reporting purposes, Trust Fund expenditures include benefit payments and administrative costs as well as debt repayments (interest and principal). Trust Fund revenue includes coal tax revenue as well as miscellaneous other revenue, such as interest payments and various fines and penalties paid by mine operators, and exclude any amount borrowed from Treasury's general fund.

[13] For reporting purposes, the Trust Fund's first decade refers to its first 10 complete fiscal years—1979 through 1989.

[14] Administrative costs include various expenditures related to the administration of the Black Lung Benefits Program such as legal, financial, and investigative support provided by DOL's Benefits Review Board, Administrative Law Judges, and the Office of the Inspector General, according to DOL documentation.

[15] This is equivalent to about $665 million and $2 billion in 2018 after adjusting for inflation.

[16] The coal tax rate increase was set to expire on the earlier of January 1, 1996, or the first January 1 after 1981 as of which the Trust Fund was free of any balance of repayable advances (which we refer to as annual borrowing from Treasury's general fund) and unpaid interest on such advances, when the tax rate would revert to its prior level of $0.50 or $0.25 per ton of underground or surfaced-mined coal, respectively, up to 2 percent of the sales price.

a result, the Trust Fund borrowed from Treasury's general fund to cover the annual differences between its expenditures and revenues, and by fiscal year 1989 the Trust Fund's outstanding debt to Treasury's general fund exceeded $3 billion.[17]

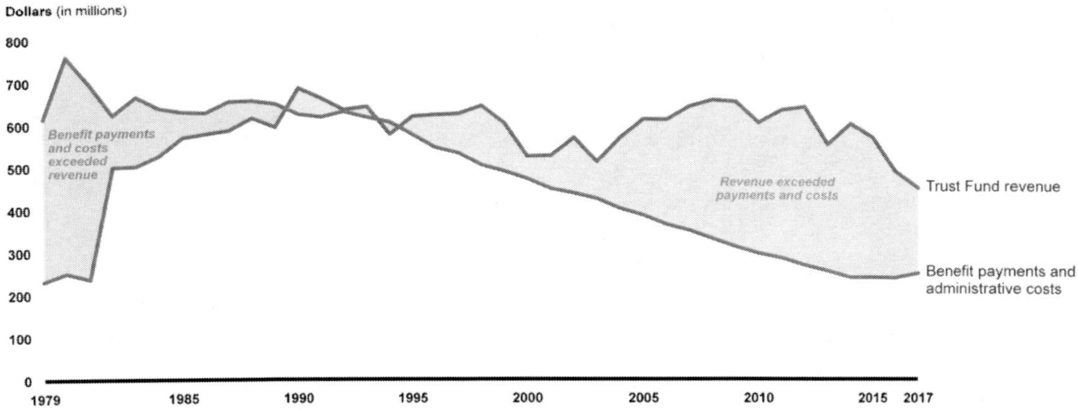

Source: GAO analysis of data from the Department of Labor and the Department of Treasury. | GAO-18-351.

Notes: Trust Fund revenue includes coal tax revenue as well as miscellaneous other revenue such as interest payments and various fines and penalties paid by mine operators. Trust Fund debt servicing costs are not included and all amounts are presented in nominal dollars.

Figure 2. Black Lung Disability Trust Fund Revenue and Black Lung Benefit Payments and Administrative Costs, Fiscal Years 1979 to 2017.

Beginning in fiscal year 1990, Trust Fund revenue generally began to exceed combined benefit payments and administrative costs, and, in fact, total Trust Fund cumulative revenue collected from fiscal years 1979 through 2017 exceeded total cumulative benefit payments and administrative costs incurred during these years. However, interest owed from earlier years of borrowing led to more borrowing and debt. From fiscal years 1979 through 1989, the Trust Fund borrowed—primarily through 30-year term loans according to Treasury officials—from Treasury's general fund at interest rates that varied from about 6.5 percent to about 13.9 percent. In fiscal year 1985, for instance, the Trust Fund paid about $275 million in interest, which was equal to about half of the total revenue collected that year.[18] Since fiscal year 1990, revenue has generally exceeded combined benefit payments and administrative costs, although interest payments on the Trust Fund's outstanding debt kept the fund in a position whereby its total expenditures continued to exceed its total revenues.[19] As a result, the principal amount of the Trust Fund's total outstanding debt to Treasury's general fund increased and exceeded $10 billion by fiscal year 2008.[20]

[17] This is equivalent to about $5.4 billion in 2018 after adjusting for inflation.

[18] This is equivalent to about $556 million in 2018 after adjusting for inflation.

[19] Since fiscal year 1990, Trust Fund revenue has exceeded combined benefit payments and administrative costs in each year except fiscal year 1994, when these costs exceeded revenue by about $29 million.

[20] This is equivalent to about $12.2 billion in 2018 after adjusting for inflation.

Legislation has been enacted over the years that was expected to improve Trust Fund finances:

- In 1981, the Black Lung Benefits Revenue Act of 1981 doubled the coal tax rates from $0.50 cents to $1 per ton of underground-mined coal, and from $0.25 cents to $0.50 cents per ton of surface-mined coal, up to 4 percent of the sales price (as mentioned previously).
- In 1986, the Consolidated Omnibus Budget Reconciliation Act of 1985 established a 5 year moratorium on interest accrual with respect to repayable advances to the Trust Fund (which we refer to as annual borrowing from Treasury's general fund), and increased the coal tax rates to $1.10 per ton of underground-mined coal, and $0.55 per ton of surface-mined coal (up to 4.4 percent of the sales price), where they have remained since.
- In 2008, the EIEA included provisions that were expected to eliminate the Trust Fund's debt. Specifically, EIEA (1) generally extended the coal tax rates at their current rates until December 31, 2018 (after which they are scheduled to decrease to their original levels of $0.50 per ton of underground-mined coal, and $0.25 per ton of surface- mined coal, up to 2 percent of the sales price); (2) provided for a one- time federal appropriation toward Trust Fund debt forgiveness (about $6.5 billion, according to DOL data); and (3) provided for the refinancing of the Trust Fund's debt that was not forgiven as a result of EIEA (which we refer to as the Trust Fund's legacy debt). Specifically, the Trust Fund's legacy debt was refinanced with more favorable interest rates, according to DOL data. Interest rates on the refinanced legacy debt range from about 1.4 percent to about 4.5 percent.

The forgiveness and refinancing of Trust Fund debt along with extending the current coal tax rates through 2018 were expected to result in annual tax revenue that could be used to pay down interest and principal on the Trust Fund's legacy debt, according to DOL and Treasury officials. These officials said that models showed that debt would be eliminated by fiscal year 2040; however, they noted that coal tax revenue has been less than originally projected due, in part, to the 2008 recession and increased market competition from other energy sources. As a result, the Trust Fund's total expenditures continued to exceed revenue and the Trust Fund borrowed from Treasury's general fund each year from fiscal years 2010 through 2017 to cover debt repayments expenditures. In fiscal year 2017, the Trust Fund's total principal amount of outstanding debt, which includes its legacy debt and the amount borrowed from Treasury's general fund that year, was about $4.3 billion (see figure 3).

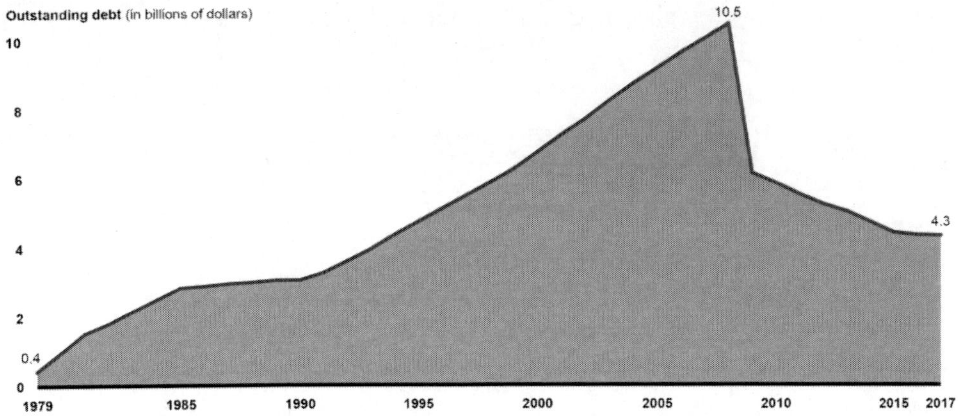

Source: AO review of data from the Department of Labor and the Department of Treasury.
Note: Amounts are presented in nominal dollars and do not include accrued interest.

Figure 3. Black Lung Disability Trust Fund Principal Amount of Outstanding Debt to Treasury's General Fund, Fiscal Years 1979 to 2017.

TRUST FUND BORROWING WILL LIKELY CONTINUE TO INCREASE THROUGH 2050, AND MULTIPLE OPTIONS COULD REDUCE FUTURE DEBT

Trust Fund Borrowing Will Likely Continue to Increase through 2050

Trust Fund borrowing will likely continue to increase from fiscal years 2019 through 2050 due, in part, to the scheduled coal tax rate decrease of about 55 percent that will take effect in 2019 and declining coal production, according to our moderate simulation. We simulated the effects of the scheduled 2019 tax rate decrease on Trust Fund finances through 2050, and in this chapter, we generally present the results of a moderate case set of assumptions (see Table 1).[21] These simulations are not predictions of what will happen, but rather models of what could happen given certain assumptions. For more information on our simulation methodology see appendix I. In addition to the moderate case assumptions, we also simulated how Trust Fund debt could change through 2050 given various other assumptions, and the full range of results for all of our simulations are presented in appendix II. Our moderate case simulation suggests that Trust Fund revenue may decrease, from about $485 million in fiscal year 2018 to about $298 million in fiscal

[21] Our simulations began in fiscal year 2016 because fiscal year 2015 was the last complete fiscal year for which DOL data were available when we began our review. Our simulations extend through fiscal year 2050 because that is as far as the EIA produces coal production forecasts which we relied on in developing our simulations relative to future coal tax revenue.

year 2019, due, in part, to the scheduled approximate 55 percent decrease in the coal tax.[22]

Table 1. Black Lung Disability Trust Fund simulations

Our simulations of future Trust Fund revenues and expenditures are based on various assumptions including those related to future coal production and future black lung beneficiaries. Given the complexities of estimating future coal production and prices and new black lung beneficiaries, our simulations are subject to considerable uncertainty and simulated values with regards to coal tax revenue and Trust Fund expenditures in future years are unlikely to be precise. For more information on our simulation methodology and the full range of results, see appendixes I and II.	
Revenue	Expenditures
Future coal production and prices are key determinants of future Trust Fund revenue because they affect the amount that is collected pursuant to the coal tax, but they cannot be known with any certainty. Therefore, to develop our simulation, we analyzed nine alternative cases that all incorporate various assumptions about how coal production and prices may evolve through 2050. These nine cases are produced by the Energy Information Administration (EIA) and reflect alternative assumptions about economic growth, oil prices, technological innovation, and energy policy.	The number of new black lung disability beneficiaries for whom the Trust Fund will fund benefits in the future is a key determinant of future Trust Fund expenditures, but cannot be known with any certainty. Therefore, to develop our simulation, we analyzed four alternative sets of assumptions about how the number of future beneficiaries may evolve over time. These assumptions were based on (1) the average growth rate of new beneficiaries for fiscal years 2003 through 2015, (2) the median growth rate of new beneficiaries for fiscal years 2003 through 2016, (3) DOL's projection of new beneficiaries, and (4) no new beneficiaries.
Moderate Case Simulation (Revenue)	Moderate Case Simulation (Expenditures)
Our moderate case simulation estimates Trust Fund revenue using EIA's reference coal case which generally assumes trend improvement in known technologies, a view of economic and demographic trends reflecting the current central views of economic forecasters and demographers, and that current laws and regulations affecting the energy sector are unchanged throughout the projection period. We also simulated Trust Fund revenue using EIA coal production and price projections that reflect alternative assumptions about economic growth, oil prices, oil and gas supply, and the Clean Power Plan,[a] and thus allow for higher and lower future coal production and prices than the reference coal case.	Our moderate case simulation estimates Trust Fund expenditures using the average growth rate of new beneficiaries for fiscal years 2003 through 2015 (-5.8%). We believe this reflects a moderate case based on historical experience, and it covers a period of time in which some coal operator bankruptcies have resulted in new beneficiaries for whom the Trust Fund will fund benefits. Other cases we analyzed resulted in higher or lower growth rates. For instance, our fourth set of assumptions assumed zero new beneficiaries each year, so using the average growth rate (-5.8%) generates more new entrants than 0, but fewer new entrants than using the median growth rate of new beneficiaries for fiscal years 2003 through 2016, which was -1.9%, making it a middle or moderate case.

Source: GAO analysis based on review of data from the Department of Labor (DOL), Department of the Treasury, EIA, and the Office of Management and Budget. | GAO-18-351.

[a] Under the Clean Power Plan the Environmental Protection Agency established guidelines for CO_2 emissions from existing power plants.

Our simulation, which incorporates EIA data on future expected coal production, also shows that annual Trust Fund revenue will likely continue to decrease beyond fiscal year 2019 due, in part, to declining coal production. Domestic coal production has declined

[22] The simulated values for Trust Fund revenue and expenditures through 2050 are presented in nominal dollars, meaning they are not adjusted for inflation.

from about 1.2 billion tons in 2008 to about 728 million tons in 2016, according to EIA.[23] Based on these projections, our moderate simulation shows that Trust Fund annual revenue may continue to decrease from about $298 million in fiscal year 2019 to about $197 million in fiscal year 2050 (see figure 4).[24]

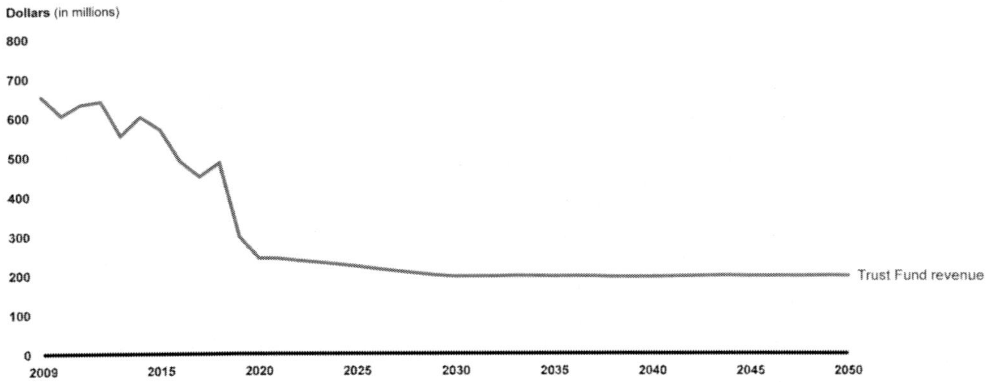

Source: GAO analysis of data from the Department of Labor and Treasury (actual data) and GAO simulation. | GAO-18-351.

Notes: Trust Fund revenue includes coal tax revenue and other miscellaneous revenue, such as interest payments and various fines and penalties paid by mine operators. Trust Fund revenue is simulated for fiscal years 2018 through 2050 and presented in nominal dollars. Moderate case simulations assume that future coal production is consistent with the Energy Information Administration's reference case, which generally assumes trend improvement in known technologies, a view of economic and demographic trends that reflects the current central views of economic forecasters and demographers, and that current laws and regulations affecting the energy sector are unchanged through 2050. Given the complexities of estimating future coal production and prices and new black lung beneficiaries, our simulations are subject to considerable uncertainty and simulated Trust Fund revenues are unlikely to be precise. For more information on our simulation methodology and the full range of results, see appendixes I and II.

Figure 4. Black Lung Disability Trust Fund Actual and Simulated Revenue Based on Moderate Case Assumptions, Fiscal Years 2009 through 2050.

With the scheduled 2019 tax rate decrease, our moderate case simulation suggests that expected revenue will likely be insufficient to cover combined black lung benefit payments and administrative costs, as well as debt repayment expenditures. Specifically, our moderate case simulation suggests that revenue may not be sufficient to cover beneficiary payments and administrative costs from fiscal years 2020 through 2050 (see Figure 5). For instance, in fiscal year 2029, simulated benefit payments and administrative costs will likely exceed simulated revenue by about $99 million.[25] These annual deficits will likely decrease over time to about $4 million by fiscal year 2050 due, in part, to the assumed continued net decline in total black lung beneficiaries.[26] Our

---

[23] U.S. Department of Energy, Energy Information Administration, *Annual Coal Report2016 (*Washington, D.C.: November 2017).

[24] This is equivalent to about $290 million and $100 million in 2018 after adjusting for inflation.

[25] This is equivalent to about $78 million in 2018 after adjusting for inflation.

[26] This is equivalent to about $2 million in 2018 after adjusting for inflation.

simulation also therefore suggests that Trust Fund revenue may not be enough to also cover the debt repayment expenditures it must continue to make through fiscal year 2040, per the payment schedule established following the 2008 EIEA.

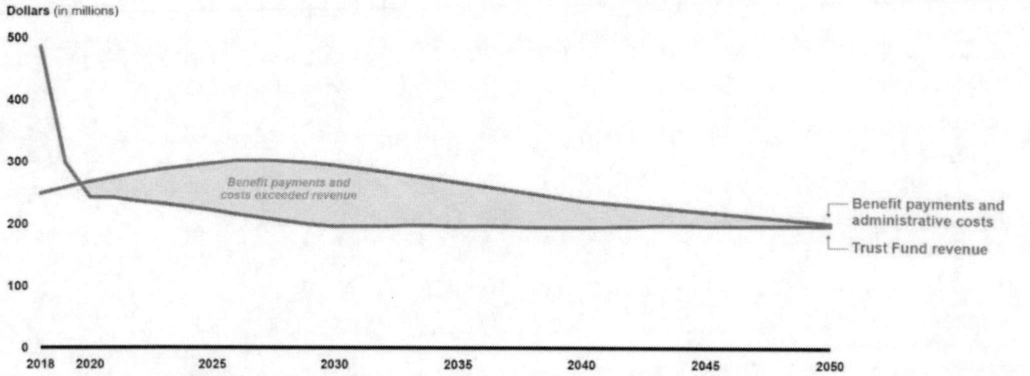

Source: GAO simulation based on data from the Department of Labor and Treasury, the Energy Information Administration, and the Office of Management and Budget. | GAO-18-351.

Notes: Trust Fund revenue and black lung benefit payments and administrative costs are simulated from fiscal years 2018 through 2050 and presented in nominal dollars. Moderate case simulations assume that future coal production is consistent with the Energy Information Administration's reference case, which generally assumes trend improvement in known technologies, a view of economic and demographic trends that reflects the current central views of economic forecasters and demographers, and that current laws and regulations affecting the energy sector are unchanged through 2050. Moderate case simulations also assume that future numbers of new black lung beneficiaries evolve over time based on the average growth rate for the period from fiscal years 2003 to 2015. Given the complexities of estimating future coal production and prices and new black lung beneficiaries, our simulations are subject to considerable uncertainty and simulated Trust Fund revenues and expenditures are unlikely to be precise. For more information on our simulation methodology and the full range of results, see appendixes I and II.

Figure 5. Black Lung Disability Trust Fund Simulated Revenue and Black Lung Benefit Payments and Administrative Costs Based on Moderate Case Assumptions, Fiscal Years 2018 through 2050.

Our moderate simulation suggests that the amount borrowed by the Trust Fund will likely increase from about $1.6 billion in fiscal year 2019 to about $15.4 billion in fiscal year 2050 (see Figure 6).[27] Although the Trust Fund's legacy debt decreases through fiscal year 2040, total Trust Fund expenditures—including combined benefit payments and administrative costs as well as debt repayments—will likely continue to exceed revenue which will require continued annual borrowing from Treasury's general fund. However, the amount borrowed by the Trust Fund could vary depending, in part, on future coal production and the number of new beneficiaries and could range between about $6 billion and about $27 billion in 2050, according to our simulations (see appendix II).

[27] This is equivalent to about $1.6 billion and $7.9 billion in 2018 after adjusting for inflation.

Adjusting Coal Tax Rates, Forgiving Interest, and Forgiving Debt Are Options That Could Improve the Trust Fund's Future Financial Position

We simulated three options that can affect Trust Fund finances through fiscal year 2050. Specifically, we simulated the effects of (1) adjusting the coal tax, (2) forgiving interest, and (3) forgiving debt. In each of the simulations, we compared the results of the option to a baseline in which the coal tax rates will decrease by about 55 percent, which we refer to as the scheduled 2019 tax rate decrease. We compare interest and debt forgiveness options to a baseline which assumes the scheduled 2019 tax rate decrease has taken effect, and that there is no interest or debt forgiveness. The simulated options are not intended to be exhaustive and we are not endorsing any particular option or combination of options.

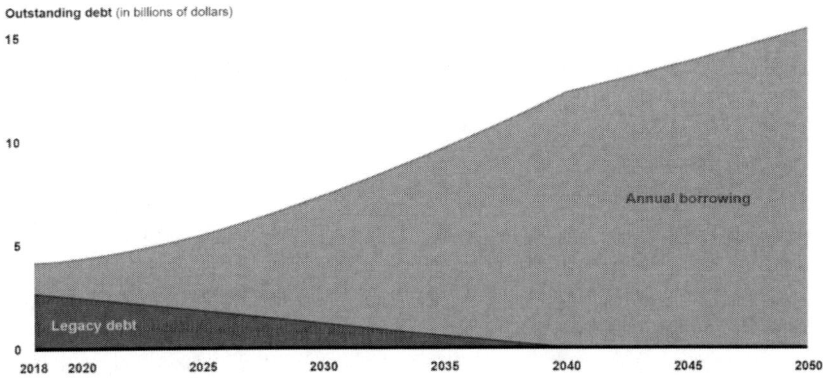

Source: GAO simulation based on data from the Department of Labor and Treasury, the Energy Information Administration, and the Office of Management and Budget. | GAO-18-351.

Notes: The principal amount of the Trust Fund's outstanding debt includes the principal amount of the Trust Fund's legacy debt—which was refinanced following the Energy Improvement and Extension Act of 2008 with repayment to be complete by fiscal year 2040—and the Trust Fund's annual borrowing from Treasury's general fund through 2050, which is simulated from fiscal years 2018 through 2050 and presented in nominal dollars. Moderate case simulations assume that future coal production is consistent with the Energy Information Administration's reference case, which generally assumes trend improvement in known technologies, a view of economic and demographic trends that reflects the current central views of economic forecasters and demographers, and that current laws and regulations affecting the energy sector are unchanged through 2050. Moderate case simulations also assume that future numbers of new black lung beneficiaries evolve over time based on the average growth rate for the period from fiscal years 2003 to 2015. Given the complexities of estimating future coal production and prices and new black lung beneficiaries, our simulations are subject to considerable uncertainty and simulated annual borrowing is unlikely to be precise. For more information on our simulations methodology and the full range of results, see appendixes I and II.

Figure 6. Black Lung Disability Trust Fund Simulated Principal Amount of Outstanding Debt to Treasury's General Fund Based on Moderate Case Assumptions, Fiscal Years 2018 through 2050.

Adjust Coal Tax Rates

Using the moderate case, we simulated four options: (1) implementing the 2019 coal tax rate reduction to $0.50 per ton of underground-mined coal and $0.25 per ton of surface-mined coal; (2) maintaining the current coal tax rates of $1.10 per ton for underground-mined coal and $0.55 per ton of surface-mined coal; (3) reducing the tax rates by 25 percent (from $1.10 and $0.55); and (4) increasing these tax rates by 25 percent (see Figure 7).[28]

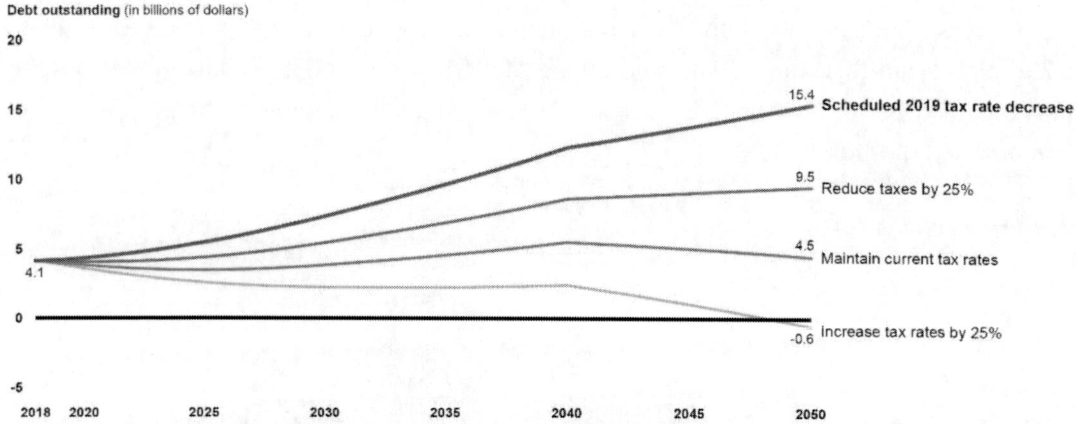

Source: GAO simulation based on data from the Department of Labor and Treasury, the Energy Information Administration, and the Office of Management and Budget. | GAO-18-351.

Notes: The principal amount of the Trust Fund's outstanding debt includes the principal amount of the Trust Fund's legacy debt—which was refinanced following the Energy Improvement and Extension Act of 2008 with repayment to be complete by fiscal year 2040—and the Trust Fund's annual borrowing from Treasury's general fund through 2050, which is simulated from fiscal years 2018 through 2050 and presented in nominal dollars. Moderate case simulations assume that future coal production is consistent with the Energy Information Administration's reference case, which generally assumes trend improvement in known technologies, a view of economic and demographic trends that reflects the current central views of economic forecasters and demographers, and that current laws and regulations affecting the energy sector are unchanged through 2050. Moderate case simulations also assume that future numbers of new black lung beneficiaries evolve over time based on the average growth rate for the period from fiscal years 2003 to 2015. Given the complexities of estimating future coal production and prices and new black lung beneficiaries, our simulations are subject to considerable uncertainty and simulated annual borrowing from Treasury's general fund is unlikely to be precise. For more information on our simulation methodology and the full range of results, see appendixes I and II. Specifically, for the range of simulated annual borrowing in 2050 associated with each tax rate change, see Table 7 in appendix II.

Figure 7. Simulated Effects of Adjusting the Coal Tax on Black Lung Disability Trust Fund Principal Amount of Outstanding Debt to Treasury's General Fund Based on Moderate Case Assumptions, Fiscal Years 2018 through 2050.

---

[28] The coal tax is subject to a maximum tax rate of 4.4 percent of the coal's sales price. Therefore, in developing our simulations, we increased, maintained, or decreased the cap by the amount we altered the tax rates. For example, in simulating a 25 percent coal tax increase we also increased the cap by 25 percent, to 5.5 percent.

Increasing the tax rates by 25 percent was the only option that eliminated simulated Trust Fund debt by fiscal year 2050, according to our moderate case simulation.[29]

Forgive Interest on Debt

We simulated three interest forgiveness options including forgiving interest on (1) legacy debt, (2) annual borrowing, and (3) all debt. Our moderate case simulation suggests that forgiving interest will not eliminate simulated debt by fiscal year 2050 (see Figure 8).

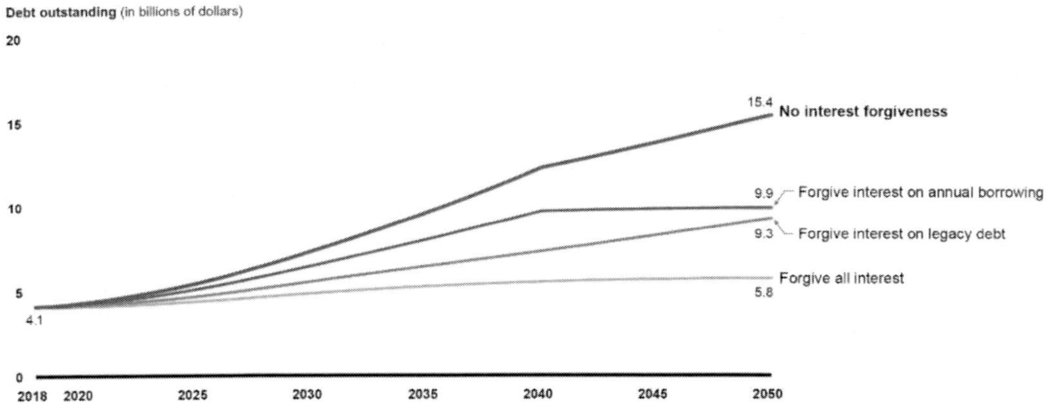

Source: GAO simulation based on data from the Department of Labor and Treasury, the Energy Information Administration, and the Office of Management and Budget. | GAO-18-351.

Notes: Options shown assume forgiveness of interest as of fiscal year 2019. We compare the results of each of these options to a baseline in which no interest is forgiven. The principal amount of the Trust Fund's outstanding debt includes the principal amount of the Trust Fund's legacy debt—which was refinanced following the Energy Improvement and Extension Act of 2008 with repayment to be complete by fiscal year 2040—and the Trust Fund's annual borrowing from Treasury's general fund through 2050, which is simulated from fiscal years 2018 through 2050 and presented in nominal dollars. Moderate case simulations assume that future coal production is consistent with the Energy Information Administration's reference case, which generally assumes trend improvement in known technologies, a view of economic and demographic trends that reflects the current central views of economic forecasters and demographers, and that current laws and regulations affecting the energy sector are unchanged through 2050. Moderate case simulations also assume that future numbers of new black lung beneficiaries evolve over time based on the average growth rate for the period from fiscal years 2003 to 2015. Given the complexities of estimating future coal production and prices and new black lung beneficiaries, our simulations are subject to considerable uncertainty and simulated annual borrowing from Treasury's general fund is unlikely to be precise. For more information on our simulation methodology and full range of results, see appendixes I and II. Specifically, for the range of simulated borrowing in 2050 associated with each interest forgiveness option, see Table 7 in appendix II.

Figure 8. Simulated Effects of Forgiving Interest on Black Lung Disability Trust Fund Principal Amount of Outstanding Debt to Treasury's General Fund Based on Moderate Case Assumptions, Fiscal Years 2018 through 2050.

---

[29] Our model does not consider how adjusting the coal tax rates could affect coal production and prices. For example, increasing coal tax rates could result in energy consumers purchasing less coal in favor of alternative energy sources.

Forgive Debt (Principal and Interest)

We simulated two debt forgiveness options by forgiving principal and interest on (1) legacy debt and (2) all debt. Our moderate case simulation suggests that both debt forgiveness options would reduce simulated Trust Fund borrowing by fiscal year 2050, but these options would not eliminate debt altogether as simulated revenue will likely not be enough to cover simulated expenditures (see Figure 9). In these cases, the Trust Fund will need to continue borrowing from Treasury's general fund to cover annual deficits, and thus accumulate debt.

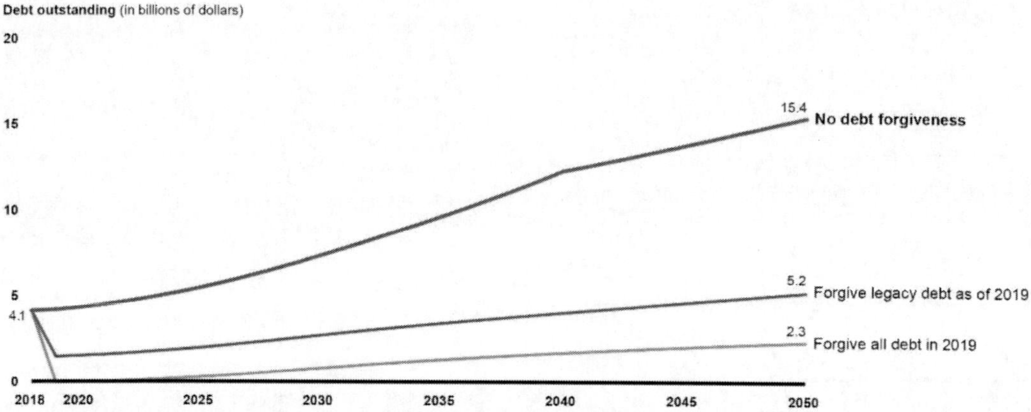

Source: GAO simulation based on data from the Department of Labor and Treasury, the Energy Information Administration, and the Office of Management and Budget. | GAO-18-351.

Notes: Each option shown assumes forgiveness of debt as of fiscal year 2019. We compare the results of each of these options to a baseline in which no debt is forgiven. The principal amount of the Trust Fund's outstanding debt includes the principal amount of the Trust Fund's legacy debt—which was refinanced following the Energy Improvement and Extension Act of 2008 with repayment to be complete by fiscal year 2040—and the Trust Fund's annual borrowing from Treasury's general fund through 2050, which is simulated from fiscal years 2018 through 2050 and presented in nominal dollars. Moderate case simulations assume that future coal production is consistent with the Energy Information Administration's reference case, which generally assumes trend improvement in known technologies, a view of economic and demographic trends that reflects the current central views of economic forecasters and demographers, and that current laws and regulations affecting the energy sector are unchanged through 2050. Moderate case simulations also assume that future numbers of new black lung beneficiaries evolve over time based on the average growth rate for the period from fiscal years 2003 to 2015. Given the complexities of estimating future coal production and prices and new black lung beneficiaries, our simulations are subject to considerable uncertainty and simulated annual borrowing from Treasury's general fund is unlikely to be precise. For more information on our simulation methodology and the full range of results, see appendixes I and II. Specifically, for the range of simulated borrowing in 2050 associated with each debt forgiveness option, see Table 7 in appendix II.

Figure 9. Simulated Effects of Forgiving Debt (Principal and Interest) on Black Lung Disability Trust Fund Principal Amount of Outstanding Debt to Treasury's General Fund Based on Moderate Case Assumptions, Fiscal Years 2018 through 2050.

Stakeholder Views and Other Options

While adjusting coal tax rates and forgiving interest or debt could reduce the Trust Fund's simulated borrowing by 2050, implementing them could affect the coal industry or general taxpayers, according to stakeholders we interviewed. For instance, a coal industry representative noted that maintaining the coal tax at its current rate would continue to burden the coal industry and increasing the tax would exacerbate the burden at a time when coal production has been declining.[30] Treasury officials noted that the costs associated with forgiving Trust Fund interest or debt would be borne by the general taxpayer since Treasury borrows from taxpayers to lend to the Trust Fund as needed.[31] These officials also said that making a one-time federal appropriation to forgive interest or debt would be the most transparent way to satisfy the Trust Fund's outstanding debt to Treasury's general fund.

In addition to the simulations, other options could affect the financial position of the Trust Fund including reducing black lung benefits, eliminating or adjusting the coal tax cap, or creating a variable coal tax. Our moderate case simulation suggests that completely eliminating black lung benefits as of fiscal year 2019 could reduce the Trust Fund's borrowing from Treasury's general fund in fiscal year 2050 from about $15.4 billion to about $6.4 billion.[32] However, doing so would generally mean that coal tax revenue would be collected solely to fund the repayment of Trust Fund debt. Another option could be to eliminate or adjust the coal tax cap, which currently prevents mine operators from paying a coal tax of more than 4.4 percent of the price per ton of coal sold. If the coal tax cap were eliminated, for instance, mine operators would pay $1.10 per ton of underground-mined coal and $0. 55 per ton of surface-mined coal regardless of price sold, which could increase revenue.[33] As an additional option, changing the structure of the coal tax to flexible rates that change based on an annual actuarial assessment of the Trust Fund could help to ensure that coal mine operators pay the necessary amount of tax to cover Trust Fund expenditures, without resulting in a Trust Fund balance or deficit.

---

[30] The burden of the coal tax is likely shared by all coal market participants, including coal companies, coal consumers, coal company employees, and other input suppliers, based on their responsiveness to changes in prices. For example, if coal consumers are less responsive to price changes than coal companies, then coal consumers will end up bearing more of the coal tax burden in the form of higher prices. However, if coal consumers are more responsive to price changes than coal companies, then coal companies will bear more of the burden through lower profits. Coal company employees and other input suppliers also share the burden depending on how responsive they are to changes in wages and other input prices relative to coal companies.

[31] The federal government borrows money from the public by issuing securities—bills, notes, and bonds—through the Treasury. Debt held by government accounts must be paid back when an account needs to redeem its securities to pay expenditures exceeding its annual receipts. From the standpoint of the government as a whole, debt held by government accounts represents amounts loaned from one part of the government to another—in other words, debt the government owes itself. For more information on federal debt, see GAO, *Federal Debt: Answers to Frequently Asked Questions: An Update*, GAO-04-485SP (Washington, D.C.: 2004).

[32] This includes eliminating all cash assistance and medical benefits.

[33] With the scheduled 2019 tax rate decrease, the tax cap will revert to 2 percent.

Multiple Options Could Reduce Future Trust Fund Debt and Would Distribute the Financial Burden Differently Among General Taxpayers and Industry

Multiple options could reduce the Trust Fund's future debt and distribute the financial burden among the coal industry and general taxpayers. We simulated whether various coal tax and debt forgiveness options could balance the Trust Fund by fiscal year 2050, whereby its simulated revenue would be sufficient to cover its simulated expenditures. These options were selected, in part, based on interviews with Trust Fund stakeholders and the availability of DOL and other data.[34] We approached these simulations from two perspectives. First, we simulated how much Trust Fund debt would need to be forgiven based on various coal tax rates. Second, we simulated the average tax collected per ton needed to balance the Trust Fund by 2050, based on certain debt forgiveness options. The simulated options are not intended to be exhaustive and we are not endorsing any particular combination of options.

Our first set of options using the moderate case simulations are based on the current coal tax rates of $1.10 per ton of underground-mined coal and $0.55 per ton of surface-mined coal, and show the amount of debt forgiveness in fiscal year 2019 needed to balance the Trust Fund by fiscal year 2050 based on certain tax rates (see Figure 10). Specifically, our moderate case simulations show the following:

- Increasing current coal tax rates by 25 percent could balance the Trust Fund by 2050 and would likely require no debt forgiveness. For this option, the simulated coal tax revenue would likely be sufficient to cover simulated Trust Fund expenditures, including combined benefit payments and administrative costs, as well as debt repayments. However, this option would place the burden solely on the coal industry that would be paying higher taxes at a time when coal production has been declining.
- Maintaining current coal tax rates could balance the Trust Fund by 2050 if coupled with about $2.4 billion of debt forgiveness. This option would distribute the burden among the coal industry and general taxpayers.
- Decreasing current coal tax rates by 25 percent could balance the Trust Fund by 2050 if coupled with about $4.8 billion in debt forgiveness. This option would burden the coal industry less than maintaining the current tax rates, but would increase the burden on general taxpayers.
- Decreasing current tax rates by 55 percent, which we refer to as the scheduled 2019 tax rate decrease, would balance the Trust Fund by 2050 if coupled with

[34] Trust Fund stakeholders that provided options to simulate include DOL, Treasury, HHS, the National Mining Association, and the United Mine Workers of America.

about $7.8 billion in debt forgiveness. This figure comprises the Trust Fund's total simulated outstanding debt in fiscal year 2019 ($6.6 billion), and an additional about $1.2 billion that would be required because the Trust Fund will accrue additional debt from fiscal years 2020 through 2050, according to our moderate casesimulations. The coal industry would bear some of the financial burden of this option, while also placing a financial burden on general taxpayers.

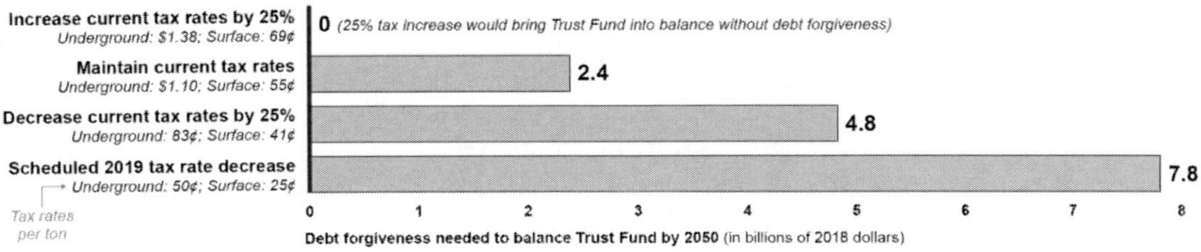

Source: GAO simulation based on data from the Department of Labor and Treasury, the Energy Information Administration, and the Office of Management and Budget. | GAO-18-351.

Notes: For reporting purposes, the Trust Fund is considered balanced when revenue is sufficient to cover expenditures. Moderate case simulations assume that future coal production is consistent with the Energy Information Administration's reference case, which generally assumes trend improvement in known technologies, a view of economic and demographic trends that reflects the current central views of economic forecasters and demographers, and that current laws and regulations affecting the energy sector are unchanged through 2050. Moderate case simulations also assume that future numbers of new black lung beneficiaries evolve over time based on the average growth rate for the period from fiscal years 2003 to 2015. Given the complexities of estimating future coal production and prices and new black lung beneficiaries, our simulations are subject to considerable uncertainty and simulated amounts of debt forgiveness needed to balance the Trust Fund are unlikely to be precise. For more information on our simulation methodology and the full range of results, see appendixes I and II. Specifically, for the range of simulated amounts of debt forgiveness associated with each tax rate change, see Table 8 in appendix II.

Figure 10. Simulated Debt Forgiveness Needed in 2019 to Balance the Black Lung Disability Trust Fund by 2050 Given Various Coal Tax Rates Based on Moderate Case Assumptions.

Our second set of options using moderate case simulations show the change in average coal tax revenue collected per ton to balance the Trust Fund by fiscal year 2050 based on certain debt forgiveness options (see Figure 11). Specifically, our moderate simulations show the following:

- Forgiving the Trust Fund's legacy debt would allow for an average tax collected of about $0.59 per ton to balance the Trust Fund by 2050. Based on certain assumptions, this could be accomplished with a tax of $0.88 per ton on underground-mined coal and $0.44 per ton on surface-mined coal.[35]

[35] The assumptions are that (1) underground-mined and surface-mined coal make up the same fractions of total coal sold as they did in 2015, about 34 percent and 66 percent, respectively; (2) the cap on coal taxes is removed; and (3) the tax on surface-mined coal is half the tax on underground-mined coal.

- Forgiving all Trust Fund debt would allow for an average tax collected per ton of coal sold of $0.47 per ton to balance the Trust Fund by 2050. Based on certain assumptions, this could be accomplished with a tax of $0.70 per ton on underground-mined coal and a tax of $0.35 per ton of surface-mined coal.

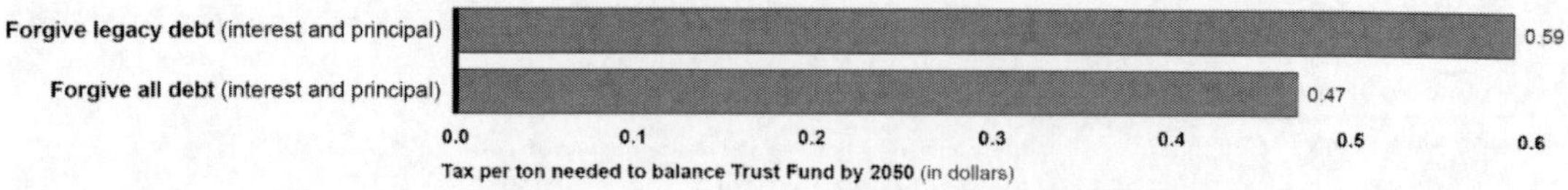

Source: GAO simulation based on data from the Department of Labor and Treasury, the Energy Information Administration, and the Office of Management and Budget. | GAO-18-351.

Notes: For reporting purposes, the Trust Fund is balanced when revenue is sufficient to cover expenditures. Legacy debt refers to Trust Fund debt that was refinanced following the Energy Improvement and Extension Act of 2008. All debt refers to the Trust Fund's legacy debt and any amount borrowed from Treasury's general fund. Moderate case simulations assume that future coal production is consistent with the Energy Information Administration's reference case, which generally assumes trend improvement in known technologies, a view of economic and demographic trends that reflects the current central views of economic forecasters and demographers, and that current laws and regulations affecting the energy sector are unchanged through 2050. Moderate case simulations also assume that future numbers of new black lung beneficiaries evolve over time based on the average growth rate for the period from fiscal years 2003 to 2015. Given the complexities of estimating future coal production and prices and new black lung beneficiaries, our simulations are subject to considerable uncertainty and simulated coal tax rates needed to balance the Trust Fund are unlikely to be precise. For more information on our simulation methodology and the full range of results, see appendixes I and II. Specifically, for the range of simulated average tax rates associated with each debt forgiveness option, see Table 9 in appendix II.

Figure 11. Simulated Change in Tax Collection per Ton of Coal Sold That Could Balance the Black Lung Disability Trust Fund by 2050, Based on Various Debt Forgiveness Options and Moderate Case Assumptions.

AGENCY COMMENTS

We provided a draft of this chapter to the Departments of Labor (DOL), Treasury, and Health and Human Services (HHS) for review and comment. DOL, Treasury, and HHS provided technical comments, which we incorporated as appropriate.

As agreed with your offices, unless you publicly announce the contents of this chapter earlier, we plan no further distribution until 30 days from the report date. At that time we will send copies of this chapter to the appropriate congressional committees, the Secretaries of Labor, Treasury, and Health and Human Services, and other interested parties.

Cindy Brown Barnes
Director, Education, Workforce, and Income Security Issues

APPENDIX I: BLACK LUNG DISABILITY TRUST FUND SIMULATION METHODOLOGY

We examined the extent to which (1) Black Lung Disability Trust Fund (Trust Fund) debt may change through 2050 and (2) selected options to improve its future financial position. We interviewed officials from the Departments of Labor (DOL), Treasury, and Health and Human Services (HHS), as well as representatives from the National Mining Association and the United Mine Workers of America. We then selected options to simulate based, in part, on these interviews and the availability of DOL and other data. These options included adjusting the coal tax, forgiving interest on some or all Trust Fund debt, forgiving some or all Trust Fund debt, or various combinations of these options. The options we simulated are not intended to be exhaustive and we are not endorsing any particular option or combination of options. Our simulations are based on various assumptions and simulate Trust Fund revenues and expenditures from fiscal years 2016 through 2050.[36] To develop these simulations, we used actual and projection data from (1) DOL for fiscal years 2015 through 2040; (2) Treasury's Office of Tax Analysis for fiscal years 2011 through 2015; (3) the Department of Energy's Energy Information Administration (EIA) for calendar years 2015 through 2050; and (4) the Office of Management and Budget for fiscal year 2017.

Black Lung Benefit Expenditures

To simulate future Trust Fund benefit expenditures, we simulated the number of beneficiaries each fiscal year, and the annual average amount of benefits received (cash assistance and medical benefits). To simulate the numbers of beneficiaries, we used DOL data on the (1) age distributions of miner and widow beneficiaries for fiscal year 2015; (2) mortality rates by age for miner and widow beneficiaries as of fiscal year 2015; and (3) numbers of beneficiaries—including married miners, single miners, widows, and miners receiving medical benefits only—in fiscal year 2015. We assumed—as DOL does in its Black Lung Budget and Liability Model—that all miners are men, all widows are women, and all spouses are 3 years younger than the miner. We also assumed that the age distribution of single miners is the same as for married miners, and that the age distribution of new miner and widow beneficiaries is the same as for miner and widow beneficiaries during fiscal year 2015. We used DOL's mortality rates to simulate the number of beneficiaries of each age and type in each year, and used those numbers to

[36] Our simulations began in fiscal year 2016 because fiscal year 2015 was the last complete fiscal year for which DOL data were available when we began our review. Our simulations extend through fiscal year 2050 because that is as far as the Energy Information Administration produces coal production forecasts which we relied on in developing our simulations relative to future coal tax revenue.

then simulate the total number of beneficiaries of each type each year (see Table 2).[37] To simulate benefit amounts, we used DOL data on (1) average monthly cash assistance for married miners, single miners, and widow beneficiaries, and (2) average annual medical benefit amounts for married miners, single miners, and medical benefit-only beneficiaries for fiscal year 2015. We assumed that each beneficiary received the average amount of cash assistance each month, increasing each fiscal year with inflation, and that each miner received the same average annual amount of medical benefits received in fiscal year 2015, increasing in the future along with inflation.[38]

Table 2. Future Black Lung beneficiaries simulation methodology

Black Lung beneficiaries	Formula
Married miner	The number of married miner beneficiaries age a in fiscal year y is equal to the number of new married miner beneficiaries age a in fiscal year y plus the number of married miner beneficiaries age a-1 in fiscal year y-1 who survived and whose spouse survived. The total number of married miner beneficiaries in fiscal year y is then the sum of the number of married miner beneficiaries of all ages in fiscal year y. Finally, we averaged the number of married miner beneficiaries by averaging the prior fiscal year's total and the current fiscal year's total.
Single miner	The number of single miner beneficiaries age a in fiscal year y is equal to the number of new single miner beneficiaries age a in fiscal year y plus the number of single miner beneficiaries age a-1 in fiscal year y-1 who survived plus the number of married miner beneficiaries age a-1 in fiscal year y-1 who survived but whose spouse did not survive. The total number of single miner beneficiaries in fiscal year y is then the sum of the number of single miner beneficiaries of all ages in fiscal year y. Finally, we averaged the number of single miner beneficiaries by averaging the prior fiscal year's total and the current fiscal year's total.
Widow beneficiaries	The number of widow beneficiaries age a in fiscal year y is equal to the number of new beneficiaries who are widows age a in fiscal year y plus the number of widow beneficiaries age a-1 in fiscal year y-1 who survived plus the number of married miner beneficiaries age a+2 in fiscal year y-1 who did not survive but whose spouse did survive. The total number of widow beneficiaries in fiscal year y is then the sum of the number of widow beneficiaries of all ages in fiscal year y. Finally, we averaged the number of widow beneficiaries by averaging the prior fiscal year's total and the current fiscal year's total.
Medical Benefit Only (MBO)	The number of MBO beneficiaries of age a in fiscal year y is equal to the number of MBO beneficiaries of age a-1 in fiscal year y-1 who survived. The total number of MBO beneficiaries only in fiscal year y is then the sum of the number of MBO beneficiaries of all ages in fiscal year y. Finally, we averaged the number of MBO beneficiaries by averaging the prior fiscal year's total and the current fiscal year's total.

Source: GAO simulation methodology. | GAO-18-351.

[37] We also assumed that there will be no new medical-benefit-only recipients.

[38] Our inflation adjustments start on January 1, 3 months after the start of the fiscal year on October 1. Therefore, in our simulations, the total amount of benefits a beneficiary receives in a fiscal year is equal to 3 months of benefits adjusted for inflation in the next fiscal year plus 9 months of benefits adjusted for inflation.

Coal Tax Revenues

To simulate future coal tax revenue, we used Treasury and EIA data to calculate (1) the amounts of underground and surface-mined coal taxed at fixed dollar amounts of $1.10 and $0.55 per ton, respectively, in 2015; (2) the amounts of underground and surface-mined coal taxed at variable dollar amounts per ton equal to 4.4 percent of the price in 2015; and (3) average prices of underground and surface-mined coal taxed at 4.4 percent of the price in 2015. We then used EIA data on projected amounts of total coal production, underground-mined coal production, lignite coal production, and coal exports, as well as projected average coal prices, for the period from 2015 through 2050 to simulate future coal tax revenues (see Table 3).[39]

Table 3. Future coal tax revenue simulation methodology

Data component	Formulas and assumptions
Coal production	We took the following steps to simulate the amount of underground- and surface-mined coal taxed at fixed and variable dollar amounts per ton for each year using data on projected coal production and coal prices for the period from 2015 to 2050: 1 We simulated surface-mined coal production as the difference between total coal production and underground-mined coal production. 2 We simulated underground-mined coal sold domestically by assuming that underground-mined coal makes up the same fraction of exported coal as it makes of total production and then subtracting exported underground-mined coal from total underground-mined coal. 3 We simulated non-lignite surface-mined coal sold domestically by first assuming that surface- mined coal makes up the same fraction of exported coal as it makes of total production and then subtracting exported surface-mined coal and lignite coal from total surface-mined coal. 4 We simulated domestic underground-mined coal taxed at a fixed dollar amount per ton by assuming production grows at the same rate as domestic underground-mined coal. We simulated domestic underground-mined coal taxed at variable dollar amounts per ton as the remainder. We simulated domestic non-lignite surface-mined coal taxed at fixed and variable dollar amounts per ton similarly.
Coal prices	We simulated the prices of underground-mined and surface-mined coal by assuming they grow at the same rate as average coal prices.
Coal tax revenues	We took the following steps to simulate coal tax revenues: 1. We simulated tax revenue from underground-mined and surface-mined coal taxed at a fixed dollar amount per ton as the fixed dollar amount per ton times production of these types of coal. 2. We simulated tax revenues from underground-mined and surface-mined coal taxed at a variable dollar amount per ton based on a percentage of the price as the percentage of price per ton times the price times production. 3. We simulated total calendar year coal tax revenues as the sum of revenues for each type of coal. 4. We simulated total fiscal year coal tax revenues as 25 percent of the tax revenues for the previous calendar year plus 75 percent of the revenues for the current calendar year.

Source: GAO simulation methodology. | GAO-18-351.

[39] Lignite coal and exported coal are not subject to the coal tax. EIA coal production data are presented in calendar years. Therefore, we developed our simulation in calendar years and then adjusted total coal tax revenue to report in fiscal years.

Other Expenditures and Revenue

We simulated other Trust Fund expenditures and revenues, including administrative costs and debt repayments (see Table 4). For our simulations, total Trust Fund expenditures are the sum of black lung benefits (cash assistance and medical benefits), total administrative costs, repayment of interest and principal on outstanding debt to Treasury's general fund, and other expenditures. Total Trust Fund revenues are the sum of coal tax revenue and other miscellaneous revenue, and exclude annual borrowing from Treasury's general fund.[40]

Annual borrowing from Treasury's general fund is the difference between total Trust Fund expenditures and revenues and is assumed to be repaid with interest the following year. If total revenues are greater than total expenditures, then the Trust Fund has a balance and would not have to borrow that year. In this case, we assumed that the Trust Fund will earn interest on that balance at the same rate on which interest would accrue on annual borrowing.

Table 4. Definitions for various Black Lung Disability Trust Fund expenditures and revenues (excluding black lung benefits and coal tax revenue)

Expenditures and revenue	Simulation methodology
Administrative costs	Sum of various expenditures in the Department of Labor's (DOL) Black Lung Liability Model, which include direct expenses, departmental management expenses, and Office of Inspector General and Treasury expenses.
Legacy debt repayments	Sum of principal and interest on the Trust Fund's legacy debt (i.e., the debt refinanced after the Energy Improvement and Extension Act of 2008).
Other expenditures	Retroactive benefits (less collections from mine operators as included in DOL's Black Lung Liability Model).
Repayment on annual borrowing	Amount borrowed from Treasury's general fund in the previous fiscal year plus interest.[a]
Miscellaneous revenue	Other miscellaneous Trust Fund revenue such as interest payments, fines, and penalties paid by mine operators.

Source: GAO simulation methodology. | GAO-18-351.

[a] When necessary for the Trust Fund to make relevant expenditures, funds are appropriated to the Trust Fund as "repayable advances," and then those advances must be repaid with interest to the general fund of the U.S. Treasury. We refer to this process as borrowing from the Treasury's general fund. According to the Department of the Treasury, the general fund includes assets and liabilities used to finance the daily and long-term operations of the U.S. government as a whole.

[40] When necessary for the Trust Fund to make relevant expenditures, funds are appropriated to the Trust Fund as "repayable advances," and then those advances must be repaid with interest to the general fund of the U.S. Treasury. We refer to this process as annual borrowing from Treasury's general fund because, for reporting purposes, we often refer to the total amount of the repayable advances made during a particular fiscal year. According to the Department of the Treasury, the general fund includes assets and liabilities used to finance the daily and long-term operations of the U.S. government as a whole.

Options That May Affect Trust Fund Finances

We simulated how the scheduled 2019 tax rate decrease and various options including adjusting the coal tax, forgiving debt interest, and forgiving debt principal and interest may affect Trust Fund finances through fiscal year 2050 (see Table 5). The options listed are not intended to be exhaustive and we are not endorsing any particular option or combination of options.

Table 5. Options that may affect Black Lung Disability Trust Fund finances

Description of simulation (implemented in fiscal year 2019)	
Scheduled coal tax rate decrease of about 55 percent	Tax on underground-mined coal decreases from $1.10 to $0.50 per ton up to the cap, which decreases from 4.4 percent of the price to 2 percent of the price. Tax on surface-mined coal decreases from $0.55 to $0.25 per ton up to the cap, which decreases from 4.4 percent of the price to 2 percent of the price.
Adjustments to the coal tax rates	Reduce coal tax rates by 25 percent. Coal tax rates decrease from $1.10 to $0.83 per ton of underground-mined coal and from $0.55 to $0.41 per ton of surface-mined coal, up to a cap of 3.3 percent of the price for both types of coal.
Maintain current coal tax rates. Coal tax rates remain at $1.10 per ton of underground-mined coal and $0.55 per ton of surface-mined coal, up to 4.4 percent of the price for both types of coal.	
Increase coal tax rates by 25 percent. Coal tax rates increase by 25 percent from $1.10 to $1.38 per ton of underground-mined coal and from $0.55 to $0.69 per ton of surface-mined coal, up to 5.5 percent of the price of both types of coal.	
Forgive interest on Trust Fund debt	Forgive interest on annual borrowing from Treasury's general fund.
Forgive interest on legacy debt.	
Forgive interest on annual borrowing from Treasury's general fund and on legacy debt.	
Forgive principal and interest on Trust Fund debt	Forgive principal and interest on legacy debt.
Forgive principal and interest on legacy debt and annual borrowing from Treasury's general fund as of fiscal year 2019.	

Source: GAO simulation methodology. | GAO-18-351.

Notes: GAO selected options to simulate based on interviews with officials from the Departments of Labor (DOL), Treasury, Health and Human Services, and representatives from coal industry and union groups, as well as the availability of DOL and other data. The options simulated are not intended to be exhaustive and GAO is not endorsing any particular option or combination of options. For our simulations, Trust Fund debt includes its legacy debt—the amount refinanced following the Energy Improvement and Extension Act of 2008 that has not yet been repaid—and annual borrowing, which is the amount borrowed in a given year from the U.S. Treasury's general fund. In developing our simulations for adjusting the coal tax rates, we increased, maintained, or decreased the maximum tax rate of 4.4 percent of the coal's sales price by the amount we altered the tax rates. For example, in simulating a 25 percent coal tax increase we also increased the cap by 25 percent, to 5.5 percent.

We simulated option combinations for coal tax rates, interest forgiveness, and debt forgiveness to demonstrate how potential financial adjustments could affect future Trust Fund borrowing from Treasury's general fund through fiscal year 2050. For options that involve adjusting coal tax rates, we estimated the amount of debt that would need to be forgiven in fiscal year 2019 for the Trust Fund's revenues to be sufficient to cover its expenditures through fiscal year 2050, assuming the Trust Fund does not borrow from Treasury's general fund after fiscal year 2018. To do so, we first calculated the real discounted present value of Trust Fund expenditures for fiscal years 2019 through 2050, including benefit payments, administrative costs, legacy debt repayments, and repayment of annual borrowing from Treasury's general fund. Second, we calculated the real discounted present value of Trust Fund revenue for the same period, including coal tax revenue and other miscellaneous revenue. Third, we calculated debt forgiveness as the difference between the real discounted present value of Trust Fund expenditures from the first calculation and the real discounted present value of Trust Fund revenues from the second calculation. When the amount of debt forgiveness is greater than the amount of debt outstanding, the Trust Fund would need an additional cash inflow in addition to forgiveness of all outstanding debt.

Amounts of debt forgiveness less than zero suggest that no debt forgiveness is required.

For options involving forgiving debt (interest or principal), we estimated the average tax per ton of coal that, if implemented in fiscal year 2019, would provide the Trust Fund sufficient revenue to cover its expenditures through fiscal year 2050, assuming the Trust Fund does not receive any advances from Treasury's general fund after fiscal year 2018. To do so, we first calculated the real discounted present value of Trust Fund expenditures for the period from fiscal year 2019 through fiscal year 2050, again including benefit payments, administrative costs, legacy debt repayments, and repayment of annual borrowing from Treasury's general fund, minus the real discounted present value of miscellaneous revenues for the same period. Second, we calculated the real discounted present value of coal production for the same period. Third, we calculated the average tax per ton of coal as the first amount divided by the second amount.[41]

To assess the sensitivity of each option, we ran each simulation 36 times using four different sets of assumptions about the numbers of future beneficiaries and nine different sets of assumptions about future coal production and prices (see Table 6). Doing so provided a range of estimates about the Trust Fund's future borrowing needs and provided insight on the sensitivity of its overall financial position relative to its various expenditures and revenues. The analysis also provided a range of estimates of the amount of debt forgiveness needed to bring the Trust Fund into balance by fiscal year 2050, assuming various coal tax rates, and the average tax collection per ton needed to do the same, and assuming various amounts of debt forgiveness.[42]

---

[41] If the average tax per ton of coal is t, then the real discounted present value of coal tax revenue in a year is the real discounted present value of t times the amount of coal produced that year. It follows that the real discounted present value of coal tax revenue for the period from 2019 through 2050 is the sum of the real discounted present values of t times the amount of coal produced in each of those years. Adjusting for inflation and discounting are multiplicative operations, so the average tax per ton can be factored out of each term in the sum. After factoring out t, the real discounted present value of coal tax revenue for the period from 2019 through 2050 is t times the sum of the real discounted present values of the amount of coal produced in each of those years. Applying the inflation and discounting adjustments to coal production in each year allows us to solve for the average tax per ton of coal, t.

[42] For reporting purposes, the Trust Fund is balanced when its revenue is sufficient to cover its expenditures.

Table 6. Future Black Lung beneficiaries and coal tax revenue sensitivity analysis

Methodology	
New entrants	The number of new black lung beneficiaries in the future is a key determinant of future Black Lung Disability Trust Fund (Trust Fund) expenditures, but cannot be known with any certainty. Therefore, to develop our simulations, we analyzed four alternative sets of assumptions about how the number of future beneficiaries may evolve over time. These assumptions were based on: 1. the average growth rate of new beneficiaries for fiscal years 2003 through 2015, about -5.8 percent; 2. the median growth rate of new beneficiaries for fiscal years 2003 through 2016, about -1.9 percent; 3. the Department of Labor's projection of new beneficiaries; and 4. no new beneficiaries.
Future coal tax revenue	Future coal production and prices are key determinants of future Trust Fund revenue, but they cannot be known with any certainty. Therefore, to develop our simulations, we analyzed nine alternative cases that all incorporated various assumptions about how coal production and prices may evolve through 2050. These nine cases were produced by the Energy Information Administration (EIA) and reflect alternative assumptions about economic growth, oil prices, technological innovation, and energy policy.[a] Specifically: • The reference case generally assumes improvements in known technologies, a view of economic and demographic trends that reflects the current central views of economic forecasters and • demographers, and that current laws and regulations affecting the energy sector are unchanged through 2050. • The high and low economic growth cases—two alternative cases—differ from the reference case in their assumptions about macroeconomic growth. • The high and low oil price cases differ from the reference case in their assumptions about oil prices. • The high and low oil and gas resource and technology cases consider alternative assumptions about oil and gas supply. • One case assumes that the Clean Power Plan is not implemented.[b] Another case considers alternative assumptions about oil and gas supply in combination with the absence of the Clean Power Plan.
Caveats and limitations	All simulations are subject to considerable uncertainty. Our results will likely be indicative of the relative effects of different options on the Trust Fund, but the simulated values of advances and other variables are unlikely to be precise. Our simulations were developed with a set of underlying assumptions, both explicit and implicit. All such simulations implicitly assume that relationships exhibited in the past will generally continue to hold over the simulation period. Our simulation model did not vary one set of assumptions based on the possible effects of other assumptions. For example, the future numbers of new beneficiaries in the model do not vary with different coal production cases. However, it seems likely that in cases where future coal production is strong, there will also be fewer coal mine operator bankruptcies and thus fewer new beneficiaries (although not all bankruptcies result in new beneficiaries to the Trust Fund).

Table 6. (Continued)

	Additionally, the model does not consider how adjusting the coal tax rates could affect coal production. However, increasing coal tax rates could result in energy consumers purchasing less coal in favor of alternative energy sources.

Source: GAO simulation methodology. | GAO-18-351.

[a] For more information on EIA coal production cases see Department of Energy, Energy Information Administration, *Annual Energy Outlook 2017* (Washington, D.C.: January 5, 2017); and Department of Energy, Energy Information Administration, *Assumptions to the Annual Energy Outlook for 2017* (Washington, D.C.: July 2017).

[b] Under the Clean Power Plan, the Environmental Protection Agency established guidelines for CO_2 emissions from existing power plants.

From the range of estimates that resulted from our sensitivity analysis, we selected cases with moderate expectations related to future Trust Fund expenditures and revenue. Specifically, for future expenditures, we assumed an average growth rate of new black lung beneficiaries for fiscal years 2003 through 2015 as a moderate case that reflects historical experience. For future revenue, we used a moderate coal production outlook based on EIA's reference case, which reflects moderate expectations about future coal production based on various assumptions about economic growth, oil prices, technological innovation, and energy policy.

APPENDIX II: RESULTS OF GAO'S BLACK LUNG DISABILITY TRUST FUND SIMULATIONS

We summarized the results of our simulations by showing the extent to which the Black Lung Disability Trust Fund's (Trust Fund) balance—the sum of tax revenue and miscellaneous revenue less expenditures—may change in fiscal year 2050 for each option simulated.[43] For example, with the scheduled 2019 tax rate decrease, our moderate case simulations suggest that the Trust Fund would likely have a deficit in fiscal year 2050 of about $15.4 billion.[44] However, because in our model the Trust Fund's financial position depends on future coal production and numbers of new beneficiaries, the alternative assumptions we analyzed generated simulated Trust Fund deficits associated with the

[43] We tracked the simulated Trust Fund balance in nominal dollars (not adjusted for inflation) to maintain consistency with historical data shown in DOL budget documents.
We also tracked the Trust Fund's balance in 2018 dollars to show how it evolves over time after adjusting for inflation. Finally, we tracked the discounted present value of the Trust Fund balance in 2018 dollars, to show how it evolves after adjusting for inflation and fully accounting for the time value of money. Adjusting for inflation and accounting for the time value of money reduce the magnitude of the Trust Fund's balance each year, and both balances and deficits are smaller. However, the relative impact of alternative policies on the Trust Fund's balance is generally the same.

[44] This is equivalent to about $7.9 billion in 2018 after adjusting for inflation.

scheduled 2019 tax rate decrease that ranged from about $6 billion to about $27 billion (see Table 7).[45]

Table 7. Summary of Black Lung Disability Trust Fund balances in fiscal year 2050 given various options and assumptions regarding coal production and new beneficiaries

	Moderate coal and new beneficiary scenarios	Average for all coal and new beneficiary scenarios	Minimum for all coal and new beneficiary scenarios	Maximum for all coal and new beneficiary scenarios
Scheduled tax rate decrease in 2019				
Nominal (dollars in billions)	-15.4	-13.6	-27.0	-6.0
Adjusted for inflation (2018 dollars in billions)	-7.9	-6.7	-10.8	-3.1
Discounted and adjusted for inflation (2018 dollars in billions)	-6.3	-5.4	-8.7	-2.5
Reduce coal tax rates by 25 percent in 2019				
Nominal (dollars in billions)	-9.5	-7.2	-19.1	1.6
Adjusted for inflation (2018 dollars in billions)	-4.9	-3.6	-8.2	0.8
Discounted and adjusted for inflation (2018 dollars in billions)	-3.9	-2.8	-6.6	0.6
Maintain current coal tax rates				
Nominal (dollars in billions)	-4.5	-1.8	-12.5	8.0
Adjusted for inflation (2018 dollars in billions)	-2.3	-0.9	-6.1	4.1
Discounted and adjusted for inflation (2018 dollars in billions)	-1.8	-0.7	-4.8	3.3
Increase coal tax rates by 25 percent in 2019				
Nominal (dollars in billions)	0.6	3.5	-7.5	14.4
Adjusted for inflation (2018 dollars in billions)	0.3	1.8	-3.9	7.4
Discounted and adjusted for inflation (2018 dollars in billions)	0.2	1.4	-3.1	5.9
Forgive interest on annual borrowing starting in 2019				
Nominal (dollars in billions)	-9.9	-8.3	-14.5	-2.9
Adjusted for inflation (2018 dollars in billions)	-5.1	-4.2	-7.4	-1.5
Discounted and adjusted for inflation (2018 dollars in billions)	-4.1	-3.3	-5.9	-1.2
Forgive interest on legacy debt starting in 2019				
Nominal (dollars in billions)	-9.3	-7.3	-19.1	0.1
Adjusted for inflation (2018 dollars in billions)	-4.8	-3.6	-7.7	0.1
Discounted and adjusted for inflation (2018 dollars in billions)	-3.8	-2.9	-6.1	<0.1

[45] This is equivalent to about $3.1 billion to about $10.8 billion in 2018 after adjusting for inflation.

Table 7. (Continued)

	Moderate coal and new beneficiary scenarios	Average for all coal and new beneficiary scenarios	Minimum for all coal and new beneficiary scenarios	Maximum for all coal and new beneficiary scenarios
Forgive all interest in 2019				
Nominal (dollars in billions)	-5.8	-4.2	-10.3	1.3
Adjusted for inflation (2018 dollars in billions)	-3.0	-2.1	-5.3	0.6
Discounted and adjusted for inflation (2018 dollars in billions)	-2.4	-1.7	-4.2	0.5
Forgive all debt in 2019				
Nominal (dollars in billions)	-5.2	-3.1	-13.7	4.2
Adjusted for inflation (2018 dollars in billions)	-2.7	-1.5	-5.6	2.2
Discounted and adjusted for inflation (2018 dollars in billions)	-2.1	-1.2	-4.5	1.7
Forgive all debt and annual borrowing outstanding in 2019				
Nominal (dollars in billions)	-2.3	-0.1	-9.4	6.9
Adjusted for inflation (2018 dollars in billions)	-1.2	-0.1	-4.1	3.6
Discounted and adjusted for inflation (2018 dollars in billions)	-1.0	-0.0	-3.3	2.9

Source: GAO simulation based on data from the Departments of Labor and Treasury, the Energy Information Administration, and the Office of Management and Budget. | GAO-18-351.

Notes: Moderate case simulations assume that future coal production is consistent with the Energy Information Administration's reference case, which generally assumes trend improvement in known technologies, a view of economic and demographic trends that reflects the current central views of economic forecasters and demographers, and that current laws and regulations affecting the energy sector are unchanged through 2050. Moderate case simulations also assume that future numbers of new black lung beneficiaries evolve over time based on the average growth rate for the period from fiscal years 2003 through 2015. See Table 6 in appendix I for a summary of alternative sets of assumptions about future coal production and prices and about future numbers of new beneficiaries.

Multiple Options

Multiple options could reduce the Trust Fund's future debt and distribute the financial burden among the coal industry and general taxpayers. We simulated how various coal tax and debt forgiveness options could balance the Trust Fund by fiscal year 2050, whereby its simulated revenue would be sufficient to cover its simulated expenditures. We approached these simulations from two perspectives. First, we simulated how much Trust Fund debt would need to be forgiven based on various coal tax rates. Second, we simulated the average tax collected per ton needed to balance the Trust Fund by 2050, based on certain debt forgiveness options.

For our first set of simulations, we calculated the amount of debt outstanding in fiscal year 2019 and the amount that would likely need to be forgiven in fiscal year 2019 for the Trust Fund to have sufficient revenues to cover its expenditures by fiscal year 2050, assuming that it does not borrow from Treasury's general fund after fiscal year 2018. For example, before any options are implemented, our moderate case simulations suggest that the Trust Fund's outstanding debt in fiscal year 2019—including both legacy debt and annual borrowing from Treasury's general fund—would likely be about $6.6 billion (after discounting and adjusting for inflation). Therefore, with implementation of the coal tax rate decrease of about 55 percent as scheduled in calendar year 2019, about 117.7 percent of that debt would need to be forgiven to balance the Trust Fund. In other words, balancing the Trust Fund would require forgiveness of $6.6 billion and an additional cash inflow of about $1.2 billion because the Trust Fund will accrue additional debt from fiscal years 2020 through 2050, according to our moderate case simulations (see Table 8).

Table 8. Estimated amount of debt forgiveness in Fiscal Year 2019 needed to balance the Black Lung Disability Trust Fund by 2050 given various coal tax rates and assumptions about future coal production and Black Lung beneficiaries

	Moderate coal and new beneficiary scenarios	**Minimum for all coal and new beneficiary scenarios**	**Maximum for all coal and new beneficiary scenarios**
Estimated discounted present value of real debt outstanding in fiscal year 2019 before implementation of any of the options listed below (2018 dollars in billions)			
Estimated debt forgiveness in fiscal year 2019 to balance Trust Fund as a percent of debt outstanding (percentage)	6.6	5.9	6.7
If coal tax rates decrease as scheduled by about 55 percent	117.7	69.0	145.6
If coal tax rates decrease by 25 percent	73.7	25.0	101.4
If current coal tax rates are maintained	36.4	0	63.9
If coal tax rates increase by 25 percent	0	0	26.5

Source: GAO simulation based on data from the Departments of Labor and Treasury, the Energy Information Administration, and the Office of Management and Budget. | GAO-18-351

Notes: For reporting purposes, the Trust Fund is balanced when revenue is sufficient to cover expenditures. Moderate case simulations assume that future coal production is consistent with the Energy Information Administration's reference case, which generally assumes trend improvement in known technologies, a view of economic and demographic trends that reflects the current central views of economic forecasters and demographers, and that current laws and regulations affecting the energy sector are unchanged through 2050. Moderate case simulations also assume that future numbers of new black lung beneficiaries evolve over time based on the average growth rate for the period from fiscal years 2003 through 2015. The coal tax is scheduled to decrease by about 55 percent beginning in calendar year 2019. The minimum estimated discounted present value of real debt outstanding in fiscal year 2019 is under the assumptions of the low economic growth coal case with no new beneficiaries. The maximum is under the assumptions of the high economic growth coal case and new entrant growth at the median for the period from fiscal years 2003 to 2016. Debt forgiveness in excess of 100 percent of debt outstanding implies that the Trust Fund would need an additional amount in addition to forgiveness of all outstanding debt in order to balance, whereby revenue is sufficient to cover expenditures.

For our second set of simulations, we estimated the average tax per ton of coal that, if implemented in fiscal year 2019, would likely provide the Trust Fund sufficient revenues to cover its expenditures in fiscal year 2050, assuming that it does not borrow from Treasury's general fund after fiscal year 2018. For example, if all principal and interest on Trust Fund legacy debt is forgiven, as of 2019, the estimated average tax that balances the Trust Fund is about $0.59 per ton (see Table 9). Based on certain assumptions, this could be accomplished with a tax of $0.88 per ton on underground-mined coal and $0.44 per ton on surface-mined coal.[46]

Table 9. Estimated average tax per ton of coal starting in fiscal year 2019 needed to balance the Black Lung Disability Trust Fund by 2050 given various debt forgiveness options and assumptions about future coal production and Black Lung Beneficiaries (Dollars per ton of coal)

	Moderate coal and new beneficiary scenarios	Average for all coal and new beneficiary scenarios	Minimum for all coal and new beneficiary scenarios	Maximum for all coal and new beneficiary scenarios
No principal or interest on debt forgiven	1.01	0.91	0.58	1.37
Starting in fiscal year 2019, forgive interest on:				
Annual borrowing from Treasury's general fund	1.00	0.91	0.58	1.37
legacy debt	0.76	0.67	0.38	1.08
All debt (legacy debt and borrowing from Treasury's general fund)	0.76	0.67	0.38	1.08
In fiscal year 2019, forgive principal and interest on:				
legacy debt	0.59	0.50	0.25	0.88
All debt (legacy debt and borrowing from Treasury's general fund)	0.47	0.39	0.16	0.74

Source: GAO simulation based on data from the Departments of Labor and Treasury, the Energy Information Administration, and the Office of Management and Budget. | GAO-18-351.

Notes: For reporting purposes, the Trust Fund is balanced when revenue is sufficient to cover expenditures. Moderate case simulations assume that future coal production is consistent with the Energy Information Administration's reference case, which generally assumes trend improvement in known technologies, a view of economic and demographic trends that reflects the current central views of economic forecasters and demographers, and that current laws and regulations affecting the energy sector are unchanged through 2050. Moderate case simulations also assume that future numbers of new black lung beneficiaries evolve over time based on the average growth rate for the period from fiscal years 2003 through 2015.

---

[46] The assumptions are that (1) underground-mined and surface-mined coal make up the same fractions of total coal sold as they did in 2015, about 34 percent and 66 percent, respectively; (2) the cap on coal taxes is removed; and (3) the tax on surface-mined coal is half the tax on underground-mined coal.

In: Black Lung Programs: MSHA, Benefits and Challenges ISBN: 978-1-53619-388-6
Editor: Ross D. Blodgett

Chapter 4

Black Lung Benefits Program: Oversight Is Needed to Address Trust Fund Solvency Strained by Bankruptcies*

Cindy Brown Barnes

Why GAO Did This Study

In May 2018, GAO reported that the Trust Fund, which pays disability benefits to certain coal miners, faced financial challenges. The Trust Fund has borrowed from the U.S. Treasury's general fund almost every year since 1979 to make needed expenditures. GAO's June 2019 testimony included preliminary observations that coal operator bankruptcies were further straining Trust Fund finances because, in some cases, benefit responsibility was transferred to the Trust Fund.

This testimony is based on GAO's report being released today, and describes (1) how coal mine operator bankruptcies have affected the Trust Fund, and (2) how DOL managed coal mine operator insurance to limit financial risk to the Trust Fund. In producing this chapter, GAO identified coal operators that filed for bankruptcy from 2014 through 2016. GAO analyzed information on commercially-insured and self-insured coal operators, and examined workers' compensation insurance practices in four of the nation's top five coal producing states. GAO also interviewed DOL officials, coal mine operators, and insurance company representatives, among others.

---

* This is an edited, reformatted and augmented version of the United States Government Accountability Office Testimony Before the Committee on Education and Labor, Subcommittee on Workforce Protections, House of Representatives, Publication No. GAO-20-438T, dated February 26, 2020.

What GAO Recommends

GAO made three recommendations to DOL to establish procedures for self-insurance renewals and coal operator appeals, and to develop a process to monitor whether commercially-insured operators maintain adequate and continuous coverage. DOL agreed with these recommendations.

What GAO Found

Coal mine operator bankruptcies have led to the transfer of about $865 million in estimated benefit responsibility to the federal government's Black Lung Disability Trust Fund (Trust Fund), according to DOL estimates. The Trust Fund pays benefits when no responsible operator is identified, or when the liable operator does not pay. GAO previously testified in June 2019 that it had identified three bankrupt, self-insured operators for which benefit responsibility was transferred to the Trust Fund. Since that time, DOL's estimate of the transferred benefit responsibility has grown—from a prior range of $313 million to $325 million to the more recent $865 million estimate provided to GAO in January 2020. According to DOL, this escalation was due, in part, to recent increases in black lung benefit award rates and higher medical treatment costs, and to an underestimate of one company's (Patriot Coal) future benefit claims.

DOL's limited oversight of coal mine operator insurance has exposed the Trust Fund to financial risk, though recent changes, if implemented effectively, can help address these risks. In overseeing self-insurance in the past, DOL did not: estimate future benefit liability when setting the amount of collateral required to self-insure; regularly review operators to assess whether the required amount of collateral should change; or always take action to protect the Trust Fund by revoking an operators' ability to self-insure as appropriate. In July 2019, DOL began implementing a new self-insurance process that could help address past deficiencies in estimating collateral and regularly reviewing self-insured operators. However, DOL's new process still lacks procedures for its planned annual renewal of self-insured operators and for resolving coal operator appeals should operators dispute DOL collateral requirements. This could hinder DOL from revoking operators' ability to self-insure should they not comply with DOL requirements. Further, for those operators that do not self-insure, DOL does not monitor them to ensure they maintain adequate and continuous commercial coverage as appropriate. As a result, the Trust Fund may in some instances assume responsibility for paying benefits that otherwise would have been paid by insurers.

Chairwoman Adams, Ranking Member Byrne, and Members of the Subcommittee:

I am pleased to be here to discuss the report we are releasing today on the need for improved oversight of coal mine operator black lung insurance.[1] The federal government's Black Lung Disability Trust Fund (Trust Fund) finances medical and cash assistance to certain coal miners who have been totally disabled due to pneumoconiosis (also known as black lung disease).[2] Black lung benefits are generally to be paid by responsible coal mine operators. However, the Trust Fund pays benefits in certain circumstances, including in cases where no responsible mine operator can be identified or when the liable mine operator does not pay.

As we reported in May 2018, the Trust Fund faces financial challenges.[3]

Its expenditures have consistently exceeded revenue and the Trust Fund has essentially borrowed with interest from the Department of the Treasury's (Treasury) general fund almost every year since 1979, which was its first complete fiscal year.[4] In fiscal year 2019, the Trust Fund borrowed about $1.9 billion to cover its expenditures, according to Department of Labor (DOL) officials.

In June 2019, we reported preliminary observations to this committee that coal operator bankruptcies were further straining Trust Fund finances because, in some cases, responsibility for benefit payments was transferred from the bankrupt operator to the Trust Fund.[5] This may occur, for instance, when the amount of collateral the Department of Labor (DOL) requires from a self-insured coal operator does not fully cover the operator's benefit responsibility should the operator become insolvent.

Trust Fund revenue is primarily obtained through a tax on coal produced and sold domestically, which we refer to in this chapter as the coal tax.[6]

The coal tax rate has varied over the years. From 1986 through 2018, the coal tax rate was $1.10 per ton of underground-mined coal and $0.55 per ton of surface-mined coal, up to 4.4 percent of the sales price. In 2019, the rate of the coal tax decreased to $0.50 cents and $0.25 cents per ton of underground-mined and surface-mined coal, respectively, up to

---

[1] GAO, *Black Lung Benefits Program: Improved Oversight of Coal Mine Operator Insurance Is Needed*, GAO-20-21 (Washington D.C.: Feb. 26, 2020).

[2] A miner's surviving dependents can also receive compensation. Black lung is caused by breathing coal mine dust, and the severity of the disease can range from mild—with no noticeable effects on breathing—to advanced disease, which could lead to respiratory failure and death according to the Department of Health and Human Service's Centers for Disease Control, National Institute for Occupational Safety and Health. See https://www.cdc.gov/niosh/docs/2019-130/default.html.

[3] GAO, *Black Lung Benefits Program: Options for Improving Trust Fund Finances*, GAO-18-351 (Washington D.C.: May 30, 2018).

[4] Under federal law, when necessary for the Trust Fund to make relevant expenditures, funds are appropriated to the Trust Fund as "repayable advances," and then those advances must be repaid with interest to the general fund of the U.S. Treasury. 26 U.S.C. § 9501(c). For reporting purposes, we refer to this process as "borrowing" from Treasury's general fund, which is distinct from the borrowing authority provided by law to some agencies. According to the Treasury, the general fund includes assets and liabilities used to finance the daily and long-term operations of the U.S. government as a whole.

[5] GAO, Black Lung Benefits Program: Financing and Oversight Challenges Are Adversely Affecting the Trust Fund, GAO-19-622T (Washington D.C.: June 20, 2019).

[6] The coal tax is imposed on the sale of all domestically produced coal with two exceptions: (1) lignite coal and (2) exported coal.

2 percent of the sales price. In 2020, the rate of the coal tax increased to pre-2019 levels. However, it is scheduled to decrease again beginning in 2021. With less revenue from the coal tax, the Trust Fund will likely need to borrow more from Treasury's general fund.

My statement summarizes the findings from the report we are releasing today, which addresses: (1) how coal mine operator bankruptcies have affected the Trust Fund, and (2) how DOL managed coal mine operator insurance to limit financial risk to the Trust Fund. In summary, we found:

- Three self-insured coal mine operator bankruptcies from 2014 through 2016 transferred about $865 million in benefit responsibility to the Trust Fund, according to DOL estimates.
    - Several other self-insured operator bankruptcies have occurred since 2016 that may also affect the Trust Fund.
    - Commercial black lung insurance helps limit Trust Fund exposure to coal operator bankruptcies.
- DOL's limited oversight of coal mine operator insurance has exposed the Trust Fund to considerable financial risk.
    - DOL began implementing a new self-insurance process in July 2019, but it lacks key enforcement procedures that could help to prevent the reoccurrence of past oversight deficiencies.
    - DOL does not monitor the commercial-insurance policies purchased by coal mine operators to secure their benefit liabilities.

We made three recommendations, and DOL agreed with them:

- To establish procedures for self-insurance renewals;
- To establish procedures for coal operator appeals; and
- To develop a process to monitor whether commercially-insured operators maintain adequate and continuous coverage.

For our report, we analyzed Bloomberg data and consulted DOL to identify coal operators that filed for bankruptcy from 2014 through 2016;[7] analyzed National Council on Compensation Insurance (NCCI) data and DOL documentation on commercially-insured and self-insured coal mine operators; and examined workers' compensation insurance practices in four states—Kentucky, Pennsylvania, West Virginia, and Wyoming—to identify relevant practices that could inform DOL's administration of coal

[7] Our search focused on the bankruptcies of parent operators rather than individual subsidiaries. Bankruptcy proceedings can vary in duration. We identified coal mine operator bankruptcies that were filed from 2014 through 2016, in part, because they were more likely to be resolved. Bankruptcies filed more recently may still be ongoing and their effects on the Trust Fund may not yet be known.

operator insurance at the federal level. We also interviewed DOL officials, coal mine operators, insurance company representatives, and officials from the National Mining Association, NCCI, National Council of Self- Insurers, and the American Academy of Actuaries, among others. A more detailed explanation of our methodology is available in our report.[8]

The work upon which this statement is based was conducted in accordance with generally accepted government auditing standards.

SOME SELF-INSURED OPERATOR BANKRUPTCIES SHIFTED $865 MILLION IN ESTIMATED LIABILITY TO THE TRUST FUND, BUT COMMERCIAL INSURANCE COVERAGE CAN HELP LIMIT TRUST FUND EXPOSURE

Of the eight coal mine operator bankruptcies we identified, three resulted in a transfer of estimated benefit liability from the coal operator to the Trust Fund and five did not, according to DOL. Figure 1 shows how many operators were self-insured or commercially insured at the time of bankruptcy, and if responsibility for benefits was shifted from the bankrupt operator to the Trust Fund. Federal law generally requires coal mine operators to secure their black lung benefit liability.[9] A self-insured coal mine operator assumes the financial responsibility for providing black lung benefits to its eligible employees by paying claims as they are incurred. Operators are allowed to self-insure if they meet certain DOL conditions. For instance, operators applying to self-insure must obtain collateral in the form of an indemnity bond, deposit or trust, or letter of credit in an amount deemed necessary and sufficient by DOL to secure their liability.[10] Operators that do not self-insure are generally required to obtain coverage from commercial insurance companies, state workers' compensation insurance funds, or other entities authorized under state law to insure workers' compensation.[11]

---

[8] GAO-20-21.

[9] 30 U.S.C. § 933(a). Employers that are not coal mine operators are not required to secure their liability with respect to employees engaged in the transportation of coal or in coal mine construction. 30 U.S.C. § 932(b).

[10] A letter of credit may only be used in conjunction with another acceptable form of collateral.

[11] According to DOL regulations, an endorsement affording coverage under the Federal Coal Mine Health and Safety Act of 1969, as amended, shall be attached and applicable to the standard workers' compensation and employer's liability policy prepared by NCCI. See 20 C.F.R. § 726.203(a). An endorsement, sometimes called a rider, amends a policy's coverages, terms, or conditions.

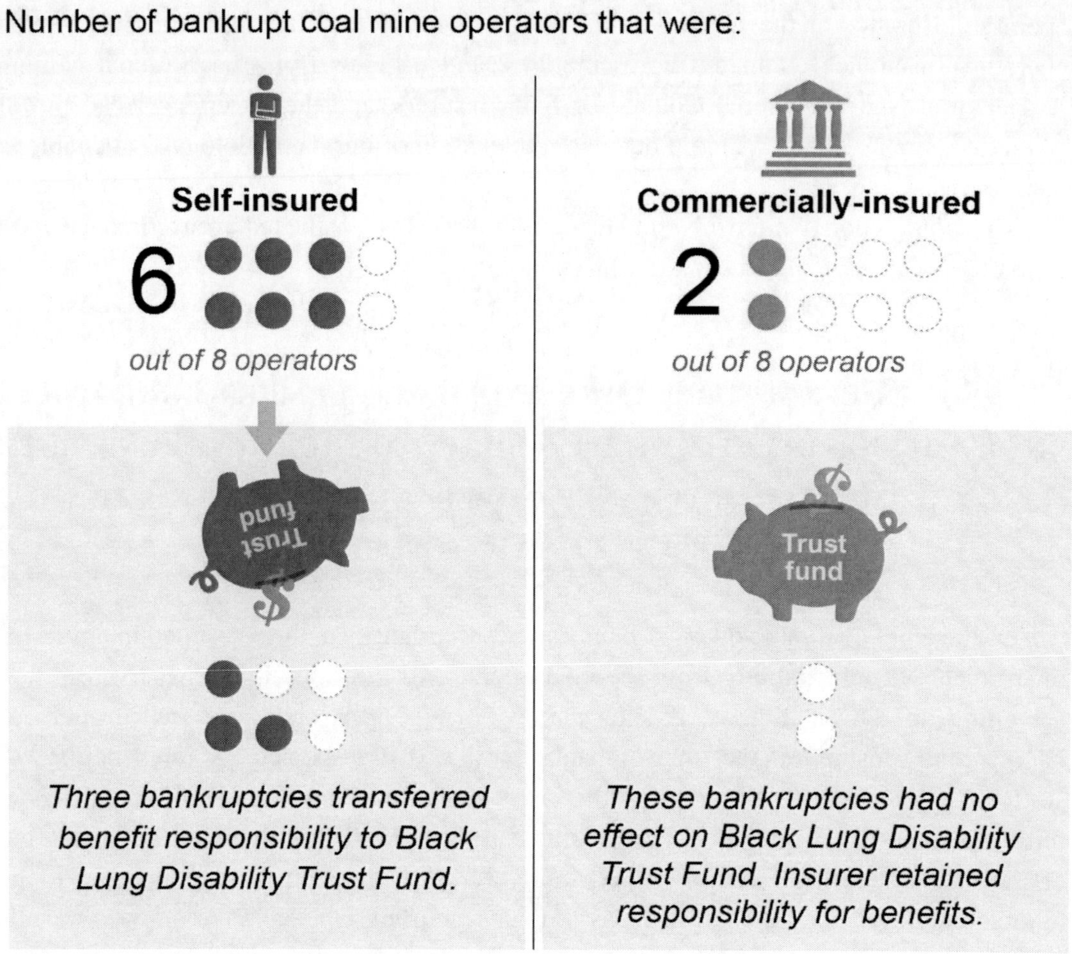

Source: Bloomberg data and Department of labor officials. | GAO-20-438T.

Figure 1. Coal Mine Operator Bankruptcies Filed from 2014 through 2016.

From 2014 through 2016, three self-insured coal mine operator bankruptcies resulted in a transfer of $865 million of benefit liabilities from the coal operators to the Trust Fund, according to DOL estimates (see table 1).[12] DOL estimates for how these bankruptcies will affect the Trust Fund have considerably increased from what DOL had previously reported.[13] In June 2019, we reported that DOL estimated that between $313 million to $325 million in benefit liabilities would transfer to the Trust Fund as a result of these bankruptcies.[14] In January 2020, however, DOL provided updated estimates stating that $865 million in benefit liabilities would transfer to the Trust Fund as a result of these bankruptcies. According to DOL, their estimates increased, among other reasons, to account for higher black lung benefit award rates that occurred from fiscal years 2016

[12] DOL officials said benefit liabilities transfers to the Trust Fund over time as claims accrue and are paid over future decades.

[13] Fiscal Year 2020 Congressional Budget Justification, Black Lung Disability Trust Fund.

[14] GAO-19-622T.

through 2019, and higher medical treatment cost inflation in recent years. Additionally, DOL's prior estimate for the Patriot Coal (Patriot) bankruptcy did not account for future claims and their effect on the Trust Fund. The amount of collateral DOL required from these operators to self-insure did not fully cover their estimated benefit liabilities. When this occurs, benefit liabilities in excess of the collateral can be transferred to the Trust Fund. For example, the collateral DOL required from Alpha Natural Resources (Alpha) was about $12 million and approximately $494 million of estimated benefit liability transferred to the Trust Fund, according to DOL.

Table 1. Self-insured coal mine operator bankruptcies that affected the Black Lung Disability Trust Fund, filed from 2014 through 2016

Coal operator	Amount of collateral at time of bankruptcy	Estimated benefit liability transferred to the Trust Fund	Estimated number of beneficiaries for whom liability has been transferred to the Trust Fund[a]
Alpha Natural Resources	$12 million	$494 million	1,839
James River Coal	$0.4 million	$141 million	490
Patriot Coal	$15 million	$230 million	993
Total	$27.4 million	$865 million	3,322

Source: Department of Labor (DOL). | GAO-20-438T.

[a] These totals include claims in active pay status as of September 2019, and estimates of newly awarded claims in fiscal year 2020 and into the future, according to DOL.

The three other self-insured coal mine operator bankruptcies we identified did not affect the Trust Fund. Specifically, Arch Coal, Peabody Energy, and Walter Energy were also self-insured operators, but DOL officials said that their federal black lung benefit liabilities were assumed by a reorganized company or by a purchaser, and therefore did not transfer to the Trust Fund.

Insurance contracts or policies to secure operators' benefit liabilities are required by law to include a provision that insolvency or bankruptcy of an operator does not release the insurer from the obligation to make benefit payments.[15] Additionally, state insurance regulation, insurer underwriting, risk management practices, and state guaranty funds help to protect the Trust Fund from having to assume responsibility for paying black lung benefits on behalf of bankrupt coal operators.[16] Thus, by being commercially insured, the two operators we identified that filed for bankruptcy between 2014 and 2016—Energy

[15] 30 U.S.C. § 933(b)(2).

[16] Property and casualty insurers, which provide black lung coverage, generally pay assessments to state guaranty funds based on the amount of premium written to finance the cost of resolving insolvent insurers.

Future Holdings and Xinergy Ltd—did not affect the Trust Fund, according to DOL (see Figure 1).

Since 2016, several other self-insured operators have also filed for bankruptcy, according to DOL officials, including Cambrian Coal, Cloud Peak Energy, Murray Energy, and Westmoreland Coal. DOL officials said that about $17.4 million in estimated black lung benefit liability will transfer to the Trust Fund as a result of Westmoreland Coal's bankruptcy. Given the uncertainty of the bankruptcy process in terms of whether liabilities will or will not transfer to the Trust Fund, however, DOL officials said that they could not speculate on how these other bankruptcies may affect the Trust Fund.

DOL's Limited Oversight Has Exposed the Trust Fund to Financial Risk, and Its New Self-Insurance Process Lacks Enforcement Procedures

In overseeing coal mine operator self-insurance in the past, DOL did not estimate future benefit liability when setting collateral or regularly review operators to monitor their changing financial conditions. DOL regulations require that collateral be obtained from operators in an amount deemed necessary and sufficient to secure the payment of the operators' liability.[17]

To determine collateral amounts under the former process, agency procedures stated that an operator's net worth be assessed by reviewing, among other factors, the operator's audited financial statements and black lung claims information. The amount of collateral was to be equal to 3, 5, or 10 years of the operator's annual black lung benefit payments made at the time of a coal operator's self-insurance application depending on its net worth. Specifically, if net worth was $1 billion or greater, agency procedures set collateral equal to 3 years of benefit payments. If net worth ranged from $500 million to $1 billion, collateral was equal to 5 years of benefit payments. If net worth ranged from $10 million to $500 million, DOL set collateral equal to 10 years of benefit payments. Agency procedures did not permit operators with net worth less than $10 million to self-insure.

DOL's former process for determining collateral did not routinely consider potential future claims for which an operator could be responsible. The agency periodically reauthorized coal operators to self-insure by reviewing an operator's most recent audited financial statement and claims information, among other things. DOL prepared memos documenting these reviews, and communicated with coal operators about whether their financial circumstances warranted increasing or decreasing their collateral.

---

[17] 20 C.F.R. § 726.105.

Regulations state that DOL may adjust the amount of collateral required from self-insured operators when experience or changed conditions so warrant,[18] but regular monitoring of self-insured operators was not conducted. In reviewing the most recent reauthorization memos for each of the self-insured operators, we found that while some of these operators had been reauthorized more recently, others had not been in decades. One operator in particular had not been reauthorized since 1988. There were no written procedures that specified how often reauthorizations should occur after an operator's initial 18-month reauthorization.

DOL has other tools available to mitigate financial losses to the Trust Fund. These include revoking an operator's ability to self-insure; fining mine operators for operating without insurance; and placing liens on operator assets.[19] Based on our review of agency documentation, however, we found instances when officials did not use these tools to protect the Trust Fund, or were hindered from doing so because of an operator's ongoing appeal or bankruptcy.

- James River. In September 2001, DOL required $5 million in additional collateral from James River Coal (James River), which would have increased its collateral from $0.4 million to $5.4 million. Although DOL did not receive the additional collateral, it did not revoke the operator's authority to self-insure, which is a potential option under agency regulations. Further, DOL had not reauthorized James River at any point from August 2001 until it filed for bankruptcy in April 2014. If James River's ability to self-insure had been revoked, DOL could have potentially prevented the Trust Fund from being responsible for claims based on a miner's employment from 2001 through 2016, when James River liquidated. Additionally, if the operator had been unable to obtain commercial insurance, the agency could have potentially fined the operator for each day it operated without insurance. Instead, no action was taken during these years and estimated benefit liability of $141 million was shifted to the Trust Fund, according to DOL. DOL officials stated that they do not have records explaining why James River did not provide the additional collateral or why they did not revoke its authority to self-insure.

---

[18] 20 C.F.R. § 726.105.

[19] DOL regulations state that the agency, with good cause shown, may revoke the authority of any coal operator to self-insure. 20 C.F.R. § 726.115. Additionally, the Black Lung Benefits Act states that DOL can fine mine operators up to $1,000 a day for operating without insurance. 30 U.S.C. § 933(d)(1). However, DOL officials said that, per the Inflation Adjustment Act, they can actually charge operators up to $2,924. DOL officials said the last time they fined a coal operator for operating without insurance was in2007, and that they do not have records of whether fines were used prior to 2007. If an operator is uninsured and is a corporation, the president, secretary, and treasurer of the operator can be liable for the assessed penalties and for benefit claims for the period in which the operator was uninsured. However, DOL officials said that they do not maintain records of those instances when DOL sought to hold company officials liable.

- Patriot. In August 2014, DOL required an additional $65 million in collateral from Patriot, increasing its collateral from $15 million to $80 million. Patriot appealed this decision and, in the 8 months that followed before Patriot filed for bankruptcy in May 2015, DOL did not obtain additional collateral, or revoke Patriot's ability to self-insure because the appeal was still pending. DOL officials said they would not typically revoke an operator's authority to self-insure during an ongoing appeal. As a result, DOL was hindered from using this enforcement tool.

Liens on operator assets can be an effective tool to protect the Trust Fund if an operator defaults on its benefit liability, but DOL officials said they are hindered from using this tool if an operator files for bankruptcy. DOL can place a lien on a coal operator's assets under federal law if they refuse the demand to pay the black lung benefit payments for which they are liable.[20] In the event of bankruptcy or insolvency, federal law states that the lien imposed shall be treated in the same manner as a lien for taxes due and owing to the United States under certain laws.[21] However, DOL officials said that operators rarely stop paying benefits until after they file for bankruptcy. Once a bankruptcy occurs, DOL officials said that they are generally prevented by the court from placing a lien and taking an operator's assets in lieu of payment of current and future benefit liability. Under bankruptcy law, DOL officials said that they have no special status over other creditors with outstanding financial claims. DOL officials said that obtaining sufficient collateral is a better way to protect the Trust Fund.

DOL's New Self-Insurance Process May Help Address Problems, but Key Enforcement Procedures Are Needed

In July 2019, DOL began implementing a new process for coal mine operator self-insurance that may help to address some past deficiencies, if implemented effectively. Among other things, DOL will require operators to periodically submit financial and claims information, including an actuarial estimate of the operator's current and future benefit liability. DOL plans to use this information to assess the insolvency risk of each operator. Depending on the results of their analysis, DOL plans to categorize the risk-level of each applicant as low, medium, or high. DOL will then set the amount of collateral required to self-insure by linking the operator's risk category to a corresponding percentage of the operator's actuarial estimated benefit liability. DOL policies state that they would require a high-risk operator to secure with collateral 90 percent of estimated benefit liability, a medium-risk operator to secure 45 percent, and a

[20] 30 U.S.C. § 934(b)(2).

[21] 30 U.S.C. § 934(b).

low-risk operator to secure 15 percent. However, in February 2020, DOL officials said they plan to revise these percentages to 100 percent, 85 percent, and 70 percent for high-risk, medium-risk, and low-risk operators, respectively.

Coal mine operators that are already authorized to self-insure will be required to submit, among other things, an annual renewal application. DOL plans to use this information to update their insolvency risk analysis. If an operator's risk category changes (e.g., from low-to medium-risk), DOL plans to send a form to the operator requiring an additional amount or type of collateral. Upon receiving the completed form, and proof that the collateral has been obtained, DOL stated that they will notify the operator that its authority to self-insure has been reauthorized.

DOL's new self-insurance process made important changes, but overlooked other key internal control improvements that are needed to protect the financial interests of the Trust Fund. DOL's new requirements for setting collateral and for the more frequent review of self-insured operators are key components of internal controls, which call for agency management to implement control activities through policy.[22] However, DOL's new self-insurance procedures do not specify (1) the duration of an operator's self-insurance authority, (2) the time frames for submitting renewal applications and supporting documentation, and (3) the conditions under which an operator's self-insurance authority would not be renewed. Our report recommends that DOL implement procedures for coal mine operator self-insurance renewal that clarifies how long an operator is authorized to self-insure; when an operator must submit its renewal application and supporting documentation; and the conditions under which an operator's self-insurance authority would not be renewed. DOL agreed with this recommendation and stated that it will ensure letters granting or renewing self-insurance authority will inform operators that their authorization expires in one year and that they must submit renewal information three months in advance of the expiration date.

DOL staff are hindered from taking enforcement action during an operator's ongoing appeal, as previously mentioned. DOL policies state that an operator may request reconsideration if its self-insurance application has been denied or if it believes the collateral required by DOL is too high to secure its benefit liability. However, DOL lacks procedures that specify, among other things, the length of time that operators have to submit supporting information. Further, DOL does not specify a goal for how much time DOL appeals decisions should take. For example, in October 2015, DOL recommended revoking Murray Energy's (Murray) authority to self-insure due to deteriorating financial conditions. Murray appealed this decision, and DOL officials said they postponed responding to the appeal until their new self-insurance process was implemented. However, Murray filed for bankruptcy in October 2019 and DOL had not revoked its authority to self-insure or requested additional collateral because Murray's appeal was still

[22] GAO, *Standards for Internal Control in the Federal Government*, GAO-14-704G (Washington D.C.: September 2014).

pending and DOL was still evaluating how much collateral it would require from the operator under its new self- insurance process.

Our report recommends that DOL develop and implement procedures for self-insured coal mine operator appeals that identify time lines for self- insured operators to submit documentation supporting their appeals and that identify a goal for how much time DOL should take to make appeals decisions. DOL agreed with this recommendation and stated that they will ensure letters denying self-insurance will inform operators that they have a 30-day appeal period (limited to one extension), and that DOL has set a goal of resolving all appeals within 90 days of the denial letter.

Commercial Insurance Oversight Improvements Are Needed

We found that DOL does not monitor coal mine operators that do not self- insure and, thus, must commercially insure their federal black lung liabilities to make certain they maintain adequate and continuous coverage as required by law. In the absence of effective DOL monitoring, we evaluated the potential risk that uninsured operators could pose to the Trust Fund. Specifically, in examining the 13 largest coal mine operators that do not self-insure, we found that some insurers erred in reporting black lung policies and in one instance an operator did not have adequate coverage.

- We found six operators (parent or subsidiary) that were not insured for the entire 3-year period from 2016 through 2018, according to our review of DOL data. When we discussed our findings with DOL, agency officials had to research each operator individually and in some cases contact the operator or their insurer to find out whether or not they had been covered. DOL concluded that these entities were insured. However, the insurers had not properly reported the federal black lung endorsement on new policies or subsequent renewals, in addition to other reporting issues.[23]
- One of these six operators also had, inadvertently, not maintained adequate commercial coverage for its mining operations in Texas, and had not self-insured those operations. In this instance, the operator obtained an excess loss policy that only pays claims once they exceed a high threshold and, therefore, is not sufficient by itself to secure the payment of the operator's benefit liability.[24]

---

[23] We found similar reporting issues with two self-insured coal operators that had subsidiaries that were commercially insured or insured by a state workers' compensation insurance fund.

[24] When we raised the issue with the operator's insurer, they said they had inadvertently omitted Texas from the list of states covered by the federal black lung endorsement on the operator's standard workers' compensation policy. According to the insurer, they have corrected the error and made the changes retroactive to the endorsement's original effective date to ensure the operator's Texas operations will be covered.

Designing processes to achieve agency objectives and respond to risks is a principle of effective internal controls.[25] Without a process to monitor operator compliance with program insurance requirements, DOL risks not identifying a lapse or cancellation of operator coverage. This could result in the Trust Fund having to assume responsibility for paying benefits that would otherwise have been paid by an insurer.[26]

Our report recommends that DOL should develop and implement a process to monitor operator compliance with commercial insurance requirements and periodically evaluate the effectiveness of this process. DOL agreed with this recommendation and stated that it will modify existing computer systems to identify lapses or cancellations of commercial insurance coverage, and require operators identified as having lapsed or cancelled coverage to obtain or provide proof of coverage within 30 days.

Chairwoman Adams, Ranking Member Byrne, and Members of the Subcommittee, this concludes my prepared statement. I would be happy to respond to any questions you may have at this time.

[25] GAO-14-704G.

[26] Another potential consequence of DOL's failure to monitor operator compliance with program insurance requirements is that responsibility for the payment of benefits can shift from operators that most recently employed a miner and are uninsured to other operators that previously employed the miner and are insured.

In: Black Lung Programs: MSHA, Benefits and Challenges ISBN: 978-1-53619-388-6
Editor: Ross D. Blodgett

Chapter 5

THE BLACK LUNG PROGRAM, THE BLACK LUNG DISABILITY TRUST FUND, AND THE EXCISE TAX ON COAL: BACKGROUND AND POLICY OPTIONS*

Scott D. Szymendera and Molly F. Sherlock

SUMMARY

The federal government pays benefits to coal miners affected by coal workers' pneumoconiosis (CWP, commonly referred to as black lung disease) and other lung diseases linked to coal mining in cases where responsible mine operators are not able to pay. In 2019, the monthly benefit for a miner with no dependents is $660.10. Benefits can be as much as $1,320.10 per month for miners with three or more dependents. Medical benefits are provided separately from disability benefits. Benefit payments and related administrative expenses in cases in which the responsible operators do not pay are paid out of the Black Lung Disability Trust Fund. The primary source of revenue for the trust fund is an excise tax on coal produced and sold domestically. If excise tax revenue is not sufficient to finance Black Lung Program benefits, the trust fund may borrow from the general fund of the Treasury.

For 2018, the tax rates on coal were $1.10 per ton of underground-mined coal or $0.55 per ton of surface-mined coal, limited to 4.4% of the sales price. These rates were established in 1986. Starting in 2019, under current law, these tax rates are $0.50 per ton of underground-mined coal or $0.25 per ton of surface-mined coal, limited to 2% of the sales price. These are the rates that were set when the trust fund was established in 1977.

The decline in the excise tax rates will likely put additional financial strain on a trust fund that already borrows from the general fund to meet obligations. The decline in domestic coal production, recent increases in the rate of CWP, and bankruptcies in the coal sector also contribute to the financial strain on the trust fund.

* This is an edited, reformatted and augmented version of Congressional Research Service Publication No. R45261, dated January 18, 2019.

The Black Lung Disability Trust Fund and associated excise tax on coal were established so that the coal industry, as opposed to taxpayers in general, would bear the burden associated with providing black lung benefits. Throughout its history, the Black Lung Disability Trust Fund has not raised revenues sufficient to meet obligations. As a result, at various points in time, Congress and the President have acted to increase the excise tax on coal, forgive or refinance trust fund debt, and modify black lung benefits eligibility. With the rate of the excise tax on coal reduced in 2019, the 116th Congress may again evaluate options for improving the fiscal condition of the Black Lung Disability Trust Fund, or other issues related to providing federal benefits to miners with black lung disease.

The federal government pays benefits to coal miners affected by coal workers' pneumoconiosis (CWP, commonly referred to as black lung disease) and other lung diseases linked to coal mining in cases where the responsible mine operators are not able to pay. Benefit payments and related administrative expenses are paid out of the Black Lung Disability Trust Fund. The primary source of revenue for the trust fund is an excise tax on coal produced and sold domestically. If excise tax revenue is not sufficient to finance Black Lung Program benefits, the trust fund may borrow from the general fund of the Treasury, which contains federal receipts not earmarked for a specific purpose.

For 2018, the tax rates on coal were $1.10 per ton of underground-mined coal or $0.55 per ton of surface-mined coal, limited to 4.4% of the sales price. Starting in 2019, under current law, these tax rates are $0.50 per ton of underground-mined coal or $0.25 per ton of surface-mined coal, limited to 2% of the sales price. This decline in the excise tax rates will likely put additional financial strain on a trust fund that already borrows from the general fund to meet obligations. The decline in domestic coal production, recent increases in the rate of CWP, and bankruptcies in the coal sector also contribute to the financial strain on the trust fund.[1]

This chapter provides background information and policy options to help inform the debate surrounding the coal excise tax rate, and other considerations related to the Black Lung Disability Trust Fund. The report begins with an overview of the federal black lung program, providing information on black lung disease and benefits under the program. The report proceeds to examine Black Lung Disability Trust Fund revenues, focusing on the coal excise tax and its history. The report closes with a discussion of policy options, evaluating various revenue- and benefits-related policy options that could improve the fiscal outlook of the Black Lung Disability Trust Fund.

---

[1] For general information on the U.S. coal industry, see CRS Report R44922, *The U.S. Coal Industry: Historical Trends and Recent Developments*, by Marc Humphries.

FEDERAL BLACK LUNG PROGRAM

The Black Lung Disability Trust Fund is used to finance the payment of federal Black Lung Program benefits under Part C of the Black Lung Benefits Act (BLBA) when a responsible coal operator does not meet its obligations under the law to pay benefits.

Black Lung Disease

Coal workers' pneumoconiosis (CWP, commonly referred to as black lung disease) is an interstitial lung disease caused by the inhalation of coal dust.[2] Like in other types of pneumoconioses, the inhalation of coal dust results in the scarring of the lung tissue and affects the gas-exchanging ability of the lungs to remove carbon dioxide and take oxygen into the bloodstream.[3] Exposure to coal dust over an extended period of time can lead to CWP and continued exposure can lead to the progression from the early stages of CWP referred to as "simple CWP," to more advanced stages of scarring referred to as "complicated CWP" or progressive massive fibrosis (PMF). There is no cure for CWP and PMF. CWP can lead to loss of lung function, the need for lung transplantation, and premature death. CWP can be identified by observing light spots, or opacities, in x-ray images of the lungs and can be classified using guidelines established by the International Labour Organization (ILO).[4]

Despite technological advances in mining dust control, mandatory chest x-rays for miners,[5] free CWP surveillance offered to miners by the National Institute for Occupational Safety and Health (NIOSH),[6] the enactment of numerous pieces of mine safety and health legislation,[7] and the promulgation and enforcement of mine safety and health standards by the Mine Safety and Health Administration (MSHA),[8] CWP persists

---

[2] For additional information on CWP, see the website of the National Institute for Occupational Safety and Health (NIOSH) at https://www.cdc.gov/niosh/topics/cwhsp/coalminingrelatedrespiratorydiseases.html.

[3] Other types of pneumoconioses include silicosis caused by the inhalation of silica dust, and asbestosis caused by the inhalation of asbestos fibers. For additional information on pneumoconioses, see the website of NIOSH at https://www.cdc.gov/niosh/topics/pneumoconioses/.

[4] For additional information on the ILO classification system, see the website of NIOSH at https://www.cdc.gov/niosh/topics/chestradiography/ilo.html.

[5] Federal law at 30 U.S.C. § 843(a) requires that each miner new to coal mining be given a free chest x-ray within 18 months of starting work, a follow-up x-ray within three years of the first x-ray, and if the follow-up x-ray shows evidence of CWP, an additional chest x-ray within two years of the follow-up x-ray.

[6] For additional information on the NIOSH Coal Workers' Health Surveillance Program, see the NIOSH website at https://www.cdc.gov/niosh/topics/cwhsp/default.html.

[7] The major pieces of enacted coal mine safety and health legislation are the Federal Coal Mine Safety and Health Act of 1969 (P.L. 91-73), the Federal Mine Safety and Health Amendments Act of 1977 (P.L. 95-164), and the Mine Improvement and New Emergency Response Act of 2006 (MINER Act, P.L. 109-236).

[8] The MSHA standards for underground coal mine safety and health are published in Chapter 1, Subchapter O, of Part 30 of the C.F.R. In 2015, MSHA revised its standards on exposure to respirable coal dust to lower exposure limits for coal miners (Mine Safety and Health Administration, "Lowering Miners' Exposure to Respirable Coal Mine Dust, Including Continuous Personal Dust Monitors," 79 *Federal Register* 24813, May 1, 2014).

in American coal miners, especially those in the Appalachian region. After reductions in rates of PMF in the 1990s, this advanced form of CWP has recently been found in Central Appalachia at rates not seen since the early 1970s.[9] In 2017 researchers discovered, among coal miners mostly living in Kentucky and Virginia and served by three federally funded Black Lung Clinics in Virginia,[10] what may be the largest cluster of PMF ever recorded.[11]

This cluster of miners with PMF includes a relatively high number of miners with less than 20 years of mining experience as well as cases of PMF in current miners. The occurrence of this advanced stage of CWP in short-tenured and current miners is noteworthy since MSHA standards require that any miner with evidence of CWP be given the option, without loss of compensation or other penalty, to work in an area of the mining operation in which the average concentration of coal dust in the air is continuously maintained at or below an established level that is lower than the permissible exposure level for all miners with the goal of preventing the progression of CWP.[12]

Federal Black Lung Program

The federal Black Lung Program was created in 1969 with the enactment of Title IV of the Federal Coal Mine Health and Safety Act of 1969 (Coal Act, P.L. 91-173, later renamed the Federal Mine Safety and Health Act of 1977 by P.L. 95-164). Section 401 of the Coal Act provides the congressional justification for the federal Black Lung Program and cites the lack of benefits for disability and death caused by CWP provided by existing state workers' compensation systems as justification for the creation of a federal program. This section also states that the program is intended to be a cooperative effort between the federal government and the states.

The Coal Act also established mandatory safety and health standards for coal mines, including standards limiting exposure of miners to coal dust and giving miners with CWP the option of being moved, without loss of compensation or penalty, to an area of the

---

[9] David J. Blackley, Cara N. Halldin, and A. Scott Laney, "Resurgence of a Debilitating and Entirely Preventable Respiratory Disease among Working Coal Miners," *American Journal of Respiratory and Critical Care Medicine*, vol. 190, no. 6 (September 15, 2014), pp. 708-709; and David J. Blackley, James B. Crum, Cara N. Halldin, et al., "Resurgence of Progressive Massive Fibrosis in Coal Miners-Eastern Kentucky, 2016," *Morbidity and Mortality Weekly Report*, vol. 65, no. 49 (December 16, 2016), pp. 1385-1389.

[10] Federal Black Lung Clincs are medical clinics that provide screening and treatment for CWP regardless of a miner's ability to pay. Federal Black Lung Clinics are supported by grants from the Department of Health and Human Services (HHS), Health Resources and Services Administration (HRSA) as authorized by 30 U.S.C. §937.

[11] David J. Blackley, Laura E. Reynolds, Connie Short, et al., "Progressive Massive Fibrosis in Coal Miners from Three Clinics in Virginia," *Journal of the American Medical Association*, vol. 319, no. 5 (February 6, 2018), pp. 500-501.

[12] 30 C.F.R. §90.3. The concentration limits of respirable coal dust are 1.5 milligrams per cubic meter (mg/m^3) of air for all miners and 0.5 mg/m^3 for miners with evidence of CWP.

mine with lower dust concentrations. The Coal Act was later amended by the Black Lung Benefits Act of 1972 (BLBA, P.L. 92-303).

Part B

The Coal Act established Part B of the federal Black Lung Program to provide cash benefits to miners totally disabled due to CWP and to the survivors of miners who die from CWP.[13] Part B only applies to cases filed on or before December 31, 1973. Part B benefits are paid out of general revenue and were initially administered by the Social Security Administration (SSA). Today, with the exception of a small number of pending appellate cases, Part B benefits are administered by the Department of Labor (DOL), Office of Workers' Compensation Programs (OWCP).

Part C

The Coal Act established Part C of the Federal Black Lung Program for cases filed after December 31, 1973, and was later amended by the BLBA. Under Part C of the BLBA, all claims for benefits for disability or death due to CWP are to be filed with each state's workers' compensation system, but only if such systems have been determined by DOL as providing benefits that are equivalent to or greater than the cash benefits provided by the federal government under Part B of the BLBA and the medical benefits provided to disabled longshore and harbor workers under the federal Longshore and Harbor Workers' Compensation Act (LHWCA).[14] If a state's workers' compensation system is not determined by DOL to meet these standards, then Part C benefits are to be paid by the each miner's coal employer, or, if no such employer is available to pay benefits, by the federal government.

In 1973, Maryland, Kentucky, Virginia, and West Virginia submitted their state workers' compensation laws to DOL for approval, but were denied.[15] To date, no state workers' compensation system has been approved by DOL under Part C of the BLBA.

---

[13] Although Part B did not originally include medical benefits, these benefits are now available to Part B claimants under Part C and are paid by the responsible mine operators or the Black Lung Disability Trust Fund.

[14] For additional information on the LHWCA, see CRS Report R41506, *The Longshore and Harbor Workers' Compensation Act (LHWCA): Overview of Workers' Compensation for Certain Private-Sector Maritime Workers*, by Scott D. Szymendera.

[15] Peter S. Barth, *The Tragedy of Black Lung: Federal Compensation for Occupational Disease* (Kalamazoo, MI: W.E. Upjohn Institute for Employment Research, 1987), p. 196.

Operator Responsibility

Because no state's workers' compensation system has been determined to be sufficient to pay benefits under Part C, each operator of an underground coal mine is responsible for the payment of benefits to that operator's miners. Operators are required to provide for these benefits either by purchasing insurance for benefits or through self-insurance approved by DOL.

A self-insured operator is required to purchase an indemnity bond or provide another form of security (such as a deposit of negotiable securities in a Federal Reserve Bank or the establishment of a trust) in an amount specified by DOL. In order to be approved for self-insurance, federal regulations require that a mine operator have been in business for at least the three previous years and have average assets over the previous three years that exceed current liabilities by the sum of expected benefit payments and annual premiums on the indemnity bond.[16]

When a claim for benefits is approved, benefits are to be paid by the "responsible" operator, which is generally the last coal operator to employ the miner.[17] If a company has acquired the assets of a mine operator, then that company is considered a "successor operator" and is responsible for the payment of claims related to the original operator.[18]

Federal Payment of Benefits and Expenses

The federal government pays benefits in cases in which the responsible operator no longer exists and has no successor operator, or is unable to pay benefits. The federal government pays benefits when an operator has not made payment within 30 days of a determination of eligibility or when benefits are otherwise due to be paid. Initially, under Part C of the Coal Act, these federal benefits were paid out of general revenue. However, pursuant to the Black Lung Benefits Revenue Act of 1977 (P.L. 95-227), these benefits are now paid from the Black Lung Disability Trust Fund established by this law and primarily financed by an excise tax on coal. If a responsible operator can later be identified, the trust fund is authorized by law to seek to recover from this operator the amount of benefits paid by the trust fund and any interest earned on these amounts.

The trust fund is also used for the following federal Black Lung Program-related expenses:

- the payment of benefits for miners whose last coal mine employment was before January 1, 1970;
- reimbursement to the Treasury for the costs of Part C benefits paid from general revenue before April 1, 1978, for periods of benefit eligibility after January 1, 1974;

---

[16] 20 C.F.R. §726.101.
[17] 20 C.F.R. §725.495.
[18] 20 C.F.R. §725.492.

- the repayment and payment of interest on advances made from the general fund to the trust fund;
- the payment of administrative expenses related to Part C of the BLBA and the coal excise tax incurred after March 1, 1978; and
- the reimbursement of coal operators who paid Part C benefits before April 1, 1978, for miners whose last coal mine employment ended before January 1, 1970.[19]

Eligibility for Black Lung Benefits

A miner is eligible for benefits if that miner is totally disabled due to pneumoconiosis arising out of coal mine employment. The survivors of a miner are eligible for benefits if the miner's death was due to pneumoconiosis arising out of coal mine employment.

Benefits are only available to miners and their survivors. The BLBA defines a miner as any individual who works or has worked in or around a coal mine or coal preparation facility in the extraction or preparation of coal. Such term also includes an individual who works or has worked in coal mine construction or transportation in or around a coal mine, to the extent such individual was exposed to coal dust as a result of such employment.[20]

Thus, other workers who may be exposed to coal dust in their work, such as railroad workers or workers at coal-fired power plants are not eligible for benefits. Persons who live near coal mines or power plants are also not eligible for benefits even if they are exposed to coal dust. In addition, while a miner's family members may receive benefits as survivors and the number of family members can increase the amount of a miner's monthly benefits, family members may not claim benefits on their own due to exposure to coal dust in the home such as from cleaning the miner's soiled clothing.

The BLBA defines pneumoconiosis for the purposes of benefit eligibility as "a chronic dust disease of the lung and its sequelae, including respiratory and pulmonary impairments, arising out of coal mine employment."[21] The BLBA directs the Secretary of Labor to develop, through regulations, standards for determining if a miner is totally disabled due to pneumoconiosis or died due to pneumoconiosis.[22]

Clinical and Legal Pneumoconiosis

The federal Black Lung Program regulations provide that the definition of pneumoconiosis includes medical or "clinical" pneumoconiosis and statutory or "legal" pneumoconiosis. Clinical pneumoconiosis is defined as follows:

---

[19] 26 U.S.C. §9501(d).
[20] 30 U.S.C. §902(d).
[21] 30 U.S.C. §902(b).
[22] 30 U.S.C. §921(b). These regulations are at 20 C.F.R.§§ 718.201-718.206.

"Clinical pneumoconiosis" consists of those diseases recognized by the medical community as pneumoconioses, i.e., the conditions characterized by permanent deposition of substantial amounts of particulate matter in the lungs and the fibrotic reaction of the lung tissue to that deposition caused by dust exposure in coal mine employment. This definition includes, but is not limited to, coal workers' pneumoconiosis, anthracosilicosis, anthracosis, anthrosilicosis, massive pulmonary fibrosis, silicosis or silicotuberculosis, arising out of coal mine employment.[23]

Legal pneumoconiosis is defined as

any chronic lung disease or impairment and its sequelae arising out of coal mine employment. This definition includes, but is not limited to, any chronic restrictive or obstructive pulmonary disease arising out of coal mine employment.[24]

Through these definitions, DOL has established that benefits are available not just to miners with CWP, but also to those miners with other respiratory diseases arising out of coal mine employment such as chronic obstructive pulmonary disease (COPD) even though these diseases are not pneumoconioses and may be linked to other factors unrelated to exposure to coal dust such as cigarette smoking.[25]

Eligibility Presumptions

The BLBA contains five presumptions used to determine if a miner is eligible for black lung benefits.[26] Three of these presumptions are "rebuttable," meaning that, in the absence of any contrary evidence, eligibility is presumed. One presumption is "irrebutable" and eligibility for Black Lung program benefits is established if the statutory requirements of the presumption are met. Three of these presumptions apply to current Black Lung Program claims while two apply only to cases filed before the end of 1981. Table 1 provides a summary of the following five presumptions provided by the BLBA.[27]

1. A rebuttable presumption that the pneumoconiosis of a miner who was employed in mining for at least 10 years was caused by his or her employment.

---

[23] 20 C.F.R. §718.201(a)(1).

[24] 20 C.F.R. §718.201(a)(2).

[25] For example, deaths due to COPD are strongly linked to cigarette smoking. The Centers for Disease Control and Prevention (CDC) estimated an average of 114,462 annual deaths due to COPD in the form of bronchitis, emphysema, and chronic airway obstruction during the period between 1997 and 2001 in the United States. Of these deaths, 79.1% were attributable to cigarette smoking (Centers for Disease Control and Prevention, "Annual Smoking-Attributable Mortality, Years of Potential Life Lost, and Productivity Losses-United States, 1997-2001," *Morbidity and Mortality Weekly Report*, vol. 54, no. 25 (July 1, 2005), pp. 625-628).

[26] 30 U.S.C. §921(c).

[27] The presumption number corresponds to the paragraph number in Subsection (c) of Section 411 of the Black Lung Benefits Act [30 U.S.C. §921(c)].

2. A rebuttable presumption that the death of a miner who worked in mining for at least 10 years and who died of any respirable disease, was due to pneumoconiosis. This presumption does not apply to claims filed on or after January 1, 1982, the effective date of the Black Lung Benefits Amendments of 1981 (P.L. 97-119).
3. An irrebuttable presumption that a miner with any chronic lung disease which meets certain statutory tests or diagnoses is totally disabled due to pneumoconiosis or died due to pneumoconiosis.
4. A rebuttable presumption that a miner employed in mining for at least 15 years, and who has a chest x-ray that is interpreted as negative with respect to certain statutory standards but who has other evidence of a totally disabling respiratory or pulmonary impairment, is totally disabled due to pneumoconiosis or died due to pneumoconiosis. This presumption may only be rebutted by the Secretary of Labor establishing that the miner does not or did not have pneumoconiosis or that the miner's respiratory or pulmonary impairment did not arise out of connection to mine employment.
5. A presumption that a miner who died on or before March 1, 1978, and who was employed in mining for at least 25 years before June 30, 1971, died due to pneumoconiosis, unless it is established that at the time of the miner's death, he or she was not at least partially disabled due to pneumoconiosis. This presumption does not apply to claims filed on or after June 29, 1982, which is 180 days after the effective date of the Black Lung Benefits Amendments of 1981. This presumption is not listed in the law as either rebuttable or irrebuttable.

Affordable Care Act Amendments

The Patient Protection and Affordable Care Act (commonly referred to as the Affordable Care Act (ACA), P.L. 111-148) included two provisions that amended the BLBA to reinstate one of the eligibility presumptions and a provision affecting survivors' benefits. The effect of these changes was to increase the opportunity to establish eligibility through the statutory presumptions and make it easier for certain survivors to receive benefits.

Pursuant to Section 202(a) of the Black Lung Benefits Amendments of 1981, the fourth presumption did not apply to cases filed on or after January 1, 1982. Section 1556(a) of the ACA removed the prohibition on applying the fourth presumption to cases filed on or after January 1, 1982. It is expected that this ACA provision will increase the number of miners eligible for benefits.

The BLBA provides that, for Part C claims, the survivors of a miner who was determined to be eligible to receive benefits at the time of his or her death are not required to file new claims for benefits or revalidate any claim for benefits, thus permitting the payment of survivors' benefits in these cases even if the miner's death was not caused by pneumoconiosis.[28] Pursuant to Section 203(a)(6) of the Black Lung Benefits Amendments of 1981, this provision did not apply to claims filed on or after January 1, 1982. Section 1556(b) of the ACA removed from this provision the exception for claims filed on or after January 1, 1982. It is expected that this ACA provision will increase the number of survivors eligible for benefits.

Table 1. Eligibility presumptions provided in the BLBA, as amended by Section 1556 of the Affordable Care Act (ACA)

Presumption Number[a]	Type of Presumption	Minimum Number of Years of Mine Employment	Basic Presumption	Exception
1	Rebuttable	10	If a miner has pneumoconiosis, then pneumoconiosis was caused by employment	None
2	Rebuttable	10	If death was from respirable disease, then death was due to pneumoconiosis	Does not apply to claims filed on or after January 1, 1982
3	Irrebuttable	None	If a miner has chronic dust disease of the lung which meets statutory standards, then he or she is totally disabled due to pneumoconiosis or died due to pneumoconiosis	None
4	Rebuttable	15	If a miner has negative chest roentgenogram, but has other evidence of respiratory or pulmonary impairment, then he or she is totally disabled due to pneumoconiosis or died due to pneumoconiosis	None[b]
5	—[c]	25, before June 30, 1971	If a miner died before March 1, 1978, then miner died due to pneumoconiosis, unless it is established that the miner did not have at least a partial disability due to pneumoconiosis at the time of death	Does not apply to claims filed on or after June 29, 1982

Source: Congressional Research Service (CRS).

a. The presumption number corresponds to the paragraph number in Subsection (c) of Section 411 of the Black Lung Benefits Act [30 U.S.C. §921(c)] and listed in this chapter.

b. Prior to the enactment of the ACA, this presumption did not apply to claims filed on or after January 1, 1982.

c. This presumption is not listed in the law as either rebuttable or irrebuttable.

[28] 30 U.S.C. §932(l).

The amendments to the BLBA provided in Section 1556 of the ACA apply to any claims filed under Part B or C of the act after January 1, 2005, that were pending on or after March 23, 2010, the date of enactment of the ACA.

Black Lung Program Benefits

Medical Benefits

Eligible miners receiving benefits under Parts B and C are entitled to medical coverage for their pneumoconiosis and related disability. This medical coverage is provided at no cost to the miner and can generally be obtained from the miner's choice of medical providers.

Disability Benefits

Eligible miners are also entitled to cash disability benefits. The basic benefit rate is set at 37.5% of the basic pay rate at GS-2, Step 1, on the federal pay schedule without any locality adjustment.[29] If the miner has one dependent (a spouse or minor child) the miner is eligible for a benefit of 150% of the basic benefit. A miner with two dependents is eligible for 175% of the basic benefit and a miner with three or more dependents is eligible for 200% of the basic benefit. Benefits may also be paid to the divorced spouse of a miner if the marriage lasted at least 10 years and the divorced spouse was dependent on the miner for at least half of the spouse's support at the time of the miner's disability. A child is considered a dependent until the child marries, or reaches age 18, unless the child is either disabled using the Social Security Disability Insurance (SSDI) definition of disability or is under the age of 23 and a full-time student.[30] The benefit rates are adjusted whenever there are changes to the federal employee pay schedules, but are not separately adjusted to reflect changes in the cost of living. Table 3 provides the benefit rates for 2019. Benefits are offset by state workers' compensation or other benefits paid on account of the miner's disability or death due to pneumoconiosis. Part C benefits, but not Part B benefits, are considered workers' compensation for the purposes of reducing a miner's SSDI benefits.[31]

---

[29] The 2018 General Schedule (Base) pay rates are available on the website of the Office of Personnel Management (OPM) at https://www.opm.gov/policy-data-oversight/pay-leave/salaries-wages/2018/general-schedule/. As there has been no legislation or presidential action to increase federal pay rates, the 2018 rates will continue in 2019.

[30] The SSDI definition of disability is provided at 42 U.S.C. §423 and generally requires that a person be unable to work full-time because of a disability. For additional information on SSDI and the definition of disability, see CRS In Focus IF10506, *Social Security Disability Insurance (SSDI)*, by William R. Morton.

[31] Section 224 of the Social Security Act (42 U.S.C. §424) provides that in cases in which a person receives both SSDI and workers' compensation benefits in a given month, the amount of the monthly SSDI benefit or the workers' compensation benefit is reduced, but not below zero, until the combined amount of the benefits equals 80% of the person's pre-disability wage depending on the type of workers' compensation benefit. In the case of Part C benefits, the persons' SSDI benefit is reduced.

Table 2. Monthly Black Lung Benefit amounts for CY2019

Category	Monthly Benefit Amount
Claimant with no dependents	$660.10
Claimant with one dependent	$990.10
Claimant with two dependents	$1,155,10
Claimant with three or more dependents	$1,320.10

Source: Office of Worker's Compensation Programs (OWCP) website at https://www.dol.gov/ owcp/dcmwc/regs/ compliance/blbene.htm.

Notes: Benefits listed are for Part C claims, which are rounded up to the nearest 10 cents. Benefits for Part B claims are the same amount as for Part C, but rounded to the nearest dollar.

The total amount paid in cash disability benefits has fallen over time, as illustrated in *Figure 1.* More is paid in cash disability benefits than is paid in medical benefits.

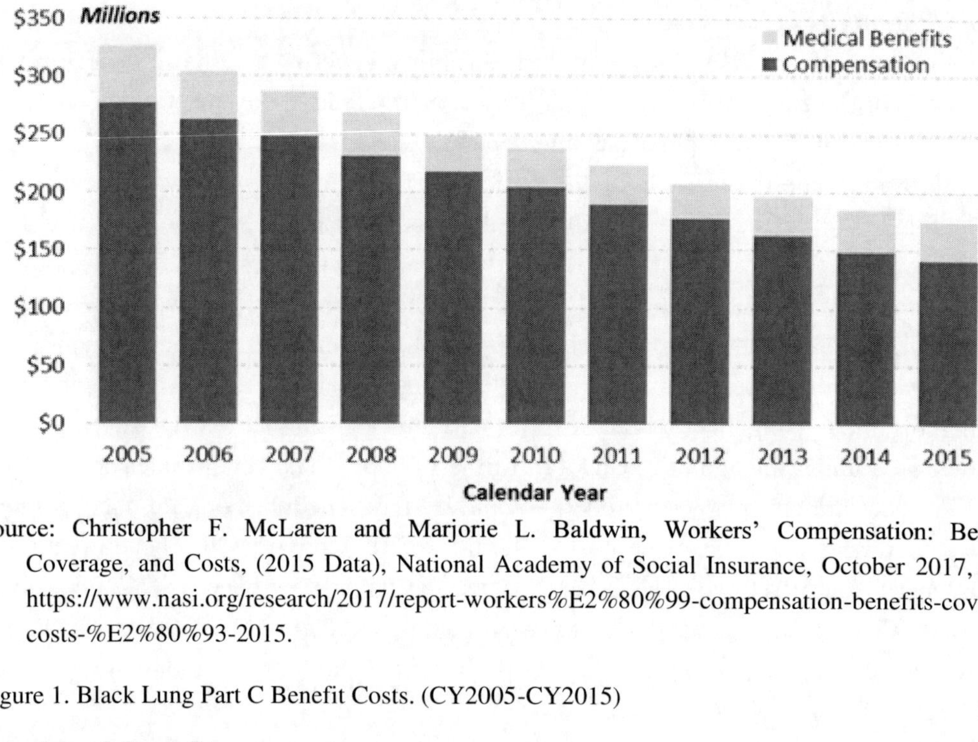

Source: Christopher F. McLaren and Marjorie L. Baldwin, Workers' Compensation: Benefits, Coverage, and Costs, (2015 Data), National Academy of Social Insurance, October 2017, p. 70, https://www.nasi.org/research/2017/report-workers%E2%80%99-compensation-benefits-coverage-costs-%E2%80%93-2015.

Figure 1. Black Lung Part C Benefit Costs. (CY2005-CY2015)

Survivors' Benefits

Certain survivors of a miner whose death was due to pneumoconiosis are eligible for cash benefits. In the case of a surviving spouse or divorced spouse, the spouse's benefit is equal to what the miner would have received and is based on the number of dependents of the spouse as provided in *Table 2.* If there is no surviving spouse, then benefits are awarded to the surviving minor children in equal shares. If there are no surviving minor children, then benefits can be paid to the miner's dependent parents or dependent siblings. If there are no eligible survivors, no benefits are paid upon the miner's death and benefits do not go to the miner's estate or to any other person, including a person named by the miner in a will. The number of miners and survivors receiving benefits has declined over time, as illustrated in *Figure 2.*

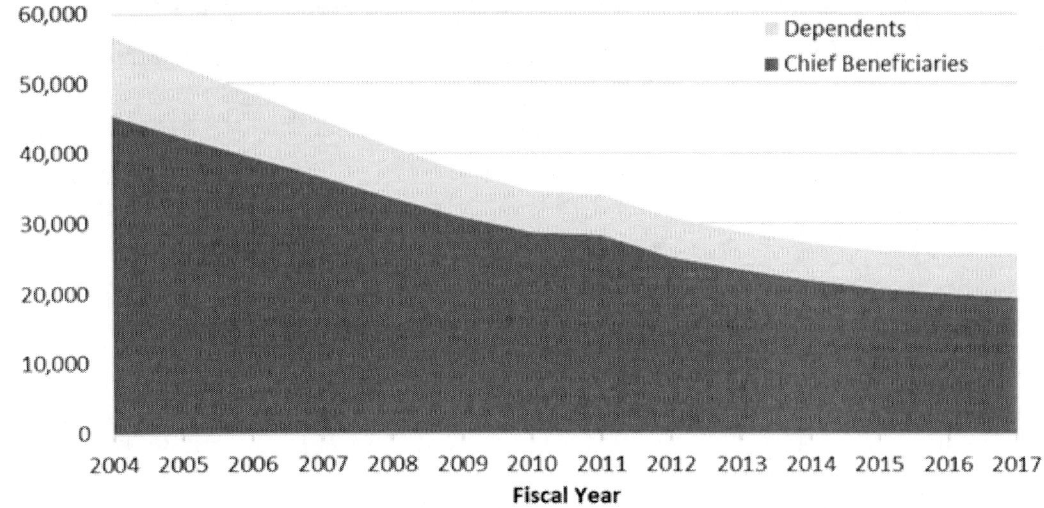

Source: Office of Workers' Compensation Programs (OWCP) website at https://www.dol.gov/owcp/dcmwc/statistics/PartsBandCBeneficiaries.htm.

Note: Chief Beneficiary is either the miner or the miner's primary survivor.

Figure 2. Black Lung Part C Beneficiaries. (FY2004-FY2017)

BLACK LUNG DISABILITY TRUST FUND REVENUES

The primary revenue source for the Black Lung Disability Trust Fund is a per-ton excise tax on coal. Historically, the coal excise tax has not generated enough revenue to meet the trust fund's obligations. Thus, additional funds have been provided from the general fund of the Treasury.[32]

The general fund includes governmental receipts not earmarked for a specific purpose, the proceeds of general borrowing, and is used for general governmental expenditures.

[32] Certain excise taxes related to Blank Lung Benefit Trusts are also deposited in the Black Lung Disability Trust Fund. Generally, since very little or no amounts have been reported for these excise taxes, a discussion of these taxes has not been included in this chapter. Black Lung Benefit Trusts are tax-exempt trusts, as described in Internal Revenue Code (IRC) Section 501(c)(21). There are no active 501(c)(21) organizations at this time.

Excise Tax on Coal

Internal Revenue Code (IRC) Section 4121 imposes the black lung excise tax (BLET) on sales or use of domestically mined coal.[33] Generally, a producer that sells the coal is liable for the tax. Producers that use their own domestically mined coal, such as integrated utilities or steel companies, are also liable for the tax.

The tax rate depends on how coal is mined. Effective January 1, 2019, the tax on underground- mined coal is the lesser of (1) $0.50 per ton, or (2) 2% of the sale price. The tax on surface-mined coal is the lesser of (1) $0.25 per ton, or (2) 2% of the sales price. Before 2019, the tax rates were $1.10 per ton for coal from underground mines or $0.55 per ton for coal from surface mines, with the tax being no more than 4.4% of the sale price. In FY2017, $229 million was collected on coal mined underground (see *Figure 3*). Nearly all of this coal was taxed at the $1.10 per ton rate. In FY2017, $200 million was collected on surface-mined coal. Just over half of this coal was taxed at the $0.55 per ton rate, with the rest subject to the 4.4% of sales price maximum tax.

On January 1, 2019, the BLET rates declined to their current levels. The rates that took effect January 1, 2019, would also have taken effect if the Black Lung Disability Trust Fund had repaid, with interest, all amounts borrowed from the General Fund of the Treasury.

The tax is imposed on "coal from mines located in the United States" and does not apply to imported coal. The tax is designed to support the Black Lung Disability Trust Fund for domestic miners. Very little domestically consumed coal is imported.[34]

The BLET also does not apply to exported coal under the Export Clause of the United States Constitution.[35] A credit or refund can be claimed if coal is taxed before it is exported.

Black lung excise tax collections have generally declined in recent years (see *Figure 3*). In FY2009, more than $650 million was collected from the BLET. In FY2017, collections were about $429 million. The decline in BLET collections follows the general decline in U.S. coal production.[36] As the price of coal rose in the 2000s, coal mined underground tended to pay the tax at a fixed rate of $1.10 per ton, as opposed to paying 4.4% of the sales price.

---

[33] The tax does not apply to lignite (brown coal).

[34] In 2017, 731.1 million short tons of coal were consumed domestically. In that same year, coal imports to the United States totaled 7.8 million short tons. Data on coal consumption and imports is available from the Energy Information Administration (EIA), at https://www.eia.gov/coal/data.php.

[35] See IRS Notice 2000-28 and CRS Report R42780, *Export Clause: Limitation on Congress's Taxing Power*, by Erika K. Lunder.

[36] See Energy Information Administration, *Average U.S. Coal Mining Productivity Increases as Production Falls*, March 7, 2018, available at https://www.eia.gov/todayinenergy/detail.php?id=35232#.

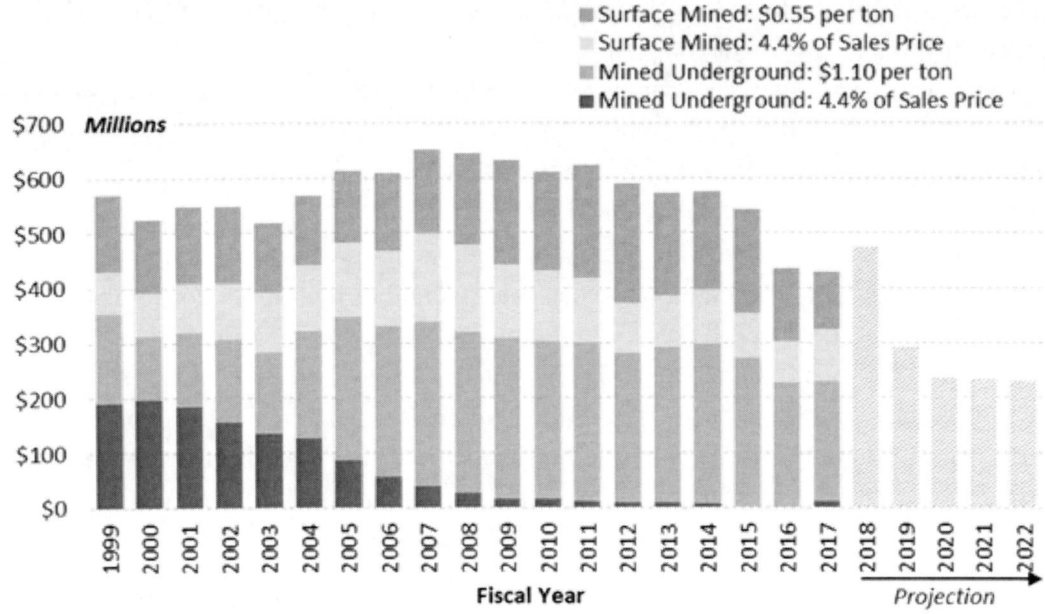

Sources: IRS SOI Bulletin Historical Table 20, available at https://www.irs.gov/statistics/soi-tax-stats-historical- table-20; and Department of the Treasury, Bureau of the Fiscal Service, Treasury Bulletin, March 2018, pp. 90-91, http://www.fiscal.treasury.gov.

Figure 3. Coal Excise Tax Collections. (FY1999 - FY2022)

In the years beyond 2018, coal excise tax receipts are expected to fall sharply, reflecting the decrease in the coal excise tax rate (see *Figure 3*).

Legislative History

The excise tax on coal was established to help ensure the coal industry shared in the social costs imposed by black lung disease. Over time, the rate of the tax has been increased, in an effort to provide sufficient revenue to meet this objective.

Establishing an Excise Tax on Coal

The Black Lung Benefits Revenue Act of 1977 (P.L. 95-227) first imposed the Section 4121 excise tax on coal. When enacted, the tax was $0.50 per ton for coal from underground mines, and $0.25 per ton for coal from surface mines. The tax was limited to 2% of the sales price. The tax was effective for sales after March 31, 1978.

Before P.L. 95-227 was enacted there was considerable debate surrounding how black lung benefits programs should be financed.[37] Various mechanisms to shift the costs of the black lung benefits program to the coal industry and its customers were considered.

[37] See U.S. Congress, Senate Committee on Finance, *Tax Aspects of Black Lung Legislation*, committee print, prepared by Joint Committee on Taxation and Committee on Finance, 95th Cong., June 21, 1977, JCS-35-77, available at https://www.jct.gov/publications.html?func=startdown&id=4028.

These debates ultimately led to the establishment of the Black Lung Disability Trust Fund and the related excise tax on coal.

There was also debate about how to structure the proposed tax. Some suggested a graduated tax, with higher rates imposed on coal with a higher British thermal unit (Btu) content, as such coal was believed to be more likely to cause black lung disease.[38] There were concerns, however, that such a tax could be difficult to administer. Other proposals suggested that coal be subject to a uniform rate, with coal mined from underground deposits subject to a higher rate than other coal (including lignite). A concern with this approach was that coal prices vary substantially per ton for different types of coal (lignite is less expensive than anthracite), meaning that the tax as a percent of the sales price could differ substantially across different types of coal. One answer to this concern is to impose an ad valorem tax, or a tax based on the sales price. Another approach that was considered was to impose a "premium rate" at a level that would fully finance the Black Lung Disability Trust Fund, giving authority to the Department of Labor to adjust the fee as necessary. The tax as enacted was the lesser of the per-unit price or the ad valorem rate of 2%.

Increasing the Rate of Tax

In the early 1980s, it was observed that coal excise tax revenues were not sufficient to meet the trust fund's obligations. The Black Lung Benefits Revenue Act of 1981 (P.L. 97-119) doubled the excise tax rates to $1.00 per ton for coal from underground mines, and $0.50 per ton for coal from surface mines, not to exceed 4% of the sales price. The higher rates were effective January 1, 1982. The doubled rates were temporary, and scheduled to revert to the previous rates on January1, 1996. Further, the rates could be reduced earlier if the trust fund repaid all advances and interest from the general fund of the Treasury. A stated goal of this legislation was to eliminate the Black Lung Disability Trust Fund's debt.[39]

The Consolidated Omnibus Budget Reconciliation Act of 1985 (P.L. 99-272) again increased the BLET rates to $1.10 for underground-mined coal, and $0.55 for surface-mined coal, not to exceed 4.4% of the sales price. The Omnibus Budget Reconciliation Act of 1987 (P.L. 100-203) extended these rates through 2013.

Increased excise tax rates on coal were again extended in 2008. Current-law rates were extended through 2018 as part of the Emergency Economic Stabilization Act of 2008 (EESA; P.L. 110-343). When extending the increased rates, Congress reiterated the original intent of establishing trust fund financing for black lung benefits, observing that

---

[38] Ibid.

[39] Background information in CRS Report 82-59 EW, *Summary and Legislative History of* P.L. 97-119, *"Black Lung Benefits Revenue Act of 1981,"* by Barbara McClure (out of print; available from the author).

it is "to reduce reliance on the Treasury and to recover costs from the mining industry."[40] It was also observed that the program's expenses had continued to exceed revenues over time, and that the debt to the Treasury was not likely to be paid off by 2013. For these reasons, "the Congress believe[d] that it [was] appropriate to continue the tax on coal at the increased rates beyond the expiration date."[41]

Borrowing and Debt

When receipts of the trust fund are less than expenditures, advances are appropriated from the general fund of the Treasury to the trust fund. These advances are repayable, and interest charged on these advances is also payable to the general fund.[42] The Consolidated Omnibus Budget Reconciliation Act of 1985 (P.L. 99-272) provided a five-year forgiveness of interest on debt owed to the Treasury's general fund. As a result, the principal amount of trust fund debt outstanding was relatively unchanged throughout the late 1980s.[43] The moratorium on interest payments ended September 30, 1990.

Throughout the 1990s and into the 2000s, the cumulative end-of-year debt of the trust fund grew, and the trust fund continued to receive repayable advances from the general fund to cover expenses. The trust fund was subject to financial restructuring when the current excise tax rate was extended until January 1, 2019, in EESA.

The Black Lung Disability Trust Fund debt was restructured in FY2009. Essentially, the partial forgiveness and restructuring allowed the trust fund to refinance outstanding repayable advances and unpaid interest on those advances. As a result of the partial forgiveness and refinancing, the cumulative debt was reduced from $10.4 billion at the end of FY2008 to $6.2 billion by the end of FY2009. At the time of the restructuring it was expected that the trust fund's debt would be fully eliminated by FY2040.[44] The trust fund's cumulative debt has trended downward since the restructuring (see *Figure 4*). However, coal excise tax revenue has been less than anticipated in recent years. As a result, current projections suggest that the trust fund debt will rise over time when considering annual borrowing as well as legacy debt. The trust fund's debt is therefore not on a path to be eliminated. By FY2050, the Government Accountability Office (GAO) projects the trust fund's debt will be $15.4 billion without any changes in current policy.[45]

---

[40] U.S. Congress, Joint Committee on Taxation, *General Explanation of Tax Legislation Enacted in the 110th Congress*, 110th Cong., March 2009, JCS-1-09, p. 302.

[41] Ibid.

[42] Repayable advances must be repaid once there is money available in the Black Lung Disability Trust Fund for such purpose.

[43] U.S. Government Accountability Office, *Black Lung Benefits Program: Options for Improving Trust Fund Finances*, GAO-18-351, May 2018, available at https://www.gao.gov/products/GAO-18-351.

[44] Ibid.

[45] Ibid.

Other Revenue Sources

In addition to revenue from the BLET and repayable general fund advances, the trust fund receives revenue from the collection of certain fines, penalties, and interest paid by coal operators and miners and reimbursements from responsible operators.

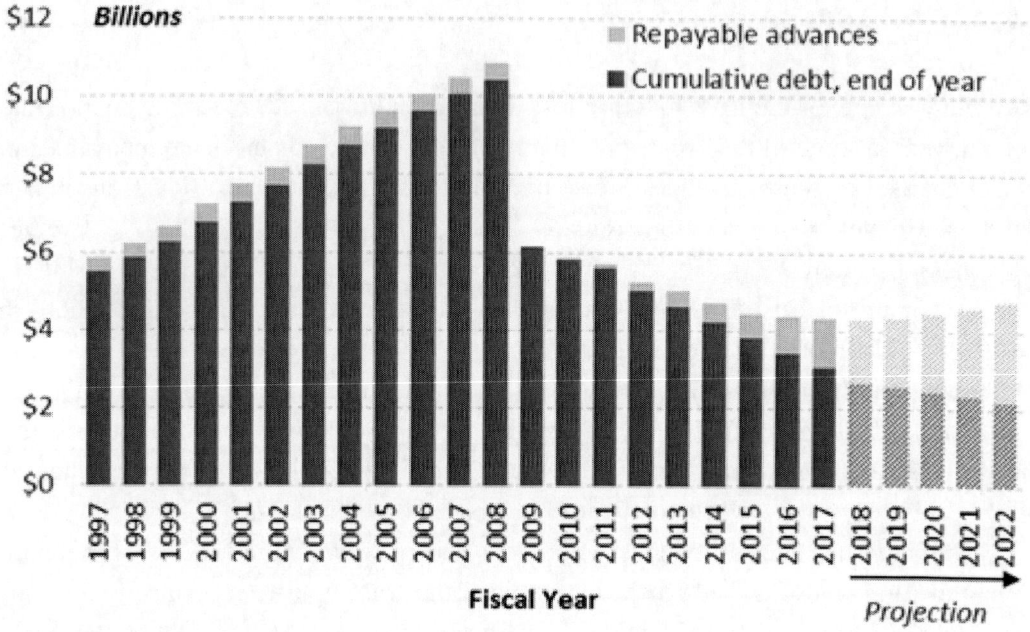

Sources: CRS graphic using data from Department of the Treasury, Bureau of the Fiscal Service, Treasury Bulletin, Annual Releases and TreasuryDirect Black Lung Disability Trust Fund Reports, Annual Releases.

Notes: Data for FY1997 through FY2017 is the cumulative end-of-year debt plus repayable advances received in the fiscal year. Data for FY2018 through FY2022 are projections. The repayable advance received in FY2009 of $6.5 billion as part of debt restructuring is not included.

Figure 4. Black Lung Disability Trust Fund Debt. (FY1997 – FY2022)

Fines, Penalties, and Interest

Part C of the BLBA authorizes the following fines and penalties for violations of the act:

- a civil penalty of up to $1,000 per day for a mine operator's failure to secure benefits through insurance or approved self-insurance;[46]

---

[46] 30 U.S.C. §933(d)(1).

- a fine of up to $1,000 upon conviction of the misdemeanor offense of knowingly destroying or transferring property of a mine operator with the intent to avoid the payment of benefits for which the mine operator is responsible;[47]
- a fine of up to $1,000 upon conviction of the misdemeanor offense of making a false or misleading statement or representation for the purposes of obtaining benefits;[48] and
- a civil penalty of up to $500 for a mine operator's failure to file a report on miners who are or may be entitled to benefits as required by DOL.[49]

The amount of these penalties and fines, as well as interest assessed, is paid into the trust fund. In FY2017, trust fund receipts from fines, penalties, and interest totaled $1.2 million. This is a small source of trust fund revenue relative to the coal excise tax, which generated $428.7 million in trust fund revenues in FY2017.[50]

Collection from Responsible Mine Operators

The trust fund is authorized to begin paying benefits within 30 days if no responsible operator has begun payment. If, after paying benefits, DOL is able to identify a responsible operator, the trust fund may seek to collect from that operator the costs of benefits already paid by the trust fund and interest assessed on this amount.[51] The amount of these collections is paid into the trust fund. In FY2017, $19.9 million was collected from responsible mine operators. The amount collected from responsible mine operators has fluctuated over time, but has averaged about 1% of total receipts since 1995.[52]

FINANCIAL CONDITION AND OUTLOOK

Various factors have contributed to the ongoing situation of trust fund expenditures exceeding trust fund revenues. Throughout the 1980s, black lung benefit payments and administrative expenditures exceeded trust fund revenue. As a result, the trust fund accumulated debt. As discussed above, over time, various efforts have been made to improve the fiscal condition of the trust fund. However, as of the end of FY2017, the trust fund remains in debt. The trust fund's cumulative debt at the end of FY2017 was

---

[47] 30 U.S.C. §933(d)(2). This offense can also result in imprisonment for up to one year.
[48] 38 U.S.C. § 941. This offense can also result in imprisonment for up to one year.
[49] 38 U.S.C. § 942.
[50] Department of the Treasury, Bureau of the Fiscal Service, *Treasury Bulletin*, March 2018, pp. 90-91, http://www.fiscal.treasury.gov.
[51] 38 U.S.C. § 934(b).
[52] Department of the Treasury, Bureau of the Fiscal Service, *Treasury Bulletin*, annual editions.

$3.1 billion.[53] The trust fund also borrowed $1.3 billion from the general fund that same year.

Projections suggest that borrowing from the general fund will increase over the next few years, even as cumulative (or legacy) debt is paid down. Under the current excise tax rates, benefit payments and administrative expenses will be approximately equal to trust fund revenues in FY2020 through FY2022 (see Figure 5). However, revenues are not projected to be sufficient to repay debt, and expenses are projected to rise over time when debt and interest expenses are included. Specifically, by FY2022, it is projected that the trust fund will borrow $2.6 billion in repayable advances from the general fund.[54]

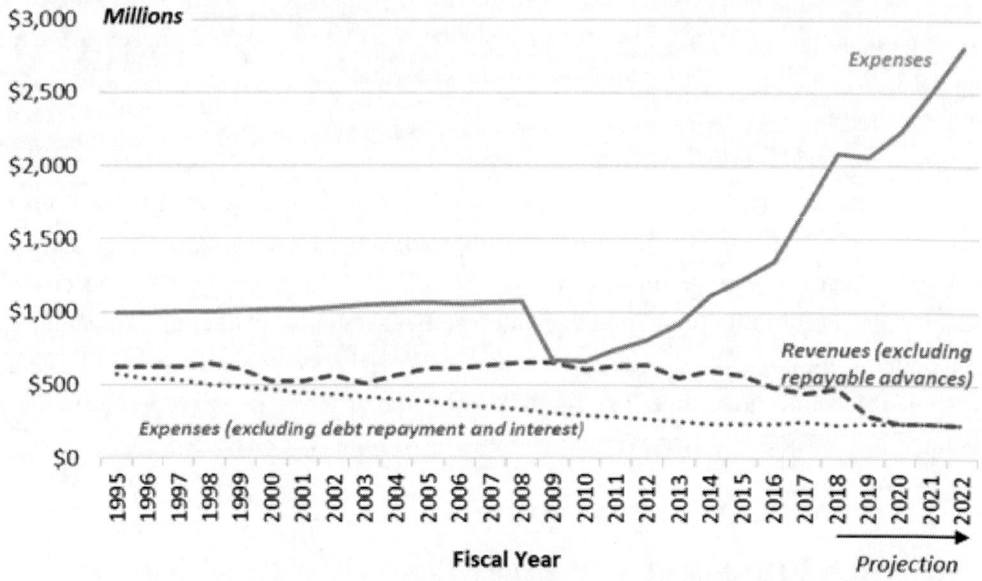

Source: CRS graphic using data from the Department of the Treasury, Bureau of the Fiscal Service, Treasury Bulletin, Annual Releases.

Notes: Revenues includes excise tax receipts; receipts reported on the Form 990BL files by 501(c)(21) black lung trusts; fines, penalties, and interest; collection from responsible mine operators; and recovery of prior year funds. Expenses include Treasury administrative expenses; program expenses and salaries and expenses at DOL; and, as indicated, interest and debt repayment expenditures. The $6.5 billion in expenses associated with debt restructuring in FY2009 is not included.

Figure 5. Black Lung Disability Trust Fund: Revenues and Expenses. (FY1995 – FY2022)

POLICY ISSUES AND OPTIONS

There are various policy options that Congress might consider to improve the fiscal condition of the Black Lung Disability Trust Fund. Broadly, increasing taxes on the coal

[53] Department of the Treasury, Bureau of the Fiscal Service, *Treasury Bulletin*, March 2018, pp. 90-91, http://www.fiscal.treasury.gov.

[54] Ibid.

industry (or maintaining 2018 rates) would pass the costs associated with paying black lung benefits onto the coal industry. Alternatively, forgiving trust fund interest or debt or financing black lung benefits out of general fund revenues would pass the costs of federal black lung benefits onto taxpayers in general. Another option would be to reduce federal black lung benefits.

Revenue Options

Additional revenue would likely need to be provided to the trust fund if the trust fund is to pay for past black lung benefits and maintain current benefit levels. Additional revenue may be needed even if past debt is forgiven (or assumed by the general fund), as anticipated trust fund revenues are not likely to be sufficient to cover anticipated trust fund expenditures.

Change the Coal Excise Tax

As discussed above, in the past, Congress and the President have opted to increase the excise tax on coal to address shortfalls in the Black Lung Disability Trust Fund. These increased rates have been temporary, and scheduled to revert back to the reduced rate if the trust fund's debt is eliminated. Congress has chosen to extend the increased rates beyond their scheduled expiration when the trust fund is in debt. One option would be to extend 2018 rates. The GAO projects that if 2018 coal excise tax rates are extended, the trust fund will have a debt of $4.5 billion in 2050 (see "GAO Options for Improving Trust Fund Finances" below).[55] GAO projections suggest that increasing 2018 tax rates by 25% would eliminate the trust fund's debt, leaving the trust fund with a surplus of $0.6 billion in 2050.

Modify Coal Industry Tax Benefits

An alternative way to raise revenue from the coal industry is to scale back or eliminate various tax expenditures, or tax preferences, from which the coal industry benefits. For example, coal producers benefit from being able to expense exploration and

[55] The data presented in this chapter are from GAO's moderate case simulations. Moderate case simulations assume that future coal production is consistent with the Energy Information Administration's reference case. Changes in economic conditions or the policy environment could lead to more or less coal production, or contribute to changes in coal prices. These changes could cause higher or lower coal excise tax revenue collections. GAO provides alternative simulations exploring how Black Lung Disability Trust Fund balances would change under a range of alternative assumptions. Under GAO's range of scenarios, trust fund debt could be between $1.8 billion and $12.5 billion if 2018 coal excise tax rates were extended. The GAO assumes that coal production does not change in response to changes in the excise tax. More on the assumptions used in GAO's moderate case simulations, and outcomes under various scenario simulations, can be found in Appendix 1 and Appendix 2 of U.S. Government Accountability Office, *Black Lung Benefits Program: Options for Improving Trust Fund Finances*, GAO-18-351, May 2018, p. 22, available at https://www.gao.gov/ products/GAO-18-351.

development costs and are able to recover costs using percentage depletion (depletion based on revenue from the sale of the mineral asset) instead of cost depletion (depletion based on the amount of the mineral asset exhausted and the amount invested in the asset). The Obama Administration regularly proposed repealing these tax incentives as part of the Administration's annual budget.[56]

It could be difficult to assign the revenues raised via the repeal of tax benefits to the trust fund. With an excise tax, it is straightforward to identify the revenue generated by the tax and earmark the revenue for a trust fund. It is not as straightforward to determine the amount of revenue that is raised through the repeal of an income tax expenditure, or direct the additional revenue raised because a certain preference is no longer in the code to a trust fund. Repeal of coal-industry tax benefits could, however, be used to offset the cost of a one-time transfer from the general fund to the trust fund.

Provide Additional General Fund Revenue

Revenue from various sources, including the general fund, could be used to supplement trust fund revenue generated from current sources. General fund revenues are not earmarked for a specific purpose, and there is generally no direct link between the source of general fund revenue and the government good or service provided. Black lung benefits were paid out of general revenue before the trust fund was established in 1977.

Trust funds are generally established when there is a link between the government benefits or services being provided and the revenue source funding those benefits or services.[57] The Black Lung Disability Trust Fund was established because Congress believed that the costs of the part C black lung program should be borne by the coal industry.[58] Financing black lung benefits with general fund revenue would weaken the link between the industry and black lung benefits, while reducing the burden on the industry associated with paying for black lung benefits.

Forgive Trust Fund Interest or Debt

In the past the Black Lung Disability Trust Fund's fiscal outlook has been improved through interest and debt forgiveness. As discussed above, in the late 1990s, there was a five-year forgiveness of interest on debt owed to the Treasury's general fund. More recently, debt was forgiven as part of the 2008 restructuring of the trust fund's debt.

---

[56] Department of the Treasury, "General Explanations of the Administration's Fiscal Year 2017 Revenue Proposals," February, 2016, available at https://www.treasury.gov/resource-center/tax-policy/Pages/general_explanation.aspx.

[57] For background information on federal trust funds, see CRS Report R41328, *Federal Trust Funds and the Budget*, by Mindy R. Levit.

[58] U.S. Congress, Senate Committee on Finance, *Black Lung Benefits Revenue Act of 1977*, S. 1538, 95th Cong., 1st sess., July 12, 1977, Report No. 95-336.

The GAO projects that if all current debt were forgiven, the trust fund would accumulate $2.3 billion in new debt by 2050. If all interest were forgiven, the trust fund debt is projected to be $5.8 billion by 2050. Forgiving the trust fund's interest or debt obligations would shift the burden of paying for black lung disability benefits from the coal industry to general taxpayers. However, a one-time appropriation to forgive interest or debt is a transparent option for satisfying the trust fund's obligations to the general fund.[59]

GAO Options for Improving Trust Fund Finances

In a May 2018 report the Government Accountability Office (GAO) projected the debt of the Black Lung Disability Trust Fund under a variety of policy scenarios. These scenarios are summarized in Figure 6. Broadly, benefit payments and administrative costs are expected to increase in the near term (into the mid-2020s), but eventually decline over time. Trust fund revenue, however, is expected to fall sharply after excise tax rates are reduced in 2019. Even if all current debt is forgiven, projections suggest trust fund revenues will not be sufficient to cover trust fund obligations, under current policy. Similarly, forgiving interest on the debt is not expected to eliminate trust fund debt over the longer term (by 2050). Extending the 2018 excise tax rates on coal is also not sufficient to achieve zero trust fund debt by 2050. However, projections suggest that increasing excise tax rates by 25% above 2018 levels would lead to a trust fund surplus of $0.6 billion by 2050.

Policies combining debt forgiveness and additional revenues may also be considered. For example, GAO projects that the trust fund would have zero debt in 2050 if 2018 coal excise tax rates were extended and $2.4 billion in debt were forgiven.

Expenditure Options

The primary expenditures of the trust fund are for the payment of Part C benefits to miners in cases in which there is no responsible operator. In order to reduce expenditures and improve the long-term financial health of the trust fund, Congress could consider several options to reduce the generosity and scope of benefits or increase the ability of the federal government to ensure that coal operators, even those who are in the bankruptcy process, pay benefits for their miners.

Reduce Benefit Amounts A reduction in the amount of Part C benefits would result in lower Part C expenditures from both responsible coal operators and the trust fund. However, as compared to other workers' compensation benefits, Part C benefits are relatively low. The basic Part C benefit rate for a single miner is equal to 37.5% of the base rate of pay for federal employees at the GS-2, Step 1 level.

---

[59] U.S. Government Accountability Office, *Black Lung Benefits Program: Options for Improving Trust Fund Finances*, GAO-18-351, May 2018, p.22, available at https://www.gao.gov/products/GAO-18-351.

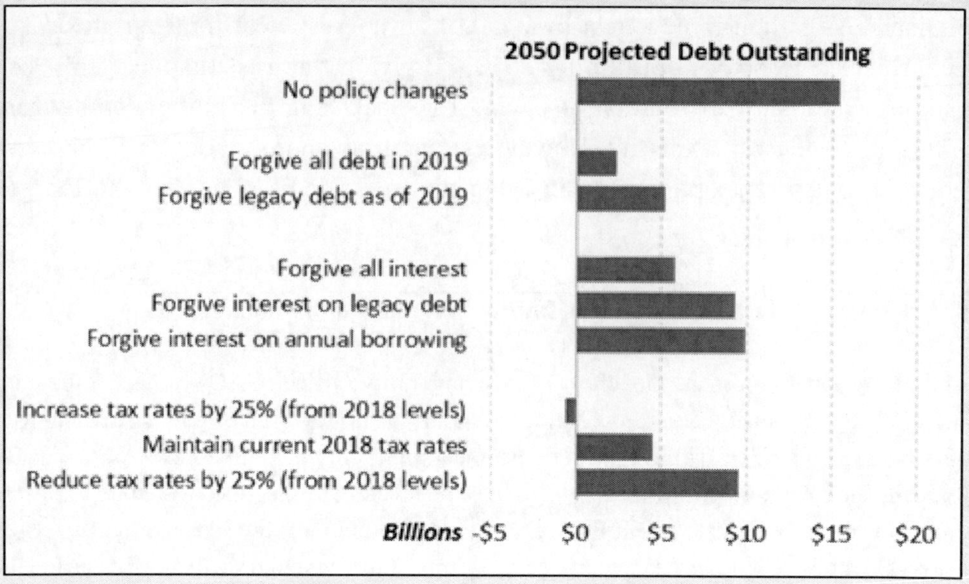

Source: CRS graphic using data from the U.S. Government Accountability Office, Black Lung Benefits Program: Options for Improving Trust Fund Finances, GAO-18-351, May 2018, p. 22, available at https://www.gao.gov/ products/GAO-18-351.

Notes: The 2050 results presented here are from GAO's moderate case simulations. Moderate case simulations assume that future coal production is consistent with the Energy Information Administration's reference case. Changes in economic conditions or the policy environment could lead to more or less coal production, or contribute to changes in coal prices. These changes could cause higher or lower coal excise tax revenue collections. GAO's moderate case simulations also assume that the number of black lung beneficiaries evolves following historical trends. Sensitivity analysis performed by GAO provides a range of estimates under various assumptions for revenues and beneficiaries associated with the policy options presented in Figure 6. This extended analysis is available in Appendix I and Appendix II of U.S. Government Accountability Office, Black Lung Benefits Program: Options for Improving Trust Fund Finances, GAO-18-351, May 2018, available at https://www.gao.gov/products/GAO-18-351.

Figure 6. Projected Debt Outstanding with Various Policy Options, 2050.

For 2019 this benefit is just over $660 per month, or under $8,000 per year. In the majority of state workers' compensation programs, the basic benefit rate is set at two-thirds of the worker's pre-disability wage, subject to statutory minimums and maximums.[60] The other workers' compensation programs administered by DOL, the LHWCA, and the Federal Employees' Compensation Act (FECA) use two-thirds of a worker's pre-disability wage as the basis for their benefits.[61] A federal worker with a

---

[60] For additional information on state workers' compensation programs, see CRS Report R44580, *Workers' Compensation: Overview and Issues*, by Scott D. Szymendera.

[61] For additional information on the FECA program, see CRS Report R42107, *The Federal Employees' Compensation Act (FECA): Workers' Compensation for Federal Employees*, by Scott D. Szymendera.

spouse or dependent in the FECA program is entitled to 75% of his or her pre-disability wage. The minimum benefit for total disability or death in the FECA program, 75% of GS-2, Step 1, is twice the amount of the Part C benefit rate. In addition, unlike the other federal workers' compensation programs and many state programs, there is no automatic adjustment to Part C benefits to reflect increases in the cost of living. Part C benefits instead increase only when federal pay rates are increased.

Restrict Benefit Eligibility

The eligibility of miners and survivors to Part C benefits could be restricted to reduce expenditures from responsible operators and the trust fund. In 1981, Congress enacted several eligibility restrictions to miners and survivors as part of the Black Lung Benefits Revenue Act of 1981, to address concerns about the financial insolvency of the trust fund. Specifically, this law removed the following three eligibility presumptions for new claims going forward:

- A rebuttable presumption that the death of a miner who worked in mining for at least 10 years and who died of any respirable disease, was due to pneumoconiosis (listed as presumption 2 in Table 1).
- A rebuttable presumption that a miner employed in mining for at least 15 years, and who has a chest x-ray that is interpreted as negative with respect to certain statutory standards but who has other evidence of a totally disabling respiratory or pulmonary impairment, is totally disabled due to pneumoconiosis, or died due to pneumoconiosis. This presumption may only be rebutted by the Secretary of Labor establishing that the miner does not or did not have pneumoconiosis or that the miner's respiratory or pulmonary impairment did not arise out of connection to mine employment (presumption 4 in Table 1).
- A presumption that a miner who died on or before March 1, 1978, and who was employed in mining for at least 25 years before June 30, 1971, died due to pneumoconiosis, unless it is established that at the time of the miner's death, he or she was not at least partially disabled due to pneumoconiosis (presumption 5 in Table 1).

In addition to removing three of the five existing eligibility presumptions, the 1981 law also removed the right of the survivors of a miner who is determined to be eligible for Part C benefits at the time of his or her death to receive survivors' benefits without filing a new claim, thus permitting the payment of survivors' benefits in the case of a current beneficiary, even if the beneficiary's death is not proven to be linked to pneumoconiosis.

Two of the restrictions put in place by the 1981 legislation were later removed by the ACA. The ACA reinstated the fourth eligibility presumption and expanded rights for survivors' benefits, thus expanding eligibility for both miners and certain survivors.

Increase the Ability of the Federal Government to Recover Benefit Costs from Responsible Operators

Under Part C of the BLBA, the federal government may recover the costs of benefits, and interest accrued on those benefits, paid by the trust fund from identified responsible operators. In addition, Part C allows the federal government to place a lien on the property and rights to property of an operator that refuses to pay the benefits and interest it owes to the trust fund. In the case of a bankruptcy or insolvency proceeding, this lien is to be treated in the same manner as a lien for taxes owed to the federal government.

However, in a 2016 letter to the Comptroller General requesting a GAO review of the trust fund, Representatives Bobby Scott, Ranking Member of the House Committee on Education and the Workforce, and Sander Levin, Ranking Member of the House Committee on Ways and Means, claimed that the number of current and potential bankruptcies among coal operators is placing stress on the trust fund.[62] Representatives Scott and Levin cited the example of Patriot Coal which, according to their letter, transferred $62 million in Part C liabilities to the trust fund when it became insolvent. In addition, this letter claims that insolvent coal operators may be able to avoid trust fund liens by continuing to make benefit payments until after the court in their bankruptcy cases has approved the sale of their assets to another company. Because the original company was never in default of its payments, no lien was filed, and these assets were able to be purchased by another company without any lien or future liability to the trust fund.

Congress may examine the issue of the impact of coal operator bankruptcies and the interaction of bankruptcy law and the BLBA's lien provisions, to strengthen both the federal government's ability to ensure that responsible operators are paying for benefits and reduce the benefit expenditures of the trust fund.

[62] Letter from Rep. Bobby Scott, ranking member, House Committee on Education and the Workforce, and Rep. Sander Levin, ranking member, House Committee on Ways and Means, to Gene Dodaro, comptroller general, September 23, 2016, https://democrats-edworkforce.house.gov/download/gao-request-letter-re-solvency-of-black-lung- benefits-trust-fund.

INDEX

A

B

C

D

E

W